Computer Studies

GCSE Computer Studies

Dexter J Booth

Pitman

PITMAN PUBLISHING
128 Long Acre, London, WC2E 9AN

A Division of Longman Group UK Limited

First published in Great Britain 1989

British Library Cataloguing in Publication Data

Booth, Dexter J.
GCSE computer studies.
I. Title
004

ISBN 0-273-03081-7

Printed and bound in Great Britain

Dedication

To my father and the memory of my late mother; also to John Schaffter, Emeritus Headmaster, and Gary Laidlaw, Head of the Physics Department, St Michaels University School, Victoria, British Columbia, Canada; people without whose humanity this book would never have been written.

Contents

Preface

This book has been written to cater for the National Criteria in Computer Studies as reflected by the regional syllabuses in the General Certificate of Secondary Education (GCSE). As such it is a suitable textbook for the GCSE Computer Studies syllabuses of all the regional examination boards including the LEAG syllabus in Computer Studies (Mature). It is also appropriate to other introductory courses in Computer Studies and will serve as a suitable text for many BTEC/HNC/HND courses in both Computing and Information Technology.

There are five sections to the work, the first being designed as an introduction to the subsequent four, each of which addresses a specific aspect of computing.

Because the GCSE is designed to appeal to all ability ranges, the content has been written in a progressive style with a number of self-help questions placed throughout the text. To further aid the student's understanding, each chapter is summarised at the end and followed by a set of short, self assessment questions, the locations of whose answers are given by their appropriate paragraph numbers. In addition, each chapter, with few exceptions, ends with a selection of exercises, typical of those that appear on GCSE Examination papers.

With the ever accelerating pace of developments in Computing technology, the computer has become an increasingly imperative influence for social change. In section five, this aspect of Computing is considered to the depth that time, space and appropriateness of the level has allowed. Whilst the recognition of the computer's influence on our daily lives and society's future is not yet fully reflected in contemporary examination papers it is anticipated that as time progresses it will become more so.

In conclusion I should like to express my gratitude to Brian Jackson who, with personal and professional care and commitment, read the first draft of the manuscript. His subsequent comments and suggestions have been incorporated into the text to the benefit of the book both in detail and as a whole.

Dexter J Booth
Huddersfield
1989

Section one

1 Chips with everything

Objectives

1 To introduce the student to the computer and to its uses by individuals, organisations and society.
2 To introduce the range and scope of computer applications.

Introduction

1 The aim of this chapter is to make you aware of the extent to which the computer and the silicon chip influence our daily lives. We shall look at computers generally without considering the details of their use. At all times you are encouraged to look around you and find computers where you might not have expected them.

Computers at a glance

2 As you read these words, computers are at work controlling and organising your life. In the highly structured society in which we live, it is necessary for computers to be used to organise and coordinate our lives—society would not work the way it does if computers were not used.

Routine tasks that were once done by human beings can now be performed more quickly and less expensively by computers. It makes sense to use computers but we must be careful not to become too dependent on them because in doing this we begin to forget how we managed before they were invented. We then become even more dependent on them because the computers remember for us, and gradually we lose our understanding of exactly how they perform each task and use them merely as tools. Do you know how much computers affect you now and how much they are likely to affect you in the future? It is essential that you do, or you may lose too much of your ability to control your own destiny.

Computers play an important part in everybody's lives; their importance is so great that without them we would not be able to live the way we do. To appreciate this, look around you to see the sort of influences that these machines have on our daily lives.

> Before you read any further, stop and think about how the computer affects your daily life; for example, at school at home and at leisure. Think about where you have seen computers in action and where they may be in action but unseen by you.

Computers for food

3 To stay alive we need food and warmth. The food we eat comes in a variety of forms: fresh food such as fruit and vegetables; 'almost-fresh' food such as frozen meat and frozen fruit juice and preserved food such as baked beans and canned soup. Whatever form of food we eat, it has to be grown, processed and delivered to the shop before we can buy it. Look at your local supermarket shelves and make a list of five fresh items, five 'almost-fresh' items and five preserved items of food. When you do this try and find out where the food was grown.

> From your list of items, find out where a computer plays its part in getting them to your supermarket shelf. Do you think the pricing of each item has involved a computer? How many of them do you think you would be able to buy if a computer had not been involved?

4 The days have long since gone when all the food we eat comes from our own locality. Now our food comes from every corner of the world. How does it get here? Have you ever thought of what a simple coffee bean has to go through before ending up in a jar of instant coffee in your kitchen?—from grower to picker to packer to buyer to transporter to manufacturer to supermarket to you. It is quite a journey, and what has to be realised is that it requires organisation.

5 Organisation means getting everything just right. You probably only buy one jar of instant coffee a week. The supermarket knows this and only orders enough coffee to supply its customers needs. The manufacturer knows this and only makes enough to supply the needs of its supermarkets and other customers. The buyer knows this and only buys enough to supply the manufacturer with what he needs. Hopefully, the grower knows this and only grows enough to supply the buyer. How does everybody know what they know? By organisation!

> How do you think the supermarket knows how many jars of instant coffee to buy each week? Do you think it uses a computer to do this? Why?

6 A jar of instant coffee is just a single item on your grocery list. You may have up to fifty items or more in your weekly shopping basket, and

1.1 Point of sale terminal with laser reader; courtesy of the Article Member Association

you can choose from thousands of items in a Supermarket. Organisation does not just mean organising your instant coffee; it means organising thousands of items and organising them on a daily basis. In addition, certain products are perishable and can not be sold after a certain date.

7 Can you imagine someone sitting down and organising every item with a pencil and paper? There are not enough hours in a day so it has to be done by computer. In some supermarkets the computer is not just in the background organising numbers of things to buy, but is up-front at the check-out. The groceries are checked out by passing them over a laser beam which reads the bar codes on each item, and each item is automatically recorded at the till. When all the items have been checked out the total bill is displayed.

> If you have a supermarket in your town that uses a laser beam to read the labels at the checkout, go and watch closely what happens. How does the checkout person know that the label has been correctly read? When it has been read, what information is shown at the till? How does the receipt differ from one where a shop does not use this sort of checkout? If you are given such detailed information on your receipt, who else has this information and what can they do with it?

Computers for warmth

8 We can keep warm in two ways: by wearing clothes and by heating our buildings. If you look at all the clothes in the shops, you will see it is just like the supermarket. Someone has to grow cotton for cotton

1.2 Control room at Oldbury Severn Power Station; courtesy the Central Electricity Generating Board.

sheets, rear sheep for woolly jumpers, and drill for oil so that someone else can make artificial fibres to make man-made cloth. Such organisation can only be controlled by computers because the task is too large for human beings to handle using a pen and paper.

9 Heating a building may be as simple to you as turning a thermostat knob, but consider what is behind that simple act when, for example, the heating is run by electricity. In simple terms the electricity is generated by boiling water to create steam, which then turns the dynamos that create the electric current. How is the water boiled? Either by burning fuel such as oil or coal or by using nuclear energy as a source of heat. Whatever system is used, a vast array of computers is required to operate and maintain an efficient supply of electricity to your home and all the millions of other homes in the country.

> Now that you have some idea of how computers can play a vital role in our daily lives, try to imagine what would happen if they were not available. How would you eat, cook or keep warm? Do you think that everything you bought would be cheaper or more expensive? Why?

Computers for everything

10 We can see that our basic needs require computers to look after them, but what about our not-so-basic needs such as television, digital clocks and watches, washing machines, telephones, hi-fi units, dish washers, microwave ovens, newspapers, mail service, credit cards, banking, bus services and even books. All these and many more require the use of computers to make themselves available to you. Some of them, for example a microwave oven, are not computers in the strict sense of the word but they have many features common to computers. This brings us to the question, what exactly is a computer?

The computer

11 There are many different makes of computer from the very large ones called **mainframe computers**, through the medium sized ones called **minicomputers** to the small ones called **microcomputers**. As you may know, a microcomputer has a **screen**, a **box** and a **keyboard**.

The screen is called a **monitor** or **visual display unit (VDU)** and is used to display words, numbers and pictures. In other words, it is the means of communication to you. The keyboard contains all the letters of the alphabet, all the numbers and several other keys, and is used to put information into the computer. Using this keyboard you can communicate to the computer. The box contains all the electrical circuits that make the computer work. These three parts may be all together in one case, or they may be separate, depending on the type of computer.

> If you have a computer at home or in school, look at it closely. Describe its appearance. Does it have any other equipment attached to it? If the monitor, keyboard and box are separate, see how they are joined together. Read about its overall description in the computer manual.

1.3A A personal computer

1.3B A microcomputer

Inside the computer

12 Some computers are easy to open, such as the Apple which allows you to lift off the lid and look inside. Others, like the IBM PC's, are more difficult to get inside and require a screwdriver. The following picture shows you the inside of a typical small computer.

Inside the computer is a board and a surprising amount of empty space. The board contains a collection of small, rectangular, black blocks, each approximately the size of a Lego brick.

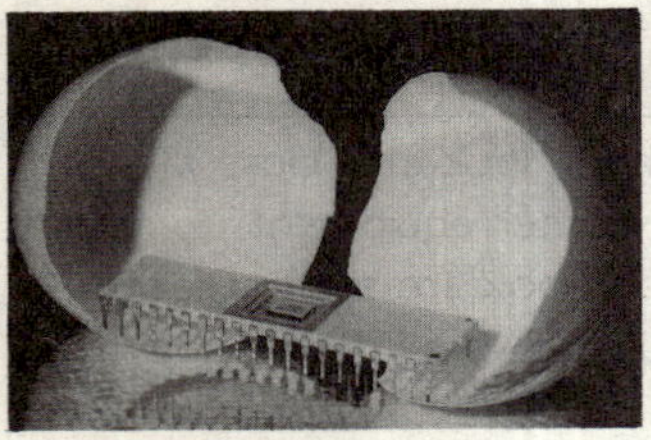

1.5 A silicon chip

13 Each block is a plug with two rows of pins that fit into a socket that is fastened to the board. It is easy to pull these out but you will need the correct tools to do so otherwise you may damage the pins on the blocks.

The pins are made of metal because electricity has to flow through them. They are the ends of wires that are connected to a silicon chip inside the block.

The chip only measures 3 mm by 4 mm. On that particular chip there are thousands of circuits, all of which are held in place inside a small 'chip' of silicon, hence its name. Silicon is a glass like substance that is made from common sand.

It is remarkable that so many circuits can be contained in such a small area. What is even more remarkable is that each chip only costs pennies to produce.

There are a number of different sized blocks on the board. Can you locate them? Each different type of chip does a different job. Look at the array of small chips set out in regular rows. Can you guess what all those small chips are for?

The computer revolution

14 Computers have been used for a long time, the first working computer in Britain being housed in a building of the University of Manchester. The picture below shows part of an early computer.

1.6 An early computer

As you see, early computers contained a labyrinth of wires and cables and a number of other bits and pieces. Every wire had to be connected by hand with the result that they were very big and expensive to make, and, as a result, expensive to use. Some of the parts that you can see in the picture are known as **thermionic valves**. This is an old-fashioned piece of electrical equipment that heats up when it is used. With so many of these valves in the computer the amount of heat created was so great that the computer had to be kept in a specially cooled room. Consequently the expense of buying and using computers meant that only very large organisations could afford them.

15 This was the situation until the late 1960's when the silicon chip was introduced. The chip replaced all the wires, cables and many of the bits and pieces, especially the thermionic valves. Suddenly computers became smaller and, more importantly, cheaper so that everybody could afford them.

> How many people do you know who have their own computer? What do they use them for? How many computers do you have in your school? What are they all used for? How many shops are there in your town that sell computers? To answer the last question you could look in the *Yellow Pages*.

16 The invention of the chip has allowed us to find so many different uses for it that we are now progressing into what is called the Information Age. We shall be looking at what is meant by this later in the book. The Information Age really refers to computers but can also be applied to the chip. It is a chip that makes your digital watch work. It is a chip that makes the panda crossing work. It is a chip that makes your microwave oven work. As mentioned earlier, these items are not computers in the real sense of the word but they have many features in common because, like computers, they are all worked by chips.

The calculator

17 The existence of the chip has allowed the electronic hand calculator to be developed.

Calculators are used everywhere, at home, at school and even for shopping. At the heart of a calculator are a number of chips that control everything. They allow the calculator to accept information when you press a button.

We call this the **input** information. When you have input all the information necessary for the calculation, the chips control the calculation. This is called **processing** information. Having completed the calculation, the chips cause the result to be displayed on the little screen.

We call this the **output** information. The calculator can therefore be called an INPUT—PROCESS—OUTPUT system.

> The calculator is like a miniature computer, but with less keys on its keyboard. It has the facility to process information—that is what goes on inside the box, and it has a screen to display results. Can you think of a fundamental difference between a computer and a calculator? As calculators become more sophisticated, this difference becomes harder to define.

Input—process—output

18 The calculator can be illustrated by the following simple INPUT—PROCESS—OUTPUT picture.

The box represents the ability of the calculator to PROCESS information. To make the calculator work we have to INPUT numbers into it by pressing buttons. When the calculator has done its calculation it displays the result on its screen. This information is the OUTPUT.

Any electronic system that uses chips can be represented by a diagram like this one—including the computer.

> How many electrical gadgets can you think of that can be represented as input—process—output? Make a list of ten and describe those that use a chip for the process part. N.B. it is not always obvious that a chip is used.

The following three examples show where the chip is used and how we separate the INPUT, the PROCESS and the OUTPUT.

The digital watch

19 Many of you will possess a digital watch. It is called **digital** because the time, to the nearest minute or second, is displayed using numbers. These watches are capable of being used as alarms by setting the time at which the alarm goes off. Here the INPUT is the setting of the time at which you want the alarm to go off, the PROCESS is the time registered by the watch up to the alarm time and when the alarm time comes round, the process causes the OUTPUT in the form of a noise—a buzz or a chime.

The panda crossing

20 A panda crossing works by displaying a green light to traffic and a red light to pedestrians. This means that traffic can pass but pedestrians must wait. When a pedestrian presses a button, there are a few seconds delay before the green traffic light changes to red and the red pedestrian light changes to green. At the same time a loud beeping noise is sounded to tell blind pedestrians that it is now safe to cross. Some seconds later the lights change again to their original colours and the traffic continues. Here the INPUT is the pressing of the button by the pedestrian, the PROCESSING of this input is what causes the lights to change after a time delay, and the OUTPUT is the colour of the lights and the beeping.

An electricity bill

21 When you read your electricity bill, you are reading the OUTPUT from the PROCESS that has calculated how much electricity you have

London Electricity

CUSTOMER ACCOUNTS OFFICE	DATE OF ACCOUNT
BENGEWORTH ROAD LONDON SE5 9AJ	29 SEP 88

MR.R HARPER & MISS R COLLYER
TOP FLOOR
216 CAVENDISH ROAD, SW12 OBY

For information on how and where to pay this account please see over →

METER READING		UNITS USED	UNIT PRICE (pence)	V.A.T. code	AMOUNT £
PRESENT	PREVIOUS				
E 05097	04397	700	5.850	0	40.95
STANDING CHARGE 27/ 7/88 TO 30/ 9/88				0	6.28

PLEASE PAY THIS ACCOUNT AT ONE OF OUR SHOW-ROOMS IF THE POSTAL SERVICE IS INTERRUPTED.

E=Estimated Reading. Please read the advice given on the back of this bill.
C=Your own reading.

YOUR REFERENCE NUMBER	YOU CAN PHONE US ON	NORMAL READING DATE	AMOUNT TO PAY
101.5743/216.637	01-733 2228	26 SEP 88	£ 47.23

1.7 An electricity bill

used and how much money you owe the electricity supplier. To set this process into action someone had to INPUT information. This information consisted of your account number and your latest meter reading. The PROCESS then used your account number to find your name, your address and your previous meter reading—all of which are stored by the computer. From this previous meter reading and the latest meter reading it works out how many electricity units you have used, and from that, how much you owe. If you look at the electricity bill shown you will see all these details printed on it.

We are all familiar with the INPUT and OUTPUT sides of these computerised systems, but how many of us are familiar with the PROCESS part of computer systems? Most of us accept it as a tool, feeding it with information and in turn, letting it feed us with information. To avoid this educated ignorance, we must focus our attention on the middle box—the PROCESS.

Summary

The computer is not only used in many different situations, its use is essential for us to maintain our living standards. The ever increasing use of the computer has become known as the Computer Revolution. This has come about because of the invention of the silicon chip which is at the heart of all computers and many other types of electrical equipment. The purpose of the chip is to control the equipment automatically, and how it does this we shall learn as we progress through this book. The original computers were large machines occupying large areas, but were expensive both to buy and to run. Consequently, only wealthy companies could afford them. As a result of the smallness and cheapness of the silicon chip, computers themselves have now become smaller and cheaper. The behaviour of any item of electronic equipment that uses a chip can be described as input—process—output, with the processing part acting on the information that is input into the equipment. When the processing is complete the results are output in some form of display, which may be on a computer screen, printed on a piece of paper or in some other form as in the case of the panda crossing.

Key Points

computers for food, computers for warmth, computers for everything, the computer assembly, inside the computer, the silicon chip, the computer revolution, the information age, electronic calculator, input-process-output, digital watch, panda crossing, electricity bill

Self Assessment questions

To make sure that you have not missed anything, try and answer the following short questions. The numbers in brackets refer to the paragraph numbers where you will find the answer.

1 How can we avoid becoming too dependent on computers and losing our understanding of basic processes? (2)
2 What evidence is available to show that we need computers to help provide us with food? (3–6)
3 Why are computers used to help provide us with food? (7)
4 What evidence is available to show that we need computers to help provide us with warmth? (8, 9)
5 Why do electricity power stations use computers? (9)
6 Name ten items of computerised not-so-basic needs (10)
7 What does a computer look like? (11)
8 What is a monitor? (11)
9 What are the monitor and the keyboard used for? (11)
10 What does the single most common component inside a computer look like? (12)
11 What is this component called? (13)
12 Describe a silicon chip? (13)
13 How different were the original computers from those of today? (14)
14 How did the silicon chip affect the availability of computers? (15)
15 In what way is an electronic calculator similar to a miniature computer? (17)
16 What is meant by 'input—process—output'? (18)
17 Draw the 'input—process—output' diagram. (18)
18 Describe the digital watch alarm system in terms of input—process—output. (19)
19 Describe the panda crossing system in terms of input—process—output. (20)
20 Describe the issuing of an electricity bill in terms of input—process—output. (21)

Exercises

1 Name **two** items of information which a library needs when a persons borrows a book.

2 Which **two** of these applications would a person working in a travel agency expect to use?

air traffic control
information retrieval
computer aided design
flight simulation
airline booking systems

3 All computer systems require at least one input device and at least one output device if they are to do a useful job. Name one input device and one output device that would be appropriate for each of the following situations:

A microprocessor system in a washing machine
An enquiry/booking system of a large airline
An arcade video game

2 What makes a computer system?

Objectives

1 To introduce some of the functions of the component parts of a computer system.
2 To introduce the need for various modes of computer operation that are suitable for particular types of processing.

Introduction

1 The purpose of this chapter is to build on the ideas of computer systems as we described them in the previous Chapter. We shall look at the different methods of inputting, processing and outputting information and this will lead us to think about methods of storing information and to the idea of the **memory**.

Your brain

2 Your brain both stores information and **processes** information. What is 2 + 2? You will automatically answer '4' because your brain has worked out the sum. In other words, it has processed information.

3 First it took signals from your eyes as you read the question. Second, it recognised it as a question and worked out the answer. Third, it produced the answer and made you say it to yourself. This is what we mean by processing information.

4 If your teacher asks you what is the capital of Brazil your brain searches its information store for the answer. If your brain has that information stored then if finds it and produces the answer—Rio De Janeiro. You may not have that information in your brain or you may not be able to recall it in which case you say nothing. But whether or not you know, your brain has still processed information.

5 Do you recognise the INPUT—PROCESS—OUTPUT at work here? The INPUT is the question, the PROCESS is your hearing the question and searching for the answer and the OUTPUT is your speaking the answer.

Make a list of other situations in which you would perform this INPUT—PROCESS—OUTPUT sequence, for example when you feel hungry, tired or angry, or even when you are riding your bicycle or going for a walk.

Your memory

6 Your brain has an ability to store information in what we call a memory. It is like a warehouse where you can store facts such as the capital of Brazil and rules such as those that tell you how to add two numbers together or how to read the words in this book.

When your brain PROCESSES information it makes use of the information stored in your memory. We say that it **accesses** the memory. We can represent this ability to access the memory by the following diagram.

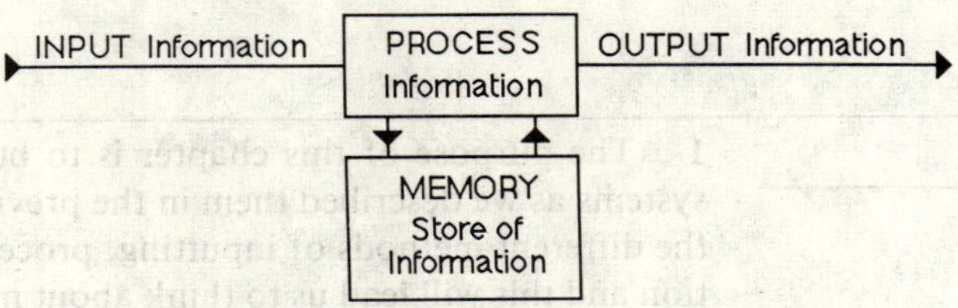

The information stored in your memory has been continually added since the day you were born. This has been done through your five senses: sight, touch, smell, hearing, taste.

In each of the following situations describe the INPUT, PROCESS and OUTPUT.

(a) You select a rose from a bush, pick it and put it in your buttonhole.

(b) You are in the lunch queue and you select a jam roly-poly for desert in preference to cheese.

(c) Someone creeps up behind you, shouts 'boo' and you jump

(d) You are sewing a button on a jacket and you prick your finger.

7 We can OUTPUT information from our memory in a variety of ways. We can speak, we can make gestures with our body, we can glare with our eyes, or we can write it down.

The computer's brain and memory

8 Look at the computer again. The **box** is like your skull and contains the computer's brain. The brain contains memory that has an ability to store information. The most important information it has to store is **how to operate** so it contains a **permanent memory** that holds information to tell it how to operate.

> Where does the analogy between the human brain and the computer break dcwn?

9 When we looked inside the computer in the last chapter we saw a number of different sized black plastic blocks or chips. These chips are responsible for doing all the work of PROCESSING information. They are collectively called the **central processing unit** or **CPU** which we shall discuss in more detail later on. The CPU accepts INPUT information, PROCESSES it and produces the OUTPUT information. The array of small chips contains a type of memory. This is not a permanent memory and the information it stores is lost when we turn the computer off. It is called **transient memory**.

Having located the computer's CPU, we must now consider how we INPUT information to it and how we OUTPUT information from it.

Input

10 A number of pieces of equipment are used to input information to the computer. The keyboard is used to type in letters and numbers. These letters or numbers form the INPUT to the CPU and as you type they simultaneously appear on the monitor screen.

1.9 Courtesy Hewlett Packard

Try entering in numbers and letters at the keyboard, even if you have never handled a computer before.

Switch the computer on (ask for help if you need it) and the monitor will display something like **A>** followed by a flashing line or square. This flashing symbol is called the **cursor**. If you press a letter on the keyboard, then that letter will appear on the screen where the flashing cursor was located and the cursor will move along one space. Try it: type in, for example, your name, e.g. DEXTER BOOTH.

You have now INPUT information to the computer—you are communicating with it. Press the ENTER or RETURN key: depending upon the type of computer you have, a message similar to the following will appear: SYNTAX ERROR *or* BAD COMMAND OR FILE NAME.

This means that the computer has not understood your communication. This is because you are not speaking its language and your name does not mean anything to it. If your computer automatically loads the BASIC language into its memory (both BBC and the Apple do this) then try typing in: PRINT "DEXTER BOOTH" followed by RETURN. It will now print your name (or mine) underneath. The word PRINT is an instruction to the computer to print whatever follows that is enclosed in double quotes. PRINT is a word it understands.

Now type in PRINT (1 + 5)/2 followed by RETURN, and the number 3 will appear. You have just instructed the computer to print out the value of the sum i.e. six divided by two

> If this is the first time you have used a computer, now is the time to experiment. See if you can make the computer do the following:
> (a) Print your address.
> (b) Print the first four letters of the alphabet each separated by six spaces.
> (c) Work out some sums. The symbol for multiplication is *.

11 Next to the keyboard is a graphics tablet.

This is a piece of equipment that allows you to draw pictures on your monitor screen. When you apply pressure at a point on the pad, a spot lights up at an appropriate place on the screen and if you draw a line on the pad a line appears on the screen. The computer has not only lit up the screen, but it has remembered where it was lit up—this information was INPUT through the graphics tablet and stored in the computer's memory. If your computer has one, try some drawing. You may need to ask your teacher to set up the graphics tablet.

12 Next to the graphics tablet is a joystick and a pair of paddles.

Those of you who play computer games will know that these are used to control the state of play during a game, such as moving a helicopter around the screen or running PAC MAN through a maze. What they do, in effect, is communicate to the computer your intentions regarding the position you want your play to be. They are

INPUT equipment—they allow you to put information into the computer. There are games you can play using the keyboard to build up your familiarity with the computer and your eye-hand response skills. Computers are practical pieces of equipment and the more hands-on experience you get the more you are going to learn about them.

13 So far we have looked at a comprehensive array of equipment which is concerned purely with inputting information into the computer. This is how the outside world **communicates** with the computer.

> Can you think of any other methods of putting information into the computer? Keep your eyes open whenever you are near a computerised system and see how many different methods you can spot in a week.

Output

14 We have already discussed the monitor, or VDU, as a method used by the computer to communicate to the outside world. On the other side of our computer is a printer.

When information appears on the monitor screen it is not permanent—it is stored in the transient memory and if you switch the computer off, you will lose your information. Often we want to keep the information produced by the computer for future reference. We therefore OUTPUT the information to the printer to produce what we call **hard copy**—a permanent printed record. If you then switch off your computer, you will still have the information.

> How many other ways can you think of that a computer uses to output information? Think of output as the computer communicating to you. You can hear, you can see, you can feel.

Input and output

15 The equipment that we have looked at so far has been dedicated to either inputting or outputting information. We call it **peripheral** equipment because it surrounds the CPU. One other piece of peripheral equipment that serves a double purpose is the box which contains all the electronics to make the computer work. Your box may have slots in the front which are called disk drives and these, not surprisingly, drive disks! Alternatively your box may not have slots in it, but will have disk drives as separate units connected to the main box.

Disk drives and floppy disks

A disk is a circular sheet of plastic enclosed within a plastic jacket. It is coated with a magnetic material and is used for storing information, in a similar way to the way the tape in a cassette stores music.

1.10A A 5¼" disk

1.10B A 3½" disk

16 However, different computers use different disks; some are 5.25 inches in diameter and quite bendy, while others are 3.5 inches in diameter and contained inside a hard plastic cover. They are called **floppy diskettes.**

17 The tape in a cassette has a magnetic coating like the diskette and the music that is stored on the tape is stored magnetically along the length of the tape. When you play music on the tape the cassette player reads the magnetically stored information and converts them into sound through the electronics of the machine. The floppy disk in the computer's disk drive works in the same way. Information is stored as magnetised spots on the disk surface and the disk drive **reads** these spots and converts them into information that can be interpreted by the computer.

18 By **reading** information stored on the diskette surface, the computer is using the floppy diskette as a method of inputting information. But not only can the computer read the information stored on the diskette's surface, it can also put information onto the diskette's surface. We call this **writing** to the diskette.

19 By writing information to the diskette the computer is using the floppy diskette as a method of outputting information. A floppy diskette therefore plays a double role as a piece of INPUT and OUTPUT equipment.

20 We shall be saying more about how diskettes and disk drives work later in the book. For now all we need to know is that the floppy disk has the ability to store information so we can call it a memory because the computer can put information onto it—by writing to the disk—and can take information off it—by reading the disk.

> Can you think of a non-computerised system which has a memory that can be used for both input and output? Try to think of three different systems.

Processing

21 In the last chapter we looked at a number of different computerised systems but they did not all process information in the same way. We shall now consider three different ways of processing information.

- real-time processing
- batch processing
- CONTROL

Real-time processing

22 Real-time processing is where information is being continually INPUT, often by hand, and immediately PROCESSED. This will also result in immediate OUTPUT and sometimes the input will depend on the output. An example of this is the theatre booking system.

23 To book seats to see a play, you go to the box office and ask if there are any seats available for the performance next Monday. The booking clerk types into the computer the word RESERVATION and the computer asks for a date to be typed in. When Monday's date is typed in, the screen fills with a plan of the seating arrangements in the theatre. A number of seats are filled with bright squares—these are the seats that are already booked. You are told that a number of seats are available in Row V, and you choose a seat in the middle, number 25. The booking clerk then types in V25 and your seat fills with a bright square. Your reservation has been made and that seat is booked. Next a ticket is issued from the printer showing you that you have reserved seat 25 in row V for next Monday's performance and you pay for the ticket.

24 This is a typical use of a real-time system. Input, process and output all happened one after the other and, more importantly, the input was **live**—it was being put in by hand and was dependent on the output. The output displayed the vacant seats which then allowed you to decide what the next input was to be.

Make a list of five real-time systems that you have seen in action. It may be useful to start with your public library.

Control processing

25 Control Processing is a form of real-time processing where the INPUT is determined by the OUTPUT but the INPUT can be **automatically** fed in. In such a situation the PROCESSING is being used to control a system by means of automatic feedback—the output is fed back to decide what the next input should be. An example of this is the automatic washing machine.

26 For example, you want to wash your jeans in a WARM WASH so they will not lose too much of their colour. You put them into the

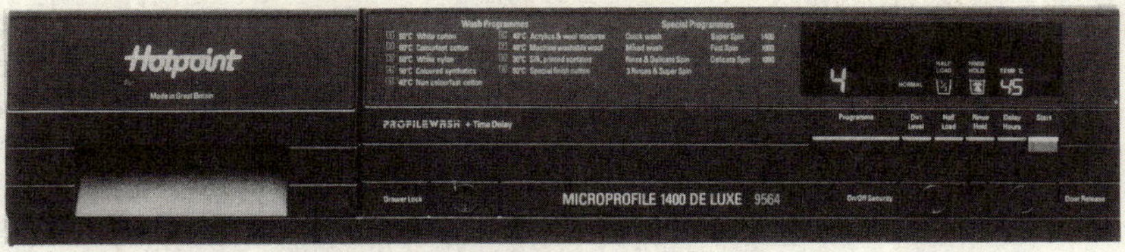

1.11 Control panel of an automatic washing machine; courtesy Hotpoint Ltd

washer, close the door and switch the machine on, setting the wash cycle to WARM and SMALL LOAD. The washer starts to fill with water. The water is cold so it has to be heated up to the correct temperature for a warm wash, 60 degrees Celsius. When the water reaches this temperature the washing machine senses it and tells the computer to switch the heater off and start to tumble wash. Here the output is the water temperature and the following input causes the heater to switch off and the tumble wash to start.

When it has finished—after a time measured by the machine—it empties the dirty water and fills up with clean water for the rinse. Again the water is cold so it has to be heated to the correct temperature for a warm rinse. The rinse complete, the machine remembers that it is a small load and so does not go into the second rinse that it would for a normal load. The machine then empties the rinse water and spins the jeans to damp dry.

Here the machine was using internal sensors to gauge the temperature of the water to move it on to the next part of the wash cycle.

27 Another obvious use of control processing is the use of a robot for welding car bodies.

In this case the robot has to sense the exact position of the two pieces of metal that are to be welded together. The position sensor outputs the information to the input which causes the welding to start.

> In the last chapter we talked about the panda crossing. Go out and watch a panda crossing in action when somebody wishes to cross the road and make a detailed report of the sequence of events that occur. Does the output determine the input? Is it automatic? Is it control processing?

Batch processing

28 Batch processing is where the INPUT information is accumulated into sizeable batches before being processed. The processing is then done, one batch of INPUT information at a time. Many commercial computer applications use batch processing as a method of delaying time-consuming computer usage to a period when the computer is not required for real-time uses such as during the night. Batch processing may also result in immediate output but the input is in no way affected by the output during the processing of the batch.

1.12 Robot production of cars on an assembly line

29 For example, you work in the wages office of a local engineering company. Tomorrow is payday so today you have to get the computer to print out the pay-slips for 1,000 people. The computer has all the necessary information for working out the wages, paying taxes and national insurance contributions provided it knows how many hours each person has worked that week.

If the system operated in real-time you would have to enter a person's name followed by the hours worked and let the computer perform the necessary calculations to produce the pay-slip at the printer. With 1,000 people this may take too long.

30 A better way to work the system would be to store the name of each person with the number of hours they worked on a floppy diskette. The computer could then read each person's details from the disk, process them and print the pay-slip. This method would allow the computer itself to control the speed at which it accepted information for processing. The computer operates at a much faster rate than a human operator and can read in employees' details in much less time than you could type them in. The process would be repeated 1,000 times resulting in the wages being ready on time. This type of processing is called batch processing.

Notice here that the input is pre-determined and is not influenced by the output at all.

> Although you may not have seen a computer doing a batch processing job, you will probably have seen the results of one many times. Make a list of three, for example, the bills that come through your letter box?

Hardware and software

31 So far we have considered the physical component parts of a computerised system. We have looked at the types of processing and seen that all the processing is controlled by the CPU—the central processing unit. What we have not considered is how the CPU works. How does it know to perform its tasks?

32 Earlier we considered the human brain's capacity to remember rules. These rules tell the brain how to work out various tasks. The CPU uses rules in the form of a list of instructions stored in its memory. This list of instructions is called a **program** and by obeying the instructions contained in the program the CPU knows how to work. When the CPU is working and obeying a sequence of instructions we say that it is **executing a program**.

33 There are two distinct parts to a computer system. First there is the physical equipment that goes together to form the computer; this is called the **hardware**. Second are the instructions that make the hardware work to perform particular tasks. These sets of instructions or programs, are called **software**.

Summary

34 Our brains store information in the form of facts and rules. The human brain accepts information, processes it and causes us to output information in a variety of different ways. The information is input to our brain through the five senses and stored in our memory. A computer also has a brain and a memory—it is called the central processing unit or CPU for short. There are many different ways that information can be put into a computer. Inputting information is the method whereby the outside world communicates to the computer. There are a number of different ways that information can be output from a computer. Outputting information is the way the computer

communicates with the outside world. All input and output equipment is external to the computer and is called peripheral equipment. A disk drive is a piece of equipment that is used both to read information from and write information to a floppy diskette.

Just as there are different methods of inputting and outputting information, there are different types of processing information. Real-time processing involves live input and simultaneous processing. The input is generally entered by hand and can be influenced by the output. Control processing is real-time processing that can be completely automatic and so proceed without human intervention. Here the input is influenced by feed-back from the output. Batch processing involves the processing of input information that has been previously accumulated into batches. During batch processing the input is not influenced by the output.

The physical components that go together to form the computer are referred to collectively as hardware. The programs of instructions that cause the computer to behave in the way that it does are collectively referred to as software.

Key points

Facts and rules, brain and memory, central processing unit (CPU), different input equipment, outside world communicating to the computer, different output equipment, computer communicating to the outside world, dual purpose disk drives and floppy diskettes, peripheral equipment, real-time processing, control processing, batch processing, hardware, software.

Self assessment questions

1 Give the three stages you go through when answering a simple question (2–5).
2 What is the name for the store of information that your brain holds? (6)
3 Name two types of information that your memory stores. (6)
4 How was information put into your memory? (6)
5 How do you output information from your brain? (7)
6 What is the most important information stored by a computer? (8)
7 What type of memory is this information stored in? (8)
8 What do the initials CPU stand for? (9)
9 What is the CPU? (9)
10 What is a keyboard used for? (10)
11 What is a graphics tablet used for? (11)
12 What are joysticks and paddles used for? (12)
13 What is all input equipment used for? (13)
14 What is the monitor used for? (14)
15 What is a printer used for? (14)
16 What is meant by the phrase 'peripheral equipment'? (15)
17 What does a floppy diskette look like? (15,16)
18 What is a floppy diskette used for? (16)
19 How does a floppy diskette store information? (17)
20 Explain why a floppy diskette can be used for both inputting to and outputting information from a computer. (18, 20)
21 Name three types of information processing. (21)
22 What is meant by real-time processing? (22)
23 Give an example of real-time processing (23–24)
24 What is meant by control processing? (25)

25 Give two examples of control processing. (26–27)
26 What is meant by batch processing? (28)
27 Give an example of batch processing. (29)
28 In what form does the CPU use the rules that are stored in the computer's permanent memory? (31)
29 What do we call a list of instructions that the computer obeys? (31)
30 What does the phrase 'executing a program' mean? (31)
31 What is hardware? (32)
32 What is software? (32)

Exercises

1 Which two of these devices are computer output devices?
graph plotter   printer   joystick   light pen
keyboard

2 Which two of these items are methods of data collection for input to a computer system?
survey forms   bar codes   printers
televisions   ROM

3 Name two examples of how computer control is used in industry.

4 Which of the following is used for transferring information from one computer to another?

flowchart
magnetic disk
printer
VDU

5 Which of the following would be used to store bookings from travel agencies?

cassette tape
magnetic disk
magnetic tape
punched cards

6 Choose an application which uses on-line processing and explain why on-line processing is used in this application.

7 Which two of these applications need to use on-line processing?

producing club membership lists
airline booking systems
printing electricity bills
producing pay slips
traffic control

8

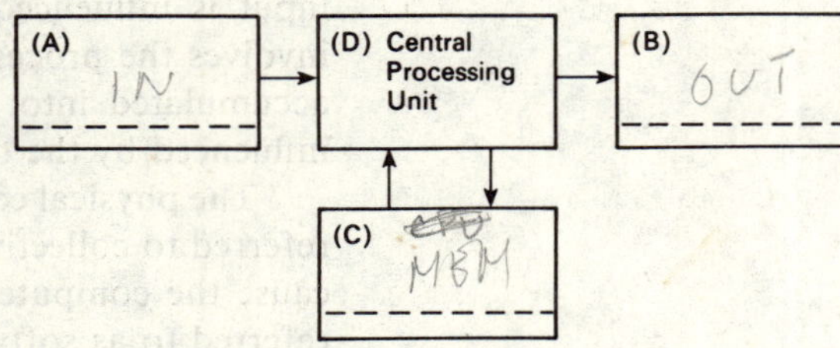

(a) The diagram above shows the flow of data in a computer system. Name the parts labelled A, B and C.

(b) In which box on the diagram would you expect to find the Immediate Access Store?

(c) Name one use of the Immediate Access Store.

9 Many banks now issue plastic cards that can be used to get cash from cash machines.

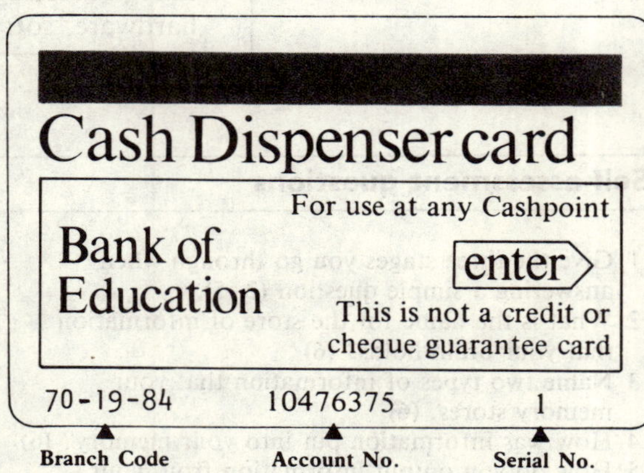

(a) How is the information about the identity of the customer held on the card?

(b) Describe the process of checking that the card user is the owner of the card.

3 *Solving problems*

Objectives

1 An introduction to the derivation of the information requirements of a system and the specification of a system in terms of the output needed, the input data and any necessary files.

2 An introduction to the formulation of solutions to problems and the communication of the solutions in appropriate ways.

Introduction

1 In this chapter we shall look at the various processes that are involved when we solve problems. These processes are illustrated by solving simple problems using both pencil and paper and a calculator. Having discussed the input-process-output diagrams in the last chapter, we will show that the solution to a problem can be represented by diagrams called flowcharts. These ideas are illustrated by showing how a problem of counting and averaging is solved using a computer. We will also discuss the use of files as stores of information, and finally, recognising the two-way communication flow between users and computers, we shall demonstrate the need for clear communication. This also includes the need for documentation, both in the form of an annotated program and a program manual.

Solving problems

2 The world is full of problems that have to be solved, some of which are difficult, and some easy. Being asked to design a new Chemistry laboratory for your school would be a difficult problem, but taking a message to the head teacher would be an easy problem.

3 However easy or difficult a problem is, the process of obtaining a solution can be separated into three stages:

- obtaining the information necessary to solve the problem
- the process of solving the problem
- communicating the solution to the problem.

4 For example, to solve the problem of taking a message to the head teacher requires you to know where the office is and how to get there.

This information is necessary to solve the problem. Without this your method of obtaining information would be to ask the way. To take the message you would use this information to find your way to the Head's office.

This is the process of solving the problem. Having arrived at the office you would pass on the message: this would be communicating the final solution to the problem.

> Describe the three parts of the problem solving process for each of the following problems
> (a) You have been invited to a party but you do not know where it is.
> (b) You want to cross a busy road.
> (c) You are miles from home and your bike has a flat tyre.

5 Do you recognise the INPUT—PROCESS—OUTPUT in action here? Solving problems follows the same pattern but with the PROCESS replaced with SOLVING THE PROBLEM.

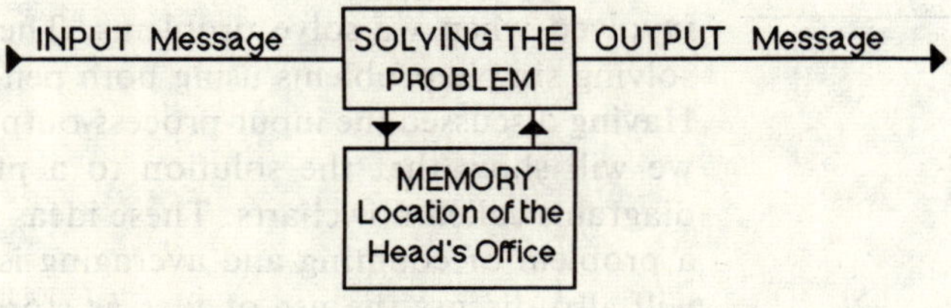

6 Because of this similarity between the processes involved in solving problems and the processes involved in using computers, computers are ideal tools for solving problems.

7 Before we can tell a computer how to solve a problem we must first know how to solve it ourselves. Let's look at the details of solving the problem of adding the numbers 142 and 379 together using a pencil and a piece of paper.

Using a pencil and paper

8 To add 142 to 379 we require information on how to add numbers together. We shall assume you already have this information. The process of adding the numbers now follows.

Task 1 Write one number below the other in column form

142
379

Task 2 Add 9 to 2 which makes 11. Write down 1 and carry 1 to the tens column

1
142
379
1

Task 3 Add 1 and 4 and 7 to make 12. Write down 2 and carry 1 to the hundreds column

1
142
379
21

Task 4 Add 1 to 1 and 3 to make 5. Write down the 5

142
379
521

The solution to the problem is 521.

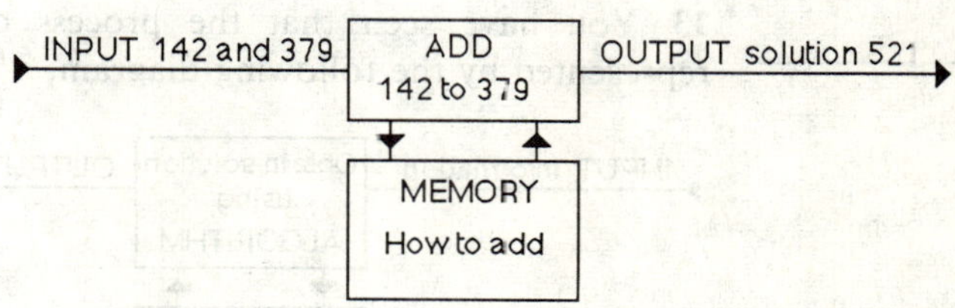

9 The process that we used to perform the addition is a procedure that we already knew and is in our memory. You will notice that the procedure consists of performing a sequence of well defined tasks.

Repeat this process by adding 9503 to 2748.

This sequence of well defined tasks is called an **algorithm**.

An algorithm is a sequence of well defined tasks that is used to obtain the solution to a problem.

10 We use algorithms to solve problems and so do computers. Some algorithms used by the computer are contained inside the computer's permanent memory in the form of a sequence of instructions. When the computer obeys one of these instructions it will perform the specific task. To illustrate this the last problem can be solved using a calculator.

Using a calculator

11 To add 142 to 379 we first enter the number **142** followed by the + sign. We then enter the number **379** followed by the = sign.

Immediately, the number **521** appears on the screen. The two numbers and the + sign form the **input information**. When we entered the = sign we told the calculator that we had finished entering the input. The calculator then used an algorithm in its memory to work out the value 521—the **processing**. Finally, the number 521 was displayed on the screen as the solution to the problem—the **output**

> Use your calculator to work out each of these sums:
> (a) (92 + 25)/6
> (b) 92 + 25/6
> (c) 12/5 + 3/7 − 7/5
> For each sum, write down exactly how you used the calculator.
> Did you use the memory?

12 We have seen how simple diagrams can help us understand the idea of input—process—output. We shall now construct some diagrams that describe the processes of solving problems.

Flowcharts

13 You have seen that the process of solving problems can be represented by the following diagram,

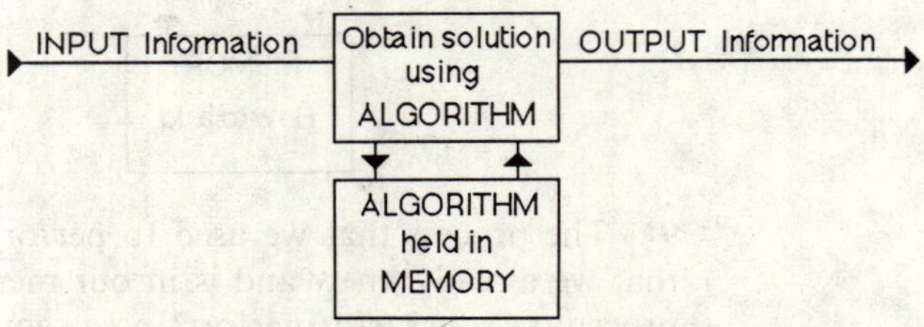

Diagrams are used to describe the various processes carried out when solving problems using a computer because they help us to visualise the individual tasks that are involved. These diagrams are called **flowcharts** because they display the way in which individual processes link together to form the complete INPUT—PROCESS—OUTPUT; they chart the flow of the algorithm. Because these diagrams are accepted all over the world as a means of describing algorithms, we have a universal agreement of what various symbols mean. For example, the symbol of a **parallelogram** is recognised as meaning INPUT or OUTPUT, whereas the symbol of a simple **rectangle** means PROCESSING. Using these conventions our earlier diagram looks like this:

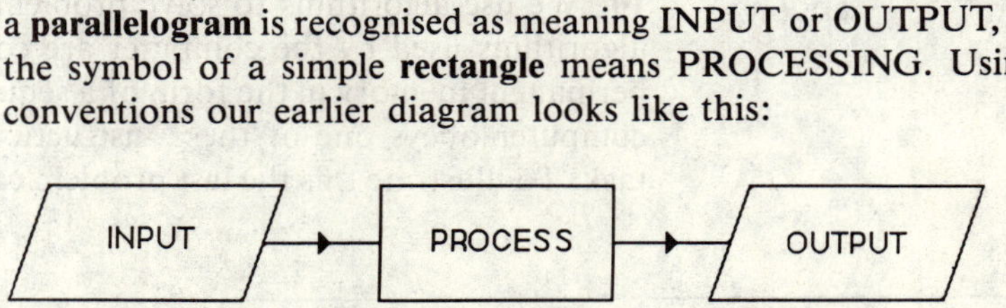

Because most flowcharts will not fit across the page the normal convention is to draw them vertically.

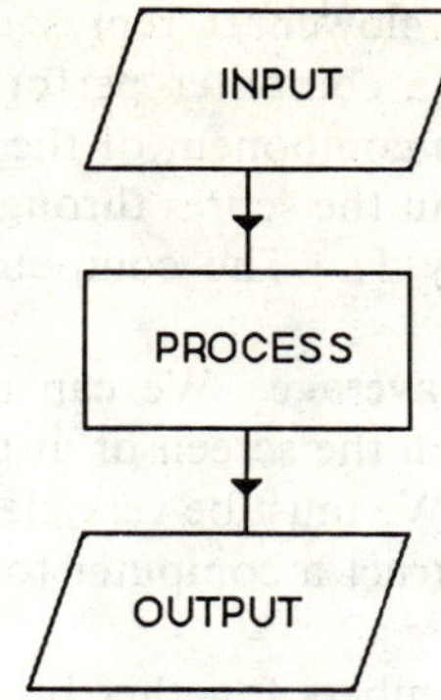

By separating the PROCESS box into the four tasks of the example where we added 142 to 379, write a flowchart to represent the way we solved the problem. Incicate in each task exactly what is being done.

A typical problem

14 The problem of adding two simple numbers together is too simple to allow us to expand on the idea of an algorithm as applied to a computer related solution. A more typical problem for which a computer is used concerns **counting and averaging**.

Counting and averaging

15 The problem is to find the average batting score of a team of 11 cricketers when the individual scores are as follows:

15, 56, 65, 42, 12, 28, 30, 15, 2, 8, 13

First, ADD up all the numbers. This gives a total of 286. Second divide the total by the number of players. This gives an average of 286/11 = 26 runs per player The following flowchart represents this simple algorithm.

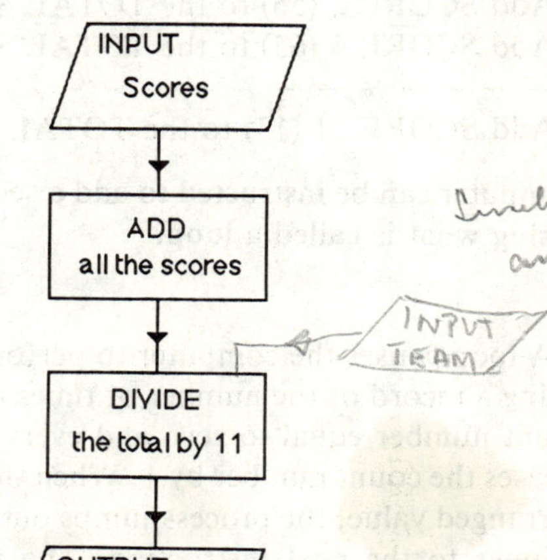

Surely the no. of players, i.e. 11 is an input!

16 Each box in the flowchart represents a component part of the algorithm. To make a computer perform this algorithm we have to make it perform each component of the algorithm in turn.
INPUT We can input the scores through the keyboard one at a time.
DIVIDE the total by 11 The computer knows how to divide two numbers.
OUTPUT the score average We can make the computer print the score average either on the screen or at the printer.
ADD all the scores We must be very clear how we added the numbers up before we can instruct a computer to do the same.

17 We added the numbers together by putting them in column form and adding first the units then the tens. This is not the only way they can be added. They can be added into a RUNNING TOTAL. The way this is done is as follows. Add the first score 15 to the second score 56 to give 71. Now add the third score 65 to this total 71 to give 136 and so on until we have added up all the scores. Note that at any time we only add two numbers together.

This is exactly the way a calculator works. Enter the number 15, press + and enter the number 56. Now when you press + again the screen reads 71—the sum of 15 and 56. When you put in the third number—65—you are really adding it to 71.

> Use your calculator to do some sums. Notice that at any time during the calculation you are only dealing with two numbers. Which two numbers are they?

18 If we instructed a computer to add the list of numbers two at a time, our instructions would look something like this:

Start with a TOTAL SCORE of zero
Add SCORE 1 (15) to the TOTAL SCORE to give 15
Add SCORE 2 (56) to the TOTAL SCORE to give 71
Add SCORE 3 (65) to the TOTAL SCORE to give 136
– –
Add SCORE 11 (13) to the TOTAL SCORE to give 286

A computer can be instructed to add a sequence of numbers in this way by using what is called a **loop**.

A loop

19 A loop causes the computer to perform a specified task repeatedly, keeping a record of the number of times it is repeated. It starts off with a count number equal to zero and every time the task is performed it increases the count number by 1. When the count number has reached a prearranged value, the process jumps out of the loop and the computer continues to the next instruction. The following diagram shows the flowchart for this loop.

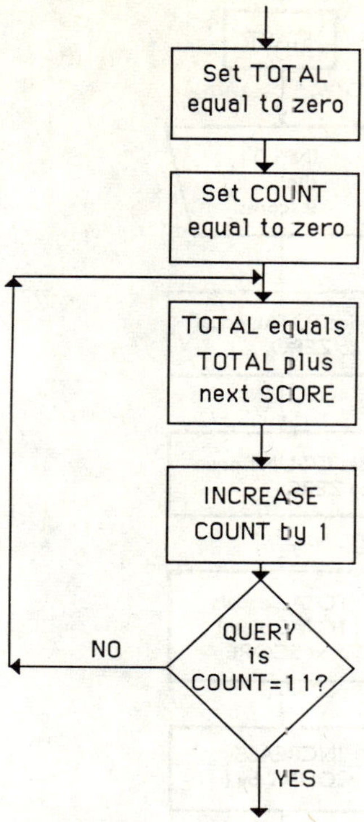

Note the **diamond** or **rhombus** surrounding the QUERY. This symbol is used when a decision has to be made.

The flow of operations travels around the loop, each time adding a score to a running TOTAL and increasing the count by 1. When the answer to the question 'is the COUNT equal to 11?' is YES, the flow of operations moves out of the loop.

If you follow the flow around the loop, you will see that it will add together the 11 scores provided that it knows what they are.

20 Note that to prepare the computer for entering the loop we set both the TOTAL and the COUNT to be equal to zero.

The flowchart that represents the complete algorithm can now be constructed by inserting this loop where the ADD box was in the first flowchart.

> Describe in words the sequence of operations necessary to add the squares of the numbers 1, 2, 3, 4 and then find the average square. Draw the flowchart that will describe the processes to solve this problem.

> If you are familiar with a programming language such as BASIC, you could try to write a program that will enable the computer to solve this problem.

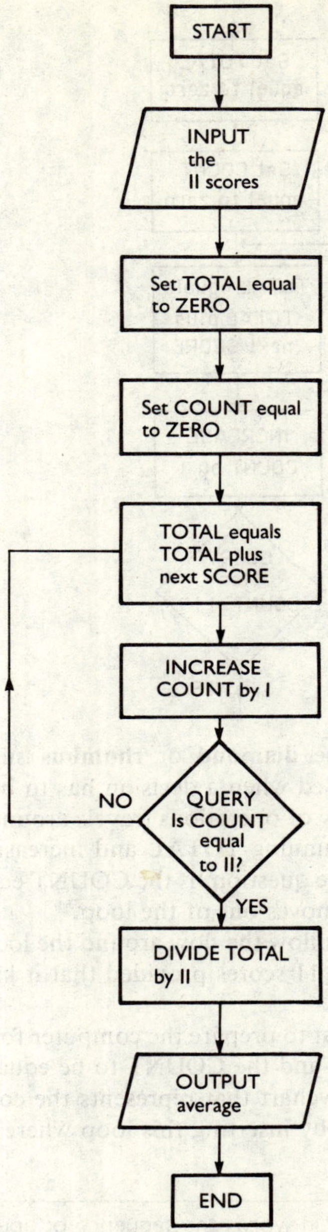

21 Counting and averaging is a simple problem for the computer to solve: it will add up the numbers and find the average in thousandths of a second. The only slow part of the process is entering the 11 scores at the keyboard—the input. This part of the system would be considerably speeded up if the scores were fed into the computer automatically, for example, by storing them on a floppy diskette in a file.

Files

22 A file is the name given to an organised store of information, organised for a specific purpose. For example, your dentist will have your dental history on record, probably on a piece of card. The card will contain your name, address, age, the current state of your teeth and a history of all the treatments that you have had up to the present date. One such card will be kept for every patient, and the whole collection will form a file, which may be kept in a filing cabinet.

1.21 A collection of records on a file

A file can also consist of computerised records kept on a diskette. The computer can then be instructed to read the records on the floppy diskette and copy them into its memory, a process that will take only microseconds. In a similar way, a program is also an organised store of information and can be stored in a file.

> Filing information is a very common process. Think of three different situations where a file of information would be kept. Could this information be kept on a diskette file?

Communication

23 Communication plays a vital role in computers. You communicate to them and they communicate to you, but it is important that communication is understood.

We shall look at two aspects of communication:

- communication from computer to user
- documentation

> Think of four situations where you are presented with a problem to solve. How do you communicate the solution to these problems. Remember that communication can also include communication to yourself.

Communication from computer to user

24 A user is any person who is using the computer. When a computer is executing a program it is likely to be in real-time and communicating to the user. This communication can consist of messages printed on the screen, sounds emitted from the speaker or information sent to the printer. Whatever the form of communication, the message transmitted must be clear and must not be ambiguous. For example, when you first turn on your computer the screen could simply produce the display: **A>** followed by a flashing line. To anyone who is unfamiliar with computers all that means is that the monitor screen is working; it is an example of unclear communication.

25 Those of you who have played games on your computer, especially old games, will be familiar with line after line of print crowded into the top half of the screen. The message may be clear once you have read it but it can take quite an effort to read it. The following is an example of bad screen display.

THIS PROGRAM WILL TAKE ELEVEN CRICKETER'S
SCORES AND WORK OUT THE TOTAL SCORE. WHEN IT
HAS DONE THIS IT WILL THEN CALCULATE THE
AVERAGE AND PRINT THIS AVERAGE ON YOUR
PRINTER. MAKE SURE THAT YOUR PRINTER IS
SWITCHED ON AND READY TO RECEIVE OUTPUT.
?-

Although the message is all there, it is hard work to read. The question mark indicates where you are to enter the scores but there is no statement telling you this. Many users, faced with that screen, would be very unsure of how to proceed from here. A much improved screen display is as follows:

<u>THE CRICKET TEAM'S AVERAGE</u>

A program to calculate the average batting score for a cricket team.

Switch on your printer and enter the eleven scores below;

1. Score 1 -
2. Score 2 -
3. Score 3 -
4. Score 4 -
5. Score 5 -
6. Score 6 -
7. Score 7 -
8. Score 8 -
9. Score 9 -
10. Score 10 -
11. Score 11 -

26 This may not be the most attractive layout but it is clear and unambiguous, leaving the user in no doubt about what the program is for and how to proceed from here.

> Define a screen display that will allow people to enter their names, addresses and telephone numbers. Do not forget to ask for the Post Code.

Having made sure that when the computer communicates to the user it does so as clearly as possible, we must now make sure that *our* communication to the user is also as clear as possible. This is achieved by **documenting** the system.

Documentation

27 Documentation comes in two forms.

- program documentation
- manuals

Program documentation

When you first write programs you will be so eager to see if they work that you will simply write code and then run it. This would make it difficult for anyone else to read and understand.

To avoid this problem, each section of the program must be accompanied by an explanation of exactly what it is doing—it must be **annotated**. This is known as **program documentation**. When a program is properly documented it should be easy for another person to read it and understand what it is doing. If in the future someone else wanted to adapt the program by adding other features they would then be able to do so.

Manuals

28 Every program should be accompanied by a printed document called a **manual**. The manual will inform a user of the features that the program provides and a description of how to use it.

> Write a user manual for a program to work out the total and average scores of a cricketer. Assume that when the program is being executed, the user has to enter only the scores at the keyboard.

Summary

There are three stages in the process of solving a problem. We require necessary information for solving the problem and if we do not possess this we must obtain it. Next comes the working that solves the problem and finally we communicate the solution. This is the familiar INPUT —PROCESS—OUTPUT again where the PROCESS is replaced by SOLVING THE PROBLEM. Before we can instruct a computer to solve a problem we must be fully aware of how we would solve it ourselves using a pencil and paper. When we analyse the problem, we reduce it to a number of simple steps. This collection of simple steps is called an algorithm. Computers use algorithms to solve problems. Many of these algorithms are stored in their permanent memory. As an aid to developing an algorithm, diagrams are used to illustrate the sequence of operations. We call these diagrams flowcharts. Often a problem is solved by repeating a sequence of tasks a number of times. This type of algorithm is called a loop. Information can be input into a computer to enable it to set about solving a problem, either through the keyboard, or from a floppy diskette. If information is input from a floppy disk then it is initially stored on the diskette in a file. The computer can then read the information that is in the file.

Finally, it is recognised that all the problem solving abilities of a computer can be wasted if there is no proper form of communication between the user and the computer. Proper communication takes the form of clear screen messages, clear printout and clear documentation. Documentation consists of two parts. First is the annotation of the program the computer is to execute, and second is the printed manual. The manual describes all that the user needs to know to use the program.

Key points

The three stages of problem solving, algorithms, flowcharts, counting and averaging, loops, files, communication, program annotation, documented manual.

Self assessment questions

1 What are the three stages of problem solving? (3)
2 Give one example of a problem whose solution demonstrates the three stages of problem solving. (4)
3 Draw a diagram to illustrate the processes involved in your answer to Question 2. (5)
4 Why do computers make ideal tools for solving problems? (6)
5 What do we need to know before we can instruct a computer to solve a problem? (7)
6 Describe the process of adding two numbers together using a pencil and paper, and draw a diagram to illustrate this. (8)
7 What is an algorithm? (9)
8 Do computers use algorithms? (10)
9 What form do algorithms take? (10)
10 When using a calculator to work out an arithmetic problem, what does entering the = sign signify to the calculator? (11)
11 Distinguish between, INPUT, PROCESS and OUTPUT when adding two numbers together using an electronic hand calculator. (11)
12 What is a flowchart? (12,13)
13 Why is a flowchart so named? (12,13)
14 What is the flowchart symbol for INPUT and OUTPUT? (13)

15 What is the flowchart symbol for PROCESS? (13)
16 Why are flowcharts drawn vertically? (13)
17 How is an algorithm related to a flowchart? (16)
18 How does a computer add a list of numbers together? (17)
19 Write a sequence of instructions to add a list of numbers together in the same way that a computer adds them. (18)
20 What is a LOOP? (19)
21 Describe how a LOOP works. (19)
22 What is the flowchart symbol for a DECISION? (19)
23 What is a file? (21,22)
24 Give one example of when a computer can make use of a file on a floppy diskette. (22)
25 List two aspects of communication as related to the computer. (23)
26 What is a USER? (24)
27 What is essential when a computer communicates to a user? (24)
28 Give an example of an unclear communication. (25)
29 How would you clarify the unclear communication example in your answer to Question 28? (25)
30 List two types of documentation. (26)
31 What form does program documentation take? (27)
32 What is a MANUAL? (28)
33 Why should you never copy commercial software?

Exercises

1 Which of the following methods of communication would leave a permanent record?

newspaper
telephone
smoke signal

2 Which of the following files would need to be updated?

1881 census data for a town
telephone directory
details of vehicles registered in the UK
results of the last general election

3 (a) Name one suitable method of reading the account number from a person's bank cash card directly into a computer.

(b) Name one validation check which can be done on the bank account number.

(c) If a cash card is stolen, how is the thief prevented from using the card to withdraw cash?

(d) Which three words from the following list would complete the following sentence?

field   tree   file   rasp   record   manual

The bank account number is one...............in a person's .... in the bank's computer..............

4 The following are two methods which could be used in a program. They are designed to test whether the variable sex is F for female or something else for male.

Method 1
If sex = "F" THEN PRINT "female" ELSE PRINT "male"

Method 2
If sex = "F" THEN PRINT "female"
PRINT "male"

(a) Which of these methods will give a strange result?

(b) Explain why this method is wrong.

5 A computer program is to be written using the following flowchart. Dry run the flowchart and name all the output produced.

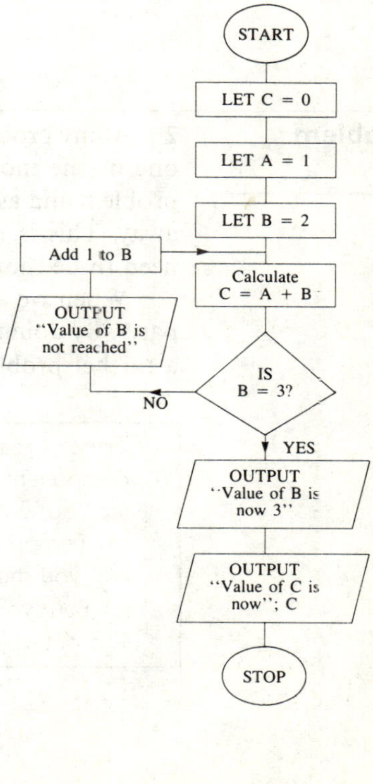

4 *Putting computers to work*

Objectives

1 To introduce the steps in the analysis, design, implementation and documentation of a system and the personnel involved with the operation of a computer system.

2 To introduce the derivation of the information required, the encoding of information and the testing of algorithms for the solution of a problem.

Introduction

1 We now apply what has been discussed in the previous three chapters to a realistic problem that could be duplicated in your classroom. A project is set up by the computer teacher at the local high school, involving the aspects of problem solving that we looked at in Chapter 3, together with the application of computers that we looked at in Chapters 1 and 2.

Practical problem solving

2 Many problems appear at first sight to be very difficult to solve, and one of the most common mistakes made by students is to look at a problem and assume that they should be able to see the solution straight away. This is rarely possible: any problem that is worth solving will need to be thought about and carefully analysed.

When we analyse a problem we break it down into its component parts. By doing this we usually find that each component part is in itself a further problem but one that we can more immediately solve.

> Try to break down each of the following problems into its component parts:
> (a) You wish to make a cup of coffee.
> (b) Tomorrow you will have a hockey match in the afternoon and you must prepare your kit tonight.
> (c) You would like to buy a new camera with a detachable zoom lens but you are not sure you can afford both.

Problems are similar to jigsaws in the respect that we solve them a piece at a time until eventually we find we have solved the whole problem. However, we solve a problem in a precisely defined manner, as shall be seen in the following mini case study.

Case study

3 In the local high school, the senior English teacher has been asked to write a short story for the school magazine. The magazine editor has restricted the size of the story to 2500 words. The English teacher is using a word processor at home on his BBC micro to produce the story but unfortunately, the first draft has run out at over 5000 words. However, his word processor does not have a word counting facility and because his style is to write a lot first and then revise many times, he anticipates spending much of his time simply counting words.

He tells the Computer Studies teacher about this in the staff room one Monday morning, just after his 5000 word count. The Computer Studies teacher, recognising his plight, suggests this might be set as a project for the students—to create a piece of software for the BBC micro that could be used by anyone to count the words in a document stored in a text file.

> How do you think they should solve the problem? Try and think the problem through and see if you can break it into its component parts.

Setting up the project

4 By Wednesday afternoon when the Computer Studies class next meets, it is clear that a number of the students have been thinking about the problem. A number of good ideas are put forward and a class discussion follows. Everyone agrees that they must organise themselves to work together to achieve a solution.

The teacher explains that any computer project can be broken down into three different stages.

- analysing the problem
- writing the computer program
- testing and running the system

Analysing the problem

5 First, the problem has to be analysed. It must be looked at in detail and broken down into its component parts. This is the job of the **Systems Analyst**.

Writing the computer program

6 Second, the work of the Systems Analyst has to be converted into a working computer program. This is the job of the **Programmer**.

Testing and running the system

7 The completed program must be tested by the programmer before it can be used as a solution to the problem. Finally, the information necessary to make the program work must be gathered, organised and entered into the system. This is the job of the **Data Manager**.

8 To make sure that work on the project is progressing satisfactorily, these three areas of activity are supervised by the **Project Manager**.

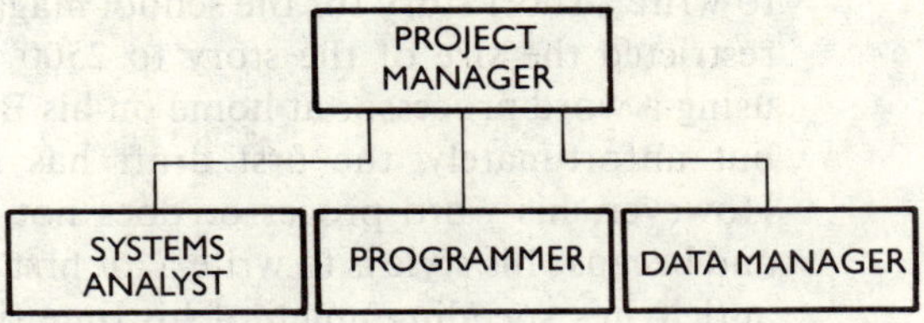

The project manager

9 The teacher suggests that the class are divided into four teams of six, each team to produce a complete solution to the problem. Within each team the students organise themselves into two people acting as systems analysts, two acting as programmers and two acting as data managers. The teacher acts as project manager for each of the four teams and explains how each particular group of two within a team are to set about their tasks.

The systems analyst

10 The problem facing the systems analysts is to examine the word processor package that the English teacher has used. From this they will be able to tell whether or not the document can be read directly from outside the word processor or whether it has to be converted into a text file first. A text file is one that contains only text characters (and possibly returns and line feeds). It does not contain any special characters that have been placed there by the word processing package and specifically devised to protect the document from being read from outside the package. Next the students have to decide how to go about counting words in a document and then how best to communicate the count to the user. They then have to break this process into a sequence of simple steps, each to be described in detail, and a system flowchart produced. This pictorially describes the whole system in terms of its individual component tasks. The results of the systems analysts' work are then passed to both the programmers and the data managers.

The programmer

11 When the programmers receive the broken down detail of the project their task is to convert the system into a computer program. This is done in stages with each component—or module—of the system being considered and tested separately. Only when this has been done can the complete program be put together. When the program is complete they test that the entire program works properly by using

sample information obtained from the data manager. This sample information will consist of a document containing a known number of words, so that when the known total is reproduced, they know that the program is correct.

The data manager

12 The data managers are responsible for making sure that all the information necessary for the system is available. They ensure that the information is gathered at the appropriate time and is prepared correctly for entry into the system. They are also responsible for entering the information into the system and notifying the project manager of any problems they incur.

The systems analyst's results

13 The systems analysts set about their task by talking to the English teacher and examining the word processor package that has been used. They soon find out that the document produced by the package is a text file and can be read directly by the BBC micro from outside the package. Next they consider how the words in the document can be counted and observing that they, as people, can count words by recognising the space between each, they realise that this is how the computer can do it as well. Assuming that every word is separated by only one space, by reading the document one character at a time the computer could simultaneously maintain a record of the number of spaces that it has read. The number of words will then be equal to the number of spaces plus 1. Why?

> The assumption that only one space divides words may be not be a very realistic assumption. For example, many typists put two spaces after a full stop to emphasise the separation between two sentences. There is another important reason why one space between two words may not be realistic—it depends on the type of word processor being used. Can you think what it is?

Finally they decide that the number of words in the document can be communicated to the user in two ways, via the printer or via the screen. While it is useful to have a hard copy of the results, the English teacher decides that it would be more convenient to see the count on the screen.

System specification

14 As a result of their discussions with the user, the systems analysts produce a system specification or **system spec.**

A document will be available stored on disk in a text file

The document is to be read character by character with a count maintained of the number of spaces encountered.

The number of words in the document will then be deduced and both displayed on the VDU screen and sent to the printer.

The program should be easily installed onto a BBC micro and executed with a minimum of effort by the user.

> Can you anticipate any other use for a program that identifies characters in a document?

The structure of the problem

15 Next the analysts must decide how to achieve this result. This is where the problem, has to be broken down into its component parts to display its **structure**. The following sequence of tasks is the structure that they finally end up with.

Task 1 The text file containing the document is opened and made ready to be read.

Task 2 The document is read one character at a time and a count of the number of spaces read is maintained.

Task 3 The number of words in the document is deduced.

Task 4 The number of words is communicated to the screen and the printer.

Task 5 The text file containing the document is closed.

The system flowchart

16 The analysts then draw a diagram to represent the description.

17 This diagram lays out the various tasks in the form of blocks. It shows how each block leads on to the next. In this way it describes the **structure** of the problem—we call this diagram the structure diagram or the **system flowchart**.

> As you follow through this project you will be counting words. With a minor modification we could insert a Task 2A to count the number of sentences in the document. Rewrite the system specification and the system flowchart to include Task 2A.

The programmer's results

18 Programming can be both fascinating and fun, especially to start with when you watch the computer do what you have instructed it to do. However, when it comes to serious program writing, a different approach must be taken. There are many bad ways to write a computer program, all of which produce similar results—bad programs. To write good programs there is only one way to proceed: program development requires discipline.

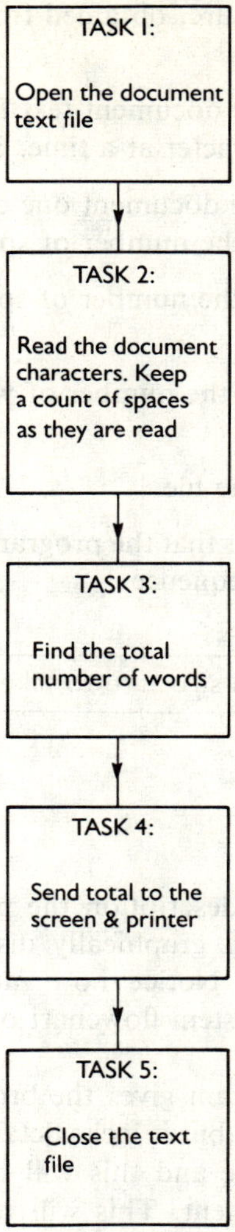

Program development

19 To develop a good program from the Systems Analyst's system specification four stages must be passed through.

- constructing the program's structure
- the program flowchart
- pseudo coding the program
- writing the final program

Constructing the program's structure

20 We have already seen that our written solution to a problem has a structure. The program has to imitate this written description of the solution so it must have a structure that is identical to the problem structure.

The program structure, obtained from the problem structure is as follows:

Task 1 OPEN the document text file and prepare the computer to read it, one character at a time. Set the space count at zero.

Task 2 READ the document one character at a time and maintain a COUNT of the number of spaces incurred.

Task 3 Add 1 to the number of spaces to obtain the number of words.

Task 4 OUTPUT the number of words to the screen and printer.

Task 5 CLOSE the file.

This structure shows that the program consists of five distinct parts, each part executed in sequence.

Rewrite the program structure to take account of Task 2A.

The program flowchart

21 From this written description the programmer is able to draw a program flowchart that graphically displays the details of how the program will operate. Notice how much more detailed this is in comparison with the system flowchart or structure diagram.

22 The structure diagram gives the broad outline of the flow of the operation of the system but it lacks detail. For example, the file is read one character at a time and this will have to be repeated for every character in the document. This will require a loop noting that the number of characters in the document is not known beforehand and which **repeats** the character read **until** the end-of-file is reached. This is best done using a REPEAT ... UNTIL loop. The flowchart on p. 47 illustrates this.

Construct a program flowchart to take account of TASK 2A

23 The next task for the programmer is to write down in detail how the object of each part of the structure is to be achieved. It would be tempting to write this detail in terms of the actual computer language to be used, but we shall avoid this temptation. Instead we shall write a pretend program and code the instructions in what is called **pseudo code**.

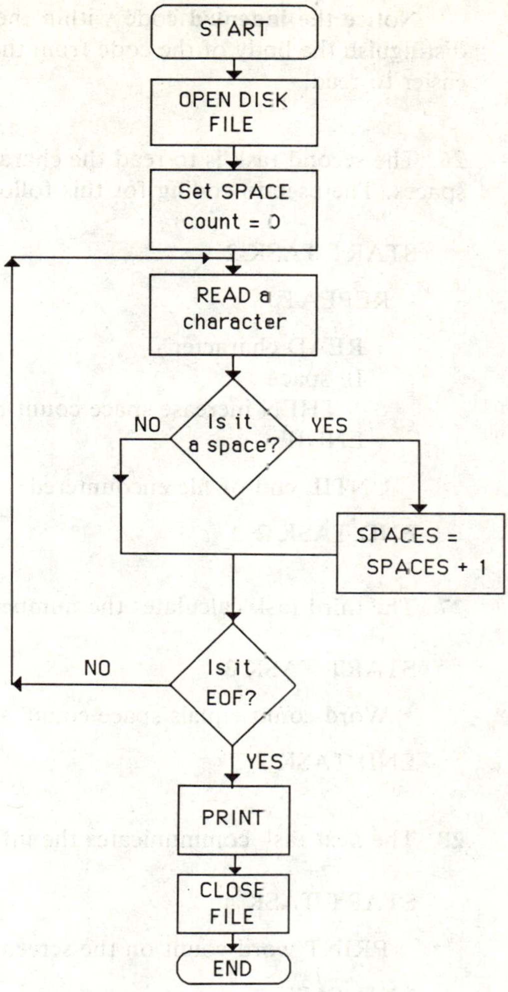

Pseudo code

24 Pseudo code is half way between the English description of the algorithm and the computer language coding of the algorithm. Its purpose is to write the sequence of instructions in English so that they can be easily checked. At the same time they are written to take on a similar appearance to the actual code, making the transition to actual code less liable to error.

25 First, the pseudo code for the first part of the structure.

```
START TASK 1

   OPEN test file
   SET space count equal to zero

END TASK 1
```

Notice the **indented** code within the START ... END. This is to distinguish the body of the code from the head and tail and so make it easier to read.

26 The second task is to read the characters and maintain a count of spaces. The pseudo coding for this follows.

```
START TASK 2

  REPEAT

    READ character
    IF space
      THEN increase space count by 1
    ENDIF

  UNTIL end-of-file encountered

END TASK 2
```

27 The third task calculates the number of words.

```
START TASK 3

  Word count equals space count + 1

END TASK 3
```

28 The next task communicates the information to the user

```
START TASK 4

  PRINT word count on the screen and at the printer

END TASK 4
```

29 Finally the test file is closed.

```
START TASK 5

  CLOSE the text file.

END TASK 5
```

Write the pseudo code for Task 2A.

30 So far we have pseudo coded each part of the structure separately. What we must now do is put the structure together. This follows, again in pseudo code.

```
START
  DO TASK 1
  DO TASK 2
  DO TASK 3
  DO TASK 4
  DO TASK 5
END
```

31 This list of instructions can be easily followed. Each is written down in a similar manner to the way computer instructions are written. However, they would not be understood by a computer because pseudo code is not a specific computer language.

32 Notice that the coding within the REPEAT ... UNTIL loop is indented. The indentation makes it easy to read and to distinguish which code is inside the loop and which code is outside it. The same applies to the coding within the IF ... THEN.

33 Now consider all that we have done.

We broke up the problem into its component parts to expose its structure. Each component part of this structure was then examined and its solution described in English and flowchart form. From here a program structure was obtained that matched the problem structure and each part was coded in pseudo code. Finally, a pseudo coded program was written that linked all these component parts together.

To complete the project we now have to write the final solution in the form of a working computer program.

Writing the final program

34 The programmer's task is to write a program that will instruct the computer to execute the tasks laid down by the system specification. We have seen that it is possible to write the sequence of instructions in plain English but this is of no use to the computer. To instruct the computer we must communicate in a language that it understands. There are a number of such languages. The most widely available language for a microcomputer is **BASIC** which stands for **B**eginners **A**ll-purpose **S**ymoblic **I**nstruction **C**ode. This is a simple language to learn and use and for this reason is provided as the standard language for all microcomputers. However, in the same way that there are different makes of microcomputer, so there are different **dialects** of BASIC. Nevertheless, all dialects of BASIC have a majority of features in common, so learning one dialect of BASIC will permit an easy understanding of them all.

35 It is from the pseudo coded set of instructions that the programmer sets about writing the final working program in a chosen **computer language**.

The BBC BASIC computer Language

36 There will be no attempt at a full treatment of the BASIC language in this book. Learning how to program effectively is one thing but learning how to code your program is another. With your computer you will also have a manual covering all the elements of programming in its particular dialect of BASIC and I would suggest that you refer to that.

For the purpose of this exercise, I shall present those elements of BASIC that are necessary to code this particular program. For more advanced coding skills refer to your manual. The dialect of BASIC that is used here is BBC BASIC because it is commonly used in British schools.

The program is given first, with an explanation of its individual parts following.

```
100 REM ************************************************
110 REM * THIS PROGRAM PROVIDES A WORD COUNT FROM A DOCUMENT *
120 REM *               STORED IN A TEXT FILE              *
130 REM ************************************************

200 REM *********************
210 REM * START THE PROGRAM *
220 REM *********************

230 PROCTASK1
240 PROCTASK2
250 PROCTASK3
260 PROCTASK4
270 PROCTASK5

280 END

291 REM *******************
292 REM * END THE PROGRAM *
293 REM *******************

300 REM **********************
310 REM * PROCEDURE LISTINGS *
320 REM **********************

1000 REM ************************************************
1010 REM * TASK 1 : OPEN THE FILE AND SET SPACE COUNT TO ZERO *
1020 REM ************************************************
1030 DEF PROCTASK1
1040     Y = OPENIN "TEXT"
1050     SPACES = 0
1060 ENDPROC

2000 REM ************************************************
2010 REM * TASK 2 : READ THE CHARACTERS AND COUNT SPACES TO EOF *
2020 REM ************************************************
```

```
2030 DEF PROCTASK2
2040      REPEAT
2050           ASKEY = BGET#Y
2060           IF ASKEY = 32 THEN SPACES = SPACES + 1
2070      UNTIL EOF#Y
2080 ENDPROC

3000 REM ***************************************
3010 REM * TASK 3 : CALCULATE THE NUMBER OF WORDS *
3020 REM ***************************************

3030 DEF PROCTASK3
3040      WORDS = SPACES + 1
3050 ENDPROC

4000 REM ********************************************
4010 REM * TASK 4 : PRINT NUMBER OF WORDS ON THE SCREEN *
4020 REM ********************************************
4030 DEF PROCTASK2
4040      VDU2
4050      PRINT "Words in document = ";WORDS
4060      VDU3
4070 ENDPROC

5000 REM ***********************
5010 REM * TASK 5 : CLOSE THE FILE *
5020 REM ***********************

5030 DEF PROCTASK3
5040      CLOSE#Y
5050 ENDPROC
```

Explanation of the coding

37 In BASIC every line of code is given a number. The value of any particular line number does not matter, as long as it is larger than the previous line number. It is a good idea to increase the line numbers in tens to allow additional lines to be inserted at a later date should that become necessary.

38 The word **REM** stands for REMark. The computer ignores anything on a line that follows this word. This is the way the program is documented for ease of reading and you will notice that the remarks are used quite freely; the golden rule is to use as many as you need to make the working of the program crystal clear to anyone else reading the coding.

39 Lines 230 to 270 refer to **procedures**. A procedure is a block of code that can be called into execution from anywhere in the program. Our program calls into execution five procedures, one after another which imitates the structure of the problem. In line 280, the word END instructs the computer that the program has come to an end, so preventing the computer from attempting to continue executing through the listing.

40 After the END instruction the procedures referred to are listed. They may be listed in any order; here they are listed in the order of execution to ease the task of another person reading the program.

41 Procedures are all defined within the instructions DEF PROCXXX and ENDPROC. The first procedure, PROCTASKI, opens a diskette file called TEXT and sets the value of the real variable SPACES equal to zero. The document is stored on the diskette under the name TEXT so to count SPACES in the document we must start off with zero spaces.

42 Procedure PROCTASK2 contains the REPEAT ... UNTIL loop. Here the computer is instructed to read the document, one character at a time by using BGET#Y and to store the ASCII value of that character in the real variable ASKEY. If the last character to be read was a space, then its ASCII code would be 32, and the following line of code would increase the value stored in SPACES by 1 using the IF ... THEN structure. This process continues throughout the entire document until the end-of-file is reached—UNTIL EOF#Y.

43 Procedure PROCTASK3 defines the number of WORDS in the document to be one more than the number of spaces. PROCTASK4 then assigns that number to both the screen and the printer simultaneously. The command VDU2 is the BBC'S METHOD of turning the printer on and VDU3 turns it off. Finally, PROCTASK5 CLOSES the file.

RUNning, SAVEing and LOADing the program

44 When the program has been written the computer can be instructed to **execute** the program by typing in the word **RUN** followed by pressing the **RETURN** key.

45 If you then turned your computer off, the program would be lost as it is resident in the computer's transient memory. To ensure that the program is saved for future use we can save it on a floppy diskette by typing in the command **SAVE "COUNT"**

46 This activates the disk drive and causes the computer to write the program coding to the diskette. The program will then be saved on the diskette in a file called COUNT. Now you can switch off the computer knowing that you have a copy of the program saved on diskette. To load the program into memory type in the following command LOAD "COUNT"

This again activates the disk drive and causes the computer to read the file called COUNT thereby loading the program into memory.

47 When the program is finished it is tested with the test information to ensure that it is working correctly. The program, complete with the test results and its manual is then passed to the data manager who is the user.

Rewrite the program to take into account TASK 2A. This program can be used with any document regardless of its size. Perform an analysis of the works of different authors: by counting the number of occurrences of vowels or particular words, some sort of comparison could be made.

Earlier you were asked to explain why the assumption that only one space separated two words may not be a realistic assumption because of the type of word processor being used. The answer is that some word processors justify the text to the right so that it appears more like the text you see in a printed book than ragged-edged as it appears when written by hand. A word processor that right-justifies text does so by inserting extra spaces between words when the original line of text does not completely fill a line. It is still possible to count spaces and deduce the number of words when this situation arises. Try to work out the algorithm for doing this and rewrite the program accordingly.

Summary

All problems require to be thought about and carefully analysed. Analysing a problem means breaking it down into its component parts, each part being a simple problem in itself. There are three stages in any computer project. The problem has to be analysed by the systems analyst, the program has to be written by the programmer and the system has to be tested and run by the data manager. The entire project is supervised by the project manager. The job of the systems analyst is to define the structure of the problem in terms of its component parts. From this a detailed description of the solution is written down, together with a structure diagram or system flowchart. The structure diagram gives the broad outline of the flow of the problem, but lacks the detail of a program flowchart. This analysis of the problem is called the system specification. The programmer has to pass through three stages when developing a program from the system specification. These are constructing the program's structure, writing a pseudo coded 'pretend' program and finally, writing the final form of the program in a computer language. The program's structure is identical to the problem structure. To aid the programmer a program flowchart is produced. Each component of the structure is then pseudo coded, and when all the component parts have been coded they are joined together in the complete pseudo coded program. Pseudo code is code in the form of conversational English but laid out in the form of computer language code. Because it is written in conversational English it is easily checked for correctness and because it is laid out in computer language style it aids in the writing of error free computer language code. A computer language is a collection of commands that is understood by the computer. The most common computer language used with micro computers is BASIC, although there are many different dialects of this the final program is written from the pseudo code.

Key points

Practical problem solving, embarking on the project, analysing the problem, writing the computer program, testing and running the system, the project manager, the systems analyst, the data manager, the system's analyst's results, the structure of the problem, the programmer's results, program development, constructing the program's structure, program flowchart, pseudocoding the program, writing the final program, the BASIC computer language, explanation of the coding.

Self assessment questions

1 What is a common mistake made by students when they first attempt to solve a problem? (2)
2 What is meant by analysing a problem? (2)
3 List the three stages in solving a computer project. (4)
4 Who is responsible for analysing the problem? (5)
5 Who writes the program? (6)
6 Who uses the finished system? (7)
7 Who acts as supervisor to a computer project? (8)
8 Describe the job of the systems analyst. (10)
9 Describe the job of the programmer. (11)
10 Describe the job of the data manager. (12)
11 What is a system specification? (14)
12 What is meant by a problem's structure? (15)
13 What is a structure diagram? (16, 17)
14 What does the structure diagram show? (17)
15 What is meant by 'hacking'? (18)
16 What does a good program require of the programmer? (18)
17 List the three stages of program development. (19)
18 How does the program structure relate to the problem structure? (20)
19 What is the purpose of a program flowchart? (21,22)
20 What job of the programmer follows the development of the program's structure? (23)
21 What is a 'pretend program'? (23)
22 What is pseudo code? (24)
23 Why is pseudo code used? (24)
24 What is meant by 'indented code' ? (25)
25 Why is code indented? (25)
26 What is a computer language? (34)
27 What do the letters of the word BASIC stand for? (34)
28 What do we call different versions of BASIC? (34)
29 What is a line number in BASIC? (37)
30 What is the meaning of REM in BASIC? (38)
31 What is a procedure? (39)
32 What does the END command signify? (40)
33 What is a real variable? (41)
34 How is a procedure declared? (41)
35 What is the purpose of a REPEAT ... UNTIL loop? (32,42)
36 What is the purpose of the conditional IF ... THEN? (32,42)
37 What is the command to execute a program in memory? (44)
38 What is the command to write a program in memory to diskettes? (45)
39 What is the command to read a program on diskette into memory? (46)
40 What does the programmer provide the date manager with? (47)

Exercises

1 For which of the following purposes is a loop used in computer programs?
- to dimension an array
- to eliminate syntax errors
- to jump out of the main program
- to repeat a section several times

2 (a) Use either a diagram or written instructions to describe a program plan (algorithm) to count the number of positive numbers, and the number of negative numbers, in a set of data. The data ends with a zero.

(b) Provide a suitable set of data to test your algorithm, together with the expected results.

5 The computer invasion

Objectives

1 To identify some of the implications of the use of computers for individuals, organisations and society.

2 To formulate a reasoned view of some of the potential effects of computer usage.

Introduction

1 In this chapter we shall look at the ways the computer is bringing about change in our lives. We shall consider some of the benefits and some of the drawbacks and finally look towards possible future developments.

The computer revolution and the information age

2 Because it is cheap and readily available, the computer is encroaching upon our lives. It is doing this at such a pace that we can call it a 'computer invasion', which like all invasions is bringing with it change.

3 Change may be for the better or for the worse. In 1066 William of Normandy invaded the shores of England and fought King Harold in The Battle of Hastings. The battle proved to be a turning point in English history. From that day on everything changed. Some things changed rapidly, like William's personal influence over the people and their daily lives and others more slowly, like the law of the land.

Some things changed for the better. The country became more united and better organised. Other things changed for the worse. The Feudal System was introduced and people's lives were dictated by the amount of land they did or did not own.

> Can you think of anything that has happened to you that has been the cause of change? How about moving house? How about moving from the junior to the senior school or having a new brother or sister? Can you imagine what your life would be like if that event had not happened? Think about the changes that it has made to your life. How many are good and how many are bad?

4 In the eighteenth century England went through another period of change, the Industrial Revolution. The power of water, be it moving or boiling, was largely responsible for this and it not only changed England forever, but also the rest of the world. Again this change had both its bad and its good effects. Amongst the good effects were manufactured goods such as clothes and imported goods such as food. During the Industrial Revolution the canals and the railways were built so that manufactured and imported goods could be moved from one end of the country to the other. Many people's lives became more comfortable. Amongst the bad effects were the working conditions: children worked from the ages of five or six, often twelve or more hours a day.

> Before the Industrial Revolution, the fastest mode of transport was on horseback. Now 400 mph in a Boeing 747 is a commonplace experience to many, and a satellite can orbit the earth in 90 minutes. Make a list of the different stages of invention that have allowed us to travel faster. What do you think the effect of this has been on the population of the world?

5 We are now experiencing the Computer Revolution which is being brought about by new technologies. This has been called the Information Age. The rapid invasion of the computer is creating a society that is becoming dependent upon information. We need information to know how to survive in the world, which is why you go to school. Your school needs information to know how to organise your lessons, how to organise what is taught in those lessons and how to find out whether you have learnt what was taught in those lessons.

Companies need information to know how to organise their business. They need to know what people want so that they can provide it. Similarly, the Government needs information so that it can govern.

Computers make the handling and communication of information easier and more efficient, not only between the computer and the user, but also between one computer system and another.

6 Computers can handle vast amounts of information. The more information becomes available, the more people demand it, and as this happens, large amounts of computerised information become a necessity for systems to work.

> Name three different aspects of your daily life where you need information. What would be the outcome if you did not have that information? List three important aspects of your daily life where a computerised system is used. What would be the effect on your life if it were not available?
> Discuss this amongst the other members of your class to find out what they think.

The Computer Revolution has brought with it change which cannot now be reversed. But change can have both advantages and disadvantages.

Advantages

7 There are many benefits that have resulted from the Computer Revolution. Look at the shops to see the vast array of different goods available.

Computers are responsible for this. Foreign travel is now possible for many more people than it used to be and at holiday times airlines are working to full capacity. At major airports planes arrive and depart every few seconds. Such timing could not be organised without computers.

Courtesy BBC Ceefax

Television is now full of computerised effects such as graphic pictures, moving titles, pictures superimposed on top of each other and film displays accompanying the news. All these are due to computers. Computers create jobs, not only in computing, but by helping to increase the efficiency of organisations they create more work.

The material benefits of the Computer Invasion are many and varied but like all agents of change, the computer also has its drawbacks.

Disadvantages

8 When a weaver's loom can be operated by a computer there is no longer a need for a weaver.

The Computer Revolution has meant that many of the more traditional manual skills are no longer needed. They can all be done by computer controlled robots. Consequently, unemployment arises in those areas where traditional skills were practised, and people begin to feel insecure. They don't understand computers and that frightens them. People become frightened by the unknown, especially when it affects their lives.

The unceasing demand for information brings with it a loss of privacy. To book a reservation on a ferry you may need to give your name, address, post code, telephone number, ages of any children and make of your car. All this information is put onto a computer, but at the expense of your privacy. Computers can be linked together by telephone and satellite, making it possible for people to access this information and remain anonymous.

> Can you think of any benefits to you that are a direct result of the computer?
> Now think of any bad effects that it has had on your life? Discuss these questions with your friends and family.

The future

9 Predicting the future is like shooting at a moving target—very unreliable. Despite that, it is still a worthwhile exercise to contemplate possibilities.

Education at the moment is mainly 'chalk-and-talk'. A variety of aids are available to help teachers put the lesson across, but more often they will stand in front of you and talk, reinforcing ideas by writing on the blackboard.

But just around the corner is Computer Based Training (CBT). Imagine that you are sitting in front of your personal computer and on the screen a lesson is in progress: a TV picture is coming from a video disk or compact laser disk slotted into the side of your computer.

You are being taught that all bodies fall equally fast when they fall under gravity and you can watch it happen. You watch the tale of Galileo dropping two spheres from the top of the Leaning Tower of Pisa and the camera focuses on the foot of the tower, just as the two spheres hit the ground together. You learn that despite their different weights the spheres of wood and lead fall equally fast.

To see the point of impact again, it can instantly be replayed. Not only can you interact with all the information in the lesson by going back over bits you did not understand, but the computer will interact with you. It will move through the lesson at a speed that matches your ability to pick up and remember information.

Think about robots doing the housework, shopping from home, booking theatre tickets from home and paying for them by the instantaneous transfer of cash from your bank account to the theatre's bank account or working from home. Many occupations require the use of a computer so if computers can be linked together via a

1.28 The DTI Autoguide—currently being developed by the Automobile Association and Plessey; courtesy AA/Plessey

telephone cable, why do they have to be in offices? With a radio phone plugged into your portable computer you could do your work on the beach!

In the same way, every car could be fitted with its own on-board computer, which could be arranged to drive the car for you. A large central computer could organise every vehicle by remote control and make sure that your journey was traffic-jam free, accident free and automatic, thereby taking the stress out of driving. A start has been made towards this with the Autoguide system. The idea is to give drivers information on how to travel to their destination. They enter their destination into a small computer fitted in the car and beacons fitted at major road junctions tell the computer which way to go. The driver is then prompted by a message and an arrow displayed on a screen. The arrow indicates left turn, right turn or straight ahead. Almost anything that involves human beings could be automated and controlled by a computer. We must always be aware of the need to adapt to change, but at the same time we must always be alert to the effects that those changes will have on us.

> Make a list of five situations where you could imagine a computer being introduced. What would be the effects? Will they benefit everybody or will some people be effected badly? Are you sure that a computer is not already doing the tasks? (There is a saying that if you have just had an idea than it is too late—it is already being developed if not done.)

Summary

10 The cheapness and usefulness of the computer causes it to be introduced into our lives at a rapid pace. The ingenuity of the computer industry is introducing new technologies and new systems. In this way they are driving the Computer Revolution. The Computer Revolution is taking us into the Information Age. Computers can handle vast amounts of information quickly, accurately and cheaply. Information is rapidly becoming the raw material that so many aspects of life depend upon. The most important aspects of the Information Age are the change that we are experiencing in our lives. Some change is for the better and some change is for the worse. It is up to each of us to adapt to the changes and to be alert to the effects that these changes will have.

Key points

> The 'computer invasion' and change, the new technologies and the Computer Revolution, the Information Age, changes for the better, changes for the worse, the future and the possible changes it may bring.

Self assessment questions

1 Why is the computer affecting our lives more and more? (2)
2 Why do we refer to the introduction of computers as 'an invasion? (2)
3 Give an example of another invasion in history that brought about great change. (2)
4 Is change all for the better or all for the worse? (3)
5 What is the cause of the Computer Revolution? (5)
6 What is meant by the phrase 'The Information Age'? (5)
7 How has the Information Age arisen (5,6)
8 Give three benefits of the 'computer invasion'. (7)
9 Give three drawbacks to the 'computer invasion'. (8)
10 How does the use of a computer create a loss of privacy?
11 Give four possible ways in which the computer could change our lives in the future. (9)

Exercises

1 (a) Although some people may lose their jobs due to word processors, advantages can be gained using them in an office.
Name two advantages gained by using word processors.

(b) So far few workers have lost their jobs to computers. Name two types of jobs in which people have had to retrain because of computers.

2 A school has a large number of computers connected as a network which it uses for computer aided learning and school administration.

(a) Name one effect that computer aided learning could have on a subject such as history.

(b) Name one reason why it might not be a good idea to process pupil records using a network system.

3 (a) Give two reasons why it is better to use robot welders rather than men.

(b) Name one way in which men are better than robot welders.

Section two

1 *The hardware assembly*

Objectives

1 To explain the functions of the component parts of a computer system

2 To evaluate the suitability of current input, output and storage devices in particular applications

Introduction

1 In Chapter 2 of Section 1 we referred to a typical microcomputer system as consisting of a **keyboard**, a **monitor** and a **box**. The box contains all the electrical circuitry that makes the computer work, the keyboard allows the user to communicate to the computer and the monitor or VDU allows the computer to communicate to the user. As this chapter progresses we shall see that there are many different kinds of computer, all of which have many features in common. We shall look at these common features, and in particular at the heart of the computer, the **central processing unit** or CPU.

The central processing unit

2 The central processing unit is the part of the computer that allows it to perform all of its functions. The way the CPU operates gives the computer its characteristics and general behaviour pattern that we come to recognise and adapt to as we use the computer. The way the CPU is constructed is referred to as its **architecture** and this architecture consists of two parts:

- the control unit
- the Arithmetic and Logic Unit (ALU).

From the names of the components of the central processing unit, try and relate this architecture to yourself. Where would your CPU be? What do you call your primary storage unit? What are your input and output devices? How are they connected to your CPU? How do your input and output devices communicate with your CPU?

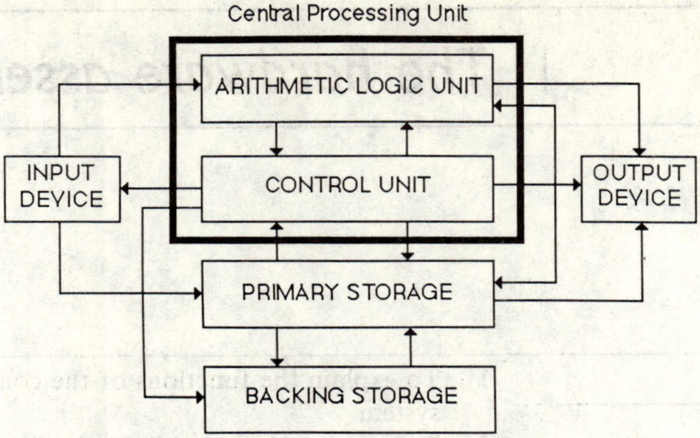

The control unit

3 The control unit controls the whole system by coordinating and organising all the operations of the computer. It obeys the instructions issued to it by various **input devices** such as the keyboard and organises the **output** to the various peripheral devices such as the printer. It also coordinates the flow of information between itself and the other two components of the CPU. It is responsible for fetching instructions that are stored in the **primary storage**, interpreting them and then issuing commands to all the hardware units that are necessary to carry out the instructions.

The control unit uses a **system clock** to synchronise all its operations. This gives off regular electrical pulses and effectively acts as a heart beat to the control unit with the number of pulses transmitted each second determining the speed at which the processor operates. The system clock speed is measured in **MegaHertz** (MHz)—millions of pulses per second. A typical microprocessor will operate at 8 MHz, although some can operate at 25 MHz.

The arithmetic and logic unit (ALU)

4 The **Arithmetic and Logic Unit** (ALU) is responsible for performing all the arithmetic and logic operations of the computer. The arithmetic operations include addition, subtraction, multiplication and division of numbers. The logic operations are used to compare numbers and include 'less than', 'equal to' and 'greater than'. The ALU can also handle text as well as numbers which we will discuss in a later chapter. Sometimes a computer will be equipped with an arithmetic co-processor which is a second microprocessor dedicated to perform arithmetic functions only. The advantage of such a co-processor is the increased speed of performing arithmetic calculations.

The CPU can be said to be the computer's brain. An encyclopaedia will tell you how your own brain is partitioned into different regions, each region performing a specific type of task. Find out where, in your brain, the regions are located that deal with control, calculations, logic and memory.

The primary storage unit

5 The primary storage unit is the computer's memory, where information is stored both permanently and temporarily. There are two distinct types of memory in the computer:

- Read Only Memory (ROM)
- Random Access Memory (RAM)

Read only memory (ROM)

6 The **read only memory** (ROM) contains all the information and instructions necessary to make the computer operate when it is switched on. This information is put into the ROM when the chip is manufactured and remains there for the lifetime of the chip. Because of its permanent nature it is said to be **hard wired** into the chip, i.e. part of the physical design of the chip. ROM contains information that is somewhere between software and hardware; it is called **firmware**, and is essential for the computer to operate. That part of the memory which contains it must therefore be capable of being **read from** but not of being **written to**, hence its name—READ ONLY memory.

ROM chips are programmed to meet the design requirements of a computer. There are, however, types of ROM chips that can be programmed to meet other specifications.

Programmable Read Only Memory (PROM) chips can be programmed by a user to perform specific functions. For example, a PROM can be used as a substitute for a program contained on a floppy disk. However, once a PROM has been programmed its final physical state is fixed and it cannot be re-programmed.

Erasable Programmable Read Only Memory (EPROM) chips are PROMS that can be **re-programmed**. They contain a window inset in the black plastic casing, through which light can be shone, so that ultraviolet light can erase the memory of the chip, leaving it in a state ready to be re-programmed. There are also EPROMs that can be erased electrically. These are EEPROMs—**electrically erasable programmable read only memories**.

2.2 An Eprom

Random access memory (RAM)

7 The second section of the primary storage unit is the part used to store **temporary information** in the form of data and instructions. The data may have been put there from an input unit or by the control unit. Similarly, the instructions may be part of a piece of software put into the main memory by the user. This part of the memory is re-useable; it can be written to, as well as read from and this ability is referred to by the words random access. RAM is held on special RAM chips and requires an electrical current to maintain the information it stores. Its contents are therefore lost whenever the computer is switched off and for this reason it is called a **volatile memory**.

> The ideas of ROM and RAM can be applied to systems other than computer systems. For example, a musical instrument has a physical construction that, in part, defines how it will sound when it is played. This is the ROM. A violin has four tuned strings that can be tuned to play and when the violin is played by pressing a finger on a string and bowing the string, even more different notes can be played. This is the RAM. How would you distinguish ROM from RAM in
>
> (a) an oven with a dial for setting the temperature?
> (b) a bicycle?

Backing store

8 For a computer to operate it requires information which the RAM is not capable of storing. For this reason it requires access to a **backing store** which is a **non-volatile**, secondary storage of information contained on a **secondary storage medium**. Backing store is used for the long-term storage of information and programs and four types of secondary storage media are in use:

- punched cards
- magnetic tapes
- magnetic disks
- optical cards.

Punched cards

9 A punched card is a stiff piece of card on which are printed numbers in regular rows and columns. The cards are placed in a keypunch machine and as the keypunch operator keys in data, it is recorded on the cards in the form of small, rectangular holes. These cards can then be read by a card reader which interprets the holes as information and sends it to the CPU. The punched card system of storing data and programs was one of the early forms of backing store and has now been largely superseded by the more efficient magnetic and optical media.

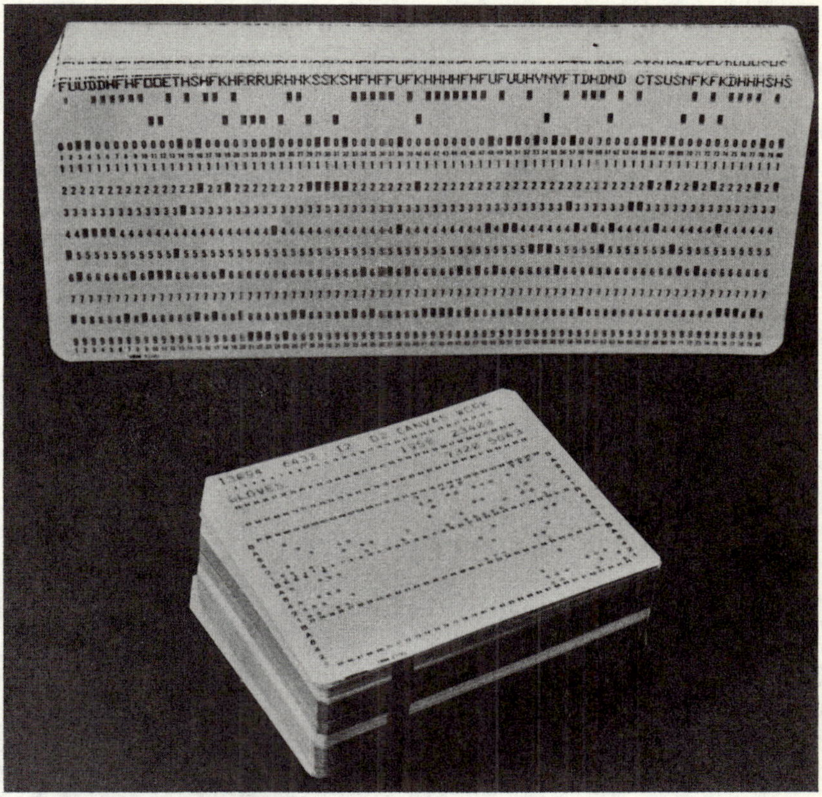

2.3 Punched cards

> A card index system is a sequence of cards used for storing information. For example, a debater could use a card index system. Each card would contain notes on one of the main topics, and could then be used during the debate as a prompt to their memory. Where else have you seen a card index system? Do you agree that it is a form of secondary storage? Why?

Magnetic tapes

10 Magnetic tape is a long plastic strip coated with a magnetic substance such as iron oxide, which works on the same principles as those that operate when you use a cassette tape in your walkman. Information can be written to the tape by the read/write head of a tape drive, and then stored as magnetised spots on the tape's surface. These spots can then be read by the same read/write head of the tape drive, converted to information that the computer can understand and sent to the CPU. Three types of tape are used:

- reel-to-reel tape
- cassette tape
- cartridge tape.

2.4 Reel-to-reel tapes

Reel-to-reel tape

11 A typical reel-to-reel tape is about 800 m long, 1 cm wide and contained on a reel about 30 cm in diameter. These tapes can hold large amounts of information and are used with the larger computer systems.

Cassette tapes

12 Cassette tape is the familiar tape that we have all used and is about 8 mm wide, comes in various lengths and is contained inside a plastic case. The early microcomputers used cassette tapes for backing store.

Cartridge tape

13 A cartridge looks like a large cassette but with wider and longer tape. Cartridge tapes are used both by large computer systems and microcomputers. A typical use with a microcomputer would be to create a copy of valuable information as a safety measure in case it were lost from its normal media storage. This procedure is known as **backing up** and should be done regularly in all computer systems.

2.5 Cartridge tape

14 Magnetic tapes suffer from one basic disadvantage: information is stored on them **sequentially**—one piece of information following another, so if a particular piece of information that is required is stored at the far end of the tape, the tape drive has to wind all the way through the tape before the required information can be read. This slows down the process of information retrieval, but this disadvantage has been overcome by the introduction of magnetic disks.

> Tapes were used to store information long before the advent of computers, for example with ticker-tape and dictaphone machines. How many different uses of tapes can you think of where information is stored?

Magnetic disks

15 A magnetic disk is a circular sheet of plastic coated with the same magnetic material as the magnetic tape. Its advantages over other forms of secondary storage are:

- access of information;
- speed of information transfer;
- amount of information stored.

Access of information

16 Information is contained on the disk surface in a series of concentric, circular tracks. The disk is made to spin by the disk drive and in doing so it passes beneath the read/write head of the disk reader. The read/write head can move backwards and forwards along the radius of the disk, thereby making it possible to access information directly.

Speed of information transfer

17 Because the disk can spin at a much faster rate than a tape can move past the tape reader's read/write head, information stored on a disk can be accessed at a much faster rate.

Amount of information stored

18 The speed at which the disk rotates also permits information to be more densely packed onto the disk surface. In this way a disk can hold far more information than a tape.

Find out how much information the disks that you use with your computer can store.

19 There are three different types of disk.

- Floppy Diskettes
- Hard Disks
- Disk Packs

Floppy diskettes

20 A floppy diskette is either 8, 5.25 or 3.5 inches in diameter and is contained inside a stiff plastic jacket. It may be single sided—information only being stored on one side—or double sided in which case both sides can be used. The magnetic material on the disk surface may be single, double or quad density. The denser the material, the more information can be stored on the disk. A floppy diskette is used with a disk drive into which the diskette is inserted. The disk drive may have one or two read/write heads. A two headed disk drive is capable of reading from and writing to both sides of the diskette without having to extract the diskette and turn it over. Floppy diskettes are standard means of storing information for use with a microcomputer.

Hard disks

21 A hard disk is made from aluminium instead of plastic and because of its rigidity can store more closely packed information than a floppy

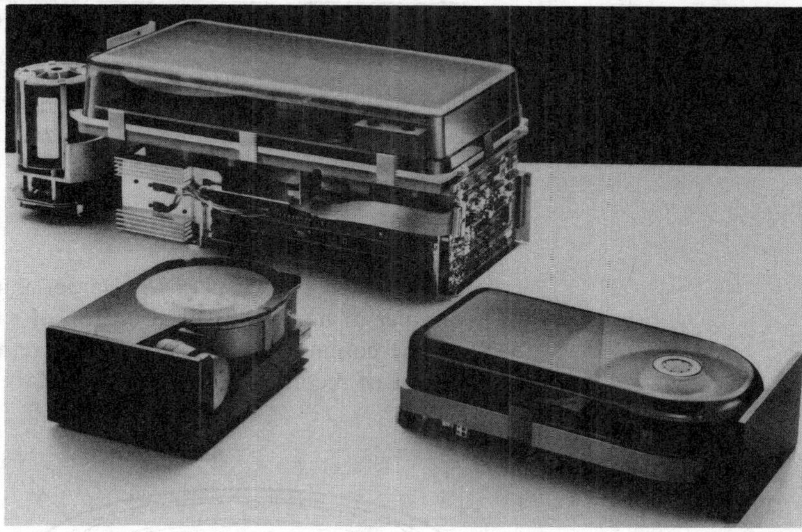

2.6 A fixed disk unit

diskette. It can also be rotated at a much faster rate than a floppy diskette, thereby permitting an even faster rate of information access. Hard disks come in a variety of forms.

(a) A **fixed disk** is a popular component for use with PC's. The hard disk is installed inside the computer and is never handled by the user.

(b) The **disk-on-a-card** is a cheaper alternative to a fixed hard disk. The card, a plastic sheet containing an amount of circuitry and the disk, is fitted into one of the expansion slots inside the microcomputer. Expansion slots are rectangular sockets located inside the computer, and are used for connecting peripheral devices to the CPU.

(c) A **Bernoulli box** is the hard disk equivalent of the removable floppy diskette. The disk is contained inside a plastic cartridge that can be inserted into and removed from a disk drive in the same way as a floppy diskette. The advantages of the Bernoulli box are two-fold. First, hard disk amounts of information can be accessed at hard disk speeds and second, like the floppy diskette, the drive is available for use with as many disks as desired. The Bernoulli box is not a true hard disk. It is a pliable plastic disk enclosed within an aerodynamically designed cartridge which employs a principle of aerodynamics first discovered by James Bernoulli in the 19th century. The principle is that when a pliable object is rotated within a specially designed cavity it becomes rigid and in this way takes on the features of a hard disk. Bernoulli boxes are available for use with microcomputers and greatly increase the amounts of useful information available to them.

Find out how much information each type of disk can store and rank them in order of size. Find out the costs of installing each one of the three hard disks and decide which of the three is the best value for money.

The disk pack

22 The disk pack is used with larger computer systems. It consists of a number of hard disks fixed on top of each other and all enclosed in a plastic container. The disk pack is removable and is a very popular means of secondary storage for the larger computer systems.

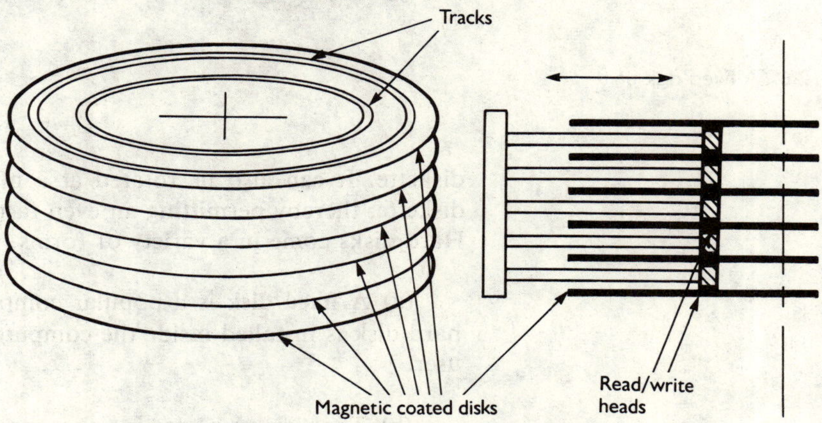

2.7 Disk Pack

Information stored on magnetic media is measured in alphanumeric characters. We shall see later that these are called BYTES. Find out how many bytes each of the different types of magnetic disks can store.

Optical disks and cards

23 Optical disks have emerged from the **compact disk** technology originally developed for the recording industry. These disks range from 10 cm to 30 cm in diameter, are made of aluminium and are read by **laser**. Optical disks are either **CD ROM** which are read-only disks, or **CD Interactive** which can also be written to. They can store information in the form of pictures and sound taken with a TV camera and microphone. Pictures are stored as single frames on the disk surface but are read in sequence to give the effect of a moving picture and form a dramatic source of information by enabling the workings of the computer to be combined with television style pictures and sound. An example of their use is with **computer based training** (CBT).

24 Optical cards are approximately the size of a credit card and can hold over two million bytes of information. They can be used to store large amounts of personal information such as medical records and employment history.

> Can you think of any systems that would benefit from using an optical disk or card? Make a list of four different uses.

Input devices

25 We have just considered some of the many ways of inputting information into the CPU. This information is, however, of a static nature. It resides on the medium, waiting to be read. Often a computer system will need more dynamic information—information that changes in time—and to cater for this, other devices are available. Devices may vary in sophistication according to the types of application for which they are being used. The suitability of one device over another will depend on the speed at which the information is input to the system, the type of information being handled and the cost of that means of inputting information. The following devices are used for inputting information.

- Keyboards
- The mouse and trackball
- Games paddles and joysticks
- Optical and magnetic readers
- Plotters
- Touch screens
- Speech recognition

Keyboards

26 The keyboard is the most common means of inputting information into the CPU. It contains keys labelled with the letters of the alphabet, the numbers 0 to 9, punctuation and grammar symbols and a number of special keys, which include:

- The cursor control keys
- Function keys

The cursor control keys

27 The cursor is a marker that appears on the monitor screen to indicate the position at which the next typed character will appear. The cursor control keys permit the cursor to be moved around the screen at will. These keys include the up, down, left and right arrows that move the cursor one space up, down, left and right respectively. They also include HOME, END, PgUp and PgDn which move the cursor to the top of the screen, the bottom of the screen, one page on and one page back respectively.

> Describe the cursor control keys on your keyboard.

Function keys

28 The function keys include those labelled F1, F2, etc, Ins, Del, Esc, Ctrl and Alt. Each one of these performs a special function and can be used for increasing the efficiency of communicating to the CPU. For example, Del is used to delete a character from the screen and in some applications is used in combination with Ctrl and Alt to delete complete words or even whole lines of text.

29 The function keys marked F1, F2, etc, are used to define a sequence of instructions. For example, in a computerised financial system, F10 may be used to leave the payroll system to move to the ledger system. Normally, this would have to be done by issuing a number of separate instructions, but instead, a sequence of instructions, called a **macro**, can be programmed into the function key. Pressing the function key then causes the computer to execute these instructions.

> How many function keys are there on your keyboard and what do they do?

> Look at the keyboard on your computer. Find out why the letters of the alphabet are arranged in this way? Do you think the reason still applies? Do you think that the layout of the keys could be improved? Why?

The mouse and trackball

30 The mouse consists of a hard ball contained in a hand-held plastic case and which rotates as the plastic case is moved around over a hard surface. As the ball rotates, the cursor moves around the VDU screen. The mouse is a very convenient means of controlling the cursor and can be used in combination with the keyboard. In addition to the hard ball, the mouse also contains a number of buttons, each of which can be used as special function keys, so reducing the need to use the keyboard.

31 A variant on the mouse is the trackball where the ball is moved directly with the palm of the hand to move the cursor around the screen.

Games paddles and joysticks

32 Games paddles and joysticks are other cursor control keys. They can also be used to input other information such as increasing or decreasing the speed of play during a games session.

> Which are your favourite computer games? Why? Is your choice influenced by the way you communicate with the computer? Are games that use joysticks, for example, more versatile than those that use the keyboard?

Optical and magnetic readers

33 There are a number of devices that read information using optical or magnetic sensing techniques. Among these are:

- Optical Bar Readers (OBR)
- Optical Character Recognition (OCR)
- Optical Mark Recognition (OMR)
- Magnetic Ink Character Recognition (MICR)
- Magnetic Strips
- Light Pens

2.8 A bar code reader; courtesy the Article Member Association

Optical bar readers (OBR)

34 An optical bar reader translates the information contained in a **bar code** into information sensible to the CPU. The bar code is in the form of a series of black and white stripes of varying widths. By relating combinations of stripes to numbers and letters of the alphabet, the bar code can be used to identify particular items in a wide variety of applications, for example, in supermarkets to code grocery items, in libraries to code books and borrowers and in computerised manufacturing systems to inform the computer that a particular job has been satisfactorily completed.

Optical character recognition (OCR)

35 Optical character recognition reads information by recognising shapes. The instrument used to read the information is called an OCR wand and can read both words and pictures.

Optical mark recognition (OMR)

36 Optical mark recognition is used to read marks made by pencil on a sheet of paper. Unlike OCR, OMR recognises position rather than shape. A typical use of this would be to mark a completed answer sheet to a multiple-choice examination. In British Columbia, Canada, the

2.9 An OCR wand; courtesy the Article Member Association

pubic examinations at the end of the last year of high school all have multiple choice sections and are marked using OMR.

> List two applications for each of the three optical readers described. Why do you think that particular method has been used in preference to any other method for each application?

Magnetic ink character recognition (MICR)

37 Magnetic ink character recognition is very similar to OCR except that the sensing device operates by reading shapes printed with magnetic ink. A typical use of MICR is for reading the numbers at the bottom of bank cheques, i.e. the bank number, the cheque number and your account number.

Magnetic strips

38 Magnetic strips are the narrow brown strips found on the backs of credit cards. These contain information coded in the form of magnetic marks and are read when the card is inserted into such devices as cash dispensers.

> List two applications for each of the two magnetic readers described. Why do you think that the particular method is used in preference to any other method for each application?

Light pens

39 The picture on a VDU screen is produced by a ray of charged particles emanating from the rear of the VDU tube and focused to a single point that scans across the inside surface of the screen. This surface is coated with a phosphorescent material that reacts to the charge by emitting light. The point of charged particles continually sweeps across the screen from top left to bottom right in a series of horizontal lines and constructs the screen display point by point. Because the time taken to perform a single screen-sweep is so short (it is called the refresh time) the viewer does not see the point of light but, instead, sees a continuous picture. The computer, however, knows exactly where the point of light is on the screen and how long it has taken to reach a given point from the top left hand corner.

A light pen is a hand held device that has a light-sensitive photoelectric cell at its tip. By placing the tip of the light pen on a VDU screen it can detect the single point of light as it passes the tip. The light that is detected is converted into electric pulses that carry information to the CPU. By measuring the time interval between the point of light starting at the top of the screen and passing the tip of the light pen, it is easy for the computer to work out exactly where the light pen is located on the screen. This permits the light pen to be used for both reading information from and writing information to the screen. For example, a light pen can be used with a graphics package to draw lines on the VDU screen.

The ability to detect the difference between light intensity makes the light pen a useful tool for reading bar codes. By wiping the pen across the bar code, the changes from light to dark and dark to light are converted into meaningful information for the CPU. As the bar code also has a start and a stop bit, the successful reading of a bar code can be indicated via the light pen, to a sound generator which emits a beep.

Touch screens

40 The touch screen is a variant on the light pen. Instead of using a light pen which is physically attached to the CPU, information regarding positions on the screen can be input simply by touching the screen. One way this is achieved is by using infra-red beams of light to form a grid pattern in front of the screen so that when the screen is touched the pattern is interrupted, thereby telling the CPU of the location. A further variant of this is the touch pad which operates by sensing the pressure of a touch. Touch pads are used on calculators, microwave ovens and a variety of computer controlled systems.

Speech recognition

41 Speech recognition operates by recognising speech patterns. Before a user can employ this means of communication with the computer, a number of words will have to be spoken into the system so that they can be translated into speech patterns and associated with specific commands. Later the user can speak to the computer, and if the speech pattern is recognised, the computer will translate it into the appropriate command. Speech recognition can be used either when the user does not have a free hand to use any other device or when security is required. For example, Jaguar Motors use speech recognition when their cars are being inspected for quality and in other organisations, doors can be automatically unlocked only when an authorised person speaks into a microphone.

> List two applications for each of these three methods of inputting information. Why do you think the particular method has been used in each application?

Key-to-disk

42 Key-to-disk is a method of storing the static information required for input at a later time. The operator of a key-to-disk system enters the information at the keyboard and this is transferred straight to the disk medium, to be read from the disk later in the usual manner. This system is used when large amounts of information have to be inputted into the computer. However, input must be checked before being assigned to the CPU which may hold up the operation if the quantity of information is large. When using a key-to-disk system, the process of converting written information into machine-readable information and ensuring its correctness can be performed independently of the computer's other operations.

> If you could talk to your computer and it could talk to you, do you think that this would be the most appropriate way of communicating in all applications? Why?

Output devices

43 There are numerous ways of outputting information from the CPU. Each will differ in sophistication according to the type of application being used, the speed at which the information is output from the system and the cost of that means of outputting information. The following methods of outputting information may be used:

- monitors
- storage media
- printers
- plotters
- Computer Output Microform (COM)
- Point-Of-Sale (POS) terminals
- speech synthesisers
- modems

Monitors

44 There are two different types of monitor or visual display unit (VDU).

- the cathode ray tube
- the flat panel display

The cathode ray tube

45 The cathode ray tube monitor (CRT) works in a similar way to a television tube. The inside of the screen is coated with a phosphorescent material that glows when it is given an electric charge. At the back of the tube an electron gun fires charged particles and when these particles hit the screen the points of impact become charged, thereby causing the phosphorescent material to glow. By using electronic techniques the beams of charged particles are made to form the familiar letter and number symbols that appear on the screen. Monitors can be either monochrome displaying in two colours only, or colour. Colour monitors use three electron guns instead of a single one at the back of the tube. Each of the guns fires electrons that stimulate one of the three primary colours—red, yellow or blue, and by mixing these, all colours can be displayed.

46 Apart from text and number displays, the CPU is also capable of causing pictures, or graphics, to be displayed on the CRT screen. To display graphics the computer must contain a **graphics card** which may be installed on manufacture or inserted into an expansion slot by the user. The graphics card contains its own CPU and interprets the information sent by the computer's CPU, causing pictures to be

PARTIAL SET OF ASCII CODES

Character	Binary Code	Decimal	Character	Binary Code	Decimal
A	01000001	65	0	00110000	48
B	01000010	66	1	00110001	49
C	01000011	67	2	00110010	50
D	01000100	68	3	00110011	51
E	01000101	69	4	00110100	52
F	01000110	70	5	00110101	53
G	01000111	71	6	00110110	54
H	01001000	72	7	00110111	55
I	01001001	73	8	00111000	56
J	01001010	74	9	00111001	57
*	00101010	42	!	00100001	33
(	00101000	40	%	00100101	37
)	00101001	41	&	00100110	38
+	00101011	43	<	00111100	60
=	00111101	61	?	00111111	63

displayed on the screen. These pictures can be either **low resolution** or **high resolution** graphics. The difference between the two resolutions is in the **pixel** size. When a monitor displays text and numbers it arranges the symbols in a regular array of 24 rows of 40 or 80 columns. The intersection of a single row and column is called a text pixel and is capable of containing a single symbol. Low resolution graphics uses pixels of the same size as text pixels and pictures are made up of a compound of pixel patterns. These pixel patterns, like letters and numbers, form part of the ASCII code.

> How many rows and columns of text characters can your monitor screen display? Find out how to produce low resolution graphics.

47 High resolution graphics uses a much smaller pixel—usually a dot that you can see when you look closely at the screen. Because the high resolution pixel is so small, pixels in the three primary colours can be packed more closely together, thereby producing the effect of more colours. While a low resolution colour monitor will display graphics in three colours, a high resolution monitor can display up to sixteen colours.

> When drawing low resolution graphics pictures, a user employs a different method from that of drawing high resolution graphics. Describe these differences and the reasons why they are different.

Flat panel display

48 As computers become smaller, lighter in weight and more powerful they are increasingly required to be portable. The monitor can be a particularly bulky piece of equipment so to increase portability the flat panel display has been developed. This does not contain a CRT but uses instead either a **liquid crystal** (LCD) or a **plasma** display. The LCD produces images by using interactions between molecules of a crystal liquid and electric voltages. Normally, the molecules of the liquid are arranged in such a way that light can pass through them. When a voltage is applied to a particular part of the screen those molecules realign themselves and in doing so prevent light from passing through them in the same direction. This produces a dark patch on the screen and by using a combination of different dark patches the alphanumeric characters can be displayed. Another method, often employed on older hand calculators is to use light emitting diodes (LEDs). These are tiny electrical components that emit points of light when electrically activated.

2.11 Toshiba's TS200 Desktop Portable 386 computer with a high resolution plasma screen; courtesy Toshiba Information Systems UK Limited

49 By using all the known technology of monitor displays, the CPU can output information to the user. The information that the monitor displays, however, is **transitory**—it does not leave a permanent record behind. Often a permanent record of the output information will need to be retained. This can be done by using **storage media** or by producing **hard copy**. Typical hard copy devices are printers and plotters.

Storage media

50 We have already considered storage media, which can not only be used for reading information into the CPU, but also for writing information from the CPU. In this way a permanent record of the output information can be made.

Printers

51 The printer is used to produce typewritten information output from the CPU. This hard copy then becomes a permanent record. Printers vary according to:

- the quality of print produced
- the method employed to print
- colour printers

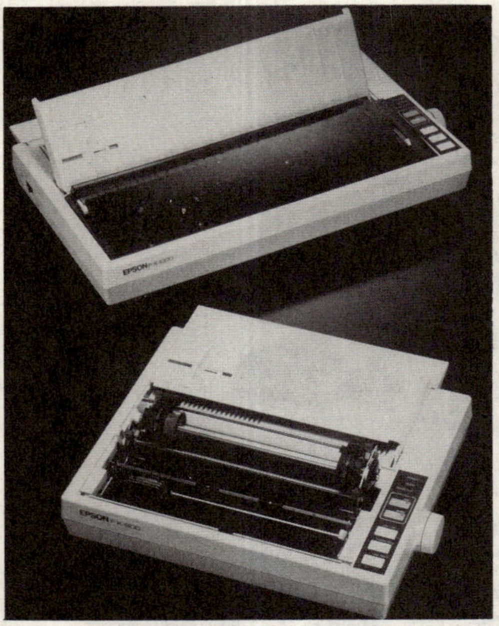

2.12A Dot matrix printer

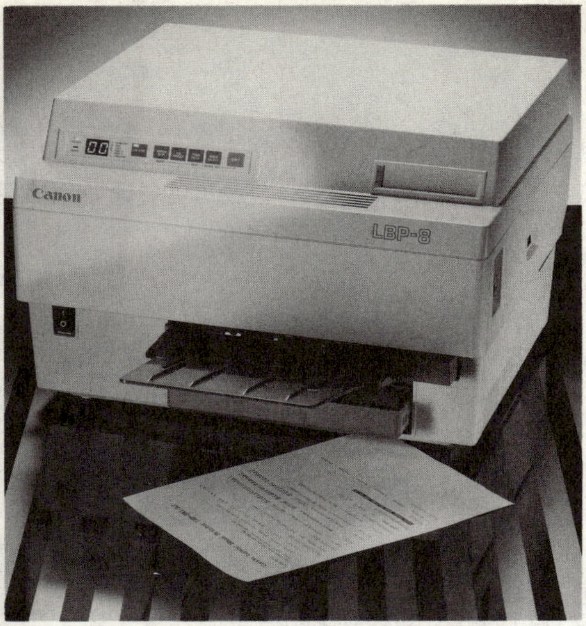

2.12B Laser printer

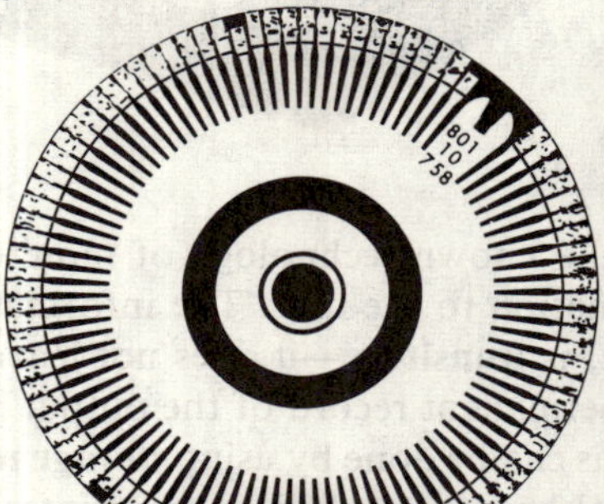

2.12D Daisy wheel

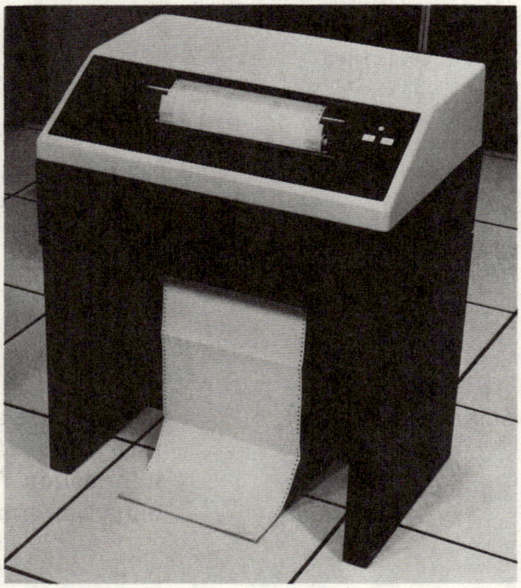

2.12C Mainframe printer

The quality of print produced

52 Print quality comes in a variety of standards.

(a) **Near-typeset quality** The appearance of the print from a near-typeset quality printer is similar to that of this book. This type of printer would be used if an effect of typeset printing were desired, such as for advertising material.

(b) **Letter-quality** A letter-quality printer will produce a print that is identical to that produced by an electric typewriter. The characters are clear and distinct. Such a printer would be used in business to produce formal letters.

(c) **Near-letter quality** A near-letter quality printer prints the characters in the form of dots. Characters printed in this way are not fully formed but by overprinting a number of times a fully formed effect can almost be achieved. This gives the effect of the near-letter quality print. This type of printer is often used as a cheaper alternative to a letter-quality printer.

(d) **Standard quality** A standard quality printer prints characters in the form of dots but with no overprinting. This quality of print is generally adequate for most purposes; for example, inter-departmental memos would only require this quality of appearance.

(e) **Draft quality** Draft quality print is composed of smaller characters made up of fewer dots. Sometimes it is called compressed print and is most used for producing rough copies of output information.

> What quality print is your printer capable of producing? Can you change the quality and if so, how would you do it?

Printers are controlled by their own internal chips, many of which can be programmed to produce a variety of different qualities of print.

> Find out the comparative speeds at which the different types of printer operate, and the comparative costs. How would you weigh cost against speed and quality?

The method employed to print

53 Printers can be classified according to the method they use to produce the print. There are two types of methods:

54 **Impact Printers** use a mechanical system to strike an inked ribbon placed between the striker and the paper. This leaves behind a printed impression on the paper. The different mechanisms that produce this effect are:

(a) **Dot-Matrix Printers** A dot-matrix printer has a print head that contains a number of pins arranged in a regular array of rows and columns. Each character of the keyboard has a corresponding pin-pattern which causes a specific selection of pins to strike the ribbon. This produces printed characters that are made up of dots. Dot-matrix printers print at a rate of between 100 characters per second for near-letter quality print to 600 characters per second for draft quality.

> Most of the printers in your school are likely to be dot-matrix printers. Look closely at the print that they produce, if necessary using a magnifying glass. See if you can count the number of dots that make up various letters and numbers.

(b) **Daisy Wheel Printers** A daisy wheel printer has a print head in the form of a spoked wheel. At the end of each spoke is a single character formed out of moulded metal. The striker is a small hammer which hits the end of a particular spoke, causing an impression of the character to be imprinted on the paper. Daisy wheel printers are used to produce letter-quality print, but because they use a rotating wheel to locate a character are much slower than dot-matrix printers. A typical daisy wheel printer will print at a rate of 30 to 60 characters per second.

(c) **Line Printers** A line printer produces print one line at a time. This is a very fast method, suitable for a larger computer system where large amounts of printed information are generated. A typical example of a line printer is the drum printer. On the outside surface of the drum are complete sets of typeface characters, each arranged around the drum's circumference. There are as many sets of characters as there are spaces across a sheet of paper and the characters are arranged so that the same character appears in a single line along the length of the drum. Because of this alignment the printer can print all the occurrences of, for example, the letter c on the line at the same time. The drum then revolves to the next character and prints all the d's and so on until the line is completely printed and the line feed causes the paper to move to the next line.

Line printers can produce print at a rate of up to 6000 lines per minute or 8000 characters per second.

55 Non-impact Printers Non-impact printers do not use a mechanical striking action to produce the print. We shall consider three such types of printer.

(a) **Ink-Jet Printers** An ink-jet printer forms each character by spraying quick-drying ink directly onto the paper. The principle is similar to the dot-matrix printer except that instead of using pins, ink is sprayed through an array of nozzles. Such a printer will produce print at a rate of around 300 characters a second.

(b) **Thermal Printers** A thermal printer, like a dot-matrix printer, uses pins. The pins are arranged to form characters and are heated electrically from pressure against heat sensitive paper to leave behind an impression of the character. Some types may use an inked ribbon, with the heat causing the ink to transfer to the paper.

(c) **Laser Printers** A laser printer is used to produce the near-typeset quality print. The laser produces a very fine beam of light which strikes the paper and leaves behind an electric charge. The ink is then attracted to the paper by the electric charge and when the paper is heated and pressed, the ink becomes fixed to the paper. Laser printers vary from those used by microcomputer systems to large commercial printers attached to larger systems. A small laser printer can print around 7 pages per minute whereas a large commercial laser printer can produce over 400 pages per minute.

> What do you consider to be the main advantages of a non-impact printer over an impact one? Are there any disadvantages?

Colour printers

56 Many printers can be arranged to print in colour. Some dot-matrix printers are arranged to take a coloured ribbon which is impregnated with the three primary colours red yellow and blue. By overstriking repeatedly any colour can be produced.

> Which primary colours go together to make
>
> (a) brown?
> (b) green?
> (c) purple?
>
> How many times must a printer re-strike to produce each colour?

Plotters

57 Plotters, like printers are used to produce printed records of output from the CPU. A plotter consists of a roller, over which a sheet of paper is placed. A pen writes on the paper with its point of contact on the roller. The pen can move laterally and the roller can rotate moving the paper backwards and forwards beneath the pen. In this way continuous lines can be drawn on the paper. Most plotters can take a number of pens, of varying colour to enable a coloured drawing to be produced quickly and with complete accuracy.

Computer output microform (COM)

58 In some situations it is not appropriate to retain all the output on paper as there is far too much of it. An example of this is the catalogue

2.13 Microfiche reader

of books held by a public library. To save space, these catalogues are contained on **microfilm** or **microfiche** which is a photograph of the printed information in a much reduced form. To avoid having to produce the printed output and then photograph it a **computer output microform** system will perform the complete process in one. A typical COM system will produce upwards of 120 000 characters per second.

> Go to your public library and look at a sheet of microfiche. Given the number of pages stored on a single sheet, can you work out how many characters that represents?

Point-of-sale (POS) terminals

59 At a point-of-sale terminal a purchase is recorded. From this information the customer's bill is automatically constructed. A number of different types of POS terminal are available, each offering different facilities. There are different ways of recording a purchase, from recording the value at an electronic till to scanning a bar code with a laser reader. With the latter type of POS, the customer's bill is itemised with a brief description of the product and the store's stock list is automatically updated.

Speech synthesisers

60 Information can be output in the form of a spoken word. The CPU translates the information to be output using a set of phonetic rules and stored sounds, which can then be used to construct words and transmit them through the computer's speaker to give the effect of speech. Speech synthesis requires a large amount of available memory and its development is still in its infancy.

Computer systems

61 Having looked at the individual hardware components that go together to form a computer system, we must now turn our attention to the complete systems themselves. Computer systems will vary in size, but can be classified as:

- mainframes
- minicomputers
- microcomputers
- supercomputers
- dedicated systems

62 It should be noted, however, that these distinctions are largely historical and are becoming more blurred as technology advances. For example, it is now possible for a microcomputer to surpass the processing capacity of what only a few years ago was thought of as a large commercial machine. Despite this it is useful to recognise that distinctions are still made.

Mainframes

63 The mainframe computer is a large system suitable for use by a large organisation. While the first general purpose, electronic computer was built in 1939—the **Atanasoff-Berry Computer** (ABC)—it was not until the 1950s that computers were built and sold as business data processing machines. These early, **first generation machines** used **thermionic valves** which generated a large amount of heat and took up a large amount of space. They were the forerunners of what are now referred to as **mainframe computers**. In the 1960s, **transistors** replaced the thermionic valves producing a consequent reduction in both size and heat generation.

A number of famous people were involved in the development of the early computers. Find out what you can about each of the following:

(a) Blaise Pascal
(b) Charles Babbage and Ada Lovelace
(c) Joseph Marie Jacquard
(d) Hermann Hollerith

The **second generation machines** saw the introduction of magnetic media for secondary storage and the development of **languages** that enabled users to program them more easily. By the end of the 1960s the **third generation computers** used **integrated circuits** on silicon chips instead of arrays of transistors. They also used keyboards and monitors for input and output.

A typical mainframe computer contains a primary storage measured in **megabytes** and processes information at a speed of up to 100 million instructions per second (mips). Users of mainframes include large businesses and institutions that process large amounts of data. Mainframes are susceptible to temperature and humidity fluctuations so are housed in specially controlled environments. These must also be secure, access only being permitted to authorised personnel. As well as processing vast quantities of data, mainframes can accommodate a large number of users simultaneously by adopting a time-sharing procedure. A CPU is 'time-shared' among a large number of terminals by switching its attention to each terminal in turn. This switching occurs at such a fast rate that the user is given the impression that the computer is entirely dedicated to their terminal.

Try to visit a mainframe computer installation to get an idea of the size and scope of such systems. You will be likely to find one in the nearest large organisation to you such as a university, polytechnic or the local authority. Talk to the people who use the machine and find out the sort of tasks it is used for.

Towards the end of the 1960s advances in microprocessor technology saw the introduction of the minicomputer.

Minicomputers

64 The early mainframes were not designed to accommodate time-sharing procedures that permitted simultaneous users; minicomputers were originally devised to overcome this deficiency. The modern minicomputer is a scaled down version of a modern mainframe with the appropriate scaling down in costs, and as such it is suitable for smaller businesses. It is easier to operate than a mainframe and both operators

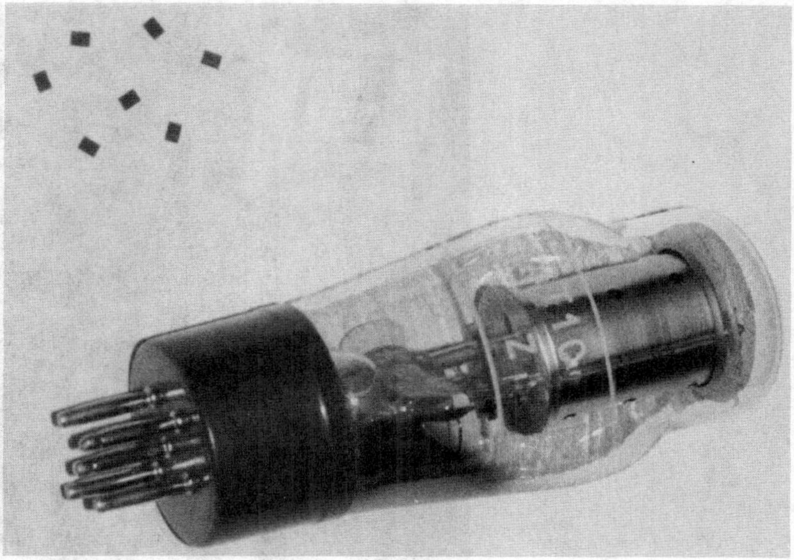

2.14 Thermionic valve with microchips. Each microchip contains over 100 transistors, each of which replaced a valve similar to this

and programmers require less training. In addition these third generation machines require less space and though they are not classified as portable machines can be moved relatively easily. Primary storage is in megabytes and secondary storage is often in the form of disk packs. Their speed of operation is usually approximately 50 mips.

Microcomputers

65 During the 1970s the first microcomputers were built. This phase of computer development is referred to as the **fourth generation** and was signified by the introduction of **large scale integration** (LSI)—the etching of thousands of transistors onto a single chip. In the late 1970s **very large scale integration** (VLSI) saw the incorporation of hundreds of thousands of transistors on a single chip. VLSI paved the way for the development of the microcomputer which continues to this day.

The microcomputer is the smallest and cheapest of all the range of computers. In 1977 Wozniak and Jobs invented the APPLE microcomputer and since then microcomputer systems have flourished. Despite their small size they are extremely useful tools, able to solve many problems more accurately and more efficiently than any other method in the same price bracket. Because of their cheapness, microcomputers are used almost everywhere, from home to school to the workplace. A typical microcomputer has a primary storage of around 512 kilobytes and a processing speed of approximately 1 mips. With the introduction of the more advanced microprocessor chips such as the INTEL 80386 and the MOTOROLA 68000, microcomputers are gaining much more processing power. For example, the INTEL 80386 currently makes available 4 megabytes of primary storage out of its eventual capability of 4 gigabytes—4 000 000 000 bytes, and operates at 25 MHz.

2.15 CRAY-2 Supercomputer; Courtesy CRAY Research (UK) Limited

Microcomputers range from the desk-top models to the light-weight, battery powered portables, called laptop models, to the small hand-held models introduced in the early 1980s.

> Describe your microcomputer. Do you know which make of microprocessor chip it uses?

Supercomputers

66 At the top of the range of general purpose computers are super-computers. The largest of these is the CRAY with a primary storage of several gigabytes and a processing speed in excess of 1200 mips.

The CRAY can manage up to 10 000 terminals but to do this it requires two smaller computers, either mainframes or minicomputers, to act as front end and back end processors. These front and back end processors coordinate all the input and output activities and so allow the supercomputer to perform its high speed calculations without hindrance. Typical uses of a supercomputer would be in the Meteorological Office where weather patterns are predicted by manip-ulating vast amounts of data. Only by holding this data in memory can the calculations be done in time to make a forecast, hence the necessity of a large and very fast machine.

Dedicated systems

Dedicated systems range from microprocessor chips inside a digital watch or electronic hand calculator to computers designed to perform a specific task such as word processing. They are controlled by a central processing unit which consists of a control unit, arithmetic and logic unit and primary storage, and they all require information to be input and they output information.

> Make a list of twelve dedicated computer systems. Could any of them be substituted by a general purpose system? If so, what would be the advantages and disadvantages?

Summary

The central processor unit (CPU) allows the computer to perform all of its functions and consists of three components. The control unit controls the hardware and memory resources and the arithmetic and logic unit (ALU) controls the arithmetic and logic functions. Primary storage consists of ROM and RAM and additional memory is provided by backing store. Backing store can consist of punched cards, magnetic tapes and magnetic disks. Information is sent to the CPU using various input devices which range from keyboards through mechanical, optical and magnetic readers to speech recognition. Information is sent from the CPU to various output devices which range from monitors, through printers and plotters to computer output microform and speech synthesis. Computer systems range from the very large general purpose supercomputers through mainframes, minicomputers and microcomputers to dedicated systems.

Key points

The central processing unit, the control unit, the arithmetic and logic unit (ALU), the primary storage unit, read only memory (ROM), programmable read only memory (PROM), erasable programmable read only memory (EPROM), random access memory (RAM), backing store, punched cards, magnetic tapes, reel-to-reel tape, cassette tape, cartridge tape, magnetic disks, access of information, speed of information transfer, amount of information stored, floppy diskettes, hard disks, fixed disks, disk-on-a-card, Bernoulli boxes, the disk pack, optical disks and cards, input devices, keyboards, the cursor control keys, function keys, the mouse and trackball, games paddles and joysticks, optical and magnetic readers, optical bar readers (OBR), optical character recognition (OCR), optical mark recognition (OMR), magnetic ink character recognition (MICR), magnetic strips, light pens, touch screens, speech recognition, key-to-disk, output devices, monitors, the cathode ray tube, the flat panel display, storage media, printers, the quality of print produced, near-typeset quality, letter-quality, near-letter quality, standard quality, draft quality, the method employed to print, impact printers, dot-matrix printers, daisy wheel printers, line printers, non-impact printers, ink-jet printers, thermal printers, laser printers, colour printers, plotters, computer output microform, point-of-sale (POS) terminals, speech synthesisers, computer systems, mainframes, minicomputers, microcomputers, supercomputers, dedicated systems.

Self assessment questions

1 What does CPU stand for? (2)
2 Name the components of the CPU. (2)
3 What are the functions of the control unit? (3)
4 How does the system clock affect the control unit? (3)
5 What units are used to measure clock speed? (3)
6 What does ALU stand for? (4)
7 What are the functions of the ALU? (4)
8 What are the logic operations used for? (4)
9 What is an arithmetic co-processor? (4)
10 What is primary storage? (5)
11 What is meant by ROM? (6)
12 What is meant by hard wired? (6)
13 What is firmware? (6)
14 Can you write to ROM? (6)
15 What is a PROM? (6)
16 What could a PROM be used for? (6)
17 What is an EPROM? (6)
18 How is an EPROM's memory erased? (6)
19 What is an EEPROM? (6)
20 What does RAM stand for? (7)
21 What does random access refer to? (7)
22 What is meant by volatile memory? (7)
23 What is RAM for? (7)
24 What is meant by backing store? (8)
25 Why is backing store used? (8)
26 List four different types of secondary storage media. (8)
27 What is a punched card? (9)
28 What does a keypunch machine do? (9)
29 What is a card reader? (9)
30 What is magnetic tape? (10)
31 How is information stored on magnetic tape? (10)
32 List three types of secondary storage using magnetic tape. (10)
33 What is reel-to-reel tape? (11)
34 What are cassette tapes? (12)
35 What is cartridge tape? (13)
36 What is meant by backing up? (13)
37 Explain the expression, 'Information is stored on a magnetic tape sequentially'. (14)
38 Name one disadvantage of magnetic tape. (14)
39 What is a magnetic disk? (15)
40 List three advantages of magnetic disk over other forms of storage media. (15)
41 What is a disk drive? (16)
42 How is information that is stored on a magnetic disk accessed? (16)
43 Can information be accessed faster from a magnetic disk or from a magnetic tape? (17)
44 List three types of magnetic disk. (19)
45 Describe a floppy diskette. (20)
46 Describe a hard disk. (21)
47 List three types of hard disk. (21)
48 What is a fixed disk? (21)
49 What is a disk-on-a-card? (21)
50 How is a disk-on-a-card fitted into a computer? (21)
51 What is an expansion slot? (21)
52 What is a Bernoulli box? (21)
53 What are the advantages of a Bernoulli box over a fixed hard disk? (21)
54 What is a disk pack? (22)
55 What are optical disks? (23)
56 What is the difference between CD ROM and CD Interactive? (23)
57 What kind of information can be stored on an optical disk? (23)
58 Give one use of an optical disk. (23)
59 What is an optical card? (24)
60 List nine different input devices. (25)
61 List two types of special keys found on a keyboard. (26)
62 What is a cursor? (27)
63 What are cursor control keys? (27)
64 What are function keys? (28,29)
65 What are the function keys marked F1, F2, etc. used for? (29)
66 What is a macro? (29)
67 What is a mouse and how is it used? (30)
68 What is a trackball? (31)
69 What are games paddles and joysticks? (32)
70 List four types of optical and magnetic readers. (33)

71 What is an OBR device? (34)
72 What is a bar code and what is it used for? (34)
73 What is an OCR device? (35)
74 What does an OCR wand read? (35)
75 What is an OMR device? (36)
76 What does an OMR device read? (36)
77 What is an MICR device? (37)
78 Give one use for magnetic ink. (37)
79 What are magnetic strips? (38)
80 What is a light pen and how does it work? (39)
81 How does a touch screen work? (40)
82 Where would you find a touch pad? (40)
83 How does speech recognition work? (41)
84 Give two uses for speech recognition. (41)
85 What is key-to-disk? (42)
86 Why is key-to-disk used? (42)
87 List eight different output devices. (43)
88 Name two types of monitor. (44)
89 Describe in brief the workings of a CRT. (45)
90 What is a graphics card? (46)
91 What is the difference between low resolution and high resolution graphics? (46)
92 What is a text pixel? (46)
93 How small is a high resolution graphics pixel? (47)
94 Distinguish between LCD, Plasma Display and LED. (48)
95 Explain the expression 'Information that the monitor displays is transitory'. (49)
96 What is hard copy? (49)
97 List three properties of printers by which two printers can be compared. (51)
98 List five different types of print quality. (52)
99 What are the two different methods used to produce print? (53,55)
100 Describe three different types of impact printers. (54)
101 Describe three different types of non-impact printers. (55)
102 How does a colour printer print in colour? (56)
103 How does a plotter produce its output? (57)
104 What is computer output microform? (38)
105 What is a POS terminal? (59)
106 What does a POS terminal offer? (59)
107 What is speech synthesis? (60)
108 List four classes of computer system. (62)
109 What was the name of the first general purpose computer ever built? (63)
110 What is a mainframe computer? (63)
111 What distinguishes first, second and third generation computers? (63)
112 What does mips stand for? (63)
113 What is meant by time-sharing? (63)
114 What is a minicomputer? (64)
115 What are fourth generation computers? (65)
116 What is meant by LSI and VLSI? (65)
117 What is a laptop computer? (65)
118 What is a supercomputer? (66)
119 Who would use a supercomputer and why? (66)
120 What are dedicated systems? (67)

Exercises

1 Which of the following is an input device only?

light pen
magnetic disk drive
printer
VDU

2 Which of the following explains the meaning of formatting disks?

arranging disks into alphabetical order
making back-up copies of disks
preparing disks for use
transferring data from disk to tape

3 A large city central library uses a computer to produce a catalogue of details for each of the 500 000 books it contains. Copies of this catalogue are output and distributed every month to all the smaller branch libraries around the city. The branch libraries do not have computer facilities of their own. Which of the following forms of output would be most suited to this task?

cassette tape
fanfolded printer paper
floppy disk
microfiche

4 A runner is training for a 1500 m race but the coach is worried about the effects of running on her heart and lungs. To monitor the runner a microcomputer system is worn on a belt around the athlete's waist. Three sensors measure the following:

breathing rate
heart rate
stepping rate.

These sensors are connected to the microprocessor which is connected to a radio transmitter. The transmitter sends the information collected to a track side computer system. This is shown in the following diagram.

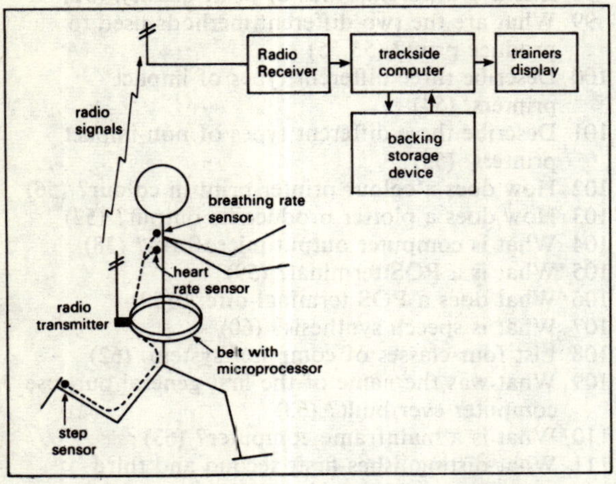

(a) Name the three inputs that are required for this data logging system.

(b) An output device is connected to the belt microprocessor. This output device is not shown on the diagram. It gives urgent information to the runner.
 (i) Describe or name a suitable device.
 (ii) Give one use for this device.

(c) The track side computer system also has an output device.
 (i) Describe or name a suitable device.
 (ii) Give one use for this device.

(d) Suggest one reason why a backing storage device is provided on the track side computer.

5 A daisy wheel printer, a dot matrix printer, and a graph plotter could all be used to produce paper output from a computer.

(a) Of the daisy wheel printer and dot matrix printer, which would be better to print business letters in an office.

(b) A dot matrix printer and a graph plotter could both be used by a fitted kitchen shop to produce the plans of a kitchen on paper. Which would produce the best results in this situation?

6 A computer controlled car park issues tickets as cars arrive. At the time of leaving the driver inserts the ticket into a payment device. The computer calculates and displays the fee and the drive inserts coins into the device to pay the fee. If necessary the machine will give change. The payment device then issues an 'exit' ticket. The driver now has a short time in which to drive the car to the exit barrier and insert the exit ticket. When the exit ticket is inserted the computer raises the barrier.

(a) Name a suitable machine readable method for encoding the arrival time on the parking ticket the machine issues.

(b) Identify three different output devices that would be connected to the car park computer system. Explain briefly what they would be used for.

(c) The control program that runs the car park system has many parts. One part works out which coins need to be ejected when change is required. For example, if the computer has calculated that the driver needs 37p in change, which coins are to be ejected?
A possible answer might be:

1 — 10p coin
5 — 5p coins
2 — 1p coins.

(i) Find another possible answer that uses fewer coins.
(ii) Suggest an alternative if there are no 20p coins or 5p coins left in the payment device.

(d) The payment device accepts 1p, 2p, 5p, 10p, 20, and 50p coins. It will use all except the 50p coin in giving change. Change is issued using the least number of coins possible.
 (i) Assuming that there are always enough of each type of coin to give the required coins in change, design an algorithm to work out how many each of the five types of coin to eject. Explain your algorithm using a diagram or words.
 (ii) Dry run your finished algorithm with 37p as the change required.
 (iii) Give a revised algorithm that will take account of some coins having run out.

7 Laser and dot matrix printers are widely used in computing. Name two other devices, which can be used for output only, and describe a use for which each device is suitable.

8 The following is a list of devices and media. State whether each is used for input or output.

mouse
graph plotter
line printer
magnetic ink character reader

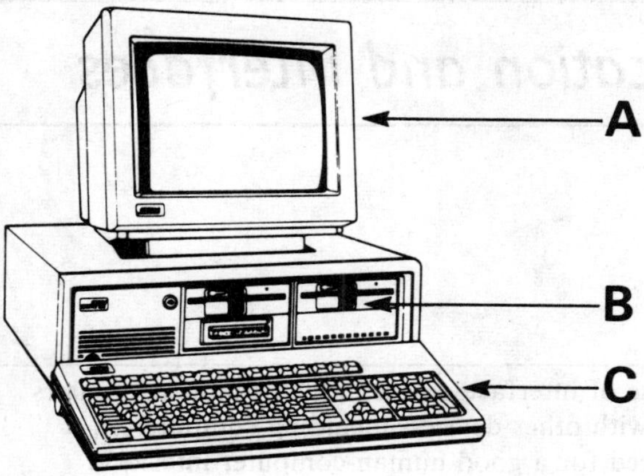

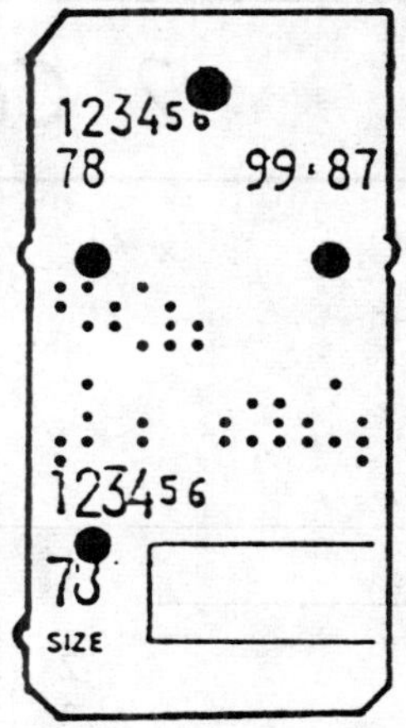

9 Name the units marked A, B and C on the above diagram of a microcomputer.

10 *Magnetic Ink Character Recognition* is most commonly used in banks. State two reasons why MICR is used in banks.

11 The following is a list of some computer devices. Which of A, B or C best describes that device.

graphics tablet	A Backing Store
speech synthesiser	B Input
disk drive	C Output.

12 For each of the following applications, is serial file access or direct file access suitable?

Sorting a file on magnetic tape
Theatre seat booking system.

13 All computers need devices for input, output and storage.

(a) Name one device used only for input.

(b) Name one device used only for output.

(c) Name one storage device.

(d) Why is an interface necessary when using a peripheral device?

14 The following diagram shows a tag similar to the ones used by clothes shops. The tags have holes punched in them to help re-order goods that have been sold.

(a) What is the name given to this type of tag?

(b) The data is printed as well as punched on to the tag. Explain why the data is printed on the tag if the computer only reads the punched data.

(c) Explain why the price of the garment is not punched on the tag.

15 (a) For each of the following applications, write down the most suitable type of output device.

Producing payslips for several thousand employees.
Producing detailed drawings for a computer aided design application.
Producing high quality letters that can be sent to business customers.
Producing listings for computer programs being developed on a microcomputer.

(b) The following payslip was printed using pre-printed stationery.

TAX CODE:	234H	NAME:	Mr A. N. Other
N.I. No.:	YZ12345A	DATE:	July 88
		PAY No:	666666
PAY AND ALLOWANCES		DEDUCTIONS	
BASIC PAY	543.00	INCOME TAX	143.00
BONUS	250.00	NAT. INS.	41.00
EXPENS.	38.51	PENSION	21.00
TOTAL	831.51	TOTAL	205.00
		NETT PAY	626.51

From the payslip above, name one item that would be pre-printed on the stationery before the payslip was produced, one item that was copied from the master file and one item that was calculated by the computer.

(c) State one reason for using pre-printed stationary in this case.

2 *Communication and interfaces*

Objectives

1 To explain the use of interface devices which enable computers to communicate with other devices, including computers.
2 To explain the need for a good human-computer interface.
3 To identify some of the implications of the use of computers for individuals, organisations and society.

Communication

1 Communication is an important part of our daily life. We communicate our feelings, our desires and our knowledge in a variety of ways; by talking, by body-language signals and by writing. It is hardly surprising then that when we invented computers to work for us we also created a need for them to communicate with each other. Computer communication is a complex process but for the purposes of this book, it is only necessary to describe the basic ideas that are involved and to demonstrate the scope and importance of computer communications.

There are four levels of computer communication:

- communication between components of the CPU
- communication between the CPU and peripheral devices
- communication between computers
- communication between computers and people

Communication between components of the CPU and primary storage

2 The two components of the CPU, the control unit and the arithmetic and logic unit, and the primary storage are activated by electric currents in the form of **pulses**. The CPU can only accept and transmit information in the form of pulses of electricity. We can represent these pulses by the following diagram.

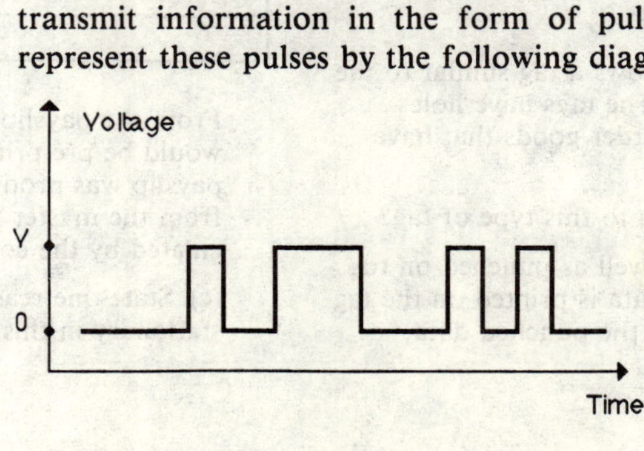

This train of pulses is quite regular. Each pulse has the same height—it represents a voltage of V volts—and each lasts for whole number multiples of a given time unit. In the diagram the first four pulses last for one time unit each and the fifth for two time units. Between the pulses there is a voltage of 0 volts, again each lasting for whole number multiples of a given time unit. Because the pulses are so regular we can code them using the numbers 0 for no voltage and 1 for V volts. The code for the train of pulses shown in the diagram is then

0010010100010110

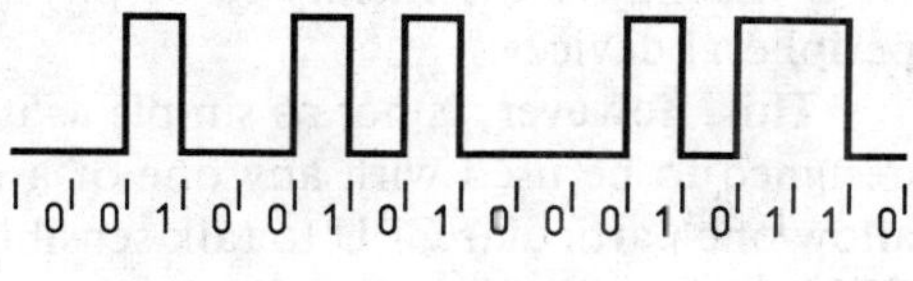

It is important to appreciate why we do this. The CPU can only understand pulses of electricity. We could then describe the train of pulses as no pulse, no pulse, pulse, no pulse, ... but this would be very cumbersome. Instead we devise the code using 0s and 1s so that we can easily describe the electric signals that are travelling around the CPU.

Write the 0,1 code sequence for the following train of pulses.

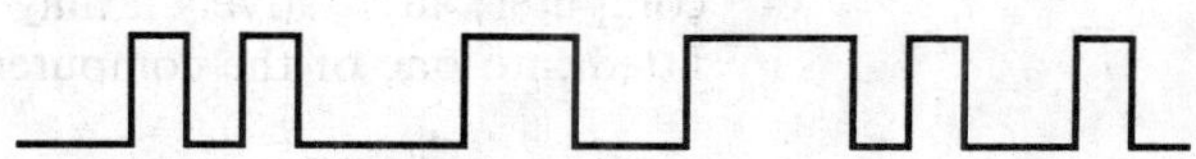

Draw the train of pulses represented by the following code.

0011010100001111001

If you are familiar with **binary numbers** you will recognise this code as a binary sequence. Having translated information that we understand into a binary sequence we can then further translate the binary sequence into pulses of electricity and transmit them to the CPU.

3 The components of the CPU communicate with each other by sending and receiving signals in the form of these regular pulses. The pulses are sent via groups of metallic wires called **buses** which connect the components together. There are three buses in the CPU:

(a) **The control bus** This is the electrical path along which the timing and controlling messages are sent to the other components.

(b) **The address bus** This electrical path transmits information dealing with the byte addresses in primary storage. The location of storage space available or used is sent via this bus.

(c) **The data bus** Data transfer travels via the data bus between primary storage, the ALU and the various input and output devices.

The binary code that we use to describe the signals that travel down the various buses is comprised of the two digits 0 and 1. For this reason we refer to this type of signal transmission as digital transmission.

Communication between the CPU and peripheral devices

4 In the last chapter we learnt how the CPU can be connected to the outside world in a variety of ways, permitting information to be both input and output. This connection enables the two-way flow of communication between the CPU and the outside world. To do this the CPU must have the facility to be physically connected to a variety of peripheral devices.

This, however, is not as simple as it sounds: peripheral devices are designed to be used with any one of a number of different CPUs. To allow one particular CPU to talk sensibly to a given peripheral then the CPU's method of communication must be matched to the method of communication of the peripheral device. This is done using a specially manufactured interface.

Interfaces

5 The interface is a piece of hardware that comes between the CPU and the peripheral device. Sometimes it is built into the body of the computer; alternatively it may be located on an interface card which is fitted into one of the computer's expansion slots.

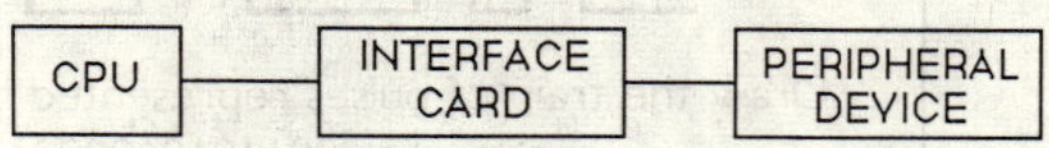

Before discussing interfaces further, we must be aware of how information is physically transmitted into and out of the CPU.

> How many peripheral devices does your computer have? Are the interfaces clearly visible? If not, look inside the computer if possible. What do the interface cards look like? How are they fitted into the computer?

Digital transmission

6 The CPU transmits information to peripheral devices via a data bus in the form of groups of electric pulses. However, some peripheral devices are so constructed that they can only receive information one pulse at a time. Hence, there are two kinds of interface.

- serial interface
- parallel interface

Serial interface

7 The serial interface permits information to be received from the CPU in groups of pulses but transmitted to the peripheral device one pulse at a time.

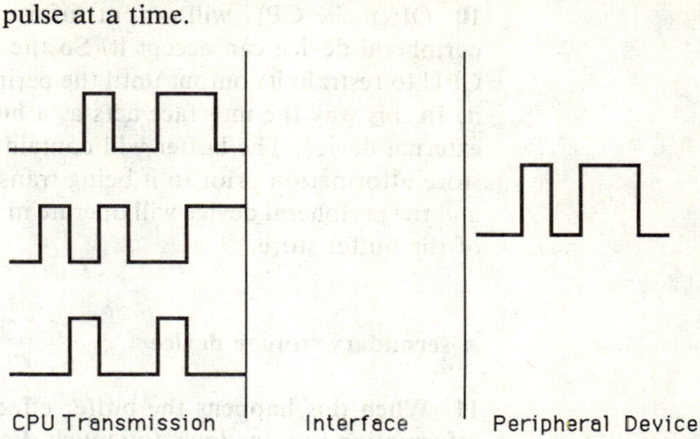

There is a standard interface connection for this called the RS 232C socket, which may be built into the computer at manufacture or may have to be inserted by the user using an interface card. A built-in RS 232C socket is located on the outside of the processor box, usually at the back. When using a card it is necessary to open up the computer's processor box and insert the card into an expansion slot. In either case the peripheral device plugs into the interface. All low cost printers are serial devices.

> If your computer has an RS 232C at the back, draw a picture of it so that you will recognise it next time you see one.

Parallel interface

8 The parallel interface permits information to be transmitted in groups of pulses at a time. There are two standard parallel interface connections called the IEEE 488 or the Centronics socket. Parallel interfaces are so called because the wires through which the information travels are grouped together in parallel. In either case the peripheral device plugs into the interface socket and, like the serial interface, can be either built-in or inserted by the user using an **interface card**. Parallel printers are much faster than their serial counterparts.

> Does your computer have a parallel interface at the back? If so which one is it? Draw a picture of it so that you will be able to recognise it the next time you see one.

Other interface facilities

9 In addition to being a means of permitting communication between the CPU and the peripheral device, the interface can also act as:

- a buffer
- a secondary storage device

A buffer

10 Often the CPU will output information at a faster rate than the peripheral device can accept it. So the interface will interact with the CPU to restrain its output until the peripheral device is ready to receive it. In this way the interface acts as a **buffer** between the CPU and the external device. The buffer will contain a small amount of memory to store information prior to it being transmitted to the peripheral device and the peripheral device will operate in bursts as it uses up the contents of the buffer store.

A secondary storage device

11 When this happens the buffer effect may cause the processing of information to slow down too much. For example, if you were printing a document and the printer could only accept a single line of print at a time from the buffer, then it would take a long time to print a complete document. To overcome this the interface can be arranged to have a large enough memory to accept a number of pages of a document at a time, allowing the printer to feed off the information stored on the interface. This is very useful with word processing because it frees the CPU to deal with other tasks. In particular, with many word processors it is now possible to print one document at the same time as editing or creating another.

> Does your printer use an interface with a buffer or does it have a secondary storage device? How can you tell?

12 Interfaces and interface cards are used to perform many different functions. They permit the CPU to output information to a disk drive, to a voice synthesiser, to a robot and many other devices. Obviously, to enable each card to perform its own dedicated task it must itself be controlled by its own CPU. Interface cards are often small, dedicated computers in their own right.

Analogue transmission

13 We have seen that the CPU can only handle information in the form of pulses of electricity which we represent by the digits 0 and 1. This information transmission is called digital transmission. There are, however, times when information is fed into the computer in the form of continuously varying signals called **analogue signals**. For example, a mouse can be moved about a flat surface in a continuous manner but the CPU will only recognise position on the screen to the nearest pixel. We need to convert the continuous signal from the mouse—the analogue signal—into a digital signal for recognition by the CPU. This is done by an interface card which contains an analogue to digital converter, in other words, a **de-modulator**.

14 There are also output devices that accept only analogue signals. A typical example of this is the older type of telephone line designed purely for voice transmission using analogue signalling. Such a telephone line can be used to allow one computer to send information to another computer. To enable this to happen the digital signal transmitted by the CPU must be converted into an analogue signal. This type of converter is called a modulator.

> Wrist watches are said to be either 'digital' or 'analogue'. A digital watch has a digital display whereas an analogue watch has the traditional long and short hands. Is an analogue watch really a true analogue device?

Modems

15 Modems are interface devices which permit a computer to send and receive an analogue or non-digital telephone line. Such a device must be capable of modulating digital to analogue for transmission and of de-modulating analogue to digital for reception. The **mo**dulator **dem**odulator interface is called a **modem**. There are two types of modem.

- the acoustic coupler
- the direct-connect modem

Acoustic coupler

16 An acoustic coupler consists of a unit containing a telephone. The computer transmits through the earpiece and receives through the mouthpiece but in both reception and transmission the electric signals are converted to sound and back again to electric signals. This makes the signals subject to distortion and considerably slows down the transmission rate. Transmission speeds are measured in baud—the number of modulations or demodulations per second—or binary digits (pulses) per second—bps.

Direct-connect modem

17 A direct-connect modem connects to the telephone line directly. There is no conversion of the signal to sound so the signal is more reliable and less likely to be distorted and the speed of transmission is higher. In addition, many of the necessary operations connected with modems can be done automatically with a D-C Modem. For example, it can have an automatic dialling facility, a variable baud rate and can respond to commands from a communications program.

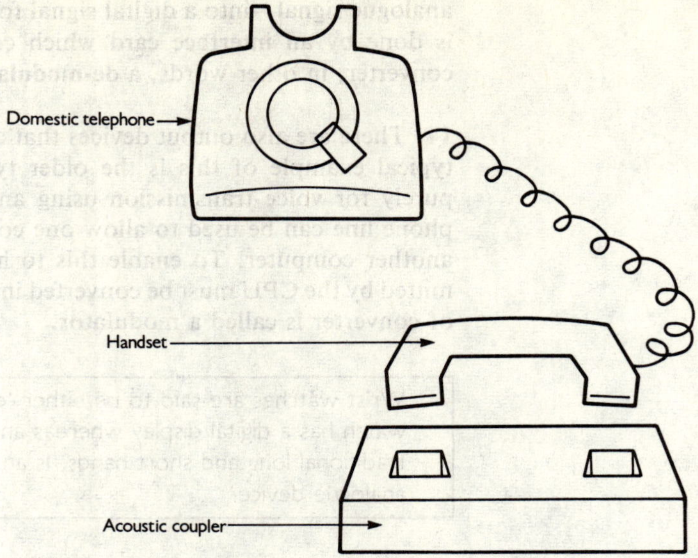

2.21 An acoustic coupler

Data transmission

18 Before a CPU can transmit or receive information to and from a peripheral device a number of rules must be satisfied and a number of procedures established. These rules and procedures are collectively referred to as a protocol and the process of establishing the fact that both CPU and peripheral device are following the same protocol is called handshaking.

A protocol defines how the information is sent and how it is received. For example, the smallest unit of information that a computer can receive is a single character. Consequently, with information arriving in a train of pulses, the printer must be able to tell where one character starts and another ends. In addition, the CPU must recognise that the printer has to resolve this problem. The resolution of the problem is a part of the protocol. Apart from character definition, data can be sent in blocks of characters enclosed within start and stop bits, this is called **asynchronous transmission**, or in blocks of characters without start and stop bits but transmitted with the sender and receiver clocks synchronised so that blocks of data can be sent in a timed sequence—**synchronous transmission**. Deciding which method will be employed is also part of the protocol.

19 As well as being able to distinguish characters, the CPU and the peripheral device must agree on the mode of transmission.

(a) **Simplex Mode** Data can only travel in one direction as in the case of information sent to a printer.

(b) **Half-Duplex Mode** Data can be transmitted both ways but only in one direction at a time, as in the case of information being sent to and received from a disk drive.

(c) **Full-Duplex Mode** Data can be transmitted both ways simultaneously as in the case of a telephone conversation.

20 During a handshake both the CPU and the peripheral device will establish agreement on the protocol after which communication can take place.

> Can you see any similarity between two computers talking to each other and two people doing the same? In what ways do you think they are similar and in what ways do they differ?

Communication between computers

21 Computers that are able to communicate with each other are said to be networked together. There are two types of network:

- the local area network (LAN)
- the wide area network

The local area network (LAN)

22 A typical LAN consists of a collection of computers and associated peripheral devices connected together in the same building by means of wire cables or optic fibres.

Wire cables

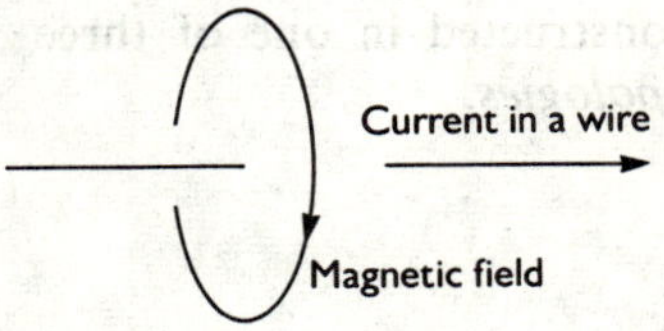

2.22 Wire cable with current and magnetic fields

23 The use of wire cables provides a convenient and cheap method of physically connecting devices together. However, in transmitting information, they give off magnetic fields, and by interacting with these it is possible to discover information that is being transmitted, thereby putting the security of confidential information at risk. Other magnetic fields in the vicinity of the cables can also interfere with the signals in the cable and corrupt the information being transmitted.

Fibre optics

24 A fibre optic is a thin tube of glass comparable in size to a human hair. The inside of the tube acts like a mirror to light signals so light can be sent down the tube, bouncing off the sides as it travels. A collection of these fibres are grouped together to form a cable which can then be used for transmitting information. The absence of magnetic fields associated with the fibre optic ensures security and integrity of the information transmitted and a further advantage is that transmission is in digital form. However, light degrades as it travels over a distance so boosters have to be installed at intervals along the cable to boost the signal. This makes the fibre optic cable a more expensive option but it

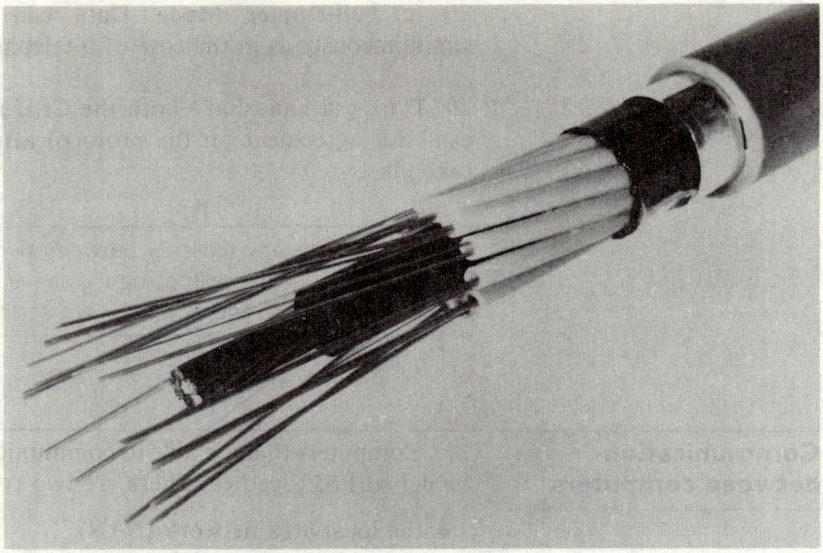

2.23 Fibre optic cable; courtesy STC Telecommunications

should be noted that *Mercury*, the telephone company, uses fibre optics to transmit information across its network.

> If you wanted to use a fibre optic cable over a long distance, where would you lay it? What do you think is the hardest problem to solve when joining two fibre optic cables together?

25 Local Area Networks are normally constructed in one of three geometrical arrangements referred to as *topologies*.

- **Star topology**
- **Ring topology**
- **Bus or tree topology**

Star topology **In this topology the computer equipment is connected radially from a central message-switching computer. All other com-**

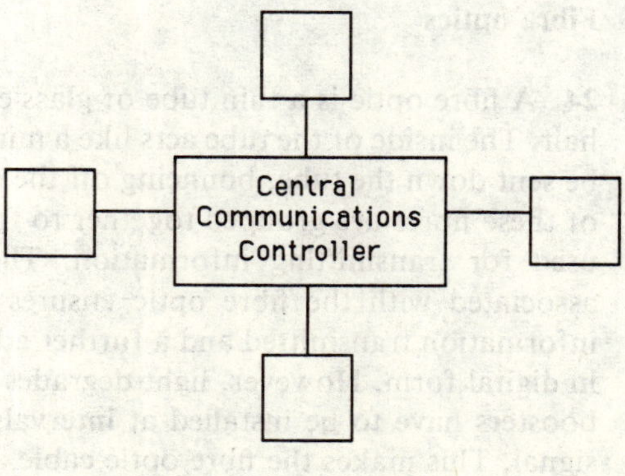

2.24 Star topology

puters on the network then communicate with each other via the central computer. The advantage of this topology is that it uses the minimum number of connection lines and only requires a single intelligent device at the centre to control the communications. The disadvantage is that the entire network depends upon the single computer at the centre.

Bus or tree topology In a bus topology all the component equipment is connected to a single cable. Computers on the bus can then communicate with each other without being routed through a central message-switching device. Data is transmitted along the bus in **packets** or **frames**—typically 8 bits long. Each packet is sent with a receiver identification and all components on the network permanently on the alert for any messages coming to them. The advantage of this topology is that once the cable has been laid, any new equipment can easily be connected to the network by a simple tap into the cable. The disadvantage is that communications between components of the network travelling in opposite directions along the bus can **collide** causing the loss of the transmitted information. Because of this a **collision detection** system has to be present to control the re-transmission of lost packets, thereby making it a more expensive option.

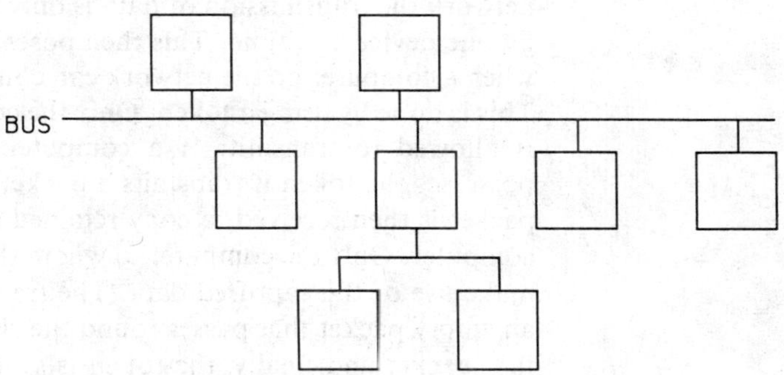

2.25 Bus or tree topology

Ring topology In the ring topology the network cable is connected to all the computers on the network in turn until they are all joined in a loop or a ring. The main feature of this topology is the direct point-to-point connections between the network computers with information travelling just one way around the ring. The advantage is that packet collisions do not occur, they are relatively cheap to install and have proven to be a very efficient and accurate means of communication.

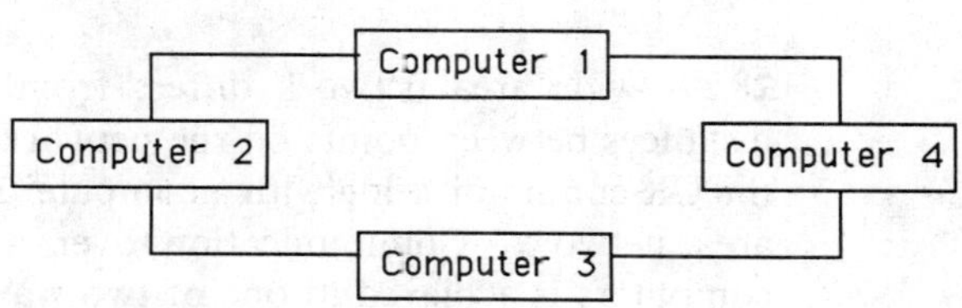

2.25A Ring topology

Communication control

27 In both the bus and the ring topology, communication between components of the topology is not controlled by a central message-switcher as it is in the star topology. Communication, however, must be controlled, or the sensible transfer of information can not reliably occur. Two methods whereby this control is instituted are:

- CSMA/CD or ethernet
- Token ring

CSMA/CD or ethernet Carrier Sense Multiple Access with Collision Detection is used on a bus network to cater for the fact that information can travel in opposing directions along the interconnecting cable and collide. When a collision occurs between two transmitted packets the data they contain is lost. The system is capable of detecting that a collision has occurred and informing the respective transmitters. The transmitters then re-transmit. Ethernet is a commercial implementation of this principle.

Token ring To avoid the problem of data packet collisions in a ring network the transmission of data is only permitted in one direction and by one device at a time. This then poses the problem of how to decide when a computer on the network can communicate and when it cannot. This is done by using a **token**. Only the computer that possess the token is allowed to transmit. If a computer wishes to transmit and also possesses the token it transmits a packet of data around the ring. This packet is then received, a copy retained and passed on in turn by each computer. Only the computer to whom the packet is addressed will then make use of the captured data. The transmitting computer then sends an empty packet that passes round the ring and clears the copies of the first packet and finally, the token is sent to the next computer on the ring and the process starts again.

> In *The Lord Of The Flies* a group of young schoolboys found themselves stranded on a desert island. One of the first problems they had to solve was how to organise group discussions so that no two boys were talking simultaneously. Find out how this was done. Can you think of other methods of controlling group discussion? In what way are these methods similar to those used in ring and bus LANs?

Wide area networks

28 A wide area network differs from a local area network by the distances between points on the network. For example, a computer in the UK communicating with a computer in the USA would form a wide area network. Communication over a WAN between two distant computers is achieved in one of two ways;

Circuit switching

A circuit switching network establishes a physical channel of communication between the sender and the receiver. This channel is then used exclusively by the two computers for the entire duration of the transmission.

Packet switching

A packet switching network does not set up a physical communication channel. Instead the sender transmits packets of data to a local packet-switching exchange. The exchange then re-transmits to the receiver. This has the advantage that data can be transmitted between two computers that individually operate at different speeds, the difference in speeds being accommodated at the exchange.

The problem of distance, however, provides its own unique solution in the use of **microwaves**. Instead of information being transmitted along cables it is transmitted through the atmosphere via **relay stations** and **satellites** to anywhere in the world. Microwave transmission is an analogue transmission and is similar to radio and television signals except that it is at very short wave lengths. Because of the short wave length it has to be boosted by relay stations every 30 miles or so. Transmission via a satellite avoids a great deal of atmospheric degrading of the signal allowing world wide communication.

2.26 Satellite dish

Communication between computers and people

29 So far we have been dealing with the lowest level of communication—the process of transmitting and interpreting signals between two machines. While recognising that this is an important part of computing technology we must also appreciate the role of communication between people and computers. This is the realm of the human-computer interface (HCI) which involves a knowledge of all aspects of human communication from the user-friendly design of presentation screens to the psychology of human-machine interaction. Part of creating a good HCI is to ensure that when a piece of software is being used, all the innermost workings of the system are transparent to the user, i.e. the user must not be aware of them. All screens presented to the user must be clear and easily read and understood. Whenever a piece of software is designed and developed the needs of the user must always be borne in mind.

> You want to display your name, address, telephone number, school form and subjects being taken on a monitor screen. Draw two layouts of how the screen will look, one to show an example of bad HCI and one to show an example of good HCI.

The communications industry

30 During the Industrial Revolution the most important commodities were raw materials. Coal, iron ore and bauxite were all essential commodities to keep the wheels of industry rolling. Today, in the Information Age the most important commodity is information and an entire industry has been created that deals solely with the creation, manipulation and transmission of information. The following are some of the components of this industry.

Common and value-added carriers

31 A carrier company is a company that provides communication services. A common carrier is licensed and regulated by the government to provide channels of communication, examples including British Telecom and Mercury. A value-added carrier leases communication channels from a common carrier and provides additional services. Prestel and Ceefax are examples of value-added carriers.

Teleconferencing

32 It is possible for a number of people, each at a different location, to be connected together so that each can see and talk to the others. This is known as teleconferencing and is becoming increasingly used for conference communication between different countries.

Telecommuting

33 This is when companies, to reduce their office costs, locate their employees in their own homes, allowing them to communicate to the company's central computer.

2.27 Oracle page display; courtesy Oracle teletext

Electronic fund transfer

34 The cash dispenser outside your bank or building society is the user terminal that allows you to access your account. At this terminal you can view the state of your accounts, transfer money from one account to another and withdraw cash. All this is accomplished through a communications system of electronic funds transfer. An advance of this system is one in which you are able to transfer cash directly from your account to a shop's account using your card for identification.

Electronic mail

35 Computers linked together can provide personal mail and message services whereby one person on the network can communicate with any other person on the same network. The electronic mail service Janet is a service that permits world wide instant mail communication and FAX or facsimile reproduction is another example. With a FAX system a document can be transmitted in its entirety to any other FAX machine anywhere in the world. A FAX machine looks like a photocopier that reads the document and transmits it via a telephone line to another FAX machine which then reproduces the image. FAX systems are fast becoming an essential business tool, and the cost of transmitting a large document to another country is substantially less than posting it airmail. In addition its great advantage is that transmission is almost instantaneous.

Information and data bank services

36 One of the advantages of computer communications is that databases can be shared, thereby avoiding the costly process of creating them for every user. Because of this companies exist purely to manage

2.28 Facsimile machine

huge data bank services and to provide information to their customers. Credit bureaux are a typical example of this facility, for example, to find out whether a credit card applicant is credit worthy or not.

Distributed data processing

37 Telecommuting consists of individuals accessing a central source of information held on a company's host computer—often using a dumb terminal. This has the disadvantage that the host computer has to perform tasks that could be done better by the telecommuters themselves. To prevent overloading the host computer and consequently slowing down the service, data can be distributed amongst the telecommuters, each of whom are equipped with their own computer, and may have information that deals specifically with their own location, such as a record of their customer's last purchases. Processing such information at the telecommuter's location saves valuable host computer time, speeds host computer response and allows applications to be tailored to local needs.

Summary

The CPU is activated by electric currents in the form of rectangular pulses, each pulse being of the same strength and lasting for a whole number multiple of a fixed unit of time. The components of the CPU and the primary storage communicate with each other down three data buses; the control, the address and the data buses. To describe these signals a binary sequence of 0s and 1s is used.

When the CPU attempts to communicate with a peripheral device it can only do so through a specially manufactured interface. The interface is a piece of hardware between the CPU and the peripheral device. It may be built into the body of the computer or located on an interface card fitted into an expansion slot. The CPU can only send and receive digital signals whereas peripheral devices may be digital or analogue. Digital transmission to a peripheral device may be serial or parallel and the interface may act as a buffer or as a secondary storage device. Analogue devices need the signals from the CPU to be modulated. Analogue signals sent to the CPU need to be de-modulated. Such a two-way interface is called a modem. Communication can be one-way only—simplex mode, two-way but only one way at a time—half duplex mode or two-way simultaneously—full-duplex mode. Communication between computers can be accomplished along wire cables, fibre optics or microwave. They communicate according to a set protocol that they establish by handshaking. A local area network consists of many users or many computers linked together in a variety of possible configurations. Communication between people and computers needs good human-computer interface. This means that the system must be user-friendly with the inner workings of the computer being transparent to the user. The communications industry ranges from carriers through electronic data transfer to distributed data processing.

Key points to note

Communication, communication between components of the CPU, the control bus, the address bus, the data bus, communication between the CPU and peripheral devices, interfaces, digital transmission, serial interface, parallel interface, other interface facilities, a buffer, a secondary storage device, analogue transmission, modems, acoustic couplers, direct-connect modem, data transmission, simplex mode, half-duplex mode, full-duplex mode, communication between computers, local area networks, wire cables, fibre optics, communication control, wide area networks, communication between people, the communications industry, common and value-added carriers, teleconferencing, telecommuting, electronic fund transfer, electronic mail, information and data bank services, distributed data processing.

Self assessment questions

1 List the four levels of computer communication. (1)
2 How is the CPU activated? (2)
3 What form do the electric currents take in the CPU? (2)
4 How do we describe the pulses of electricity that are transmitted through the CPU? (2)
5 Why do we code the sequences of pulses of electricity passing through the CPU as a binary sequence? (2)
6 How are the components of the CPU physically connected? (3)
7 What are the control, address and data buses? (3)
8 What is meant by digital transmission? (3)
9 What is required between the CPU and a peripheral device before they are able to communicate to each other? (4)
10 What is an interface card? (4,5)
11 List two types of interface for digital transmission. (6)
12 What does a serial interface do? (7)
13 What is an RS 232C socket? (7)
14 What does a parallel interface do? (8)

15 Name two types of parallel interface. (8)
16 List two functions of an interface card. (9)
17 What is a buffer? (10)
18 How can an interface card act as a source of secondary storage? (11)
19 What is an analogue signal? (13)
20 What does a de-modulator do? (13)
21 What does a modulator do? (14)
22 What is a modem and why is it so called? (15)
23 List two different types of modem. (15)
24 How does an acoustic coupler work? (16)
25 How does a direct-connect modem differ from an acoustic coupler? (17)
26 What is a communications protocol? (18)
27 What is meant by handshaking? (18)
28 What is the difference between synchronous and asynchronous transmission? (18)
29 Distinguish between simplex, half-duplex and full-duplex modes. (19)
30 Name two types of computer network. (21)
31 Name two methods of cabling two computers together. (22–24)
32 What problems does a wire cable suffer from when transmitting information? (23)
33 What is a fibre optic? (24)
34 How does a fibre optic cable overcome the problems associated with transmitting data via a wire cable? (24)
35 Describe three LAN topologies. (25)
36 How are communications controlled in a ring LAN and a bus LAN. (27)
37 What is a wide area network? (28)
38 Name a third means of transmitting information from one computer to another. (28)
39 What is meant by HCI? (29)
40 What does user-friendly mean? (29)
41 What does it mean when we say that 'the innermost workings of a system with good HCI are transparent to the user'? (29)
42 List seven participants in the communications industry. (30–37)
43 How does a common carrier differ from a value-added carrier? (31)
44 What are teleconferencing and telecommuting? (32,33)
45 What is EFT? (34)
46 What is electronic mail and how does it differ from FAX? (35)
47 What do information and data bank services provide? (36)
48 What is distributed data processing? (37)

Exercises

1 A travel agent uses an on-line booking system to book seats on aircraft flights. The telephone system is used to communicate between the travel agency and the airline's computer.

(a) Name one advantage of travel agencies being connected on-line to the airline's computer in this way.

(b) Which of the following secondary storage devices do you consider to be most appropriate for the airline's computer? Give one reason for your choice.

a magnetic tape unit	a cassette tape machine
a floppy disk drive	a fixed disk store

(c) Whilst booking a seat for a customer there is a power failure at the travel agency which lasts for an hour. Give one possible effect of this delay in communication.

2 State whether each of the following devices gives an analogue or digital output.

joystick fire button
sundial
radio loudspeaker

3 A computer centre holding personal data can be accessed from a remote terminal. The centre decides to use a cable buried in the ground between the centre and the remote terminal.
Name two advantages to the computer centre of using such a cable rather than the normal telephone system.

4 Several computers in a factory share information through interconnecting wires. The way the computers are connected is an example of

computer networking
information retrieval
on-line processing
time-sharing

5 Some schools and colleges have networks of computers.

(a) Name two advantages of a network of computers.
(b) Name one disadvantage of using a computer network.

6 A remote terminal is connected to a central mainframe computer via the telephone lines.

(a) What device is needed at each end of the telephone line?
(b) What task does this device perform?

7 Which of the following best describes the task of a modem?

allows several programs to run at the same time
converts digital signals to analogue (and back again)
converts positions on a grid to co-ordinates
decodes teletext signals

8 The water tank in the following diagram uses a computer to help keep a head of water between two sensors placed at points A and B.

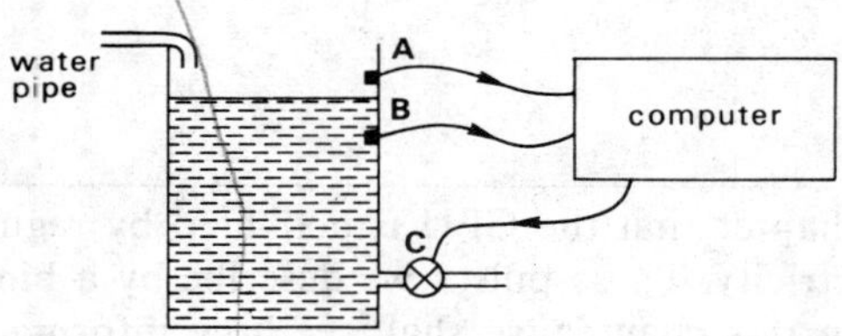

Describe how the system works, showing clearly where feedback is being used.

9 The users of a school computer network share a high capacity disk drive and a single printer.

(a) Two users of the network want to print out long documents at the same time. Name two ways in which the network software could handle simultaneous requests for the printer.
(b) Before the school had a computer network it used stand alone computers each storing its data in its own single disk drive. Give one advantage and one disadvantage to the school of having the computers connected as a network.

10 A greenhouse has a window which can be opened or closed under computer control. It also has a heater which can be switched on or off by the computer.
An electronic thermometer is connected to the computer to measure the temperature inside the greenhouse.
As it is a very hot day, the window is open and the heater is off. At night there is a dramatic fall in temperature.

(a) How will the computer know about changes in temperature?
(b) List the two steps that the computer will take as the temperature falls.

11 (a) What is communications software?
(b) When would communications software be used?
(c) Explain the difference between Ceefax/Oracle and Prestel.
(d) Why is a modem often needed to transmit data between computers over a telephone link?
(e) Describe an application which is likely to use communications software.

3 Low level languages

Objectives

1 To explain the need for encoding information into concise, standardised and unambiguous form for computer processing.

2 To represent integers, characters and instructions in computer format.

3 To describe the characteristics of the two low-level programming languages.

Introduction

1 We saw in the last chapter that the CPU is activated by regular, rectangular pulses of electricity. These pulses we describe by a binary sequence of 0s and 1s. In this chapter we shall see how information can also be coded as a binary sequence and how, by appropriate circuitry, this information is translated into electrical pulses and sent to the CPU.

Case Study

2 Joey's father owned a coffee bar. He had recently installed a new machine for serving soft drinks and was, this week, serving limeade, lemonade and carbonated water. Each drink was served through a tap, and Joey was put in charge of operating the machine.

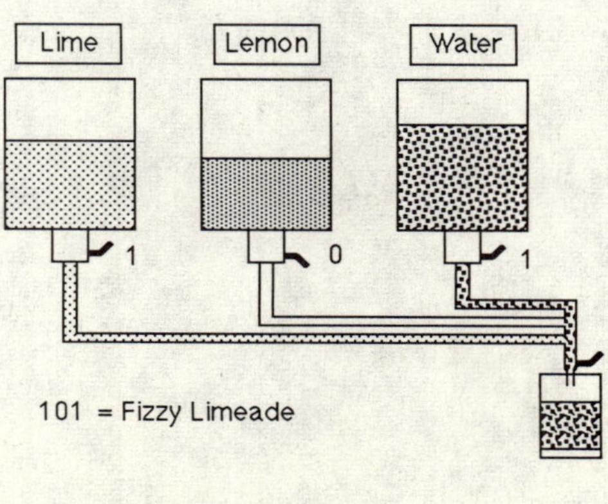

To speed up his service, Joey devised a code. If a tap was up to let liquid flow out it was given the number 1. If a tap was down then it was given the number 0. Combinations of three numbers then formed his code. For example, 001 stood for fizzy water, 010 stood for lemonade and 100 stood for limeade. Combinations such as 101 stood for limeade and fizzy water mixed. Joey realised that these code numbers could be thought of as binary numbers, each having a decimal value.

$$\text{Binary } 001 = 0 \times 2^2 + 0 \times 2^1 + 1 \times 2^0 = 1 \text{ Decimal}$$

$$\text{Binary } 010 = 0 \times 2^2 + 1 \times 2^1 + 0 \times 2^0 = 2 \text{ Decimal}$$

$$\text{Binary } 100 = 1 \times 2^2 + 0 \times 2^1 + 0 \times 2^0 = 4 \text{ Decimal}$$

$$\text{Binary } 101 = 1 \times 2^2 + 0 \times 2^1 + 1 \times 1^0 = 5 \text{ Decimal}$$

What is the decimal value of each of the following binary numbers?

1) 110
2) 101101
3) 11.11

What is the binary form of each of the following decimal numbers?

1) 21
2) 126
3) 1.25

One day Joey was so busy that when he was asked for a 101 he accidentally served a 111. His customer took a sip and his eyes lit up. 'Hey Joey, this is great', he said 'what do you call it?' Joey looked at the customer, looked at the machine, saw the tap settings at 111 and quickly replied, 'Seven-up!'

3 The point of this mini case study is that:

Taps are examples of **two-state** devices. They can be on or off.
The states of a two-state device such as a tap can be represented by the two numbers 0 and 1 respectively.
Using the numbers 0 and 1 the state of a collection of two-state devices is represented by a sequence of 0s and 1s—a binary number.
The state of a tap can be changed, if it is on it can be turned off and if it is off it can be turned on. At any given time when the states are set the machine can be said to have a memory—it remembers the current settings.

Because the soft drinks machine can be said to remember the settings of the taps we say that the machine is storing information.

Storing information

4 Any machine that has more than one state can be said to store information. A vacuum cleaner is either on or off. In either state it can be said to be storing the information that it is on or off. A weaver's loom stores information of a more complicated nature. When a weaver sets his loom to weave a fabric with a particular design, the loom remembers the settings and the fact that the loom has not forgotten the settings is shown by the patterned fabric that it weaves as the weaver works. Computers also have memories which are very similar to that of the soft drinks machine.

> Make a list of as many two-state devices as you can. Would it be appropriate to describe the two states by 0 and 1 for each of the devices?
> Make a list of four different ways of storing information.

Computer memory

5 A computer's primary storage, its memory, consists of a collection of two-state devices. These devices are electronic cells that can be either **charged** or **uncharged**. We represent the state of an uncharged cell by the number 0; of a charged cell by the number 1. As a result the combined state of a number of such cells is represented by a binary number. For example, if we had three cells that were respectively charged, uncharged, charged then this combination would be described by the binary number 101. Using computer jargon we would say that these three cells together contained the binary number 101 which equals the decimal number 5.

Although the cells cannot contain anything except charge, by saying they contain a number allows us to build up a useful mental picture of the computer's memory. The diagram that follows displays our three electronic cells as boxes. If a box is empty (cell uncharged) it is said to contain the number 0 and if it is full (cell charged) it is said to contain the number 1.

> We have already discussed how the CPU is activated by electric pulses which can be described as a series of 0s and 1s. You can now see how information moves. When information is sent from an input device it is translated into electric pulses. These pulses are sent to the CPU and charge or discharge the appropriate memory cells. The computer system works by electricity but we describe what is happening electrically by using binary numbers.
> For example, we may want to send the number 7 to the CPU from the keyboard. Assume that our keyboard translates 7 as 111 in binary. Using diagrams, show how the number 7 is sent by us to the CPU.

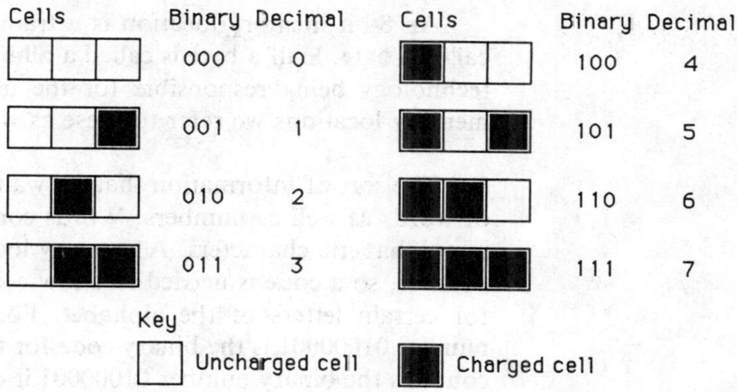

What are the binary and decimal values of the contents of each of the following groups of 4 cells?

1. 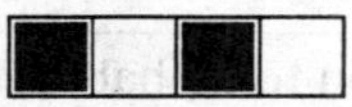

2. 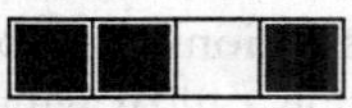

Draw groups of 4 cells that contain the following numbers:

1) 0110
2) 14

Bits

6 Because we consider each electronic cell to contain either of the **binary digits** 0 or 1, we refer to the information that each cell stores as a bit. The bit is the fundamental unit of information stored in a computer's memory. In all modern computers the electronic cells are arranged in groups of 8, 16 or 32. These groupings of cells are called **memory locations** and depending on the computer may be either 8-bit, 16-bit or 32-bit memory locations. Because the bit is too small a unit of information to handle we talk about the **contents** of memory locations.

Bytes and words

7 An 8-bit memory location can contain any one of **256** different binary numbers ranging from

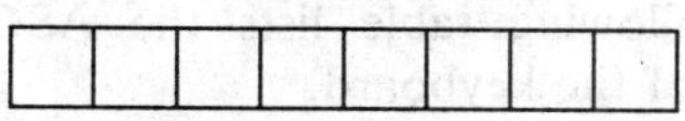 00000000 binary = 0 decimal up to

 11111111 binary = 255 decimal.

What is (a) 127 decimal as an 8-bit binary number?
(b) 11001101 binary as a decimal number?
Represent both of these numbers as charged and uncharged states of 8-bit registers.

An 8-bit memory location is a traditional unit of memory and is called a **byte**. Half a byte is called a **nibble**. With developments in chip technology being responsible for the introduction of 16 and 32 bit memory locations we refer to these as **words**.

8 The sort of information that we want a computer to store consists of words as well as numbers. Words consist of letters of the alphabet i.e. alphabetic characters. A memory location can only store a binary number, so a code is needed to allow certain binary numbers to stand for certain letters of the alphabet. For example we say the binary number 01000001 is the binary code for the capital letter A so if a byte contains the binary number 01000001 it can also be said to contain the letter A.

Coding

9 In addition to alphabetic characters, grammar symbols such as the full stop (.) and the comma (,) need to be stored in the computer. The following illustration is a typical computer keyboard with a variety of different symbols, all of which will have to be coded.

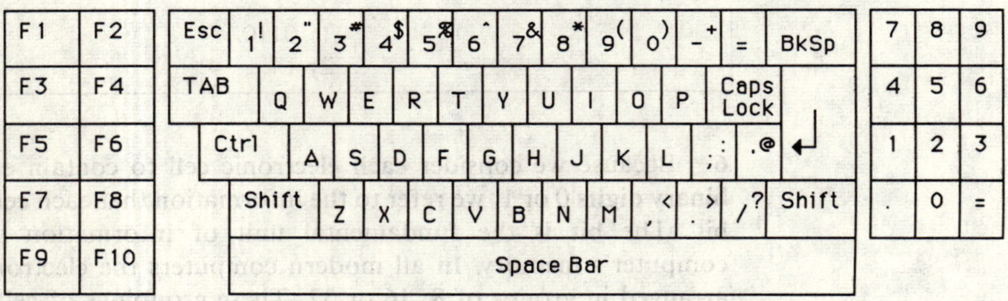

In order to obtain some form of agreement between different computer manufacturers, a standard code has been devised. This is called **The American Standard Code For Information Interchange** or **ASCII** (pronounced askey) for short.

ASCII codes

10 The following table lists the ASCII Codes for some of the characters of the keyboard.

Partial set of ASCII codes

Character	Binary Code	Decimal	Character	Binary Code	Decimal
A	01000001	65	0	00110000	48
B	01000010	66	1	00110001	49
C	01000011	67	2	00110010	50
D	01000100	68	3	00110011	51
E	01000101	69	4	00110100	52

F	01000110	70	5	00110101	53
G	01000111	71	6	00110110	54
H	01001000	72	7	00110111	55
I	01001001	73	8	00111000	56
J	01001010	74	9	00111001	57
*	00101010	42	!	00101001	33
(	00101000	40	%	00100101	37
)	00101001	41	&	00100110	38
+	00101011	43	<	00111100	60
=	00111101	61	?	00111111	63

Note that the codes are given in both binary and decimal form. It is obviously easier to think of the capital letter A being coded as 65 decimal rather than remembering 01000001 binary.

The ASCII code was devised at a time when the maximum memory location size was 8-bits. Since then technology has developed 16- and 32-bit memory locations, and as a result these larger memory locations can contain more than one 8-bit binary number, enabling computers to store much more information i.e. their memories have been increased.

Memory size

11 It would be natural to measure the size of a computer's memory by the number of memory locations that it contains. However, this would give an unreliable measure because of the different sizes of different memory locations. Instead, the size of a computer's memory is measured by the number of characters that it can store. A character occupies 8 bits—a **byte**. Consequently computer memory size is measured in bytes—or more accurately in **kilobytes**.

$$1 \text{ Kilobyte (Kb)} = 2^{10} \quad \text{bytes} = 1024 \text{ bytes.}$$

Most Personal Computers have a standard memory of 256 Kb, although 512 Kb or even 640 Kb is quite common. Larger machines have memories measured in megabytes or even gigabytes where

$$1 \text{ Megabyte (Mb)} = 2^{20} \text{ bytes} = 1\ 048\ 576 \text{ bytes}$$

and

$$1 \text{ Gigabyte (Gb)} = 2^{30} \text{ bytes} = 1\ 073\ 740 \times 10^9 \text{ bytes}$$

If a monitor screen can display 25 rows of 80 characters per row, how many screens-full does each of the following represent?

(a) 1 Kb
(b) 1 Mb
(c) 1 Gb

Byte addresses

12 Computers contain a large amount of bytes, each of which can contain information. To control this information we need to know where each particular byte is located, and for this purpose **byte addresses** are used, or in the case of 16- and 32-bit machines, **word addresses**. A byte address describes the actual location of a byte on the chips.

Numbers

The important point to notice about the ASCII codes is that they represent symbols i.e. the characters of the keyboard. This means that the ASCII code for 1 does not represent the actual number 1 but the symbol 1.

If a byte contains the binary number 01000001 then the computer is faced with two alternatives. It can interpret this number as the capital letter A or it can interpret this number as the number 65. The computer interprets the contents of its bytes according to the instructions it is given which we shall look at later in this chapter. For what follows we shall assume that the computer has been instructed to interpret the byte contents as actual numbers.

When we see the binary number 0101 we can easily translate this into its decimal form because the numeral 0101 is shorthand for

$$\begin{aligned} & 0\times 2^3 + 1\times 2^2 + 0\times 2^1 + 1\times 2^0 \\ & = 0\times 8 + 1\times 4 + 0\times 2 + 1\times 1^0 \ (2 = 1) \\ & = 4 + 1 \\ & = 5 \text{ decimal} \end{aligned}$$

Even fractional numbers follow the same pattern. For example, the binary numeral 11.101 stands for

$$\begin{aligned} & 1\times 2^1 + 1\times 2^0 + 1\times 2^{-1} + 0\times 2^{-2} + 1\times 2^{-3} \\ & = 1\times 2 + 1\times 1 + 1\times (1/2) + 0\times (1/4) + 1\times (1/8) \\ & = 2 + 1 + 0.5 + 0 + 0.125 \\ & = 3.625 \text{ decimal} \end{aligned}$$

Notice the **point** in 11.101—in a binary number we call it a binary point.

> To practice this, convert the following decimal numbers into binary form:
>
> (a) 2125 (b) 212.5 (c) 21.25 (d) 2.125
>
> Now convert the following binary numbers into decimal form:
>
> (a) 1101 (b) 110.1 (c) 11.01 (d) 1.101

Distinguishing whole numbers from fractional numbers

13 We can easily distinguish the whole binary number **11101 binary = 29 decimal** from the fractional binary number **111.01 binary = 7.25 decimal** by the binary point—that is the purpose of the point.

How does the computer distinguish between a whole number and a fractional number? Although it does not use a binary point it recognises that it distinguishes the numerals that are to the left of the point from those that are to the right. The binary point is not stored by the computer but its notional position is dictated by the software that controls the arithmetic processes. This can be done in two ways.

Fixed point arithmetic

14 In fixed point arithmetic fractions are stored in the same way as integers with the binary point in a fixed position. The problem with fixed point codes is that the range of numbers that can be represented is greatly restricted so to overcome the limited range imposed by this, floating point arithmetic was devised.

Floating point arithmetic

15 In floating point arithmetic the binary point is floated to the left most end of the binary number. This means, for example, that we must change the number **111.01** to $\mathbf{.11101 \times 2^3}$.

This is called the **normalised floating point format** of the number 111.01. Notice the curious mixture of binary and decimal numerals. In a consistent binary format we should write $\mathbf{.11101 \times (10)^{11}}$.

The number .11101 is referred to as the **mantissa** and the power 3 is called the **exponent** which in binary form is 11.

> Write the following binary numbers in floating point notation.
>
> (a) 1011.101
> (b) 0.01
>
> What is the decimal value of each of these numbers?

By using the normalised floating point notation we have effectively split our single number 111.01 into two sets of numerals—11101 and 11.

These two sets of numerals are stored in different bytes to enable the computer to recognise the first as the mantissa and the second as the exponent. By this means the computer recognises the combination of the two numbers as $.11101 \times 2^3 = 111.01$ (exponent 11 written as power 3 here).

If a particular computer uses one 8-bit byte to store the mantissa and one byte to store the exponent, what numbers do each of the following represent? (The first byte is the mantissa)

(a) 01010101 00000111 (b) 01101101 00011101
(c) 01111101 10101010 (d) 00110011 01011101

What is the largest number that can be represented?

Negative numbers

16 When we use a pencil and paper we distinguish a negative number from a positive number by using the minus sign. For example 101 binary = 5 decimal and − 101 binary = − 5 decimal.

A computer uses the feature of a negative number that, when added to its positive counterpart, produces **zero**. 5 + (− 5) = 0.

If we have the binary number 00110101 binary = 53 decimal we need to find the binary number that when added to it gives zero 00000000. We can almost do this. Consider the binary number 11001011 and add it to 00110101, i.e.

```
  00110101
+ 11001011
 ---------
 100000000
```

The result is a 9-bit number 100000000, which when stripped off the leading 1 leaves 00000000 – zero.

Though it might seem artificial to strip off the leading 1, if the computer has 8-bit bytes it is easy to lose the leading 9th because there is nowhere for it to go. For this reason we agree to represent 11001011 binary as − 00110101 binary.

To make sure that you understand this procedure, add the binary numbers 01011101 and 10100011. What does 10100011 represent?

Next we need to know how the computer recognises the fact that the number stored as 11001011 binary = − 00110101 binary = − 53 decimal and not 303 decimal.

The reason is that the leading bit—the bit at the left—is a 1. All numbers stored with a leading bit as 1 are interpreted as negative and all those with leading bit 0 are interpreted as positive.

The final problem to solve is how, given 00110101, we arrive at the number 11001011. This can be done by an ingenious method known as **two's complement**.

Two's complement

17 Take the number 00110101 and exchange all the zeros for ones and all the ones for zeros to give 11001010. Now **add** 1 to give 11001011. This is the two's complement method of obtaining a negative number from a positive number.

> Find the two's complement of each of the following binary numbers.
>
> (a) 00110011
> (b) 10110100
>
> What is the binary form of 23 and − 23. Do they add to zero?
> Using binary numbers and two's complement form, subtract 25 from 34.

> A particular computer stores numbers in single 8-bit bytes.
> How would it represent;
> (a) 25 (b) −25 (c) 145 (d) − 145 (e) − 93 (f) − 1
> What is the largest positive number and largest negative number that can be represented using an 8-bit byte?

Range of numbers

18 If a computer used only a single 8-bit memory location to store its numbers it would have a very restricted arithmetic. The largest positive 8-bit binary number is 01111111 binary = 127 decimal. The negative of this number (its two's complement) is 10000001 binary = − 127 decimal though this is not the smallest integer that can be represented. The smallest is 100000000 binary = − 128 decimal. The reason for this is that the binary number 00000000 is its own two's complement.

Using a single byte to represent numbers would greatly restrict numerical calculations. To overcome this problem the computer uses a number of bytes to store numbers. For example, both the Apple and the IBM PCXT uses two bytes so that the range of integers that can be represented range from 01111111 11111111 binary = 32767 decimal to 10000000 00000000 binary = − 32768 decimal.

This is still quite restrictive. The BBC has a range from 2,147,483,647 to − 2,147,483,648 because it uses four bytes per number.

Arithmetic inaccuracies

19 Because of the way numbers are stored in a computer, numerical inaccuracies can occur during arithmetic operations. Although integer arithmetic is completely accurate, numbers are restricted by their range; for example, a computer that can only store fixed point numbers in the range 32767 to – 32768 will signal **overflow** if a number is used that is outside this range. The range can be increased by employing floating point arithmetic but even here numbers are restricted by their representation; for example, if a computer can only deal with numbers that have nine or less significant digits, then even in floating point notation they will have to be rounded to the ninth significant figure. Herein lies the source of inaccuracy and there is no way of solving the problem. The best that can be done is to use more bytes per stored number and thereby reduce—but not eliminate—the level of inaccuracy.

> A particular computer can represent numbers to only nine significant figures. What values would it give to each of the following decimal numbers?
>
> (a) 0.1234567654 (b) 0.0080000076 (c) 0.00000000022354768765
> (d) 376.129348725 (e) 1000.0000090 (f) 638562913.7

Dynamic memory

20 We have seen that the contents of the bytes in the computer's memory can be understood by the computer to represent keyboard characters or numbers. The fact that the contents of the bytes in the computer's memory can be changed makes the computer's memory **dynamic**. The next question to ask is WHY does the computer change the contents of bytes? The answer is because it is INSTRUCTED TO.

The accumulator register

21 We learned in Chapter 1 of this section that the CPU contains a section called the arithmetic logic unit, the ALU. Within this are a number of groups of **special bytes** called **registers**, one of which is called the **accumulator register**. The accumulator plays a central role in computer arithmetic: adding two numbers together must be done within the accumulator. For example. To add 25 to 14 where byte number 8 contains the number 25 and byte number 9 contains the number 14.

add the number 25 from byte 8 to the accumulator
add the number 14 from byte 9 to the accumulator

The accumulator now contains the number 39.

Copy the number 39 from the accumulator into byte 10.

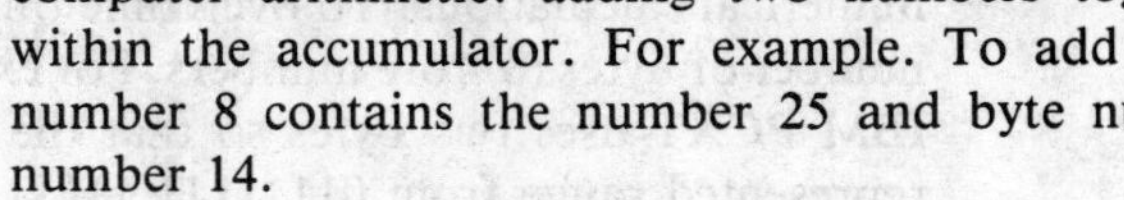

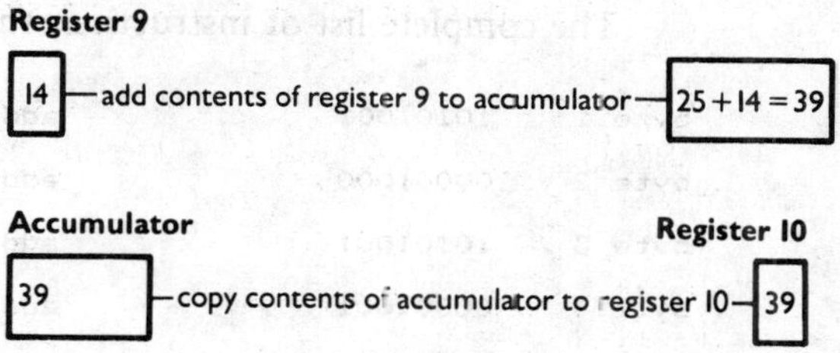

Describe how the accumulator is used to add 123 to 247.

Binary coded instructions

22 Instructions are stored in the computer's memory as binary numbers. These numbers form part of the set of ASCII Codes. For example, the instruction to load the accumulator has the ASCII Code 177 decimal which is 10101001 in binary. There are a number of instructions dealing with the handling of the contents of bytes called the **Binary Coded Instruction Set**.

Having described the processes involved in adding 25 to 14 we shall place the necessary instructions in bytes 1 to 7.

The first instruction is to add the contents of byte 8 to the accumulator. This instruction has the binary code 10101001 and byte 8 is referred to as 00001000. The instruction will then take up bytes 1 and 2 as follows:

byte 1	10101001	add to accumulator contents of –
byte 2	00001000	address of byte 8

Bytes 3 and 4 then contain the instruction to add the contents of byte 9 to the accumulator

byte 3	10101001	add to accumulator contents of –
byte 4	00001001	address of byte 9

The next instruction in bytes 5 and 6 tell the computer to move the contents of the accumulator to byte 10. The instruction to move the contents of the accumulator is 10001101, so bytes 5 and 6 contain the instructions

byte 5	10001101	transfer contents of accumulator to –
byte 6	00001010	address of byte 10

Finally the computer is instructed that the instructions have come to an end. The binary code for this instruction is 11101010 and this is placed in byte 7.

byte 7	11101010	end of instructions

The complete list of instructions then appears as

byte 1	10101001	add to accumulator contents of
byte 2	00001000	address of byte 8
byte 3	10101001	add to accumulator contents of
byte 4	00001001	address of byte 9
byte 5	10001101	transfer contents of accumulator to
byte 6	00001010	address of byte 10
byte 7	11101010	end of instructions
byte 8	00011001	25
byte 9	00001110	14

This list of instructions is called a **program** and is our method of communicating to the computer. For this reason we say that the program is written in a **language**. The language that consists of these binary coded instructions is called **machine code**.

> Assuming that bytes 12 to 15 contain the following numbers 123, 51, 74, 209, write a machine code program (a set of binary coded instructions) that will add these three numbers together and place the result in byte 16.

Instructing the computer using machine code can be a long task and with so many different instructions it can be difficult to remember all the codes in their binary format. To instruct the computer using the binary coded instructions you would need to constantly refer to a manual to obtain the codes. For this reason, a **mnemonic** code has been devised called **assembly code**.

Assembly code mnemonics

23 A mnemonic is an aid to the memory. It often takes the form of a sentence that when remembered helps you to remember something else. For example, the sentence—'stalaCtites hang from the Ceiling and stalaGmites sit on the Ground' is a useful way of remembering which are which. The mnemonic code for using binary coded instructions is made up of acronyms which are words formed from letters contained in other words. For example, the acronym for LoaD Accumulator is LDA. Because the acronym LDA helps the memory remember what the instruction is, it is called a mnemonic. For each binary coded instruction there is a mnemonic and the complete list of mnemonics is called assembly code. The previous list of instructions would read in assembly code as

byte 1	LDA	LoaD Accumulator with contents of
byte 2	00001000	address of byte 8
byte 3	LDA	LoaD Accumulator with contents of
byte 4	00001001	address of byte 9
byte 5	STO	STOre contents of accumulator in
byte 6	00001010	address of byte 10
byte 7	NOP	No OPeration (Stop Here)
byte 8	00011001	25
byte 9	00001110	14

Assuming that bytes 12 to 15 contain the following numbers 123, 51, 74, 209, write a set of instructions in assembly code mnemonics that will add all these numbers together and place the result in byte 16.

Low-level programming languages

24 The two languages that we have seen so far are;

- the binary machine code language
- the mnemonic assembly code language

Both of these languages deal with the contents and addresses of specific bytes and as such are interacting with the computer's memory at its closest or lowest level. For this reason these languages are called **low-level languages**. In the following chapter we shall be looking at other languages that do not require the programmer to interact at the low level of memory. These languages are called **high-level languages**.

Summary

25 A computer memory consists of electronic cells that can be in either a charged or an uncharged state. These states are described by the binary digits 0 and 1 which are called bits. The electronic cells are arranged to form groups of 8, 16 or 32 depending on the make of computer. These groupings are referred to as 8-bit bytes and 16- or 32-bit words. Using the bits 0 and 1 to represent the states of each electronic cell allows us to describe the contents of bytes as binary numbers. Because there is a need for the computer to store information in the form of keyboard characters, the ASCII code has been devised to relate specific binary numbers to specific keyboard characters. The contents of bytes can be interpreted either as coded keyboard characters or as numbers. A positive number is interpreted as the direct decimal value of a byte's binary contents. Negative numbers are represented in two's complement form which permits the computer to identify negative numbers. Fractional numbers can be represented using the floating point format of mantissa and exponent or fixed point format.

Because every computer contains thousands of bytes and because any particular byte must be identified, each byte is given an address. This address locates each component BIT of the byte on the memory chips. Using the byte addresses and the byte content it is possible to make the computer execute instructions. This gives a third possible interpretation of a byte's contents—as an instruction. Issuing such instructions to the computer is known as programming. In binary form these instructions are awkward to use so a mnemonic code has been devised to make programming easier. This mnemonic code is referred to as assembly language. Both the binary coded and mnemonic coded instruction sets are referred to as low-level languages. The 'low-level' refers to the fact that programming in these languages involves reference to specific bytes. In a high-level language this is not the case.

Key points

Two-state devices, bits 0 and 1, binary numbers, storing information, the computer's memory as electronic cells, bytes, words and their contents, keyboard characters and ASCII codes, byte addresses, integer and fractional numbers, mantissa and exponent form of a binary number with a decimal point, fixed- and floating-point arithmetic, two's complement and negative numbers, dynamic memory and instructions, the binary coded and mnemonic coded instruction sets, machine code, assembly code, low-level and high-level languages.

Self assessment questions

1 What is a two-state device? (2,3)
2 How do we represent the states of a two-state device. (2,3)
3 How do we represent the combined state of a collection of two-state devices. (2,3)
4 What is meant when we say that a machine stores information? (4)
5 What does a computer's memory consist of? (5)
6 What is a BIT and what is a byte? (6,7)
7 How many BITs are there in a byte? (6)
8 How many different binary numbers can a given 8-bit byte store? (7)
9 What sort of information do we want a computer to store? (8)
10 How do we relate the contents of a byte with the keyboard characters? (9)
11 What do the letters ASCII stand for? (9)
12 Why was the ASCII code devised? (9)
13 What is a BYTE and how many are there in a KiloByte, a MegaByte and a GigaByte? (11)
14 What is a byte address? (12)
15 What is a fractional binary number? (13)
16 What is fixed point format? (14)
17 What is floating point format? (15)
18 What is a mantissa and what is an exponent? (15)
19 How does the floating point format enable a computer to distinguish between a whole number and a fractional number? (14,15)
20 What is the significant effect of adding a negative number to its positive counterpart? (16)
21 How can a computer distinguish between a positive number and a negative number? (16)
22 What is meant by two's complement? (17)
23 What affects the range of numbers stored by a computer? (18)

24 What are the causes of arithmetic inaccuracies within a computer's operation? (19)
25 How can the level of arithmetic inaccuracy be reduced when designing a computer? (19)
26 Why is a computer's memory dynamic? (20)
27 What is the accumulator? (21)
28 How does the computer use the accumulator when adding two numbers? (21)
29 What is the binary coded instruction set? (22)
30 What does the word mnemonic mean? (23)
31 What is the mnemonic assembly instruction set? (23)
32 What is a program? (24)
33 What is the major difference between a low-level language and a high-level language? (25)
34 Name two low-level languages. (25)

Exercises

1 Which of the following is a bit?

Eight bytes
Either 0 or 1
The base for hexadecimal notation
The same as a word

2 What is a group of eight bits called?

3 Write the number 6 in binary.

4 A coding scheme for the numbers 0 to 9 and the characters A to Z has the following bit pattern.

	Bit pattern
0	0 0 0 0 0 0 0 0
1	0 0 0 0 0 0 0 1
2	0 0 0 0 0 0 1 0
9	0 0 0 0 1 0 0 1
A	0 1 0 0 0 0 0 1
B	0 1 0 0 0 0 1 0
Z	0 1 0 1 1 0 1 0

(a) Write down the bit pattern for
(i) the number 3
(ii) the character C

(b) Modern computer keyboards allow a wider range of characters than those shown above. Suggest three types of characters that are missing from the above coding scheme.

5 The following is part of a message that is being sent from the terminal to the central mainframe.

Typed letter	Binary pattern sent	Binary pattern received	Letter displayed
I	00001001	00001001	I
space	00000000	00000000	space
A	10000001	10000011	C
M	10001101	10001101	M
space	00000000	00000000	space
J	00001010	00001010	J
O	00001111	00001111	O
H	10001000	10001000	H
N	10001110	10001111	O

Even parity bit ↙ letter code (in 10001110: first bit is the even parity bit, the remaining bits the letter code)

(a) What is a group of 8 bits that represents one of the letters called?

(b) What is even parity?

(c) How does the mainframe computer know that the message is wrong?

6 A computer uses a word length of 8 bits. Machine code instructions are represented by 3 bits for the operation code followed by 5 bits for the address. The instruction JUMP 23 is represented by:

1 0 1 | 1 0 1 1 1
operation code | address

(a) How many different addresses can be directly addressed?

(b) Most programmers would prefer to write the instruction JUMP 23 as JUMP start.
(i) Give one advantage of using a name such as start.
(ii) Name the system software which would convert the instruction JUMP start into machine code.

(c) The computer stores numbers in two's complement form. The number +15 is stored as:

0 0 0 0 1 1 1 1

How would −15 be stored?

7 A computer uses 8 bits to represent integers in two's complement form.

(a) What is the bit pattern for the highest positive number that the computer can hold?

(b) What is the denary value of this number?

8 The graphics symbols of a particular microcomputer are designed on a grid of sixteen squares as shown below.

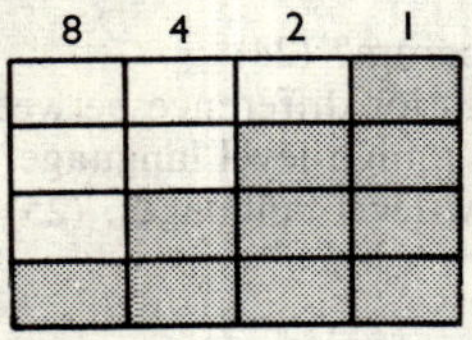

Binary pattern	Decimal Value
0 0 0 1	1
0 0 1 1	3
0 1 1 1	7
1 1 1 1	15

Each row on the grid is represented by the decimal equivalent of a four bit binary pattern. Each symbol is stored in two bytes of computer memory.
The symbol above is created by the command CHAR 1, 3, 7, 15.

(a) Shade squares on the following grid to show the symbol that would be created by the command CHAR 7, 15, 6, 14.

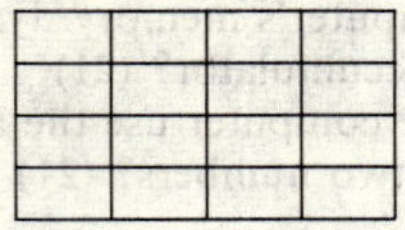

(b) What command would produce the graphics symbol shown below?

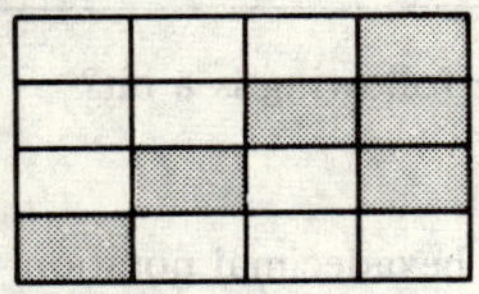

(c) Explain the meaning of each of the terms *bit* and *byte*.

4 High level languages

Objectives

1 To describe the characteristics of various high level languages
2 To introduce the idea of a non-procedural language

First and second generation languages

1 From the early days of computing, programming has been recognised as a difficult process. This difficulty comes from two sources: first the complexity of the computer system that we try to instruct and second the complexity of the applications that we try to devise. The latter is one we have very little control over and although we can develop disciplined methods to attack problems, they will still exist. The complexity of the computer itself however, we can do something about.

As time goes on we try to program even more complex processes with the result that programming becomes even more difficult. Programs can contain many thousands of lines of code, each of which has to be constructed individually and as programs become longer, so the complexity grows. The aim of a programming language is to reduce this complexity to manageable proportions.

You have already learnt that computers were originally programmed in machine code. The central processor unit is instructed by pulses which are coded as a sequence of 0s and 1s. Specific sequences of 0s and 1s form machine code—the lowest level programming language. This is referred to as the first generation language. Programming in machine code is a long and tedious process and greatly prone to error. Apart from having to deal with the cumbersome nature of the code itself, the programmer also had to know exactly how the computer worked. The development of the assembly language, the second generation language, went some way towards simplifying the writing of programs by using simpler code but it still required a detailed knowledge of how the computer hardware operated.

Third generation languages

2 By the 1950s a need was seen to create a language that permitted the programmer to instruct the computer and comprised standard mathematical English which did not require the programmer to possess a

detailed knowledge of the computer's workings. This was achieved in 1957 with the introduction of FORTRAN—the first of the third generation languages. There soon followed a multitude of other third generation languages, each for its own reason.

FORTRAN

3 FORTRAN was designed as the language to be used by users of IBM computers. Its name comes from **FORmula TRANslator** and it was the first **high level language** to be devised. It was designed specifically for scientists and engineers who were required to perform highly complex mathematical calculations.

A sample of FORTRAN code follows.

```
C     PROGRAM TO FIND THE SQUARE OF A SET OF NUMBERS
      X = 0
5     Y = X * X
      PRINT, X, Y
      X = X + 1
      IF (X.LT.10) GO TO 5
      STOP
      END
```

Line 1 This is a **comment** line as indicated by the C. The computer takes no notice of this line as it is there only to identify what the program does for the benefit of anyone else who reads it.

Line 2 The letter **x** is a **variable**. By variable we mean that a number can be **assigned** to that letter. Here we assign the number 0 to the variable X.

Line 3 The variable Y is assigned a value that is equal to the value of X multiplied by itself. i.e. X squared. Note that this line of code is **numbered** with the number 5. This is so that the line can be referred to later in the program.

Line 4 The computer is instructed to PRINT the values of X and Y. This may be at a printer or it may be at a monitor.

Line 5 Here the value of X is increased by 1.

Line 6 In this line of code we have a **condition** statement. The letters LT stand for less than so the code reads

If the value of X is less than 10 **go to** line number 5.

If X is less than 10 the computer will jump back to the line labelled 5 and continue executing the code from there. If X were not less than 10 then the computer would move to the next line of code which is Line 7.

Line 7 The computer is instructed to **STOP** execution of the program.

Line 8 **END** indicates the end of the program.

Write a short FORTRAN program to PRINT the values of a sequence of two numbers, their sum, their difference, their product and their quotient. The first values of the two numbers will be 1 and 2 and they will both increase by 3 until their product is greater than or equal to 400.

4 FORTRAN was a very successful language and is still in use today. As well as using standard English it also uses **subroutines**. A subroutine is a block of code within a program that can be called into use during the execution of the main program.

```
C     PROGRAM CONTAINING SUBROUTINES

        ( Lines of Code )

      CALL SUBR1

      CALL SUBR2

      STOP

      END


      SUBROUTINE SUBR1

        ( Lines of Code )

      RETURN

      END


      SUBROUTINE SUBR2

        ( Lines of Code )

      RETURN

      END
```

The subroutine is invoked using CALL and terminated by END. The RETURN command returns execution to the line following the CALL command.

5 Despite its success amongst scientists and engineers, FORTRAN is less suitable for manipulating very large database files because it lacks non-numeric operations. To overcome this deficiency the Conference On Data Systems Language (CODASYL) in 1959 devised the COBOL language.

COBOL

6 The name COBOL comes from **COmmon Business Oriented Language** and was designed specifically to manipulate large database files and business applications. Whereas FORTRAN uses a brief form of English, COBOL uses descriptive English which makes it easier to understand and easier to follow the program's logic. It is, however, a tedious language to use and programs in COBOL are usually longer than their equivalents in other high level languages. Both FORTRAN and COBOL are well established with great investments having been made in operational systems and despite their deficiencies they are likely to be used for many years to come.

```
IDENTIFICATION DIVISION.
PROGRAM-ID. PRODUCT OF A NUMBER.
REMARKS.  THIS PROGRAM DOES WHAT THE FORTRAN ONE DID.

ENVIRONMENT DIVISION.
CONFIGURATION SECTION.
SOURCE-COMPUTER. ( Here follows the name of computer 1 )
OBJECT-COMPUTER. ( Here follows the name of computer 2 )

DATA DIVISION.
WORKING-STORAGE SECTION.
77  QUANTITY 99 VALUE ZERO.
77  QUANT-SQUARE 999
PROCEDURE DIVISION.
P1    PERFORM PRODUCT.
      PERFORM PRINT.
      PERFORM INCREASE.
      PERFORM REPEAT.

      STOP RUN.

PRODUCT.
 MULTIPLY QUANTITY BY QUANTITY GIVING QUANT-SQUARE.

PRINT.
 DISPLAY QUANTITY, QUANT-SQUARE.

INCREASE.
 ADD 1 TO QUANTITY GIVING QUANTITY.
```

```
REPEAT.

 IF QUANTITY LESS THAN 10 PERFORM P1.
```

7 Note the length of the program compared with that using FORTRAN. However, COBOL was not devised to do what FORTRAN did, but what it could not do.

8 Every COBOL program has four **divisions** which must be stated as shown. The **identification** division identifies the name of the program—the PROGRAM-ID. The **environment** division identifies the computers that are being used—there may only be one, in which case computer1 has the same name as computer 2. The **data** division is where the **variables** are declared. Here we declare that we are going to use two variables QUANTITY and QUANT-SQUARE. The number 77 indicates that they are going to be whole numbers and the number 99 indicates that QUANTITY will have up to two digits. 999 shows that QUANT-SQUARE will have up to three digits. Also the starting value of QUANTITY is set at ZERO.

9 The procedure division contains the body of the program instructions. Like FORTRAN, COBOL uses subroutines which are called into action by using the command PERFORM. Each subroutine is identified by a name or by a P reference, hence the label P1. The letter P is used because in COBOL a subroutine is called a **procedure**. Notice, that COBOL uses the word DISPLAY instead of PRINT.

The following code demonstrates the ease with which COBOL can handle files and strings.

```
INPUT-OUTPUT SECTION.

FILE-CONTROL.

    SELECT RECRDS           ASSIGN TO MAG-TAPE.

    SELECT LABELS           ASSIGN TO PRINTER.


DATA DIVISION.

FILE SECTION.


FD RECRDS

    LABEL RECORDS ARE OMITTED

    DATA RECORD IS RECD.


01 RECD.

    02 PART-NUMBER      PICTURE IS X(6).

    02 PART-NAME        PICTURE IS X(10).
```

```
FD LABELS
     LABEL RECORDS ARE OMITTED
     DATA RECORD IS LABEL.

01 LABEL
     02 LINE-OF-PRINT   PICTURE IS X(10).

WORKING-STORAGE SECTION.
01 END-OF-DATA         PICTURE IS X(3).

PROCEDURE DIVISION.

OPEN INPUT RECRDS
     OUTPUT LABELS.

     MOVE 'NO' TO END-OF DATA.
     PERFORM RECRD-READ.
     PERFORM LABEL-PRINT UNTIL END-OF-DATA IS EQUAL TO 'YES'.

CLOSE RECRDS
      LABELS.

STOP RUN.

RECRD-READ
     READ RECD RECORD AT END MOVE 'YES' TO END-OF-DATA.

LABEL-PRINT
     MOVE PART-NUMBER TO LINE-OF-PRINT.
     WRITE LABEL BEFORE ADVANCING 1 LINE.
     MOVE PART-NAME TO LINE-OF-PRINT.
     WRITE LABEL BEFORE ADVANCING 1 LINE.
     PERFORM RECRD-READ.
```

The purpose of this code is to read a part number and a part name from a file record on a mag-tape and then to print the part number and name on a label. This process is repeated for all the records in the file.

> Write the data division and the procedure division of a COBOL program to DISPLAY the values of a sequence of two numbers and their sum. The starting values of the two numbers are both 0. One number increases by 1 and the other number increases by 2, as long as their sum is less than 100.

10 FORTRAN was designed specifically for the IBM computers which meant that it was **machine-dependent.** From a desire to devise an international programming language that could be used on different makes of computers, the programming language ALGOL was introduced in 1958.

ALGOL

11 ALGOL—from **ALGOrithmic Language**—took many of the features of FORTRAN but made them available to many different machines. It was the first machine-independent language. Unfortunately it did not address the problem of string handling that COBOL had done. Strings are collections of characters as opposed to collections of number digits. It was, however, a simple and easy to use language. A section of ALGOL code now follows.

```
begin
      integer x
      begin
        for x:=1 step 1 until 10 do
          prod := x*x
      end
end
```

12 For the first time code was written in blocks, each block starting with begin and finishing with end. Coding within a block is intended to make it easier to read. Like COBOL, variables are declared—here x is declared to be an integer variable, a whole number.

13 Because ALGOL was machine independent it had no commands that permitted information to be either input or output to the CPU. To do so required a knowledge of the specific computer system that was being used. To overcome these shortcomings the programming language Pascal was developed.

Pascal

14 Named after the French mathematician and inventor of the first mechanical adding machine, Blaise Pascal, this language was developed in 1968 specifically to teach the concepts of **structured programming**

and **top-down** program design. Top-down design will be discussed further in Section 3. There are a number of different dialects of Pascal but UCSD Pascal is probably the most popular. A section of Pascal code follows

```
PROGRAM SQUARE (OUTPUT);

VAR  X:INTEGER;

VAR  Y:INTEGER;

BEGIN;

    X:=0;

    REPEAT;

      Y:=X*X;

    WRITELN (X,Y);

      X:=X+1;

    UNTIL X=10;

END;
```

15 You will notice that a number of features here are similar to ALGOL. The program declares that OUTPUT will be used as well as declaring the variables X and Y. There is a block of code within the words REPEAT .. UNTIL. This is called a control structure and will be discussed further in the next section. Clearly, WRITELN is an instruction to write a line to an output device, a printer or a monitor. Note that all lines of code must end with a semicolon (;).

> Write a short Pascal program to PRINT the values of a sequence of two numbers, their sum, their difference, their product and their quotient. The first values of the two numbers will be 1 and 2 and they will both increase by 3 until their product is greater than r equal to 400.

BASIC

16 BASIC, the **Beginners All-purpose Symbolic Instruction Code** was originally devised in 1964 to provide students with an easy to learn language that could be used interactively on time sharing computer systems. Because of its simplicity it is the language that is provided with all microcomputer systems. There is no standard BASIC and dialects abound. The original BASIC was not a structured language so it was not suitable for solving problems by considering their structure. It uses code line numbers and the GOTO command used in FORTRAN and as a result, early attempts to program in BASIC ended up with an execution sequence like a tangled knot. This has been referred to as **spaghetti coding** and has put back the discipline of computer programming to the early days of assembly code. A number of attempts have been made to overcome this lack of structure, only when Pascal was devised was the problem realistically overcome.

C

17 The language **C** was developed by Bell Laboratories in the USA (now AT&T) as a simple language that possessed features of both high and low level programming. Like Pascal it is a structured language and like assembler, gives control over hardware and peripherals. A section of C code now follows.

```
main()   /* This program is like all the others*/;
{
     int quantity;
     int step;
     quantity =1;
     step = 1;
     while quantity < 10 {
          printf ("%2.0d %4.0d\n", quantity,
          quantity*quantity);
          quantity = quantity + step;
     }
```

18 Here the program commences with the statement main () and what follows on that line is a comment enclosed with /* .. */. Like ALGOL and Pascal, C uses blocks of code but instead of using begin .. end, uses { .. }. Again variables are declared and in this program we have used the **while** control structure.

Within the print statement are some formatting rules inserted between quotes " .. ".. These are %2.0d%4.Od\n.

19 This indicates that there will be two numbers printed, the first a decimal number—d with 2 digits before the decimal place and none after, and the second a decimal with 4 digits before the decimal place and none after. The \n tells the computer to print the new line and return characters so that the next output will appear below the previous output.

> Write a short program in C to PRINT the values of a sequence of two numbers, their sum, their differences, their product and their quotient. The first values of the two numbers will be 1 and 2 and they will both increase by 3 until their product is greater than or equal to 400.

Artificial intelligence

20 The languages that we have looked at so far have been concerned with tackling the standard types of problems that computers are good at: arithmetic, data management, recording and manipulating information, controlling machinery and many other tasks. But as computers become more sophisticated, so the problems they can tackle become more involved and the one thing they cannot do is to think for themselves; they have to be instructed to do everything down to the very smallest detail. We can think for ourselves, we can accept information, we can reason and we can make decisions. Computers can accept information and make decisions but they cannot reason. It is, however, possible to program computers to make them appear to reason. This is called **artificial intelligence**.

21 Reasoning is a very different process from simply manipulating information and because of this, languages that are ideal for manipulating information are very hard to use to simulate reasoning. To overcome this a number of high level languages have been devised, for example **LISP** and **PROLOG**, to make the programming of simulated reasoning easier. Coding in PROLOG is quite different from programming in all the other high level languages we have considered as can be seen from the following:

```
predicates

     goodat(symbol,symbol)

     because(symbol,symbol)

     cando(symbol,symbol).


clauses

     goodat(alan,maths).

     goodat(betty,english).

     goodat(colin,french).

     goodat(deborah,maths).


     because(engineering,maths).

     because(science,maths).

     because(communicating,english).

     because(writing,english).

     because(translating,french).

     because(teaching,french).


     cando(Person,Subject):-

          goodat(Person,Subject).
```

```
cando(Person,Job):-
        because(Job,Subject).
        goodat(Person,Subject).
```

The predicates are similar to variables except that the only values that they can take are true or false. For example, if, when the program were run, the user entered

goodat(alan,maths)

the response would be true since goodat(alan,maths) is a valid clause. If, on the other hand, the user entered

goodat(deborah,french)

the response would be false since that is not a valid clause. The principle behind the running of the program is that the computer will look through the list of clauses to find a match with the user's entry. The match may not be declared explicitly but may be inferred from using the logical structure of the declared clauses. For example, if the user entered

cando(alan,X)

the response would be

maths
engineering
science

since alan cando maths and because alan can do maths he can also do engineering and science. The maths is explicit but the engineering and science are inferred. Such inferences are made by PROLOG's inference engine which is the name given to the coding within PROLOG's structure that draws inferences from the explicit clauses. The inference engine is constructed using a system of logic devised originally by the Ancient Greeks and codified by George Boole in the nineteenth century—it is called Boolean logic. Boolean logic was the first attempt to explain in mathematical terms the principles behind the reasoning process—or what we call intelligence. By embodying Boolean logic within PROLOG's inference engine the first important steps toward artificial intelligence have been made.

Procedural and non-procedural languages

22 A procedural language deals with how a problem is to be solved. A program written in a procedural language describes step by step the procedure to be followed by the computer when solving a problem. The high level languages we have discussed so far are procedural languages. The success of a language for programming a problem is related to the ease with which complicated tasks can be programmed. This not only

simplifies the task of writing the program but also reduces the risk of error. For this reason a number of **non-procedural languages** have been devised which concentrate not on how but on **what** is to be accomplished. These languages are classified as fourth generation languages.

Fourth generation languages

23 Fourth generation languages, or 4GL's for short, permit programs to be constructed using short, English, easily understood and easily remembered commands. There is no single 4GL that stands out as a landmark because such a language is of little use without a database facility to accompany it. As a result 4GL's are all part of application packages, examples including dBase, SMART and ORACLE. Three uses of a 4GL are as:

- application generators
- database query languages
- report generators

Application generators

24 An application generator will permit a program to be written that will construct a database, permit information to be entered into it, permit records to be updated, calculations to be performed and output produced. The following is a typical short program written in the 4GL that accompanies the SMART suite of software.

```
COMMENT ***********************************
COMMENT * LOAD AND ENTER CUSTOMER RECORDS *
COMMENT ***********************************
unload all
load CSTMRS screen CSTMRS
order key [1]
enter
key update
```

25 The first three lines are COMMENT lines which are ignored by the CPU and merely serve to describe what the program does to anyone else reading it.

The fourth line **unloads** all files that are currently in the memory and automatically saves them to disk. This is done to make as much primary storage space available as possible.

The fifth line **loads** the file that is stored on disk under the name CSTMRS. If the file is too large for the available primary storage then only a portion of the file is loaded into memory with the remainder being accessible using a system of **paging**. Associated with this file is a particular screen display which is also loaded using the screen command.

The sixth line orders all the records in the file against the key field number 1. This field contains the customer's name so now all the records are arranged with the customers' names in alphabetical order.

The seventh line permits the user to enter records at will and on completion, a key is pressed on the keyboard to tell the computer.

The last line regenerates all the **key files**. These are the files that are associated with each key field and which contain the order in which records should appear if they were to be ordered by a particular key.

> A recipe book contains a collection of recipes of soups, lunches and supper dishes. If you were to convert that recipe book to a card index how would you go about it? You could computerise your card index with an application generator.

Database query language

26 A database query language will permit extensive queries to a database. For example, if a database contains details of a company's customers then the query language will permit all customers who live in Wales to be listed quickly and easily.

The following is an example of querying a data base written in the SMART 4GL. Notice the economy of code and the similar structure to the previous example.

```
COMMENT ************************************

COMMENT * LOAD AND QUERY CUSTOMER RECORDS *

COMMENT ************************************


unload all

load CSTMRS screen CSTMRS

order key [1]

query sales < 1000 screen
```

In this case **query** will list all those customers whose previous month's sales were less than 1000 on the screen.

> From a card index of recipes, how would you locate the cards that deal with lunches? How would you locate those recipes that deal with cold lunches? A database query language would enable the records to be located in a computerised system with ease.

Report generators

27 Report generators permit extensive manipulation of data contained in a database. The manipulated data can then be extracted and used to form a report that can be output to the printer. For example, if a database contains a file that records every sale representative's sales for each month of the year, then a report can easily be generated to list each sales representative by name, and their last month's sales compared with this month's sales.

The following coding shows how the SMART 4GL can be used to produce a report.

```
COMMENT ************************************

COMMENT * LOAD AND REPORT CUSTOMER RECORDS *

COMMENT ************************************


unload all

load CSTMRS screen CSTMRS

order key [1]

report print CUSTREP printer
```

Here the last line of code would cause a search of the CSTMRS file to find all the relevant information to be included in a **report**. This report, whose structure is predefined and stored in the file CUSTREP, would then be output to the printer.

> If you wanted your card index of recipes to have its own index listing particular recipes against card numbers, then to find a particular recipe you could simply look it up in the index. How long do you think it would take you to create such an index if the card index contained 1000 recipes? With a report generator it would not take much longer than it would take to print it from a computerised file.

Summary

To reduce the complexity of coding instructions to a computer in either machine or assembly code, the high level language FORTRAN was devised for use by scientists and engineers. This uses standard mathematical English and also employs subroutines—pieces of code used repeatedly—which can be called into use during the execution of instructions in the main body of the program. COBOL was devised because the early versions of FORTRAN only possessed limited non-numeric operations that were required for handling database files. COBOL is a structured language with four divisions: any variables used in COBOL must first be declared in the data division. COBOL, like FORTRAN also uses subroutines except that in COBOL they are referred to as procedures. Both FORTRAN and COBOL were machine-dependent, though COBOL less so, and a need was seen for a simple language that was machine-independent. For this reason ALGOL was devised. ALGOL uses blocks of code, each block starting with begin and finishing with end. Using this block structure ALGOL programs can be more easily read. Unfortunately ALGOL was so machine-independent that it had no routines for inputting or outputting information. To overcome this deficiency, Pascal was devised. Pascal is a structured language that is ideal for use when developing programs based on top-down design. The high level language BASIC was developed with students in mind. Unfortunately, the early forms of BASIC were not structured. They also contained the GoTo command which allowed unconditional branching around the program. The liberal use of this command developed bad habits in program design and spaghetti coding. The language C was developed as a simple language containing features of both high and low level languages.

The demands of artificial intelligence require a different approach to problem solving from that for which the existing languages are used. LISP and PROLOG are two examples of languages that were devised to meet these demands. PROLOG uses an inference engine to draw inferences from explicitly stated clauses. The inferences engine makes use of a system of logic that was first codified by Boole—it is called Boolean logic.

All languages, high or low level, are either procedural—they instruct the computer *how* to perform an operation—or they are non-procedural—they instruct a computer *what* to do. Non-procedural languages are referred to as fourth generation languages—4GLs—and are intrinsic features of application generators, database query languages and report generators.

Key points

First and second generation languages, third generation languages, FORTRAN, COBOL, ALGOL, Pascal, BASIC, C, artificial intelligence, procedural and non-procedural languages, fourth generation languages, application generators, database query language, report generators

Self assessment questions

1 Give two reasons why programming is a difficult process. (1)
2 Name the first generation language. (1)
3 Name the second generation language. (1)
4 Name the first third generation language. (2)
5 Why was FORTRAN devised? (2,3)
6 What is a subroutine in FORTRAN? (4)
7 Why was COBOL devised? (5)
8 How many divisions are there in COBOL? (8)
9 What is meant by declaring variables? (8)

10 What is a subroutine called in COBOL? (9)
11 Why was ALGOL devised? (10)
12 What are blocks of code? (12)
13 Why was Pascal devised? (13,14)
14 What is meant by spaghetti coding? (16)
15 What are the two main features of C? (17)
16 What is artificial intelligence? (20)
17 Name two languages used to program artificial intelligence applications. (21)
18 What is the difference between an explicit clause and an inferred clause in PROLOG? (21)
19 What does an inference engine do? (21)
20 What does a procedural language aim to do? (22)
21 What does a non-procedural language aim to do? (22)
22 What type of language is a 4GL? (22)
23 List three uses of a 4GL. (23)
24 What is an application generator? (24)
25 What is a database query language used for? (26)
26 What is a report generator? (27)

Exercises

1 1 A High Level Language is slow to execute.

2 A High Level Language is easy for people to read and write.

3 This is because it is close to human language.

Write three statements like these about a Low Level Language.

2 An advantage of a program written in an assembly language rather than a high-level language is that it is faster to
debug
execute
learn
write

3 From the following lists match the introduction type with the appropriate instruction.

Instruction	Type
SAVE	arithmetic
OR	logic
JUMP	control
SUBTRACT	data transfer

5 Operating systems

Objectives

1 To describe the functions of operating systems
2 To explain the need for translation programs

The early days of computer operation

1 When the first general purpose computers were developed they were operated by highly qualified people who were required to know how the computer and all its peripherals functioned. These early computers could only run one program at a time and each program performed a very specific task. One would load data into primary storage, another would process the data and a third would output the results of the processing. The operations of the computer, the resources and the management of the memory were all under the control of the programmer and the operator.

To operate such a computer, each stage required careful preparation. For example, to input data a number of relay switches on the computer had to be set, which told the computer that data was going to be entered. Then the data reader, card reader or punched tape reader had to be prepared and set into operation. Consequently, operating these early computers was a time consuming task, during which time most of the equipment was idle. If the computer was outputting information then you could neither input data nor process data. Computer resources were being wasted and with the high cost of the machines, wasted time and resources meant wasted money. What was required was a collection of programs to enable the computer to manage its own resources—an **operating system**.

Operating systems

2 As the name implies, an operating system is a system of different programs that work together in unison to maintain the operations of the computer.

Operating systems were first introduced in the 1960s to allow the computer to control its own resources, execute its own programs and manage its own data. The operating system assists users in the sharing of resources and uses service programs to take care of standard tasks that are used repeatedly. In brief, the role of the operating system is to control and manage the hardware, to provide the most efficient use of available equipment and memory resources and to act as an interface between the computer and the user. In effect it makes the computer easy to use by taking care of all the difficult problems itself.

> There are many examples of operating systems used by machines other than computers. For example, all cars have a choke that cuts off the air supply to the petrol-air mixture that makes a car engine work. Some cars have choke controls and others have an automatic choke. An automatic choke is part of the car's operating system. Make a list of four other examples like this.

The components of an operating system

3 The collection of programs that make up the operating system can be grouped as follows:

- control programs
- supervisory programs
- service programs

Control programs

4 The control programs control and manage all the hardware and memory resources of the computer. They allocate resources as and when they are needed. For example, they regulate and time the activities of the CPU, they allocate the primary storage when it is required and they schedule the data to be received and transmitted via the various input and output devices.

Supervisory programs

5 The supervisory programs form the most important component. They control all other operating system programs and any application programs that are being used. They also control the activities of the hardware. For example, the supervisory programs will activate the disk drive as and when it is to be required for data transfer.

> During the operation of a computer program you are asked to enter three numbers at the keyboard. As you do so the numbers appear on the monitor screen. When you have finished these three numbers their totals are output to a printer. Where do the operating system's control and supervisory programs come into use during the execution of this program?

Service programs

The service programs provide system services to the user. These programs are contained within two categories.

Utility programs

6 Utility programs provide a set of services that are often required when running a program. They permit files to be saved to and loaded from storage media, and to be copied, renamed or deleted. They activate the printer, the keyboard and all other peripheral devices, and they are able to format a disk in preparation for storing information.

Formatting Before a disk can be used to store information it has to be prepared by allocating areas on its surface. This process is called formatting the disk. Every disk stores information on its surface within a number of **tracks** in the form of concentric circles. When a disk is formatted, each one of these tracks is magnetically divided into a number of sectors and each sector is numbered. One or more of the tracks are reserved for the **catalogue** in which a list of the names and locations will be kept of all files stored on the disk.

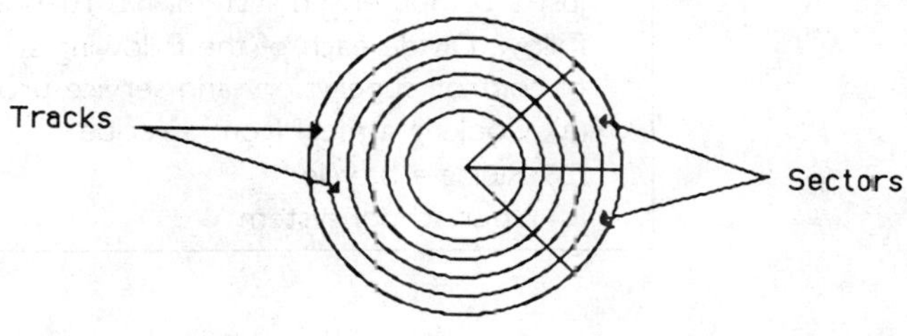

2.47 Track sector arrangement on a disk surface

> Find out how the disks that you use with your computer are formatted. How many tracks do they have? How many sectors is each track divided into? Which track contains the catalogue. On the disk envelope is a small hole beside the larger one. The disk inside has one too. Turn the inside disk until the two holes are aligned. Why do you think those are there?

System aids

7 There are numerous system aids provided by the operating system to assist the user when developing a program. Any errors in a program experienced at run time will be located and identified by the operating system. **Syntax error** is a common expression seen when first attempting to program a microcomputer. This is a message from the operating system telling the user that something is wrong with the program's coding. The computer will not locate a logic error however; these must be located by the programmer.

Locating and correcting errors in a program is referred to as **debugging**. The operating system may identify the error or it may require the program to be **traced** for the error to be found. Tracing is a facility offered by the operating system that prints a reference to code as it is executed so that the user can locate where in the program the error has occurred. In a BASIC program a trace will print each line number as it is executed.

> Find out how the TRACE facility works on your computer.

Other system aids include **subroutines** that are frequently used within a program. For example, square roots, the trigonometric expressions and other such mathematical subroutines are all provided by the operating system.

> Think of an operating system as a set of rules that must be obeyed and a set of instructions that must be executed. Any system, not just a computerised system, has rules and a set of instructions to follow. Divide each of the following systems into the three divisions of control, supervisory and service programs
> (a) Cooking a meal from a recipe
> (b) Riding a bicycle
> (c) Your school system

Translators

8 To enable the operating system to act as an intermediary between the user and all the component parts of the computer, the system must be capable of accepting information from the user in the user's language. The computer does not understand English or any other such language, so some means of translating into the computer's language must be provided.

9 The United Nations in New York is an organisation which permits the leading statesmen of the world to assemble together to debate the world issues of the day. It is similar to Parliament in the UK except that it does not have any power to enact laws.

When the statesmen gather together their debates are conducted in every language of the world. This form of communication would be of very little use if it were not for a large number of translators who translate speeches from one language into all the other languages represented in the United Nations.

Similarly a computer needs to understand our language. We communicate to it in a high level language because we can understand that language and use it to create the instructions necessary to perform the task we have in mind. But as we saw in Chapter 3 of this section, the computer only understands the on/off states of its internal switches. Consequently, we need to translate the language we have used into the language that the computer uses.

There are three different types of translators.

Assemblers Assemblers were the first translators and are used to translate assembly language into machine code. The lowest level of language that we use to instruct the computer is the mnemonic assembly code. This code is translated into machine code by an assembler. The assembler is a piece of software that recognises the mnemonic codes, looks them up in a look-up table and then replaces them with the appropriate machine coded instruction.

Compilers A compiler translates a program written in a high level language into machine code. The program as written in the high level language is referred to as the **source code** and the compiled machine coded program obtained from it is called the **object code**. The computer executes the object code whereas we write and read the subject code.

Interpreters An interpreter translates a program written in a high level language into machine code, one line at a time, as the program is being executed. As each line of code is translated it is executed. The machine coded form of the program is not stored as object code, so every time the program is executed it has to be re-interpreted. BASIC on a microcomputer is executed through an interpreter.

Each of the following requires the use of a translator. Which uses a translator that performs like a compiler and which uses a translator that performs like an interpreter?

(a) A book translation
(b) A speech translation being translated as it is given
(c) Setting the controls of a washing machine
(d) Riding a bicycle

Operating system storage

10 Most computers have their operating system stored in secondary storage which is accessible from a system resident device such as a hard or floppy disk or tape drive. When the computer is switched on the appropriate secondary storage device is also switched on and the operating system is loaded into the CPU's primary storage. If the operating system is very large then only essential parts of the supervisory programs are loaded and when other parts of the operating system are needed they are loaded as necessary and deleted after use. Alternatively, the operating system may be part of the firmware, as is the case with the BBC microcomputer.

> Inside the manual that comes with your computer you may find a memory map that describes which sections of RAM are used for what purpose. By consulting this manual or otherwise, find out where in RAM your operating system is placed when it is loaded.

Types of operating system

11 Just as there are different types of computer system, so there are different types of operating system. Each type of operating system offers facilities that are appropriate to the computer system in which it is used.

Single program operating system

12 A single program operating system will permit one application program to be run at a time. It will permit both real-time processing, where the user is interacting with the computer during the execution of the program and batch processing, where a series of programs are run in sequence. As batch processing is not done in real-time it is the operating system that acknowledges the termination of one program and initiates the execution of the next program.

Multi-user operating systems

13 A multi-user operating system will permit a number of users to **appear** to use the computer system at the same time. The computer's resources are **time-shared** among the users, each user having exclusive use of the resources at any one time. The **time slices** during which any one user has access to the computer can be as small as 2 milliseconds. This is a long time for many of the computer's operations and because all operators are offered a time-slice in turn, every user has the impression that they have exclusive use of the computer all the time.

> When someone tries to speak to you when you are on the phone talking to someone else, you are being time-shared or multi-used. Can you think of other instances of this?

Multi–programming operating system

14 A multi-programming operating system gives the appearance of running more than one program at a time. Different areas of primary storage are reserved for each program and any particular program can be called into operation by the user at any time. An example of a piece of multi-programming software is the program Sidekick which is a combination of diary, notebook and calculator that can be called into use at any time

> Can you think of the last time you tried to do two things at once, for example trying to walk upstairs reading a book? Think of other situations where you tried to do two things at once but found you couldn't? If you had to stop doing one thing to do another then you were multi-programming.

Virtual storage operating system

15 The virtual storage operating system was originally devised to cater for programs that were too large to be wholly contained within primary storage. Even today, with large amounts of primary storage available, it is not unusual for the size of RAM available to be too small to accommodate the needs of a particular application program. In this case a virtual storage operating system will permit data to be moved between primary and secondary storage as and when the primary storage proves to be too small. This gives the user an *impression* of a computer with a large memory, especially if the secondary storage is a multi megabyte hard disk. Many professional word processors use this facility. If the RAM available is too small to accommodate a complete document then only a few pages will be in RAM at any one time. Any other pages that are required will then be brought in from the secondary storage, room being made for them by dumping current pages from primary storage to secondary storage. Another aspect of virtual storage is called **spooling**. Spooling is the process of sending output to a disk file and then printing that output directly from the file, thereby freeing the CPU to do other tasks.

> Most people use a virtual storage system. If you can not remember a certain fact but know that you once knew it, then you can look it up in a book: that is your virtual storage system.
> How many times in the last week have you used a virtual storage system?

Virtual machine operating system

16 Multi-programming and timesharing can bring users into conflict over shared resources. Consequently the idea of the virtual machine has been devised to give each user the impression that each has control over the entire computer i.e. each user has what appears to be a separate copy of the physical machine. In such a virtual machine operating system, different users can even use different operating systems simultaneously.

This facility allows different application programs to use the operating system appropriate to them. The overall control of such a system is under the supervision of a virtual machine operating system.

Portability of operating systems

17 A BBC microcomputer uses a different operating system from the one used on an IBM PC. As a result of this, software written for the BBC cannot be run on an IBM, i.e. it is not portable from one computer to another. Not only is the software not portable, but neither is the operating system. This lack of portability of operating systems means that much software has to be duplicated before it can run on different computers, which is wasteful, especially if the duplication involves a lot of re-writing. As a result, a number of operating systems have been devised that are capable of being used on a variety of different computers. **CP/M** Control Program/Microcomputers, is an operating system designed to be portable between different makes of microcomputer while **UNIX** is an operating system designed to be portable across the range of all computers from microcomputers to mainframes.

Neither of these operating systems are **user-friendly** and so the problem of developing an easy-to-use, portable operating system remains. One outcome of this situation is the proliferation of **clones**.

Clones

18 Clones are copies of computers, designed to use the same operating systems and software. The Apple microcomputer developed by Wozniak and Jobs, immediately led the market for small computers with the result that a considerable amount of software was written for it. A computer is of no use without software so other manufacturers copied the Apple to produce Apple clones, using the same operating systems and software.

> If you look through a typical monthly computer magazine you will see advertisements for computers that are described as PC compatible. What do you think that means?

When IBM first marketed their PC they used an operating system called PC DOS which is a far more versatile and superior operating system to Apple DOS. IBM PC sales soon overtook Apple sales with the result that more software was being written for the PC than was for the Apple. The clone manufacturers then switched their attention to IBM clones, but IBM had patented their PC DOS. Consequently MS DOS emerged which is sufficiently similar to PC DOS to enable IBM software to be run on them, yet different enough to prevent breach of the copyright laws.

Summary

The first general purpose computers were only capable of running one program at a time and each program had a very specific task. The operations of the computer, and the resources and management of the memory were all under the control of the programmer and the operator. An operating system takes all this responsibility of the operator and puts it under the control of the computer. The most important part of the operating system consists of the supervisory programs as they control all other programs in the operating system. Tasks that are required repeatedly are catered for by various service programs. These range from utility programs to system aids. Three types of translation programs are used to translate into machine code instructions issued in higher level languages. The operating system is stored in secondary storage and loaded into RAM when the computer is switched on. There are various types of operating system available including single program, multi-user, multi-programming, virtual storage and virtual machine operating systems. Most operating systems are designed to be used with a particular computer. UNIX and CP/M are two examples of operating systems that are portable. This lack of portability of operating systems has also led to the manufacture of clones.

Key points

The early days of computer operation, operating systems, control programs, supervisory programs, service programs, utility programs, formatting, system aids, translators, assemblers, compilers, interpreters, operating system storage, types of operating system, single program operating system, multi-user operating system, multi-programming operating system, virtual storage operating system, virtual machine operating system, portability of operating systems, clones

Self assessment questions

1 Why were operating systems developed? (1,2)
2 List the three types of programs in an operating system. (3)
3 What functions do control programs perform? (4)
4 What functions do supervisory programs perform? (5)
5 List two types of service programs. (6–7)
6 What services do utility programs provide? (6)
7 What is meant by formatting a disk? (6)
8 How is data stored on a disk's surface? (6)
9 What are system aids? (7)
10 What is a trace? (7)
11 What is debugging? (7)
12 What are translators and why are they needed? (9)
13 What does an assembler do? (9)
14 What does a compiler do? (9)
15 What are the differences between source code and object code? (9)
16 What does an interpreter do? (9)
17 Where is an operating system stored? (10)
18 List six types of operating system. (11–17)
19 What is the difference between real-time and batch processing? (12)
20 How does a multi-user operating system cater for many users. (13)
21 How does a multi-tasking operating system cater for more than one program? (14)
22 What does a true multi-programming operating system offer? (14)
23 What does a virtual storage operating system offer? (15)
24 What does a virtual machine operating system offer? (16)
25 What is meant by the portability of an operating system? (17)
26 List two portable operating systems. (17)
27 What is a clone? (18)
28 Why are clones manufactured? (18)

Exercises

1 Name two of the functions of a computer operating system.

2 An operating system is essential to any general purpose computer system. This is true whether the computer system is a central mainframe with many users, some using remote terminals, or a personal computer with only one user. Describe three tasks that must be performed by the operating system.

3 (a) Name a commonly used high-level computer language.

(b) Name the two different types of translators that are used with a high-level language.

(c) What is the main difference between the methods of operation of these two types of translator?

(d) Name the type of translator that is used for a low-level language.

(e) Name the type of instructions that the computer hardware actually uses.

4 A computer program is to be written using one of two languages. Language A is interpreted and language B is compiled. Name one advantage of using each language.

5 A computer program written in a high-level language must be translated before it can be executed. Which of the following describes this process?

Object code → compiler → source code
Object code → interpreter → source code
Source code → assembler → object code
Source code → compiler → object code

6 Apart from games and entertainment software, most commercially produced software is either an application package or a utility program.

(a) Give one example of an application package.
(b) Give one example of a utility program.

7 (b) Any good applications package has these features regardless of the task it is to do.
It must be <u>robust</u>.
In order to sell well it must be <u>portable</u>.
It must be <u>reliable</u>.
Explain each of the <u>underlined</u> terms. You may use examples to help you do this.

8 The following list shows four items of software. Each one is either an 'Applications Package' or a 'Utility Program'. For each item, decide which type it is, giving a reason why you would use it for each.

screen dump program	database program
wordprocessing program	disk copying program

9 The contents of four files are shown as follows:

A	B	C	D	
27	93	34	27	60
36	60	39	34	93
38	34	45	36	97
97	39	60	38	102
	102	93	39	
	45	102	45	

(a) State how utility routines could have been used to produce files C and D from files A and B.

(b) Describe the function of one other utility routine.

10 The Euclid Microcomputer is supplied with 512 Kbytes of RAM and a 20 Mbyte Hard Disk. The Operating System, a BASIC Interpreter and a COBOL Compiler are on the Hard Disk.

(a) What is RAM and what is it used for?

(b) What is the function of an interpreter?

(c) What is the function of a compiler?

(d) Write down one advantage and one disadvantage in using a compiled language rather than an Interpreted language.

(e) For what types of application are
(i) COBOL and (ii) BASIC
particularly suitable?

(f) What are two advantages of having a Hard Disk rather than the more usual Floppy Disk?

(g) The Euclid Microcomputer is also supplied with a mouse and a WIMP user interface. (WIMP means "Windows, Icons, Mouse, Pointers.)

(i) What is a mouse? How is a mouse used?
(ii) What are the advantages in using a WIMP user interface instead of the more common text Operating System command lines?

11 Students use terminals on-line to a central computer.

(a) What type of operating system must the computer have?

(b) Describe how the system works to share computer time between the students using the system.

6 Applications packages

Chapter objectives

1 To compare the purposes of utility programs and applications packages and identify their appropriate uses.
2 To describe the range, scope and use of applications packages.

Introduction

1 Utility programs are programs that are part of the operating system that permit the handling of files. They permit the transfer of data and the sorting, searching and merging of files. Their use within an application is very restrictive because usually the application demands more than simple utility routines. As a result, applications and application packages have been developed with more sophisticated facilities than those offered by the utility routines. An applications package is a program written to solve a particular problem and may be

- a bespoke Application Package
- an off-The-Shelf Application Package

Bespoke application packages

2 A bespoke application package is a program that is written for a specific user to solve a specific problem. For example, in the last section a computer teacher had a program written to compute the number of words in a document. When the manual is also included we call the whole package a bespoke package. Bespoke packages can be written in-house or by employing a professional programmer employed by a consultancy company.

Find out what a 'bespoke tailor' is?

Off-the-shelf application packages

3 A whole industry has been created specifically to provide software for computers—from micros to mainframes.

> Go to a computer shop and ask to have a look at their software catalogue. See if you can sort the different packages into types, for example games, financial packages, information packages.

There are two types of off-the-shelf package.

- specific application packages
- general application packages

Specific application packages

4 Specific applications packages are programs written to perform a particular job. However, unlike bespoke packages they are not written for a specific customer but rather for a general type of customer. For example, a stock control program is designed to deal specifically with stock but can be used by anyone who needs to control their stock. As a result, they may be restricting because it may be necessary to adjust your stock control system to the way the program works.

The decision must therefore be made whether to pay more for a bespoke system to be written to match your needs exactly, or to save money by buying a specific application package and adjust your own system accordingly.

Typical of specific application packages are:

(a) **Accounting systems** An accounting system can range from a simple accounts-receivable system which keeps a track of debtors and creditors to a full ledger system that maintains a company's complete ledger system. Some of these systems are designed for use by any company while others are designed for specific companies only, such as bookmakers or petrol filling stations.

(b) **Payroll packages** These range from straightforward wage payments to complex multi-company, weekly wages and monthly salary organisers.

(c) **Financial analysis systems** A Financial Analysis System will use all the information contained in the various ledgers and permit forcasts of future company performance to be made. They will also allow a company to create a realistic budget for the following year and then analyse comparisons between budget targets set and actual targets achieved.

(d) **Stock control systems** These systems range from straightforward accounting of stock held, issued and delivered, to complex systems where stock levels are optimised to reduce costs. If you hold too much stock you spend too much storing it. If you hold too little you hold up production which also costs money. Balancing these two requires a deal of sophisticated mathematics—which can be handled easily by a computer.

(e) **Estate agents** Software available to estate agents permits the administration of both commercial and residential properties. The system will retain full information on a property and match against a potential customer's requirements. It can also maintain a file of potential customers, organise mail shots of appropriate properties, record appointments and produce publicity material.

(f) **Travel agents** Travel agents can be provided with software to take care of hotel reservations, airline bookings, specific holiday bookings and complete tour operations. Many of them use Videotex which links them to a data bank of graphical information, permitting customer's to see what it is they are paying for.

The range of specific applications software available is huge. A visit to your local library to look at the **Software Users' Year Book** will soon convince you of the scale and scope of software available.

> From your local computer shop's catalogue, select four different specific application packages. Go to your public library and look up those packages in the *Software Users Year Book*. Make a note of what the book has to say about each package and look through the *Year Book* to see if there are other, better packages available. If they are better, explain why.

General application packages

5 Specific application software may not be appropriate to your particular needs or may cost more than you are willing to pay, in which case you may require a package that is half-way between bespoke software and specific applications software and which allows you to construct your own application package. These are known as general applications packages and include:

- Word processors
- Spreadsheets
- Databases
- Graphics packages
- Communications package
- Expert systems

Word processors

6 The invention of the typewriter towards the end of the nineteenth century revolutionised the processing of commercial correspondence enabling it to be produced faster and more efficiently. Now, with the introduction of the word processor, a second revolution has occurred.

A word processor is a computer program that enables the user to manipulate text displayed on the monitor screen and then instruct the printer to produce a hard copy of that text. Text can be entered into a document faster because mistakes can be very simply edited later. Paragraphs and even whole documents of pre-written text can be inserted into a document without needing to be re-typed and documents can be stored on disk instead of on paper in a filing cabinet. Word processors are faster, more efficient and use very little space.

Word processing systems may be stand-alone systems, dedicated only to word processing, or they may consist of a PC running the appropriate software. Whichever system is used they all have facilities and features in common.

> Do you think it is better to buy a dedicated word processor or to buy a word processor program to run on your micro? Explain your reasons.

Screen display

7 When a word processor is being executed the monitor screen will display a number of features. A status line will appear either at the top or bottom of the screen and there will be a large area in the centre of the screen in which the document is displayed. In the area where the text is displayed will be a cursor which is usually flashing. The cursor is the marker which indicates where the next typed character will appear on the screen and it is flashing to catch your attention.

```
DOCUMENT : Letter          PAGE :   1   LINE :    8    COL : 10
------------------------------------------------------------------
Dear Reader

This is an extract from a document called Letter that is
being displayed on a word processor screen.  Notice the
status line at the top and a list of commands at the bottom.
The highlighted block is where the cursor is located and as
you see from the status line it is on line 8 column 10.
         █
------------------------------------------------------------------
 COMMAND LIST 1 : Load  Save  Print  Window  Copy  Move
                  Delete  Undo  Spell-check  Page-break
```

The **status line** describes the name of the document you are currently typing, the page number of the document and the position of the cursor on the screen, this position being given in terms of line and column numbers. On some word processors the bottom or top few lines of the screen will display a list of commands which can be used when creating a document.

> Run your word processing software and examine your screen display. Make sure that you understand what everything refers to, then try entering text at the keyboard.

Commands

8 Instructions are issued to the computer during the execution of a word processor by using commands. These may be selected from a menu of commands displayed on the screen, by using the function keys or by using special key combinations. For example, to save the document on disk, either the function key F10 may be used or the combination ⟨CTRL-S⟩, depending upon the word processor you are using. Whichever type of word processor you use, the commands will be described in the manual.

> Find out the commands on your word processor that allow you to
>
> (a) save a document
> (b) load a document.

Cursor and document control

9 A document is created by entering the text at the keyboard. As this is done the cursor moves across the screen to the next vacant location, but unlike a typewriter, it is not necessary to press return at the end of every line. As you type the words are automatically adjusted to wrap round from the end of one line to the beginning of the next. This feature is called wordwrap. If you do press return then the cursor moves to the start of the next new line which is the start of a new paragraph in the document.

It is also possible to make the cursor move about the screen by using the cursor control keys. These may be up, down, left or right arrows coupled with the home and end keys, or where special keys are used, they will be described in the word processor manual.

As well as moving the cursor, the document itself can be made to move by using either the PgUp or PgDn keys or specially designated keys, again listed in the manual. Using these keys the document will scroll backwards or forwards one page at a time.

> Find out which keys control the cursor on your computer. When you have done this use the word processor to write a note that explains how these keys are used to move the cursor around the screen and the screen around the document.

Windowing

10 Another feature of many word processors is windowing. This permits the screen to be split into a number of different areas, usually two, and to display a different document in each window, thereby permitting both documents to be viewed simultaneously. There will be a special command to put the word processor into **window mode**.

```
DOCUMENT : Letter          PAGE :  1   LINE :          COL :
Dear Reader
This is an extract from a document called Letter that is
being displayed on a word processor screen.  Notice the
status line at the top and a list of commands at the bottom.
The highlighted block is where the cursor is located and as
DOCUMENT : Memo   (Active) PAGE :  1   LINE :    3     COL : 51
Dear Reader
The screen is split showing another document here.█
  COMMAND LIST 1 : Load   Save   Print   Window   Copy   Move
                   Delete  Undo  Spell-check   Page-break
```

> What is the command to put your screen display into window mode?
> How do you move from one window to another?

Text editing

11 The main purpose of the word processor is to permit text editing which consists of entering text and then editing by correcting mistakes. This editing can take a number of different forms.

(a) **Inserting or overwriting** If a mistake has been located in the text displayed on the screen, place the cursor at the appropriate location and re-type at the keyboard. Depending upon the choice of the user, the new type will either be overwritten or inserted. If it is inserted, the type to the right of the insertion will automatically move on to make room for the insertion.

(b) **Copying, moving and deleting** Single characters, lines or whole blocks of text can be copied or moved to a different location in the document. This is done by marking the beginning and ending of the appropriate text and issuing the appropriate command. In the same manner, text can be completely deleted from the document.

> With your word processor, how do you insert text, overwrite text copy text, move text and delete text?

(c) **Undo** If you delete some text from the document and then immediately realise that you should not have done, your word processor may have the facility for the deletion to be undone. Issuing this command will restore the deleted text.

(d) **Search and replace** If you have used a word or phrase frequently in a document and you later realise that it has been used incorrectly, then using the search and replace commands, every occurrence of the word or phrase in the document can be automatically replaced by the word or words of your choice. Searching and replacing can also be done selectively with the user making the decision whether or not to replace at each occurrence of the word or phrase.

> Find out how you can search a document and replace text within a document with your word processor.

(e) **Spell checking and thesaurus** Many word processors have a facility that checks all the spelling in a document. This is done by consulting the word processor's dictionary and comparing spellings. Any incorrect spelling can then be identified and automatically corrected with the correct word from the dictionary. Not all the words you use will be in the dictionary and so these will also be selected as misspelt even though they are not. In this case, issuing the appropriate command will leave them as they are.

In addition to a dictionary some word processors also possess a thesaurus which can be used to suggest synonyms. For example, the synonyms listed on my word processor for document are archive, monument and record. I could use any one of these as a substitute for document by selecting it from the thesaurus.

(f) **Saving and loading** When a document has been created it can be saved to disk by issuing the appropriate command. When this command is issued the user is asked to give the document a name and the computer saves the document in a file with that name. At any later stage the document can be loaded and displayed on the screen by identifying it by its file name. The security of a document can be ensured by assigning it a password. This prevents the document from being loaded without giving the password.

(g) **Printing and merging** A hard copy of the document can be obtained by instructing the computer to print the document. Some word processors also have the facility to merge two documents together by printing selectively from both documents. For example, if one document contained a standard letter and a second document contained a list of names and addresses then a circular could be printed with each letter containing the standard letter in its body, but each headed by a different name and address. This is how mailing companies manage to send you a **personalised** letter.

Describe how to print a document with your word processor

(h) **Formatting** The ultimate aim of a word processor is to produce a typewritten document. For this reason we must be able to control the appearance of the text as it appears on the paper. This process is known as formatting and a number of facilities are available to enable us to get the appearance we require.

- **Justification**—the alignment of text.
- **Left-justified**—text appears with the first characters of every line immediately under each other.
- **Right-justification**—the same but to the right hand side. If print is not right-justified it is said to be **ragged edged**.
- **Centring**—text can be centred on the page to give a symmetric appearance.
- **Margins and tab setting**—Left hand and right hand margins can be set as can tab settings. A tab setting permits type to be inset from the left by pressing the tab key.

Describe how you would justify, centre, set margins and tabs with your word processor.

- **Hyphenation**—when text is right justified this may only be achieved by placing additional blank spaces between words, which gives a document an uneven appearance. There may be a facility for the automatic insertion of hyphens to overcome this problem.
- **Widows and orphans**—it is not good printing practice to end a page with a single line of a new paragraph—a widow—nor to start a new page with the last line of a paragraph—an orphan. Some word processors can automatically adjust the text to prevent widows and orphans.
- **Character enhancing**—many word processors allow enhanced characters to be printed. These characters may be larger than normal or even smaller. They may be in bold-face type, underlined or italicised.
- **Line spacing**—documents may need to be printed double or triple spaced. By issuing the appropriate command the printer will comply although the spacing does not appear on the monitor screen.
- **Page breaks**—word processors may be page-oriented or document-oriented. A page-oriented word processor will only bring one page at a time into memory whereas one that is

document-oriented will bring the entire document into memory. If the word processor is document-oriented, then a marker will appear between each page to indicate a page break. Some word processors use **virtual memory** by swapping portions of the document between primary and secondary storage. This is an automatic process and gives the impression of a large primary storage—hence the use of the word virtual.

- **Headers and footers**—a document may require the same heading to appear on each page. This is known as a header and it can be formatted for inclusion into the document. In the same way footers—at the end of each page of the document—can be formatted. A typical display in a footer is the page number.

> From the list starting hyphenation and ending headers and footers, how many of these facilities does your word processor offer?

On-line help

Using a word processor requires remembering a list of commands and to assist the user, many word processors will have an on-line HELP facility. By issuing the appropriate help command, a list of commands and their meanings will be displayed, which being on-line and available for use as you create a document, makes it an invaluable aid.

> Does your word processor possess an on-line help facility? If so then how do you access it?

Spreadsheets

12 To show an example of a spreadsheet we will compare the cost of buying a car by taking a loan over one, two, or three years. We shall construct the following table where the interest on the loan has been calculated at 10% simple interest.

Loan Period	1 Year	2 Year	3 Year
Cost Of Car	10,000	10,000	10,000
Interest 10%	1,000	2,000	3,000
Total Cost	11,000	12,000	13,000

The format of this table is in regular **rows** and **columns** i.e. it is a spreadsheet.

If, having drawn up this spreadsheet, we found out that the interest rate had been changed to 11% simple interest then the three interest values would have to be changed along with the corresponding Total Costs and a new spreadsheet drawn up.

Loan Period	1 Year	2 Year	3 Year
Cost Of Car	10,000	10,000	10,000
Interest 11%	1,100	2,200	3,300
Total Cost	11,100	12,200	13,300

If there were hundreds of rows and columns all with entries that depended upon each other this would be a very tedious task. Fortunately, however, the electronic spreadsheet enables us to re-draw the second sheet simply by changing the 10% to 11% which **automatically updates** the interest values and total costs. Spreadsheets are used frequently in many situations and the first electronic spreadsheet, VisiCalc, was probably one of the most important developments in microcomputer software.

> The number of applications to which a spreadsheet can be put is almost endless. Name four different applications.

An electronic spreadsheet—hereafter referred to simply as a spreadsheet—is a computer program that permits numbers, entered in a regular array of rows and columns, to be manipulated at will. The spreadsheet can be constructed so that the value of one number can be made to depend on the value of a second number. In other words, if the second number is changed the spreadsheet automatically re-calculates the value of the other. In this way complicated spreadsheets can be constructed that allow the user to apply the **'What if ...'** principle. What happens to all the other numbers if we change this number? The possibilities for projecting the consequences of different situations is endless.

The spreadsheet is an ideal tool to use whenever data has to be tabulated in this form, regularly and with varying data such as, for example, summarising monthly sales figures, listing weekly stock despatches or totalling and averaging students' marks.

13 To distinguish between spreadsheet meaning the program and spreadsheet meaning the tabulated data we shall hereinafter refer to the latter as the worksheet.

Screen display

14 The worksheet consists of a number of boxes or cells arranged in regular rows and columns. Along the top of the screen is displayed the column address of each cell and down the left hand side the row address of each cell. Addresses may be in the form of numbers, letters or both, and are combined to give the **cell address** which identifies the exact location of the cell.

At the bottom of the screen will appear the status line, prompt line and possibly a list of commands. The status line describes the name of the current worksheet and the position of the cursor in terms of the address of the cell containing it. The cursor may be a simple flashing line or a highlight filling an entire cell and the prompt line will display a prompt for future action such as Do you wish to recalculate?. The commands are the various instruction options available to the user when manipulating the spreadsheet.

	1	2	3	4
1	Period	1 Year	2 Year	3 Year
2	Car Cost	10,000	10,000	10,000
3	0.10	1,000	2,000	3,000
4	TOTAL	11,000	12,000	13,000
5				
6				

```
Input:
Status: Worksheet : Cars                    Active cell: r1c1
Prompt:
Command list: Load Save Copy Delete Move
```

Also displayed will be an **input line** where the data is keyed before it appears in its designated cell. This allows the contents of a cell to be edited or changed.

> Run your spreadsheet software and examine the screen display. Make sure that you understand everything that is displayed on the screen. Try entering information from the keyboard into the spreadsheet.

Cursor and sheet control

15 The cell containing the cursor is referred to as the **active cell** as it is ready to receive an entry. This can be changed simply by using the cursor control keys.

Scrolling

Only part of the worksheet will appear on the screen at one time. To view other parts the worksheet must be scrolled either left/right or up/down by using the control keys as described in the spreadsheet manual. For example, on a PC PgUp and PgDn will move the worksheet up and down a screen at a time and CTRL in combination with the left and right arrows will move the worksheet left and right, a screen at a time.

> Describe how you move the cursor from cell to cell using the cursor control keys. How can you scroll around the worksheet?

Windowing

Some spreadsheets permit the screen to be split into a number of windows with a different worksheet in each window. This is a very useful feature if all the worksheets are linked to each other. Linking two worksheets together enables the contents of one worksheet to affect the contents of the other, for example, a set of twelve monthly sales projections coupled with a summarised annual projection.

> Can you window your screen? What are the commands that do this?

Data entry

16 Each cell on a worksheet is capable of containing:

Numbers

Numbers are entered straight from the keyboard and appear in the cell in a pre-defined format. They can appear as whole numbers or decimal numbers to a particular number of decimal places. If desired, they can also appear in scientific notation.

Text

Text is again, entered directly from the keyboard and, provided the first character is not a number, the spreadsheet automatically recognises the entry as text. Many spreadsheets permit **spillover** where the text contents of a cell, being larger than the cell width, spill over into the adjacent cell.

> Enter numbers and text into a worksheet that reproduces the appearance of the CAR spreadsheet at the beginning of our discussion of spreadsheets. You will not be able to perform any calculations with this sheet yet. This exercise is simply to practice moving around the worksheet and entering numbers and text.

Formulas

A formula can be entered into a cell, provided the user indicates first that a formula is to be entered. On some spreadsheets this is done by starting the entry with = followed by the formula. Formulas can be constructed by combinations of the arithmetic symbols with cell addresses, for example: (r1c4 + r29c33)/r2c5 adds together the contents of cells row 1 column 4 and row 29 column 33, and then divides by the contents of cell row 2 column 5.

> Find out from your spreadsheet manual
>
> (a) How individual cells are referred to, for example r1c2.
> (b) How groups of cells are referred, for example r1:4c2:5 which means from rows 1 to 4 and columns 2 to 5.
> (c) How a formula is entered into a cell.
>
> Enter the number 5 in r1c1, the number 7 in r1c2 and the formula r1c1+r1c2 in r1c3.

Spreadsheets also have a large number of in-built functions such as SUM, AVERAGE and MAX. Using these, coupled with cell addresses, formulas can also be constructed. For example SUM (r2:4c3) will compute the sum of the contents of cells from row 2 column 3 to row 4 column 3.

> Look in your spreadsheet manual under *Spreadsheet Functions* and find out what functions are available. In the earlier worksheet, replace the formula in r1c3 by the formula SUM (r1c1:2)

Cell addresses and cell references

17 Every cell has an address which locates its position in the worksheet, for example r2c5 is the address of the cell at the intersection of the second row and the fifth column. When cell addresses are used in formulas they are called cell references and these can be in one of two forms.

Absolute and relative cell references

18 In a formula, another cell can be referred to by its position on the worksheet—its absolute address or by its position relative to the formula cell—its relative address. The difference between these two forms of cell reference will be in the notation used. For example in cell r3c4 a formula may be used that uses the cell reference r2c5. This may refer to the cell in row 2 and column 5.

If the cell reference were in the form r[– 2]c[5], this may refer to the cell 2 rows up and 5 columns to the right. All spreadsheets have their own notations for relative and absolute cell reference and these will be described in the manual.

> Read your spreadsheet manual and make a note of how your spreadsheet distinguishes between absolute and relative cell addresses. You might also read the manual's description of the meaning of absolute and relative cell addresses.

Calculations and recalculations

19 The spreadsheet can be in either automatic recalculation mode or manual recalculation mode, the difference being that the sheet recalculates either automatically or when commanded to. When a spreadsheet recalculates, all the formulas are calculated afresh. When the contents of a cell are changed, recalculation is automatically prompted if those contents affect any other cell contents. The worst offence here is the circular reference where the recalculation never ceases because of a circular relationship between cells. For example:

Cell 1 affects Cell 2
Cell 2 affects Cell 3
Cell 3 affects Cell 1

Many spreadsheets will recognise a circular reference and not perform the recalculation but issue a warning of the situation.

> Construct a worksheet that has a circular cell reference in it. If you are unsure how to do this, enter the formula r1c2 * 10 in cell r1c1 and the formula r1c1 * 5 in cell r1c2. See what happens when the spreadsheet tries to calculate.

Sorting

20 A row or column of numbers can be sorted in ascending or decending order by marking the row or column and issuing the sort command.

Copying, moving and deleting

21 The contents of a cell or block of cells can be copied or moved to another cell or, if desired, deleted altogether. Before any of these three procedures can be carried out the cell or block of cells must be marked. The method of marking cells varies according to the spreadsheet that is used. One method is to locate the cursor in the top left-most cell of the block, press a special command key, then move the cursor to the bottom right-most cell of the block and press a second special command key. An alternative to repeated marking is to name a cell or block of cells, and manipulate their contents by identifying them by name.

Inserting rows and columns

22 Often during the construction of a worksheet you will find that you have not left enough space to enter all the necessary information. This problem can easily be overcome by inserting blank rows and columns. When this is done, all the information currently on the worksheet moves over to accommodate the new blank rows and columns. For example, if you inserted a column, then all the cell contents to the right would move one column to the right to make room for the new column. If the cells that move hold formulas containing cell references then problems may occur. It is always advisable to check the worksheet's formulas before inserting rows or columns, to ensure that the cell references in those formulas are still correct.

> Enter a column of numbers, not in numerical order, into the cells r1:10c1. Sort the numbers into
>
> (a) ascending order
> (b) descending order
>
> Copy the contents of the cells r1:10c1 to cells r1:10c2. Move the contents of cells r1:10c1 to cells r1:10c3. Delete the contents of cells r1:10c1.
> Insert a column of cells between the first and second columns.
> Insert two rows of cells between the first and second rows.

Graphics facilities

23 Spreadsheets often have graphics facilities permitting a variety of graphs to be drawn using the data available on a worksheet. A graph is a picture that represents the relationship between two sets of numbers. Since a worksheet can have sets of numbers arranged in rows or columns it makes an ideal source of data for plotting a graph. The types of graphs available include:

- line graphs
- bar charts
- histograms
- pie charts
- scatter graphs

24 Computer graphics come in two forms. Text Graphics and High Resolution Graphics which we shall discuss when we consider graphics packages.

> If your spreadsheet offers a graphics facility, read the manual and draw as many different types of graph as are offered.

Formatting

25 One of the requirements of a worksheet is that it displays its information in a neat, ordered and well-presented manner. To achieve this a number of formatting options are available, which can be applied to a single cell or to the worksheet as a whole.

Column widths

The default column width may be too small or too large to accommodate its contents. For example, a column width of 10 characters would be unnecessarily wide to contain a single character. Column widths can be altered to suit the cell content.

Justification

Text and numbers can be arranged within a cell so that they are left-justified, right-justified or centred.

Number formats

Numbers can appear as whole numbers or decimal numbers to any desired number of decimal places. They can also appear in scientific notation.

Cell locking and unlocking

The contents of any particular cell can be locked, preventing its contents from being changed. This feature is especially useful if the worksheet is being manipulated to find the effect of different values of some of its data, and will ensure that cells are not changed by accident. Any locked cell can be unlocked, after which its contents can be changed.

Titles

Because only a small portion of the entire worksheet is visible at any one time, it is often desired to range around the sheet to view different parts of it. When you do this, row and column labels that you may have on the worksheet could move off the screen preventing you from knowing what the data you see refers to. The titles option allows you to fix a number of rows at the top of the screen which will remain on the screen as you range through the worksheet. Any labels that you place in a titled area will then remain visible as you range around the worksheet.

Character attributes

If you require a copy of the worksheet to be printed, a number of character attributes are available to allow certain parts of the printout to be emphasised. These include:

- boldface
- underline
- enhanced characters

How many of the formatting facilities does your spreadsheet offer? Does it offer any that are not listed here?

Saving, loading and printing a worksheet

26 A worksheet can be saved to the disk as a file under a given name, so that at a later time it can be re-loaded into memory by identifying its given file name. To prevent unauthorised access to the information on the sheet, many spreadsheets permit passwords. Once a password has been attached to a worksheet, it cannot be loaded without knowing the password.

Worksheets can be printed and will appear as they do on the screen. If a worksheet is too wide to be accommodated on the width of your printer it may be possible to print in compressed mode in which case all the characters are compressed to allow the width of the paper to accommodate the width of the worksheet.

How do you save a worksheet with your spreadsheet? How do you load and how do you print a worksheet?

On-line help

27 When using a spreadsheet you may need to refer to the manual to find out how to perform a particular task. Many spreadsheets provide an on-line HELP facility in addition to the manual, which can be accessed as you use the spreadsheet to avoid constant recourse to the paper manual.

Does your spreadsheet have an on-line HELP facility? Do you know how to access it?

Data managers

28 Data managers may be either of the following general types;

- file managers
- database manager systems (DBMS)

File managers

29 A file manager is a program that stores and manipulates information held in a file. It will permit the file to be created by defining the

form of the contents of each record and then permitting records to be entered into the file. At a later time it will then permit access to the file for updates or queries such as changing records or finding particular records. The file manager will only handle a single file at a time and typical applications are simple examples of lists of names and addresses or lists of recipes.

More complex applications, however, require more than one file to be handled at the same time. For example, an order-invoicing application will require both a customer file and a stock file to be handled simultaneously. Also, many files are required by more than one system. For example, a customer file may be needed by both the accounts package and the order-invoicing package. The file manager, handling only one file at a time is not suitable for these more complex situations so a database management system would have to be employed.

Database management system

30 A database management system (DBMS) is a program that stores and manipulates information held in a database. More than one file can be accessed at the same time so the data stored in one file can be used in combination with that of another. The advantages of this system over a simple file manager are that duplication of information is unnecessary and updates need only be done once.

> Before you read any further, make sure that you remember how a file is constructed. What is a field? What is a record? What is a file?

Database managers

31 A database is a collection of files, each consisting of a collection of records which in turn is made up of a number of fields. A database manager permits the creation of files and the subsequent manipulation of those files.

Screen display

32 A typical screen display consists of an area to display a record from a file and a status line. The status line describes the name of the file

```
  Name : Dr DJ Booth

  Address :  Department of Computer Studies & Mathematics
             The Polytechnic
             Queensgate
             Huddersfield, W Yorks

  Post Code : HD1 3DH    Tel : 0484 22288   Fax 0484 516151

Status : File Name : ADDRESS                  Record Number 1

COMMAND LIST 1: Load    Save    Print    Sort    Search    Goto
```

currently being viewed and the record number of the specific record being viewed. In addition the screen may display a list of the commands that are available for use when manipulating the database.

File creation

33 A file consists of a collection of records similar in principle to a card index. Each record in a file is identical in form but different in content. To create a file the user must first define the record structure. This is done in a **data dictionary**.

Data dictionary

34 A data dictionary lists the name, type and length of each **field** in a record.

Field Number	Field Name	Field Type	Field Length
1	Name	Alphanumeric	25
2	Adcress-1	Alphanumeric	45
3	Adcress-2	Alphanumeric	45
4	Adcress-3	Alphanumeric	45
5	Adcress-4	Alphanumeric	45
6	Post-Code	Alphanumeric	8
7	Telephone	Numeric	10
8	Fax-Number	Numeric	10

The screen display shows a data dictionary with eight fields defined. The first six are alphanumeric which means that they can contain any character from the keyboard. The seventh and eighth fields are both numeric and can only contain numbers. The lengths of the fields are maximum lengths: they must always be long enough to contain the necessary information, although the contents of a field need not fill all the available space.

Screen creation

Having defined the data dictionary, the data manager will permit a screen to be designed to provide the most attractive layout for each record. For example, to computerise a company's manual invoicing system the screen should be designed to look similar to the actual invoice, rather than just have the fields listed one under another.

Passwords

A password can be attached to any file to prevent unauthorised access to the information it contains.

> If your data manager allows you to define a screen, find out how this is done. Does your data manager permit passwords?

Entering data

35 Having defined the data dictionary and the screen for a particular file you will have a complete template for every record. Now, all that is needed is to fill the file with records by entering data into each record in turn. Do this field by field until the record is complete, before moving on to the next record.

Often data required for one file is already contained in another file. For example, a customer's name and address will be needed for both an invoice and a despatch note. To avoid having to type data into a record that is already in another file, some data managers employ lookups.

Lookups

A lookup is a means of linking two files together and transferring data from one to the other. For example, a file of customers, each with a customer number, can be looked up from a second file of invoices so that when you type in the customer's number on the invoice, their name and address will automatically be copied onto the invoice.

> Set up a name and address file similar to the one previously displayed. This will involve defining the data dictionary, defining the screen and then entering records into the file.
>
> When you are familiar with this process look at the data manager manual to see if it is a file manager or a database manager. If it is a database manager, read the information on lookups.

Adding, updating and deleting records

36 Existing records can be added to by entering new records. They can also be amended or updated by viewing them and changing appropriate field contents. Unwanted records and whole files can also be deleted.

> When you have created your name and address file, make sure that you know how to enter additional records, update those records and delete records from the file.

Manipulating a database

37 Information held in a database can be manipulated in a variety of ways.

Sorting

When records are entered into a file stored on a tape they are said to be in **sequential order**, i.e. they are stored in the sequence in which they were entered into the computer. Often records are required in a different sequence from that in which they were entered. For example, a file of invoices may be required in the order of customer account number or in the order of the date at which their payment becomes due. The problem then is in re-sorting them into the desired order.

Within a file a record can be identified by a selected field within each record. This is called the **key** of the record and the only restriction imposed on the key is that all records have key fields with unique entries. For example, the field containing the record number could be the key as no two records should have the same number. Using this means of identifying a record within a file, all the records can be re-sorted into the desired order. The end result of a sort is a new file with the records physically rearranged into the desired order.

An alternative method of sorting can be employed if the file is stored on a disk. If the records are required to be sorted against a particular field, such as customer names in alphabetical order, then an index file is created that contains the values of the key field in the order that is desired. When the file is displayed it can then be sorted by reference to this index file and will appear in the required order. This sorting process differs from the key sort in that no new file is created—the coupling of the file with the index file merely gives the appearance that the records have been rearranged.

> Find out how key fields are defined in your data manager. Make the first field (Name) in your name and address file into a key field. Then sort the records on that field so that they can be viewed in alphabetical order.

Searching

A file can be searched for records that satisfy certain conditions. For example, all those invoices that were issued over 30 days ago.

GoTo

It is possible to **goto** any particular record in the file and display it on the screen.

Scroll

All the records in a file can be scrolled through by displaying them one after another automatically. When the record being looked for appears then the scroll can be turned off.

Relations

A new file can be created from two existing files by establishing a link and defining a relationship between the existing files. The new file will then contain records created from those records in the two existing files that satisfy the relationship. The link is made by identifying corresponding fields in the two files. Information from the two existing files can then be compared and combined according to a number of different relation types. For example, by using the relation type **intersect**, a record will be placed in the new file for every match between the link fields.

Windows and linking

38 By dividing the monitor screen into a number of different windows, records from more than one file can be viewed at the same time. By linking files, information entered into one file can affect the information content of other files.

Printing and report generation

39 Files can be printed record by record. Reports can also be generated and sent to the printer. A report generator will take information from records in the file and produce an analysis of the information according to the criterion given. For example, from a file of invoices, it can list the values of all the invoices and their final totals. In line with desires for neat presentation of reports, report generators can also permit headers, footers and various format facilities to allow information to be arranged on the report as you wish it.

Copying, saving, loading and passwords

Files can be copied, saved, loaded and password protected.

On-line help facility

40 Like all quality software the data manager provides an on-line HELP facility to avoid constant recourse to the paper manual when in difficulties.

> Read the manual to your data manager and find out whether it offers all of these facilities. Make sure that you know how they are accomplished and how you access your on-line HELP if it is available.

Graphics packages

41 It has been said that 'a picture is worth a thousand words' and there is no better way to display general information than to draw a picture. Information you wish to convey may range from the relationships between two sets of data to the spiritual feeling of a landscape and it is for this reason that graphics packages exist.

There are two basic types of graphics available on a computer,

- text graphics
- high resolution graphics

Text graphics

42 When a computer monitor screen displays text the screen is divided into blocks, each block being capable of displaying a single character. Most screens can display 25 rows of text, each row containing a fixed number of characters. These blocks are called text **pixels** and if you look closely at the screen you will see that each text pixel is comprised of an array of dots. Every character is then formed by a specific arrangement of highlighted dots.

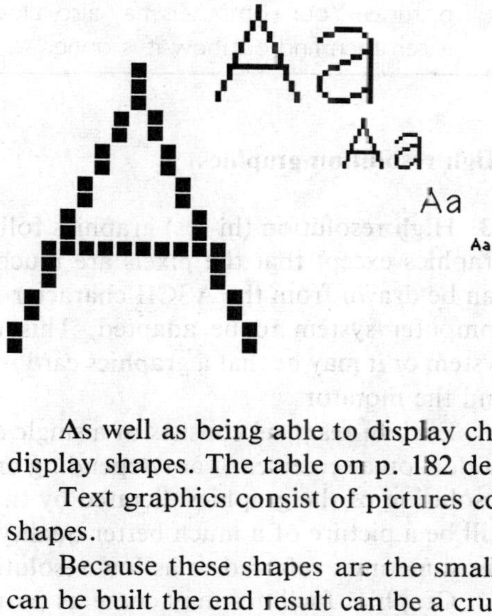

As well as being able to display characters, the computer can also display shapes. The table on p. 182 describes these shapes.

Text graphics consist of pictures composed from this collection of shapes.

Because these shapes are the smallest units from which a picture can be built the end result can be a crude drawing, but the quality can be improved by using high resolution graphics.

ASCII Graphic Character Codes

Character	Code	Character	Code	Character	Code
░	176	└	192	╨	208
▒	177	┴	193	╤	209
▓	178	┬	194	╥	210
│	179	├	195	╙	211
┤	180	─	196	╘	212
╡	181	┼	197	╒	213
╢	182	╞	198	╓	214
╖	183	╟	199	╫	215
╕	184	╚	200	╪	216
╣	185	╔	201	┘	217
║	186	╩	202	┌	218
╗	187	╦	203	█	219
╝	188	╠	204	▄	220
╜	189	═	205	▌	221
╛	190	╬	206	▐	222
┐	191	╧	207	▀	223

Find out how to put your computer into text graphics mode. When you can understand this procedure find out how to draw pictures. Your computer may also allow you to generate sounds. If it can then find out how it is done.

High resolution graphics

43 High resolution (hi-res) graphics follow the same principles as text graphics except that the pixels are much smaller. While text graphics can be drawn from the ASCII character set, hi-res graphics require the computer system to be adapted. This may be part of the standard system or it may be that a graphics card is required to interface the CPU and the monitor.

Each hi-res pixel consists of a single dot on the screen. The number of dots on a screen can vary depending on the size of the screen and the resolution of the graphics dictated by the graphics card, but the result will be a picture of a much better quality and definition. Text graphics are sometimes referred to as low resolution (lo-res) graphics.

Graphics facilities may come as part of another facility such as a spreadsheet or database or as stand-alone packages.

> If your computer offers high resolution graphics, find out how to put it into hi-res graphics mode and learn how to draw pictures. A few simple commands will allow you to do this.

Graphics offered by spreadsheets and databases

44 Because spreadsheets and databases are used to store data in a regular form—entries in rows and columns or filed in a number of records—they make ideal sources of data for drawing graphs.

- Line graphs
- Bar charts
- Scatter graphs
- Pie charts
- Titles and annotation
- Grid For accurate drawings such as building plans a grid is supplied against which lines and shapes can be drawn. The grid may also be supplied with a **ruler** to help maintain accuracy.
- Copy, drag and delete Sections of a picture can be copied to another part of the picture or deleted altogether. If you are using a mouse to input the drawing on the screen a shape can be moved from one part of the picture to another by dragging it.
- Cut and paste Another variant of copying and deleting can be accomplished by cut and paste. Here a selected component of the picture is cut which takes it off the screen and saves it in another part of memory—sometimes referred to as a **clipboard**. The contents of the clipboard can then be pasted onto another part of the picture or even onto another picture.
- Reduce and expand Selected parts of the picture can be enlarged or reduced in size as desired.
- Rotate If you require a printed copy of the picture that is too wide for the paper in the printer, you can rotate the picture through 90 degrees to print it so that it fits onto the paper. Not only can shapes be rotated but their **mirror images** can sometimes be obtained.

Stand-alone graphics packages

45 The advantages of a stand-alone graphics package lie in its comprehensive ability to **draw** general shapes that do not rely on data for their generation. The screen display will have an area reserved for drawing and a **prompt area** that displays either **commands** or graphic **options** available. Like a spreadsheet the screen only displays a portion of the area onto which pictures can be drawn so the package will provide a means of moving around the drawing board.

- **Drawing** When you draw a picture using a pencil and a piece of paper you use a number of aids to help you, such as rulers, erasers, colours, shading and compasses. Graphics packages also provide these facilities by issuing the appropriate commands
- *Lines and boxes* Straight lines can be drawn between any two points on the screen as can rectangular boxes. Boxes may have sharp or rounded corners, and the thickness of the lines can be varied between a number of options.
- *Fill* The boxes and closed shapes can be filled with a pattern selected from a pallette of patterns and, if you have a colour monitor, colours are available as well.
- *Freehand lines* Depending on the method used by the computer, you may also be able to draw freehand lines and shapes. These will be possible, for example, if you are using a mouse or a graphics tablet.

> Drawing pictures with a graphics package is fun. Make sure you appreciate all the facilities that your graphics package offers. Check the ones listed here first and then find out if your package offers additional features. Look out for the zoom facility which allows you to draw in the fine detail.

- **Zoom** When you draw a picture the individual pixels are too small to be plotted individually. To enable very fine detail to be drawn in, a zoom feature permits you to zoom into a portion of the picture which is displayed magnified, with the individual pixel represented as small rectangles within the zoomed area.

Communications packages

46 A communications package is a computer program designed to control communication between two computers. The computer being communicated to is called the **host** computer. Before two computers communicate with each other they must:

- recognise each other
- agree how to transfer data

Recognise each other

47 To allow a computer to communicate with another computer it must be given a communication profile. This communication profile describes the computer in terms that the host computer can understand and recognise. The profile will contain details of physical information dealing with the transmission of data such as the type of modem used, the type of terminal that the communicating computer will emulate and the speed at which data will be transmitted i.e. the baud rate.

- **Emulation** To emulate means to copy behaviour. The communicating computer must behave like a terminal to the host computer and this is known as **terminal emulation**. Various types of terminal can be emulated but the most common is the **dumb terminal,** from which all computers can accept information.

What is a dumb terminal?

Agree how to transfer data

48 Once a computer is identifiable by its communication profile it must establish a communication protocol with the host computer. The protocol has two functions,

- handshaking
- line discipline

Handshaking Handshaking is the name given to establishing the physical connection and agreeing the type of protocol to observe between two computers to enable them to communicate.

Line discipline Line discipline controls the actual transmission, and reception of data. It defines how characters and words start and end and it handles errors in transmission by detecting and correcting them.

There is a similarity between computers establishing protocols with a handshake and two people meeting. They shake hands, they start to talk and as the conversation develops they establish certain protocols. Can you describe this process showing the similarities between people communicating and computers communicating?

Types of protocol

49 A protocol is an agreed set of rules between a transmitter and a receiver of data that controls the flow of data from one to the other. Before data transfer can take place an agreed protocol has to be established between the transmitter and the receiver. By using the established protocol the transmitter can send data knowing that the receiver is in a state to receive it. There are two series of protocols, the X-series which control digital transmission and the V-series which control analogue transmission. Numerous different X-series protocols are in use but they are only of two basic types:

Text protocols A text protocol allows information to be transmitted in characters. Examples of such protocols are **XON/XOFF** which uses the signal XON to start transmitting and XOFF to stop.

Binary Protocols A binary protocol transmits data as a stream of bits. Examples of such protocols are **Xmodem** and **Kermit**. Xmodem is generally used between micros whereas Kermit can be used to link micros to larger machines.

Dial, answer and hanging up

50 For two computers to communicate with each other they must be connected by a communication channel. When communication is not taking place then this channel is **closed**. To open the channel the terminal will **dial** the telephone number of the host computer which can be arranged to automatically **answer** the phone and establish contact. When the communication is complete the communication channel is then closed by hanging up.

Communication package features

51 Once communication has been established a number of features are available within a communications package to assist in the transmission of information.

Autodialling The communicating computer can be made to automatically dial the host computer and the host computer can be made to automatically answer and establish the link.

Duplex The two computers can be set to either half or full duplex mode.

Downloading and uploading Downloading allows data to be sent directly from a media file and uploading allows data received to be immediately stored in a media file or transmitted to a printer.

Capture buffers A data **buffer** is provided so that any information received can be viewed and edited before being stored in a media file. This permits only required data to be saved.

Encryption The security of data is an ever present problem, especially if it is being transmitted via a microwave radio signal. Many communication packages provide an encryption facility to code and de-code information as it is sent and received. Anyone intercepting such information would be presented with a garbled message that could not be deciphered without the encryption key.

> Consider the follow ng code that reverses the order of the letters in the alphabet:
>
> Letter: A B C D E F . . . X Y Z
> Code : Z Y X W V U . . . C B A
>
> Write a program that will accept alphabetic input and print out the coded form.

Expert systems

52 An expert system is a computer program that displays the expertise of an expert.

Computers can be made to perform many of the tasks associated with an intelligent human mind. For this reason many people believe that computers can be designed to possess what we think of as 'intelligence'. Human intelligence is not an easy attribute to define but the ability to reason and make decisions must come within its definition. As a result, the first developments in **artificial intelligence** or computer intelligence concerned such reasoning and decision-making. This is the realm of expert systems.

Artificial intelligence and expertise

53 An expert is someone who has a special knowledge and who, using that special knowledge, can make decisions that a person not possessing such knowledge could not make. For example, a medical doctor has a special knowledge of medicine and using this special knowledge could decide to take out your appendix. A lawyer has a special knowledge of the law and can plead in court on your behalf.

54 We all use our cwn special knowledge and expertise to make decisions that affect our lives, and developments in artificial intelligence have asked the questions:

- how do we make decisions?
- how can we instruct a computer to make those decisions?

How do we make decisions? We make decisions by using rules together with facts. For example, if we take the **rule** IF today is Sunday THEN we do not go to work, and the **fact** today is Sunday, then we apply the fact to the rule and make the **decision** not to go to work.

How can we instruct a computer to make decisions? This simple example displays the essence of how an expert system works. Every expert system has three parts:

- **A knowledge base** This is similar to a database except that it contains rules.

- **An inference engine** This applies facts to the rules of the knowledge base and infers decisions.
- **A user interface** The user interface permits a user to interact with the expert system to enter facts that permit the expert system to make decisions.

Expert system tool

55 An expert system tool is a computer program that permits the user to create and use an expert system. The program provides the **inference engine** and the **user interface**. The user must then provide the **knowledge base** with the rules.

Rules Any area of expertise that involves decision making can, in theory, be reduced to a set of rules of the form **IF** condition **THEN** conclusion.

Rules may be **well defined** rules, like those of the highway code, or they may be instinctive, when a decision is made without consciously applying a rule.

While well defined rules can be entered into a knowledge base directly in their IF ... THEN ... form, instinctive rules have to be derived from examples of what you would do in certain situations.

When the knowledge base has been constructed the expert system is complete and ready for use. Unlike a more conventional program which follows a specific sequence of instructions, an expert system will ask questions. The responses by the user to these questions give **truth values** to the **conditions** that are embodied in the rules. The expert system then reacts to the truth values and continues to ask questions until it has sufficient information to produce a decision.

Integrated software

56 Integrated software is a collection of programs, called a **suite of programs** that share the same data in a similar way to spreadsheets. We learnt that some spreadsheets could not only handle the data on a worksheet, but also use that data to construct graphs. We shall look at three types of integrated software;

- Integrated suite of programs
- Integrated operating environment
- Utility multi-programming

Integrated suite of programs

The SMART Software Suite, Open Access and Symphony are three packages of software that combine word processing, spreadsheet and data management in one integrated whole. When using this software only one application is being used at any time but any data within the application can be used by any of the other applications. This has the obvious advantage that data need not be duplicated, thereby saving not only storage space but also user time in that data is not required to be entered into the system.

Integrated operating environment

An integrated operating environment uses a **window manager** that permits independent applications from different manufacturers to work together in an integrated manner.

Utility multi-programming

Multi-programming is the apparent simultaneous execution of more than one program. It is apparent because what is actually happening is that each program is being executed on a time-sharing basis by a single CPU. It appears to be simultaneous because the time slices are so small. An example of this is the program SideKick which is a utility program that can be used as a calculator, a clock, a diary or as a notepad. This program is designed to be used concurrently with any other application and operates in the background. A single keystroke will bring it to the foreground to permit it to be manipulated.

Multi-user software

57 Some applications software packages are designed to be used by more than one user at the same time. A typical situation is a PC with additional terminals or two or more PC's on a network accessing the same software. With multi-user software, file management requires special consideration to prevent confusion.

If two people access the same file at the same time, then any amendments to the file by one user could be confused with those of the other user. To prevent this a system of locking is used so that when a file is accessed by two users, the first person accessing the file **locks out** the second user. This means that the second user may be able to view the file but will not be able to amend it in any way. In this way updating a file can only be done by one person at a time.

Sometimes file locking is too restrictive and locking a whole database file may negate the whole purpose of multi-using. Instead, **record locking** is employed so that only individual records are locked at any one time.

Summary

The utilities offered by a computer's operating system are inadequate to meet the demands made of data management. For this reason a whole industry has grown that writes and markets applications software packages. These packages can be bespoke designed, which is an expensive option, or bought off-the-shelf. Off-the shelf packages are either specific or general: specific packages will perform a specific task like financial analysis, or booking holidays, while a general package offers features that permit a number of different applications to be generated from the same package. The general packages considered are word processors, spreadsheets, data managers, graphics packages, communication packages and expert systems.

A word processor is a text editor with a range of editing, formatting and document handling facilities.

An electronic spreadsheet is an arrangement of cells in regular rows and columns. Each cell is capable of holding text, numbers or formulas. By using formulas the contents of one cell can be made to be dependent on the contents of other cells. Recalculation over a worksheet permits 'what if ...' projections to be made.

There are two kinds of data manager. The file manager only allows one file to be resident in memory at a time which restricts the possible uses of such a system. A database management system allows many files to be resident in memory simultaneously, thereby allowing interaction between different files in the database. The DBMS package will have facilities to create and manipulate files.

Graphics can be high or low resolution and are sometimes offered by spreadsheets or data managers. Stand alone graphics packages have facilities to enable very intricate pictures to be constructed.

A communications package is a facility that makes the setting up of a communications link between two computers relatively straightforward. Like all such general applications packages, it can be used to permit connections to be made at any time by a user who has no knowledge of the finer intricacies of communications. In effect, the communications package sets up the link and all the user has to do is request the link to be turned on.

Expert systems are the most widely used aspect of artificial intelligence and are proving to be a valuable application for decision-making in the absence of a resident expert. Expert systems applications can be generated by using an expert system tool.

Many application generators are integrated suites of software that will enable interactions between their component parts, for example between the spreadsheet and the database. Other facilities offered are the integrated operating environments that permit different proprietary software to be used in an integrated environment. Integration has the advantage of avoiding the duplication of data.

Multi-programming and multi-user software are becoming more widely used as more and more companies recognise the advantages of relatively cheap microcomputer facilities.

Key points

Bespoke application packages, off-the-shelf application packages, specific application packages, accounting systems, payroll packages, financial analysis systems, stock control systems, estate agents, travel agents, general application packages, word processors, spreadsheets, data managers, file managers, database management system, graphics packages, text graphics, high resolution graphics, graphics offered by spreadsheets and data managers, stand-alone graphics packages, communications packages, expert systems, artificial intelligence and expert systems, expert system tools, integrated software, multi-user software.

Self assessment questions

1 Distinguish between utility programs and application packages. (1)
2 List the two categories of application packages. (1).
3 What does the word bespoke mean? (2)
4 What is a bespoke application package? (2)
5 List the two categories of off-the-shelf application packages. (4)
6 What is a specific application package? (4)
7 List four different types of specific application package. (4)
8 Name two types of company that would use a specific application package. (4)
9 Why were general application packages developed? (5)
10 List six forms of general application package. (5)
11 What is a word processor? (6)
12 What would a status line contain on a word processor screen display? (7)
13 How do you move around a word processor document? (8, 9)
14 What is meant by 'windowing' with a word processor? (10)
15 List nine facilities offered by most word processing packages. (11)
16 Distinguish between inserting and overwriting into a word processor document. (11)
17 What is meant by merging? (11)
18 What does formatting a document involve? (11)
19 What is on-line HELP? (11)
20 What is a spreadsheet? (12)
21 What are the advantages of an electronic spreadsheet? (12)
22 What is a worksheet? (13)
23 What, in a spreadsheet, is a cell? (14)
24 What three types of input can be put into a cell? (16)
25 What is spillover? (16)
26 Name three typical in-built functions you would expect with a spreadsheet. (16)
27 What is a cell address? (17)
28 Distinguish between relative and absolute cell addresses. (18)
29 What is a circular reference? (19)
30 What is meant by marking a block of cells? (21)
31 What facilities does formatting offer in a spreadsheet? (25)
32 List the two different forms of data manager. (28)
33 What is a file manager? (29)
34 What does DBMS stand for? (30)
35 What is a database management system? (30, 31)
36 What is a data dictionary? (33, 34)
37 What is meant by a record template? (33)
38 What is a lookup? (35)
39 What is a key field? (39)
40 What is an index file? (37)
41 List one type of relationship that can be used to create a new file from two existing files. (37)
42 What is a report? (39)
43 Distinguish between text and high resolution graphics. (41–43)
44 What is a pixel? (42, 43)
45 Why do some spreadsheets and databases offer graphics facilities? (44)
46 List nine features that could be offered by a stand-alone graphics package. (45)
47 What is a communications package? (46)
48 What two sets of conditions must be met before two computers can talk to each other? (46)
49 What is a communication profile? (47)
50 What is the baud rate? (47)
51 What is meant by terminal emulation? (47)
52 What is handshaking? (48)

53 What does line discipline control? (48)
54 What is the difference between a text protocol and a binary protocol? (49)
55 List five features that could be offered by a communications package. (51)
56 What is an expert system? (52)
57 List the three components of an expert system. (54)
58 What is an expert system tool? (55)
59 List three different categories of integrated software. (56)
60 What is an integrated suite of programs? (56)
61 What is an integrated operating environment? (56)
62 What is meant by utility multi-tasking? (56)
63 What is meant by locking in a multi-user system. (57)
64 Name the two levels at which locking can occur in a multi-user database. (57)
65 Why is locking necessary? (57)

Exercises

1 A single computer can be used for many different applications. Which part must be different for each application?

The central processor
The operating system
The output device
The software

2 A new accounts package for small businesses is to be released by a software house. The package is designed to perform the following tasks:

- print out a bill for each order sent out by the business.
- print out a payment slip to go with all bills paid by the business.
- record the details of all the goods bought and sold by the business.
- keep a record of all stock held, and update this record when goods are sold or received.
- keep and update the financial records of the business, e.g. how much money is in the bank, how much is owed to the business, how much is owed by the business, profits, losses etc.

(a) Name four essential items of hardware that would be required to run this sort of package.

(b) There are both advantages and disadvantages for small businesses in buying packages like this accounts package. Name two advantages and two disadvantages, to a small business, of buying a ready made package from a software house, rather than commissioning one for its particular needs.

(c) The programmers employed by the software house have written a user manual to be supplied with the package. Describe three sections that should be included in this user manual and explain the benefit that the user might gain from each of these.

(d) The programmers have also written the detailed program documentation which is kept by the software house. Describe three sections of this documentation and explain why they are included.

3 A file is an organised collection of .... records. Which of the following words below completes this definition?

Alphabetic
Alphanumeric
Numeric
Related

4 The following screen display is produced when the manager of a company loads an integrated office software package.

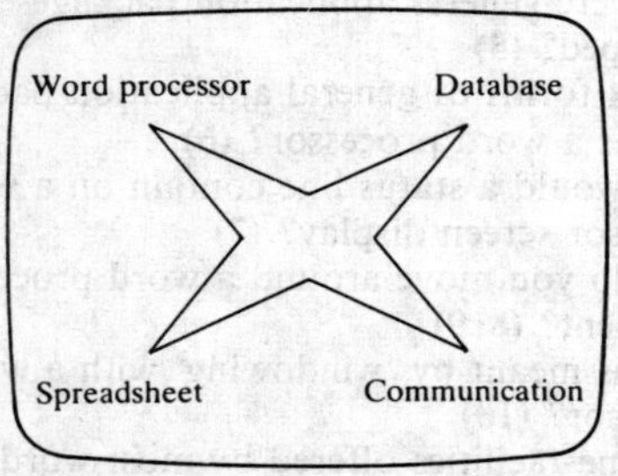

Which of these four should be selected in order to predict the possible profit of the company in three months time?

5 (a) (i) What is a database?
(ii) Describe one application of a database.

(b) (i) What is a computer network?
(ii) Describe one application which would make use of a network.

(c) (i) What is CAD?
(ii) Describe one application which would use CAD.

(d) (i) What is office automation?
(ii) Describe the effects that office automation might have on a company.

6 A large company is soon to buy a network of microcomputers for use in general office work.

(a) Draw a diagram to show the links between the various devices you would expect to be attached to the network.

(b) (i) Describe three facilities you would expect to be available in word processing software.
(ii) How would the use of word processing software change the work carried out by typists?
(iii) Suggest two advantages to the public of introducing word processing in commercial organisations.

(c) Name two other types of software that would be useful in an office and give an example of the use of each.

(d) What new security problems would you expect to encounter as a result of the introduction of this network? Explain how you would deal with them.

7 A disc jockey with a collection of about two thousand albums, wishes to index them using a computer. He needs to be able to find albums with a particular title, performed by a particular artist or written by a particular composer.

(a) His alternatives are either to buy an existing software package, or to write software specially.
(i) Give two advantages of buying an existing package.
(ii) Give two advantages of buying specially written software.

(b) If the disc jockey were to buy a package, what type of computer software package would be most suitable?

Information	Type	Size
Title	String	50 Characters
Price	Numeric	5 Characters

(c) What type of backing store should he buy for this application?

(d) When planning the record structure, a table such as the one shown on this page should be completed. Suggest four more items that might be required.

(e) For the problem outlined above, he would probably need to use some key fields.
(i) What is meant by a key field?
(ii) What key fields would be required for this application.

(f) Describe a suitable non-computer system for this application.

(g) A friend of yours has a hundred albums to index similarly, and does not own a computer. Would your advice be to buy and use a computer, or to use the method you have described in part (f)? Give reasons for your answer.

8 A school keeps a file on its pupils. Some of the information stored on each pupil is as follows:

Pupil Number	Name	Date of Birth	Age
123	Allen, R.	21.12.76	11
073	Brown, P. R.	10.10.74	13
009	Clarke, R. V.	28.06.72	15

(a) State which field is the key field.

(b) What is data validation?

(c) How can age be validated.

(d) Suggest an extra field that could be added, giving one reason for your choice.

9 (a) A wide range of information can be accessed by users from viewdata systems such as Prestel. The following diagram shows the stages necessary for a user to access a particular page of information. From the following list, choose suitable statements for the stages marked A–F on the flowchart on p. 194.

enter page number
enter password
dial computer
load communications software
download software
does the page exist?
exit code selected?
copy page
enter a key word

(b) Name the main charges that would be made for accessing information from Prestel. Do not include in your answer the cost of any equipment or software.

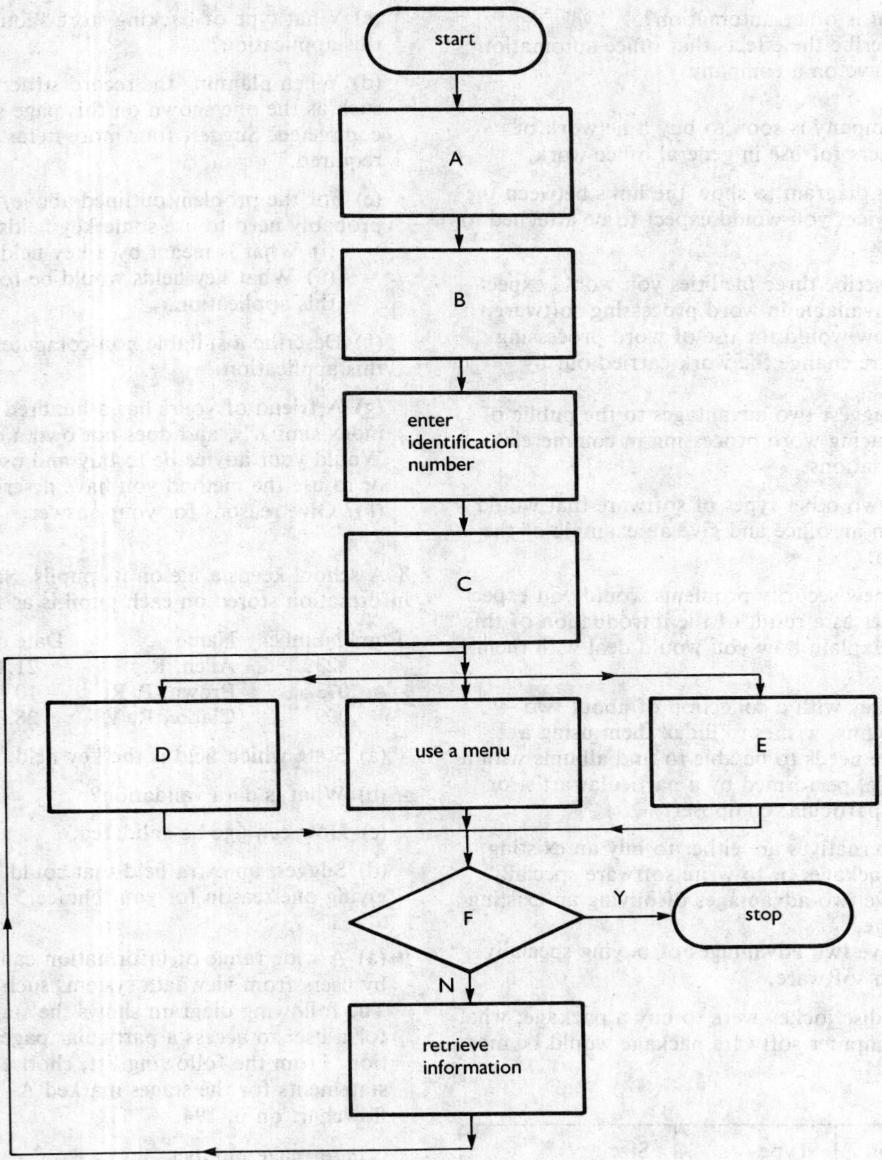
start
A
B
enter identification number
C
D
use a menu
E
F
Y
stop
N
retrieve information

Section three

1 What is the problem?

Objectives

1 To define what is meant by an information system
2 To understand the role of the systems analyst
3 To appreciate the need for close communication between all parties involved in the development process to achieve the stated aims of the information system.

Computerising a manual system

1 Throughout our daily life situations are handled manually that are capable of being controlled by a computer. The pelican crossing that we discussed in Section 1 is a typical example of an automated system, and one which when controlled manually would be very costly and, on certain roads, even dangerous.

2 There are many business situations where the introduction of a computer would be of great benefit, especially where a particular task is performed repetitively and where speed and accuracy are essential. Other situations may require frequent access to stored information which by a manual system would be slow and labour intensive. In addition, computerising complicated mathematical processes that were required would not only speed up the process but also guarantee accuracy.

Describe three other manual systems that have been computerised to produce a relatively cheap alternative to the manual system.
Can you think of any computerised systems that have no manual equivalent?
List three computerised systems that are:

(a) faster
(b) cheaper
(c) more accurate

than their manual equivalents.
Can you think of at least one computerised system that would be of little benefit?

3 Whatever manual system is to be computerised the end result must be of benefit to the organisation. The purpose of introducing computerisation is to provide a system that is easier and cheaper to operate, works faster and more accurately and provides more valuable information.

Systems

4 We have already used the word system and shall continue to do so, so we must know exactly what is meant by the word. We define a system as a combination of people, computers and work practices connected together to achieve **a common aim**. For example, a company payroll system consists of the staff employed in the wages office, the computers and computer programs they use and the day-to-day tasks that they perform to ensure that the wages are paid on time each week. All such systems handle information and for this reason they are referred to as information systems. A business or organisation may have a number of information systems. Some of these may interact with each other while others may be stand-alone systems. Regardless of the type of complexity of the information system, it will convert data into information so we must be sure of the distinctions between data and information.

Data and information

5 Data consists of individual numbers and characters that have neither context nor meaning. Information is data within a context and with some meaning. For example, the characters B559UAT have neither context nor meaning. When they are printed onto a car number plate as B 559 UAT they have context and they have meaning—B denotes the year of registration, 559 denotes the car registration number issued against the letters UAT which denote the town where the car was registered.

Data forms the INPUT into an information system and information forms the OUTPUT—information is data PROCESSED to give it context and meaning.

Information system development team

6 Whatever information system is required, its creation requires much planning, not just in writing the computer program and then using it, but in considering its effects on both people and their jobs.

Developing a successful information system requires continual communication between those who will use the new system—the managers and the users—and those who are responsible for creating the system—the analyst, designer and programmers.

With any project three different categories of people are involved.

- the management and users
- the systems analysts and designers
- the programmers

The management and users

7 The project will be initiated by management because they are the people who recognise the need for the information system and will decide exactly what they want from the system and how it will fit into the business. At the other end of the scale are the personnel who will operate the system and whose needs must also be taken into account. If they are currently operating a manual system then the introduction of a computerised system will change their work practices and possibly even their roles within the company.

> Do you think that managers alone can decide which systems need to be computerised or do you think they should consult others? Why?

The systems analysts and designers

8 For a small project the systems analyst and designer may be just one person while a larger one will involve a team of individuals led by a Project Leader. Systems analysts and designers will analyse the problem to be solved and produce a design for the information system that will enable it to be developed by the programmers.

The programmers

9 It is the programmers' responsibility to write the software necessary to meet the systems analyst and designer's specifications.

The role of the systems analyst

10 While the decision to introduce a new information system is made by the management of a company or organisation, its creation and physical installation are the responsibility of the systems analyst.

The systems analyst's task is to ensure that the management's desires are communicated correctly to the programmer and that the programmer produces a program that achieves the management's desires. The manager is the expert in running the department but is usually unable to create the information system required, either through lack of ability or through lack of time. Instead, computer professionals are employed to create the information system that is required and the analyst's job is to create a clear understanding between them.

The system is then subjected to a development process during what is called the information systems life cycle, the period of time starting at its inception by management and running through its use to its eventual removal or redesign.

> Apart from systems analysis skills, what other skills do you think a systems analyst requires?

The information system life cycle

11 We have already seen that the process of solving problems can be described by using the principle of INPUT—PROCESS—OUTPUT.

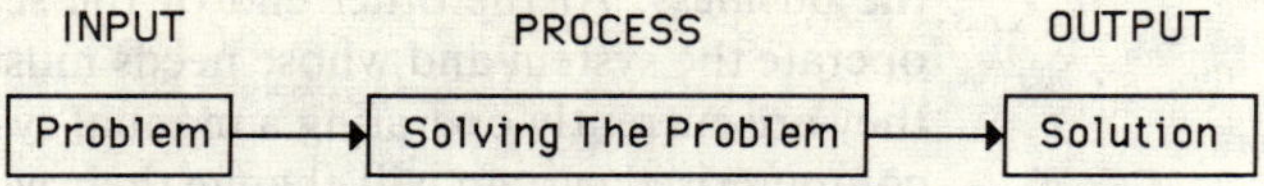

The Information System Life Cycle consists of four parts:

- **Defining and analysing the problem** An analysis of the current manual system, prompted by a problem or a desire to improve efficiency and the quality of the output.
- **Designing the solution** The development of a design of a proposed solution to the problem.
- **Developing the solution** Writing the programs that will convert the design into a working information system.
- **Implementing and maintaining the solution** The installation and consequent use of the new information system. The installed system is maintained by being continually monitored and amended as required until it is either removed or replaced.

In the next four chapters we shall look at each of these aspects in turn.

> Draw a diagram to illustrate how these four parts fit into information system life cycle.

Project documentation

12 During the development of the project, all the tasks performed by the individual members of the team will be documented. The purpose of this is to permit anyone to check the state of the project at any time. Many large projects take months or even years to complete, during which time the personnel involved may change. Anyone newly introduced to the development team must be able to find out exactly what has been done and what remains to be done. Only by maintaining a written record of activities can this be successfully accomplished. With any project a series of documents will be maintained.

- Project Manual details all the steps taken to date in the development of the project.
- System Manual contains all the technical details of the information system.
- Program Manual contains all the details of the work completed by the programmers, alongside the technical details of the programs.
- Operators Manual describes the details of the procedures to be followed during the actual operation of the information system.

- User's Manual a simplified version of the operators manual, designed to be used by those who are likely to want information from the system but who are not involved in operating it.

Who, in the information system development team, do you think should be responsible for writing which manual?

Summary

The purpose of computerising a manual system is to produce a system that is easier and cheaper to operate, works faster and more accurately and provides more valuable information. An information system consists of the hardware, the software and the people and procedures involved in its operation. It is created by a team consisting of the management and end-users, the systems analysts and designers and the programmers. It is the duty of the systems analyst to ensure proper communication between all parties concerned and to make certain that the end result exactly fits the needs and desires of the management.

Every information system has a life cycle. Any identified problem is subjected to analysis, design, development and implementation and maintenance. All information systems are accompanied by the appropriate documentation.

Key points

Computerising a manual system, systems, data and information, information system development team, the management and users, the systems analysts and designers, the programmers, the role of the systems analyst, the information system life cycle, defining and analysing the problem, designing the solution, developing the solution, implementing and maintaining the system, project documentation, project manual, system manual, program manual, operators manual, users manual.

Self assessment questions

1 What is meant by computerising a manual system? (1)
2 List three types of situation that would benefit from a system being computerised. (2)
3 What is the purpose of computerising a manual system? (3)
4 What is meant by the word 'system' in the context of this chapter? (4)
5 Why are information systems so called? (4)
6 What does an information system do? (4)
7 What is the difference between data and information? (5)
8 List three categories of people involved in an information system development team. (6)
9 What is required to develop a successful information system? (6)

10 Describe the role of the managers and users in relation to the development of an information system. (7)
11 Describe the role of the systems analysts and designers in relation to the development of an information system. (7,10)
12 What is the responsibility of the programmer? (8)
13 What is an information system's life cycle? (10,11)
14 List the four parts of an information system life cycle. (11)
15 What happens during the stage of defining and analysing a problem? (11)
16 What is meant by developing the solution? (11)
17 What is meant by maintaining an information system? (11)
18 What is the purpose of project documentation? (12)
19 List five manuals that should accompany every information system. (12)
20 What is the project manual? (12)
21 What is the system manual? (12)
22 What is the program manual (12)
23 What is the operator's manual? (12)
24 What is the user manual? (12)

Exercises

1 In which of the following would be found instructions about how to 'run' a piece of software?

program flowchart
program listing
sales information
user manual

2 Which of the following describes a data capture form?

a document for collecting information
a manual for a disk drive
a network of computers
an error check list

3 For each of the following items state whether its data type is string or numeric.

a town name, e.g. Banbury
the number of words in a sentence, e.g. 11
a car registration number, e.g. B353AXB

4 At which of the following stages in a systems analysis should staff reactions to increased computerisation first be considered?

design
feasibility study
implementation
monitoring

5 A company is considering implementing a computerised stock control system.

(a) Name two activities which are involved in analysing the existing manual system.

(b) Which type of computer personnel is most involved with the investigation of the manual system?

6 A supermarket uses point-of-sale terminals.

(a) In what order should the following steps be carried out at the terminal when an item is being purchased.

look up price
input item code
work out change
input money given

(b) Name two methods of inputting the item code at the terminal.

(c) The record for each item on the computer file contains its price and the number left in stock. What change is made to this record when an item is sold?

7 Give one reason why a flow diagram is often a part of program documentation.

8 Which three of the following items would be found in the user documentation of a word processing package.

what commands to use to carry out functions
how to touch type
how to load the package
examples of screen layout
program listing
how data moves round the CPU

9 A stock control applications package is to be written requiring different types of documentation at different stages of its development.

(a) Explain the need for different types of documentation.

(b) What types of documentation would be produced at the following stages in the development of the stock control package ?

10 Which of the following is essential in a user manual?

a description of subroutines
a list of variables
input and output details
program listing

2 *Defining and analysing the problem*

Objectives

1 To formulate solutions to problems and communicate the solutions in appropriate ways.
2 To explain the need for encoding information into concise, standardised and unambiguous form for computer processing.

Terms of reference

1 It is the responsibility of management to identify the problem that is to be solved and this must then be defined exactly in a document called the Terms Of Reference. The terms of reference describe what the information system is to achieve—the objectives of the project. They will also describe the scope and the constraints of the investigation and the resources that are available to the project team developing the project.

- **The objectives** A description of what the information system is expected to achieve. For example management may be looking for ways to save money so a typical objective would be to reduce the running costs of the wages office by up to 50%.
- **The scope and constraints** A description of how far the investigation is to go, coupled with a description of what is not to be done. For example, if a project were to deal with a stock control system the scope may be restricted to stock control to the exclusion of the invoicing system. The constraint may be to retain a particular procedure in its current form such as location of stock within the warehouse.
- **The resources** Resources will include the personnel available to work on the project as well as the money available for the successful completion of the project.

As soon as the terms of reference are agreed by management they are passed to the systems analyst to permit a **feasibility report** to be prepared.

Library project
Imagine you are the Chief Librarian of a local library and you wish to computerise the loan system from the music section. The music section provided records and cassette tapes for its borrowers as

> well as complete music manuscripts. The main section of the library has already been computerised and book loans are recorded as borrowed by a lender using a bar reader. Write the terms of reference of this project.

The feasibility study

2 As soon as management have produced the terms of reference, the systems analyst sets about a feasibility study to assess the different approaches that can be taken to achieve the objectives laid down in the terms of reference. The systems analyst must assess whether the information system is technically possible on the following criteria. Is the equipment available to perform the tasks required? Is it possible to use that equipment within the existing organisation? Will the operators need any training? The financial aspects must also be considered. Is it going to be cheaper than the old system? If it is going to be expensive, will the benefits gained outweigh the costs involved? Finally the impact of introducing a new information system on the employees must also be considered. Will it cause redundancy? Will it adversely affect the staff? How much disruption of current working practices will it involve?

The feasibility study also concerns itself with a review of what the new system will require. What sort of computer is recommended? What sort of input units are to be used? What sort of output units are required? How will the system be operated and by how many people? This part of the study is not a detailed investigation of the project, but an overview.

When the study is complete a report is given to management who must then decide whether or not to proceed with the project. If they decide to proceed the project leader or systems analyst is given authorisation and a thorough analysis of the system starts.

> **Library project**
> Now imagine that you are a systems analyst brought in by the Chief Librarian to develop the music section's lending system. Write a feasibility report to follow on from the Terms of Reference written earlier.

Sources of information

3 The systems analyst must find out all there is to know about the current system before a new one can be designed. Three primary sources of information are available to them:

- personnel
- written records
- observation

Personnel

4 By interviewing the personnel involved the systems analyst can assess how people view the current system and how they feel about the introduction of a new system. If a large number of personnel are involved then a questionnaire may be used.

Written records

5 Written records describe how the details of the current system operates. Typical records are the style of invoices used, the layout of stock records and the form of payslip currently in use.

Observation

6 Often, talking to people and reading records will not reveal every aspect of a system. By watching the system being operated a systems analyst can learn about working practices, for example, if an order is being given over the telephone, the way the order form is filled out will suggest possible improvements in its design.

When all the information about the old system has been gathered it must be carefully analysed to enable the new system to be designed.

> **Library project**
> Describe how you would gain knowledge from the current lending system in the music section of the library.

Data analysis

7 The new information system—like any other system—will consist of data being INPUT, then PROCESSED and information being OUTPUT. Processing will involve many component stages and the design of the system will involve itself with how the data flows through the processing part of the system. A number of tools are available to the analyst to assist this process.

- systems flowcharts
- decision tables

Systems flowchart

8 A systems flowchart describes graphically the route taken by the data through the system from input to output.

For example, the process of paying a company's wages bill could be described by the simple systems flowchart on p. 207, following where the arrows indicate the direction in which the data flows.

> **Library project**
> Draw a systems flowchart for the library system in the music section of the main library.

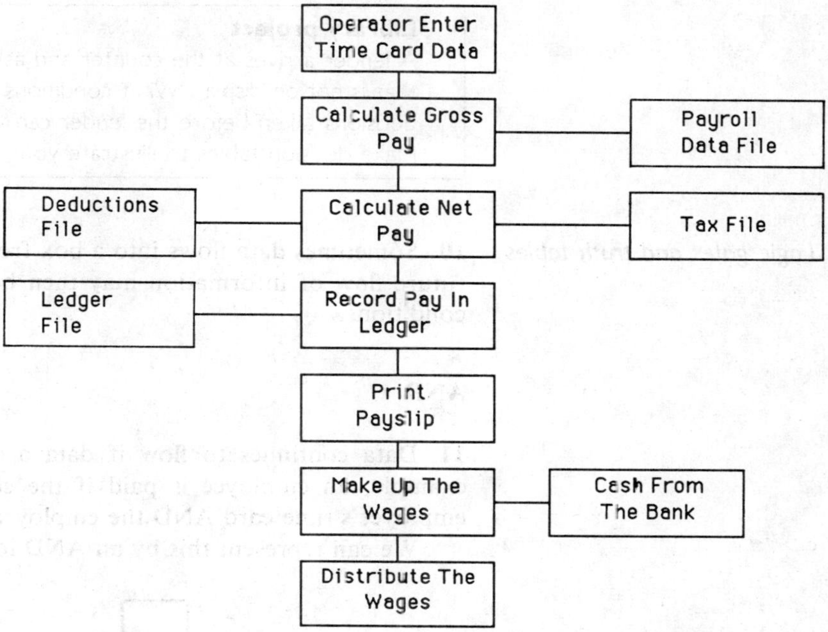

Decision tables

9 A decision table is a means of displaying alternative decisions for different circumstances. A list of conditions and rules are laid out to describe particular courses of action. For example, assume that you wish to know whether or not to use an umbrella.

There are two conditions that must be met in order for an umbrella to be used: first it must be raining and second, it must not be windy or you may damage your umbrella. There are also two rules: to use the umbrella or not to use the umbrella. We can couple these conditions and rules in the following decision table.

CONDITIONS				
It is raining	T	T	F	F
It is windy	T	F	T	F
RULES				
Use umbrella	N	Y	N	N
Do not use umbrella	Y	N	Y	Y

By writing out decision tables such as these, the analyst obtains a clearer picture of how the current system operates and how the new system must behave to achieve its objectives.

> **Library project**
> A lender arrives at the counter and asks to borrow a rare record that is not on display. What conditions must be satisfied and what decisions taken before the lender can walk away with the record? Make decision tables to illustrate your answer

Logic gates and truth tables

10 Sometimes data flows into a box from more than one source. The future flow of information may then be determined by one of three conditions.

AND

11 Data continues to flow if data arrives from both sources. For example, an employee is paid if the computer has a record of the employee's time card AND the employee's tax code.

We can represent this by an AND logic gate as follows.

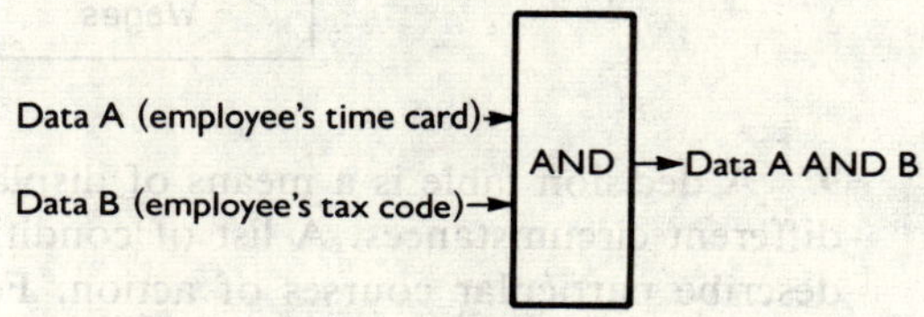

This can also be represented by a **switching circuit** as follows,

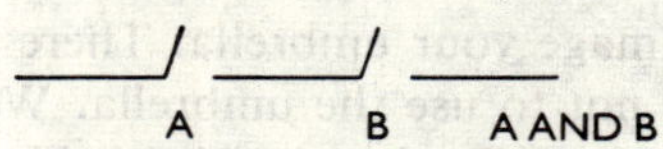

Here data will flow from beginning to end of this circuit only if switches A AND B are ON.

OR

12 Data continues to flow if it comes from either one OR the other source. For example, an employee is either male or female. Either way the employee is paid. We can represent this by an OR logic gate as shown.

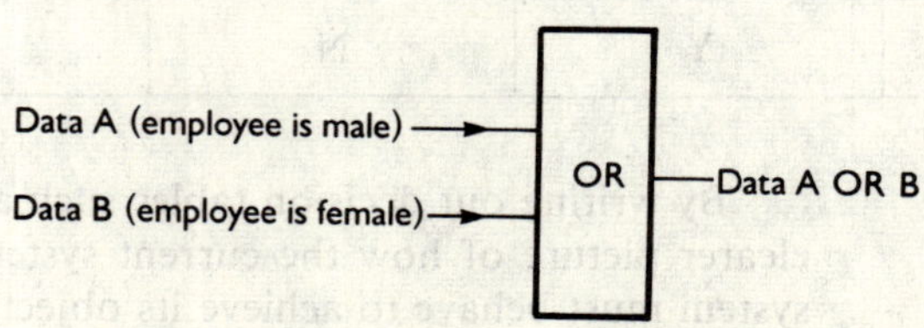

This can also be represented by a switching circuit as shown:

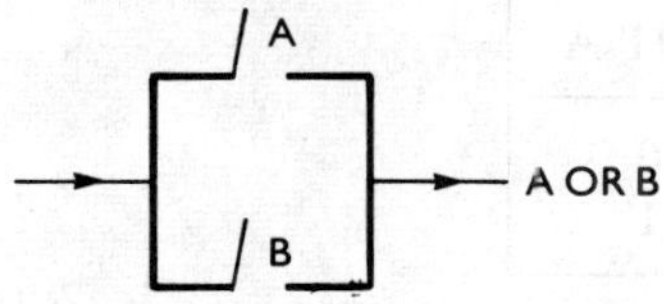

Data will flow from beginning to end of this circuit if one **OR** the other of the switches are ON.

Truth tables

13 An alternative way of describing these two gates is to use truth tables. The truth tables for AND and OR are as follows:

A	B	A AND B	A OR B
0	0	0	0
1	0	0	1
0	1	0	1
1	1	1	1

In this table 1 represents true or data flow and 0 represents false, or no data flow. For example, if data flows through A but not B (represented by 1 and 0 respectively on the second row then A AND B has no data flow but A OR B does have data flow.

Inverter

14 A mathematician called Boole showed that by including a third logic gate called an inverter or a NOT gate, then these three gates would be sufficient to describe all logic.

We can represent the **NOT** gate as follows;

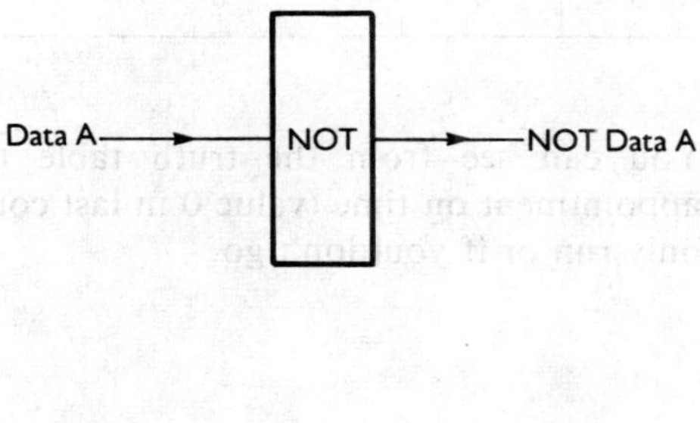

The truth table is quite simple:

A	NOT A
1	0
0	1

By appropriate use of combinations of these three gates, any logic diagram can be represented and its truth values found. To illustrate this, imagine you are almost late for an appointment but realise that you can arrive on time if you alternately walk and run or if you go by bicycle. You cannot run all the way because it is too far. This is the logic circuit.

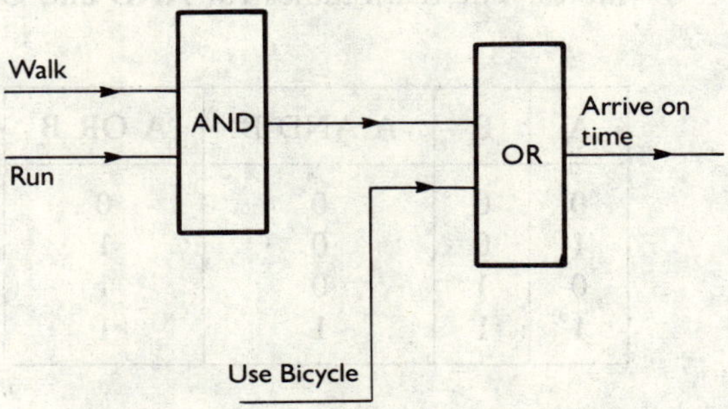

The truth table for this combination of gates as follows:

Walk	Run	Bike	Walk AND Run	(Walk AND Run) OR Bike
1	1	1	1	1
1	1	0	1	1
1	0	1	0	1
1	0	0	0	0
0	1	1	0	1
0	1	0	0	0
0	0	1	0	1
0	0	0	0	0

You can see from the truth table that you will not make the appointment on time (value 0 in last column) if you only walk, if you only run or if you don't go.

Library project

A borrower can borrow a record if:

(a) the borrower has a card AND
(b) the borrower presents the card at the desk

OR

(c) the borrower has a card AND
(d the borrower produces identification AND
(e) the borrower signs for the record.

Draw the logic circuit for this and illustrate with the truth table.
Show that NOT (A AND B) is identical to (NOT A) OR (NOT B)

Input and output formats

16 Data has to be input into the system and information output. As a consequence we must be sure that what we enter and what is output are what we expect, by formalising the processes. We do this by designing the layout of the screens for input and the screens and printout for output, using **layout charts** to facilitate this process.

Layout charts

A layout chart is a piece of paper, ruled off into text pixels into which a character can be written. Using such a layout chart a screen display can be easily designed.

Library project

Design a screen display that provides the user of the library system with a menu—a list of options available with the system.

Summary

Any new information system will be initiated by management in a document called the terms of reference. This document will lay out the objectives, the scope and constraints and the resources available for the information system. From this document the systems analyst prepares a feasibility report which is an overview of the new systems requirements in terms of hardware, software and personnel and procedures. The systems analyst has a number of tools to assist in the early (and later) stages of the analysis and design of the new information system. These include the system flowchart and decision tables.

Key points

Terms of reference, objectives, scope and constraints, resources available, feasibility study, sources of information, personnel, written records, observation, data analysis, systems flowcharts, decision tables.

Self assessment questions

1 Whose responsibility is it to identify the problem? (1)
2 Name the document in which the problem is identified. (1)
3 What do the terms of reference contain? (1)
4 What is meant by the objectives of an information system? (1)
5 What is meant by the scope and constraints of an information system project? (1)
6 What is a feasibility study? (2)
7 Who writes the feasibility report? (2)
8 What does the feasibility report describe? (2)
9 Where does a systems analyst obtain the information necessary to write a feasibility report? (3–6)
10 What does observation achieve that other means do not? (6)
11 What does data analysis involve? (7)
12 List two tools that the systems analyst has available for designing information systems. (7)
13 What is the purpose of a system flowchart? (8)
14 Why are decision tables used? (9)

Exercises

1 Which of the following is suitable for storing in a fixed length field of 6 characters?

address
birthplace
date of birth
name

2 (a) Suggest two programming languages that might be used when writing new programs for a stock control system.

(b) The following phrases refer to the capture, input and checking of data:

verify, magnetic ink encoder, data capture, optical mark reader.

Which of these phrases would best be used to complete the following sentences. *Each phrase is to be used once.*

(i) When a cheque is paid into a bank, a .... will be used to print the amount of the cheque in the space provided.
(ii) Collecting information to be processed by a computer is called ....
(iii) .... can detect marks made on specially prepared source documents.
(iv) To .... data means to check that it has been accurately copied from one medium to another.

3 (a) A company lends people money to buy such items as cars, hi-fi, and washing machines. When the loan is agreed the customer is given a book of payment slips with which to repay the loan in monthly instalments. With each payment the customer sends a payment slip that is used to update that customers account.
All accounts are held in a mainframe computer system and every day a large number of payment details are received and input to the computer system. Suggest one reason why batch processing would be most suitable for the application described.

(b) The company has set up a batch processing system to update the customers' accounts. A batch is a collection of similar documents (in this case payment slips) which are grouped together for input to the computer. A batch control slip is added to the front of each batch on which extra information is written about the batch of payment slips. The extra information on the control slip is used to monitor the progress of the batch and reduce errors during data preparation.

(i) What is written on the batch control slip to help prevent documents from being missed or input twice to the computer.
(ii) In what way is this information used to help detect being missed or input twice to the computer.

(c) The system needs to produce a magnetic tape of all the transactions ready for an update program run on the mainframe computer. The data preparation department has the following computer hardware:

a minicomputer,
a disk drive
a magnetic tape drive,
16 VDU/keyboard terminals linked to the minicomputer,
an operators console.

Design a data preparation system that would be suitable for the above application. Your answer may be either a description of the steps necessary to prepare the batch tape or a systems flow diagram of these steps. In your design, include methods to ensure error free data entry.

(d) On transferring its accounts from a manual to a computerised system the management of the company hoped to improve the operation of the company. Describe two benefits to the company of using the computerised system.

4 (a) Explain what the following flowchart symbols represent.

(i)

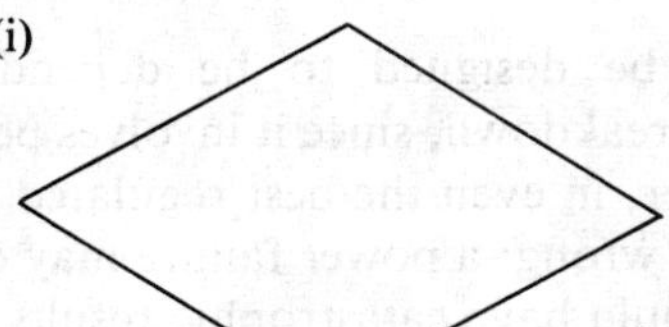

(ii)

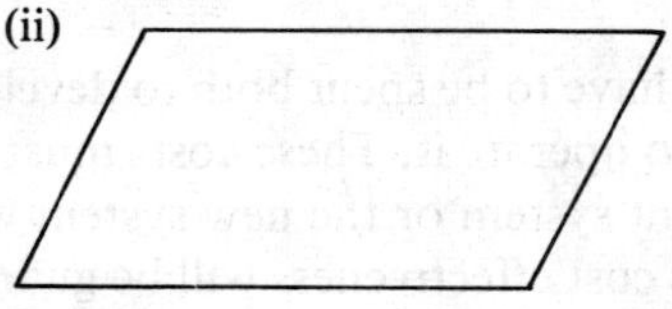

(b) Why are flowcharts used in computing?

(c) Explain the difference between a program flowchart and a system flowchart.

5 Which of the following is output by the flowchart below?

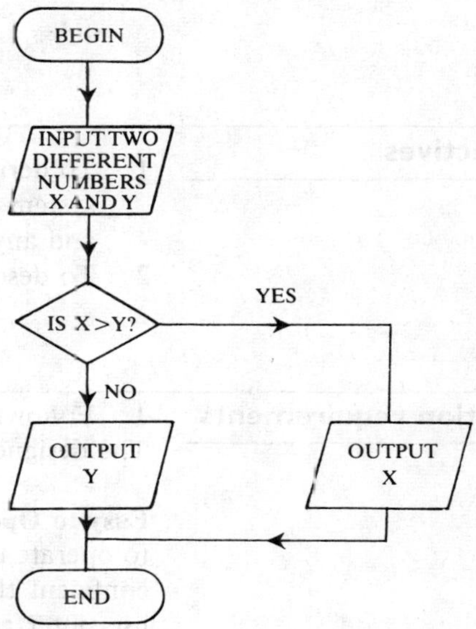

the first number
the larger number
the second number
the smaller number

6 A computer file on a school computer is to be introduced to contain records of all pupils and produce form lists. Each record will consist of the pupil's name, home telephone number, date of birth, medical problems and comments.
Draw a diagram to show a suitable structure for a pupil record. Use as an example John Simpson, telephone (0273) 61322, born on 21st June 1973, suffers from asthma. Indicate on your diagram any fields which should be of fixed length.

3 Designing the solution

Objectives

1 To derive the information requirements of a system and specify a system precisely in terms of the output needed, the input data and any necessary files.

2 To describe the organisation of files

Solution requirements

1 Following data analysis the information system can be designed. The designer must ensure that it is:

Easy to Operate In many cases untrained personnel may be required to operate the system after only a short training period. They must be confident that what they are doing at any time is correct so a clear user-interface is essential. When designing hardware, requirements it is best to use well-established equipment which is more reliable and less subject to unknown faults.

Dependable The system must be designed to be dependable in minimising errors and continual breakdown, since it involves personnel and their work practices. However, in even the best regulated systems there will be times when things go wrong: a power failure may occur in the middle of processing which could have catastrophic results if there were not an adequate backup procedure installed with the system.

Cost-effective Money will always have to be spent both to develop and install an information system and to operate it. These costs must be less than the costs of running the current system or the new system will not be cost-effective. In most situations cost effectiveness will be guaranteed because fewer personnel will be required to operate the new system. As wages and salaries will account for at least 50% of the cost of running any system, a reduction in labour costs can be far more significant than any capital involved in purchasing new equipment.

Library project
How would you ensure these requirements for the library system?

System analysis and design

There are two aspects of design associated with any information system

The logic design

2 The logic design deals with the flow of information through the system which can be illustrated by system flowcharts.

The physical design

3 The physical design deals with the actual files that are used, the style and content of both the output and input data and the hardware necessary to accomplish the objectives of the project.

When analysing and designing a system it is best to keep these two aspects separate for as long as possible, thereby simplifying the process of arriving at the final complete design. At the logic design stage the management, users and systems designers are in continual consultation to ensure that all available user experience is captured. Furthermore it allows the user to make sensible contributions to the design process even if they have little or no experience of data processing.

There is no single fixed way of designing a system. Two methods are commonly used although neither is used to the exclusion of the other. Usually a combination of methods is used at different stages of the design process. The system designer never starts from scratch: existing systems in the company and personal experience generally mean that by the time the system design stage has been reached the designer will have a clear idea of what is required. Then, by using various methods, together with the designer's experience and consultation with management and users, the design evolves. The process of design is as much an intellectual process as it is a strict formal process.

The two methods of system analysis and design we shall consider are

- Prototyping
- Top-Down Modelling

Library project

Distinguish between the logical design and physical design of the library system.

Prototyping

4 Using an application generator with a 4GL the system designer can construct simple applications very quickly. In this way applications can be created, amended and extended within a cycle of consultations with the management which opens up the possibilities of demonstrating to management various different options and allowing them to choose the one they prefer. This has the advantage of close and continued

interaction with the people who have written the terms of reference, who can now appreciate possibilities that would be advantageous to incorporate. In short, management become closely involved in the development of their own system.

Micro based 4GLs such as SMART, Symphony or Open Access are used as tools by systems designers for creating prototypes for use on larger machines. As soon as the prototype has been agreed by the management, the designer knows exactly what is required of the system and can use a more formal solution, coded in another language if desired.

Library project

The systems analyst arranges a meeting with the Chief Librarian for a prototyping session. What would you expect to be discussed at this session?

Top-down modelling

5 Top-down modelling is a process of starting with the basic INPUT —PROCESS—OUTPUT model and breaking it down into its smallest components. First the desired output from the system is tightly defined; second, the files necessary to support the information system are designed; third, the required inputs are similarly defined and finally the processing tasks are considered. Each processing task is broken down into smaller tasks resulting in a series of **modules**, each of which can be programmed separately with a minimum of effort. The advantage of this approach to design is further adopted at the programming stage.

Outputs

6 The main considerations in the design of the output are the requirements of the users of the system. The output must convey all the information that is required of the system so the design of its layout is important. The output required from a system depends on:

Who is going to use it?

The choice of whether to use simple text and numbers or text, numbers and detailed graphics depends upon the particular personnel to whom the output is intended. For example, a warehouse clerk will need only a columnar display of items by name and number, while the warehouse manager may need an analysis of sales from stock, presented either numerically or graphically. While a graphic presentation would be of less detailed use it may be sufficient to point out necessary features that need urgent attention in a more striking manner.

What should be output?

It is very tempting to produce too much information and this can cause confusion. For example, if the financial department wanted a list of late paying customers there would be little point in issuing a list of debt due by all customers.

How permanent is the output?

Some output will be in the form of a written record such as a ledger entry, while other information may be of a more temporary nature. For example, information output that need not be read by any personnel but is required at a later date by the computer as input is best stored on media until it is required. Other output may be stored on media but only for a fixed period of time, after which it is of no further use. Weekly records of stock in grandfather files, for example, are only required for a limited period, after which time they can be deleted. Archival storage is another problem which is best solved by storing on magnetic media or even microfiche rather than paper.

> **Library project**
> What can you say about the output from the library system in reference to those who are going to use it?
> What should be output and in what form from the library system?
> How permanent is the output for the library system likely to be?

Files

7 A file consists of a collection of records, each of which consists of a number of fields. The files are a collection of characters and they form the smallest unit of data within a file. A file is created by specifying the number and lengths of each field in a record, and is filled by entering records one at a time.

Every file is specified by a data dictionary which specifies details of the fields constituting a record.

Data dictionary

8 The following is a typical data dictionary for a customer file.

FIELD NAME	FIELD DESCRIPTION	FIELD TYPE	FIELD SIZE
CUSTNAME	Customer Name	Alphanumeric	30
ADDRESS1	First line of address	Alphanumeric	20
ADDRESS2	Second line of address	Alphanumeric	20
ADDRESS3	Third line of address	Alphanumeric	20
TELEPHON	Telephone number	Numeric	12
POSTCODE	Post Code	Alphanumeric	10
FAX	FAX number	Numeric	12

Note the field type. Alphanumeric means that any character on the keyboard can be used when entering this type of field, while numeric means that the field will only contain numbers. The field sizes refer to the maximum number of characters that can be contained.

Library project

Construct a data dictionary for any files that are going to be used in the library system. How many are currently available?

9 During the operation of an information system there will be times when large amounts of data are stored on the various media. This stored information has to be organised using files. There are two aspects to file design.

- file organisation
- file type

File organisation

10 There are two types of file:

- sequential access files
- random access files

Sequential access files

11 In a sequential file records can only be accessed in the sequence in which they were entered. This is the situation when the files are stored on a tape. To access a particular record in the file will then require going through each record in turn until the desired one is found. This slows down the process of file access, especially when a file contains a large number of records. If, however, the files are stored on disk then access to individual records can be considerably speeded up by using random access files.

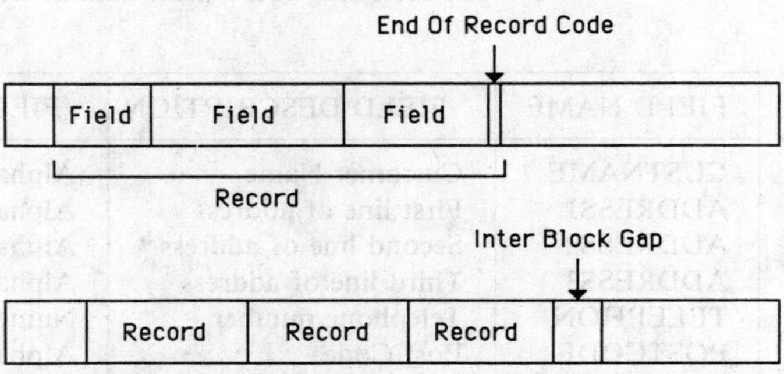

3.9 Sequential records on a tape

Random access files

12 In a random access file the location on the disk surface of every record is known. This means that it is possible to locate a specific record without going through any intervening ones. This has the effect of making access to records much faster.

> **Library project**
> When would you use either a sequential or a random access file?

File type

13 Files can be distinguished according to their use within the system. We shall consider seven types of file.

- Master files
- Transaction files
- Reference files
- Archival files
- Working files
- Backup files
- Report files

Master files

14 Master files contain information that is continually being referenced such as that relating to customers, sales, and stock and which will, from time to time, have their contents amended. A master file may contain records of two types of data: first, data that is of a semi-permanent nature such as a name and address, and second, data which is less permanent, for example, the number of hours worked during the previous week. The first is called reference data whereas the second is called dynamic data in view of its changing nature.

Transaction files

15 Transaction files contain data and information that has been both input into and output by the system. They are files holding temporary information. Some of which can be used to amend Master Files.

Reference files

16 A reference file will contain information that is of a permanent nature, the bulk of which remains unchanged. A database of files containing graphical information for the display of Ordnance Survey maps is an example of a reference file.

Archival files

17 An archival file will hold historical information for permanent storage, which may never be used again but is kept for historical purposes.

Working

18 A working file is one that is created and may even be deleted during the execution of a program. The user may not even be aware of its existence. For example, during multi-user access of the same file the records will be locked against the second and subsequent persons accessing the file. The information relating to the locking may be stored in a separate file which is deleted as soon as record locking is no longer necessary.

Backup files

19 A backup file is a copy of a file. Its purpose is to guard against any loss of information from the system due to accidental loss or damage to the system's files. Backup copies must be kept of all files and procedures for backing up any files that have been changed must be followed, to ensure the safety of any new information within the system.

Report files

20 A report is an organised summary of information held within the system. The report may be displayed on the screen but more usually it well be sent to the printer. All reports contain summarised information obtained from the system's files, which will be placed within a defined layout as to how and where on the report it should be placed. A report file will be used to store information relevant to a particular report. The information it will contain will refer to the layout of the report and from which files information is to be obtained to go into the body of the report.

Library project

Which of the library system files are

(a) the master files
(b) the transaction files
(c) the reference files
(d) the archival files
(e) the working files
(f) the report files

Input

21 Much of the data used by an information system will have to be entered into the system at some time or another. This will be done by an operator interacting with the computer via the prompts and messages that are displayed on the VDU screen. When designing the input for an information system the designer must consider its likely users. Appropriate input techniques must be applied, for example, using a light pen or laser reader to read the bar codes at a supermarket would be more appropriate than a keyboard.

Whatever method of input is selected, the computer will have to communicate with the user, most likely via the VDU monitor. Careful consideration must therefore be given to the design of screen layouts to avoid, for example, allowing too much information to be read as this soon becomes counter-productive. When data is to be entered via a keyboard to appear on screen, a highlighted marker indicating where it will appear is essential. The guiding principle is only to display what is absolutely necessary, while at the same time producing an attractive appearance. Try to avoid flashing screens: after long periods of use they can become very annoying. Colour is useful if you can employ it but be careful not to put two colours that clash next to one another, and use muted colours rather than bright ones. Sound effects are also useful especially if you wish to sound a warning, although again, overuse can be irritating.

Windows are another useful device especially if a selection from a list of options produces a further selection from a second list of options. In this way much screen information can be retained in memory but withheld from view until it is needed. The internal workings of the system should be completely transparent to the user, while the screen should display only what is necessary.

Data will often have to be entered into the system from a written form, such as a stack of cards. When transferring data from the card onto the screen, it is a good idea to make the screen look as near to the card in appearance as possible so that there is a one-to-one correspondence between the card being read and the screen display.

All entries should, if possible, be located sequentially on the screen to allow the operator to know where to look for the required information.

> **Library project**
> Describe the inputs needed for the library system.

Input and output formats

22 Data has to be input into the system and information has to be output. As a consequence we have to be sure that what we are entering and what is output are what we expect. To ensure this we must formalise the processes of input and output. We do this by designing the layout of the screens for input and the screens and printout for output. To facilitate this process we make use of layout charts.

Layout charts

A layout chart is a piece of paper ruled off into text pixels into which a character can be written. By using such a layout chart a screen display can be easily designed.

> **Library project**
> Design a screen display that provides the user of the library system with a menu—a list of options available with the system.

Program flowcharts

23 A program flowchart is similar to a system flowchart but it allows greater detail. It allows decisions to be displayed and indicates which hardware and storage media is to be used, and as such it can be a useful device for designing the solution to a problem. The flow of data through the system is illustrated by using the six National Computer Centre (NCC) flowchart symbols:

Terminator that signifies the start and end of a program or subroutine.
Operation that signifies an operation that does not move data from one location to another nor makes a decision.
Subroutine that signifies a self contained program block.
Input-output that signifies data being moved from one location to another.
Decision that signifies branching.
Connector that signifies the end of a data flow line on one page that extends over to another page.

The following system flowchart illustrates part of the payroll system in greater detail.

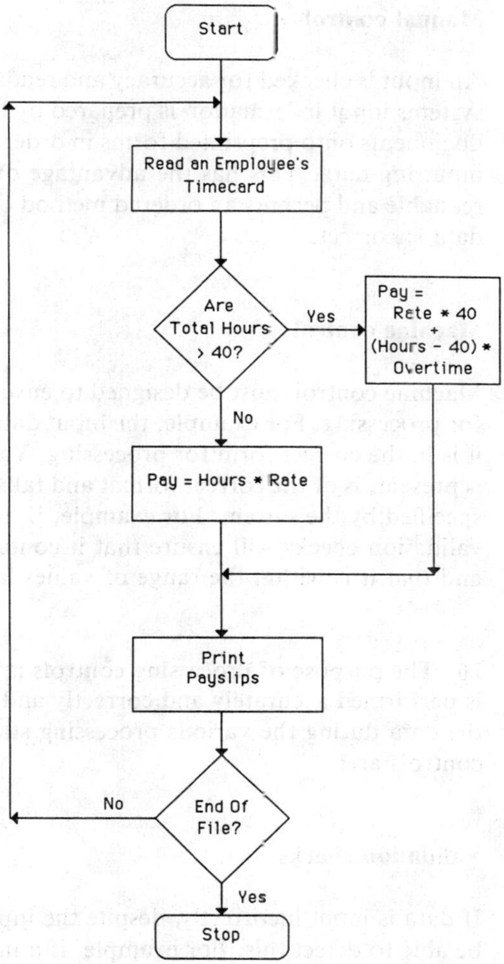

Error control

24 Problems are likely to occur in even the best regulated families so it is essential to recognise this to be able to guard against them. Errors are guarded against by imposing several controls on the system which affect:

- Input
- Processing
- Output

Input controls

25 The purpose of input controls is to ensure that all data input is done so correctly and completely. There are a number of ways to ensure this.

Manual control

All input is checked for accuracy and readability. For example, in many systems input information is prepared by transposing data from source documents onto preprinted forms in order to standardise the process of inputting data. This has the advantage of ensuring that input data is readable and permits an ordered method of manually checking that the data is correct.

Machine control

Machine control must be designed to ensure that the data is acceptable for processing. For example, the input data must be **validated** to ensure it is in the correct form for processing. Validation ensures that all data is present, is of the correct format and falls within the prescribed ranges specified by the system. For example, if a number is to be entered, the validation checks will ensure that it contains no alphabetic characters and that it is within the range of values laid down by the system.

Processing controls

26 The purpose of processing controls is to ensure that the processing is performed accurately and correctly and to ensure the integrity of all the data during the various processing stages. Examples of processing controls are:

Validation checks

If data is input incorrectly, despite the input controls, the system must be able to detect this. For example, if a number is to be entered into a field then the system must be able to detect the presence of a non-numeric character and permit the user to re-enter the correct data.

Hardware checks

Hardware checks prevent the system from failing due to user error when operating the system. For example, if a report is expected at the printer and the user has forgotten to switch the printer on or to check the supply of paper, the system should be able to anticipate this and either issue a warning or halt processing until the situation has been rectified.

Output controls

27 The purpose of output controls is to ensure that the correct output is produced and the processing cycle of the information system comes to the correct conclusion. This aspect of control deals more with working practices than with computer operation and includes:

Log books

Log books record the work received for processing and the various outputs required to ensure that all the different stages of processing are complete. They also record the distribution of hard copy to ensure that the entire processing cycle is complete.

Library project
What sort of error control would be necessary on the library system?

Development of the software

28 The third stage in the construction of an information system concerns the development of the software. Software is made up of a suite of programs, each program being a set of instructions to the computer to perform a series of tasks. The software is developed by the programmer but at all times the systems analyst must ensure that the programmer is producing what management desires.

The software that constitutes the core of the information system can be developed in a variety of ways;

- Applications package
- Bespoke program
- Application generator

Applications package

29 An applications package that already exists to satisfy the requirements of the proposed information system will be the cheapest option, but because applications packages are written to cover a wide variety of situations, a particular package may not exactly match the terms of reference of the project. From a costing point of view it may be desirable to adjust the terms of reference to suit the features of the package.

Bespoke program

30 At the other end of the cost scale, the bespoke program can be written from scratch to match exactly the specifications laid out in the terms of reference and the system design. Programming is a time consuming task and a program may take many days, weeks or even months to complete, thereby incurring high costs.

Application generators

21 The applications generator is a compromise between the applications package and the bespoke program and is becoming increasingly used in the development of information systems. A typical application generator will contain a database and a 4GL and be designed for use by people who are not professional programmers.

Library project

Which software option would you recommend for the library system and why?

Summary

The design of an information system should produce a system that is easy to operate, dependable and cost-effective. When designing a system the logical design is kept separate from the physical design for as long as possible. There are two design methods discussed, namely prototyping and top-down design methods. Prototyping permits user interaction in the design stage while top-down modelling breaks the system into its smallest sub-unit resulting in a set of easily coded modules. System design involves determining the outputs, the files needed and the inputs necessary. Files are collections of records, each record being a collection of fields, and they are defined by using a data dictionary. Files are either sequential or random access. In addition there are a number of different types of file. Error controls guard against errors in input, processing or output.

Key points

Solution requirements, easy to operate, dependable, cost-effective, design methods, systems analysis and design, prototyping, top-down modelling, output, who is going to use it? what should be output? how permanent is the output? files, data dictionary, file organisation, sequential files, random access files, file types, master files, transaction files, reference files, archival files, working files, backup files, report files, input, error control, input controls, processing controls, output controls, the development of software, applications package, bespoke program, application generator.

Self assessment questions

1 Name three requirements to be met by any solution to a problem. (1)
2 What is meant by saying that a system is easy to operate? (1)
3 What is meant if a system is said to be dependable? (1)
4 What is meant by a computerised system being cost-effective? (1)
5 Distinguish between logical design and physical design. (2–3)
6 What can you say about the design process? (2–3)
7 List two design methods (3)
8 What is prototyping? (4)
9 What does top-down modelling involve? (5)
10 What three questions must be answered prior to deciding on the output from an information system? (6)
11 How is a file specified? (7,8)
12 What is meant by field type and field size? (8)
13 List and distinguish between two file organisations. (9–13)
14 On what media would you expect a sequential access file and a random access file? (11,12)

15 List seven organisational files. (13)
16 What is a master file? (14)
17 What is a transaction file? (15)
18 What is a reference file? (16)
19 What is an archival file? (17)
20 What is a working file? (18)
21 What is a backup file? (19)
22 What is a report file? (20)
23 What must the designer bear in mind when considering the input to a system? (21)
24 What can you say about input requirement to a system? (21)
25 What are layout charts? (22)
26 What is the purpose of a program flowchart? (23)
27 List three types of error control that can be imposed on a system. (24)
28 What are input controls? (25)
29 What are processing controls (26)
30 What are output controls? (27)
31 List three possible software options available to the designer. (28–31)

Exercises

1 Which of the following is used to guard against accidental loss of data?

keeping back-up copies of files
keeping files under lock and key
keeping terminals under lock and key
using passwords

2 What is a key field in a record used for?

arranging the file
file protection
storing the file
updating the file

3 The following table shows part of a pupil file.

Name of pupil	Date of birth	Form	Tutor
Peter, Simon	290575	1B	RKA
Rea, Andrew John	130675	1A	JMB

How many records are there?

4 Explain what is meant by serial access and direct access. Give an example of a backing storage device which uses each of these methods of access.

5 Five different options are to be available on the menu of a program that is to be written.

load a file   sort the file   save the file
print the file   finish

Design a suitable screen layout from which the user could select one of the above options.

6 Give one reason why large programs are often written in modules.

7 Either magnetic tape or magnetic disk can be used as backing storage on most commercial computer systems.

(a) Which must use serial access and which can use direct access?

(b) for each of the following computer applications, decide whether a disk system or a tape system is appropriate. In each case give a reason for you choice.

Storage of flight details in air airline booking system
Storage of records needed to calculate the weekly wages in a factory
Storing the frames that make up the PRESTEL database at British Telecom.

8 Look at the systems flowchart which outlines a computerised payroll system.

(a) What are the media used to store files "A" and "B".

(b) On the diagram on p. 228 locate the following:

a scratch (work) file.
a master file
a transaction file.

(c) State one reason why the data is sorted in the process labelled "C" on the diagram?

9 KM plc is a high fashion clothes company that sells knitwear. It does much of its business using telephone sales. Customers place their orders from a catalogue using the telephone. They give their account number, and then the catalogue code number and quantity of each item they want.

The telephone sales staff enter the information into a computer system using a keyboard and VDU as

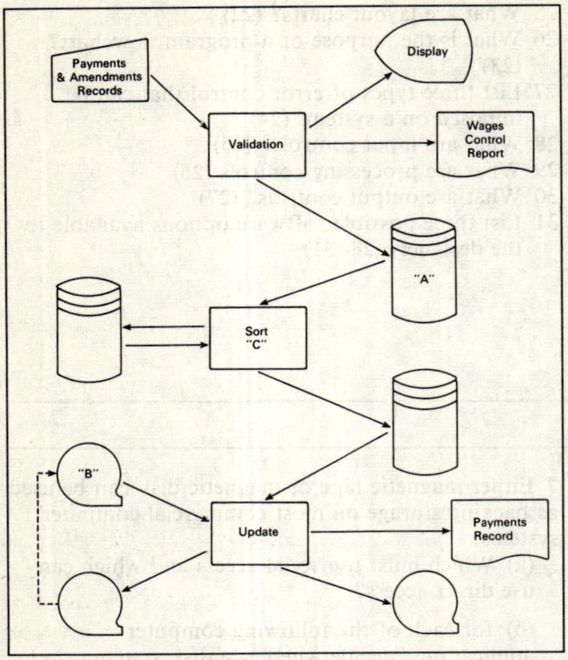

the customer gives them the information over the phone. While the telephone sales staff are dealing with the order the computer accesses several files. One of these files is the *customer file*, giving details about KM's customers, and another is the *product stock file*, giving details about the knitwear that KM stocks.

When the customer has finished giving the details, the order is stored in the computer system. The complete order is printed out ready for the dispatch department to make up the parcel of clothes. Each order is taken in turn and the parcel made up by the dispatch department. The parcels are then stacked ready for Post Office collection.

(a) For both the *customer file* and the *product stock file*, list the fields that might be a typical record, and give an example data item for each. You will need at least four fields in each record.

(b) For each file which is the key field?

(c) Describe how the product code given in the catalogue could be designed so that it could be checked by the computer.

(d) Describe two checks the telephone sales staff might make as they enter an order into the computer to ensure that the customer's order is correct.

(e) Design a suitable format for the printed instructions to the dispatch staff. Draw a diagram to show your proposed layout. Explain briefly why you have included each item.

(f) Many people are worried that personal data held on computers could be misused. (This includes being used for purposes other than that for which it was collected.) Describe two ways in which the data collected by the system described in this question could be abused and suggest what the abuse might be and who might want to do it.

4 Developing the solution

Objectives

1 To formulate solutions to problems.
2 To communicate solutions in appropriate ways.

Programming concepts

1 Programming appeals to many people for many reasons, whether it is the satisfaction of making a machine perform a sequence of tasks you have told it to do, the feeling of achievement when you master a particularly difficult problem, or the enjoyment of communicating successfully, albeit with a machine. However, many bad practices have developed as a result of self-tuition in programming.

These bad practices tend to emerge from not thinking about the program before starting to code it. As a result the program develops by solving individual problems as they occur. For example, you want the computer to print out the number 15 so you type in:

```
100 N = 15
110 PRINT N
```

This will work but if, to print out the numbers 1 to 15 you amend the code:

```
100 N = 1
110 PRINT N
120 N = N + 1
130 GOTO 110
```

then how do you stop the computer? The program will run forever and the only way out of this dilemma may be to turn the machine off, which will result in you losing your program.

You must think about the problem in a disciplined way and adopt a good programming style. There are many ways of programming a problem but you must learn how to program properly.

> Try this code out for yourself. Have you ever come across this problem before?
> Have you ever written a program and looked at it later, to find that you have difficulty in understanding it? Why do you think this is so?

> Many programs that appear in magazines are hard to understand. Why do you think this is so?
> Many people regard a program as their own personal property so that it does not require clear documentation. Do you agree with this viewpoint? Why?

To learn how to program properly we must consider:

- program qualities
- structure

Program qualities

2 Before we can develop good programs we must know what constitutes a good program.

A good program must first of all be **correct**—it must contain no bugs. Much research is currently being done to develop a method of proving programs to be correct or incorrect using highly sophisticated mathematical techniques. We must adopt the best programming style and test our programs with realistic test data. Assuming our program is correct, it must also be **easy to understand, maintain and update**. It should be designed and written in a manner that can easily be read and its logic understood. If this condition is met then any amendments of additional features can be inserted with relative ease. The program should be **efficient, reliable and flexible**. To be efficient it must perform its processing quickly and use its resources effectively. To be reliable and flexible it must perform as expected, yet without being too rigid in the demands it places on the operator. For example, if the operator is required to enter a number, the program should not accept an alphabetic character, but if this is done in error it should take appropriate action to allow the operator another try.

To achieve these objectives the correct programming style must be adopted. This means adopting a **structured approach** to writing programs.

> Write a small block of code that will accept an input at the keyboard but will only accept either Y for yes or N for no.

Structure

3 Even the most complex program logic can be expressed in terms of three simple control structures:

- sequence control structure
- selection control structure
- repetition control structure

Sequence control structure

4 The sequence control structure is the simplest of the three: it simply executes statements one after another in sequence. The following

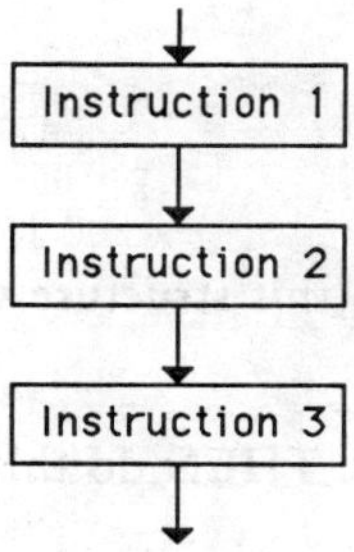

BASIC code is an example of this control structure:

```
100 VALUE = 100
110 TAX = VALUE * 0.15
120 COST = VALUE + TAX
130 PRINT COST
```

Selection control structure

5 This presents a choice from a number of options depending upon whether a condition is true or false. The simplest selection control structure is the: IF condition is true THEN do this ELSE do that.

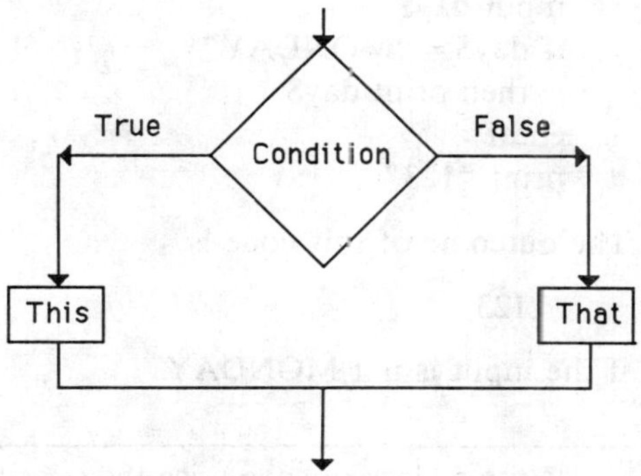

An example of this structure is:

```
input day$
if day$ = "MONDAY"
  then print day$
  else print "NOT MONDAY"
endif
print "123"
```

The outcome of this code is either

MONDAY
123

if MONDAY is input or

NOT MONDAY
123

if MONDAY is not input.

There is a variant on this structure where **do that** is simply **do not do this.**

If condition is true THEN do this

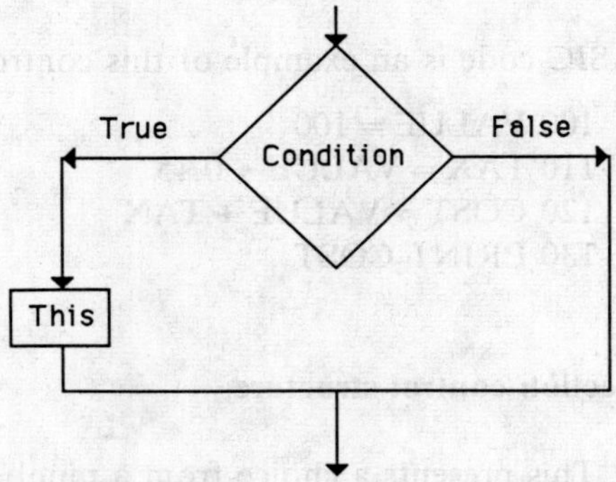

For example:

```
input day$
if day$ = "MONDAY"
   then print day$
endif
print "123"
```

The outcome of this code is

123

if the input is not MONDAY.

> Write a block of code using the selection control structure that will accept an input of a greeting. The output should produce HELLO, GOOD MORNING if you input HELLO and just GOOD MORNING of you input anything else.

6 A more complex variant of the selection control structure is where the single condition is replaced by a number of conditions. If any particular condition is true (and only one is allowed to be) then a particular option will be selected. This takes the following form:

```
If condition 1, condition 2, ... , condition n
THEN CASE 1
     CASE 2
     ......
     CASE n
ENDIF
```

where each CASE corresponds to a particular condition.

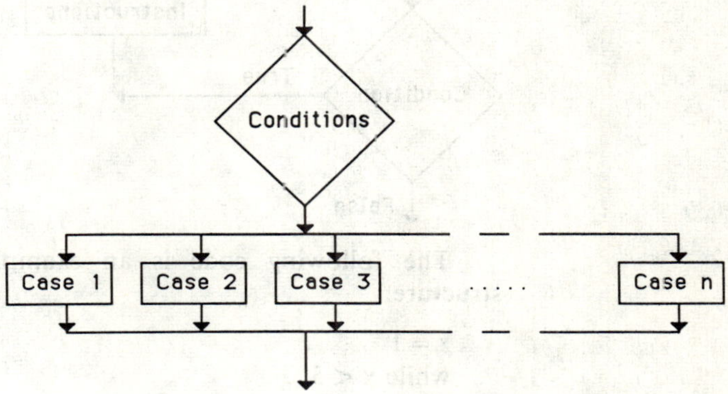

A typical use of this extended selection control structure would be:

```
input choice
if choice = 1, choice = 2, choice = 3
   then do proc-one
        do proc-two
        do proc-three
   else do proc-quit
endif
```

Here, the value of choice input determines the particular proc-xxx that is executed.

> Use this extended selection control structure to enable a user to select from a displayed menu. If the option number 1 is selected then ONE is printed, if option number 2 is selected then TWO is printed. Construct the code to allow a repeat selection to be made if a number other than 1 or 2 is entered.

Repetition control structure

7 The repetition control structure, also referred to as a LOOP, is used to execute a set of instructions repetitively until some condition is satisfied.

There are two basic types of repetition control structure, differing only in the outcome of the condition. The first causes a set of instructions to be repeated WHILE a certain condition is TRUE and to stop the repetition when the condition is FALSE.

DO WHILE condition is true

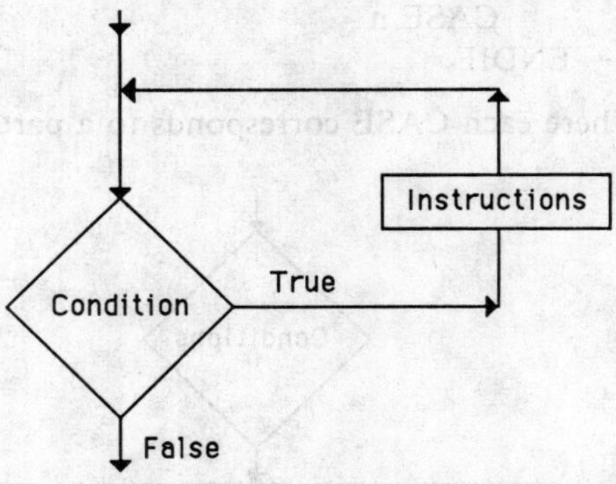

The following code is an example of the repetition control structure:

```
x = 1
while x < 5
  print x
  x = x + 1
endwhile
```

The outcome of this code is the following printout:

```
1
2
3
4
```

> Use this repetition control structure to accept a letter of the alphabet at the keyboard and then print out all the letters of the alphabet in sequence from A up to and including the letter input.

8 The second repetition control structure causes a set of instructions to be repeated UNTIL a certain condition is TRUE and to continue the repetition when the condition is FALSE.

The following code typifies this variant of the repetition control structure:

```
x = 1
repeat
  print x
  x = 1 + 1
until x = 5
```

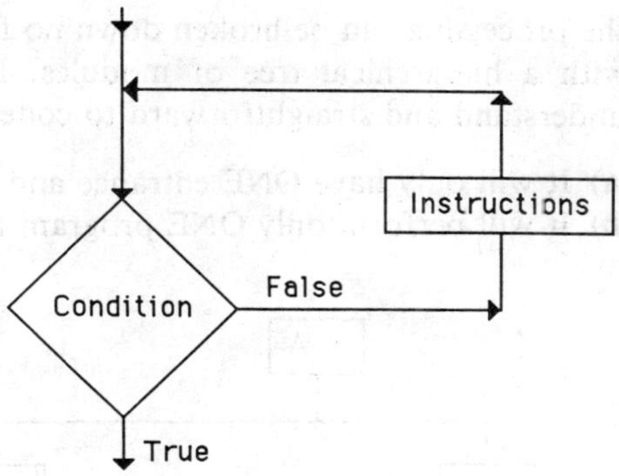

What is the outcome of this block of code? Write a block of code using the repetition control structure to accept a letter of the alphabet at the keyboard and then print that letter and all subsequent letters of the alphabet in order.

9 A fourth control structure that is commonly used is the unconditional branching performed using the GOTO instruction. This control structure is to be avoided at all costs as it lies at the root of many bad programming practices. Liberal use of the GOTO command produces programs whose logic moves around the coding like a snake inside a tree. Such coding is often referred to as spaghetti code because of its convoluted logic. Spaghetti code is like a ball of knotted string which gets more knotted as you try to unravel it.

The exclusive use of the sequence, selection and repetition control structures as the basic building blocks of your program form the first step in developing program style.

The second step is to look at the problem as a sequence of sub-problems and to adopt a top-down modular approach to the construction of programs.

Top-down modular programming

10 We discussed top-down modelling in the last chapter and we now apply the same principles to the programming phase of the project development. There are three main steps to follow:

Defining the output, input and major processing units

When this is done the programmer should know exactly what input and output is required and should have identified the processing as distinct from the input and output.

Refining the major processing unit

The major processing unit is now broken down into smaller and smaller tasks. This creates a hierarchical structure to the processing and when the processing can be broken down no further, the programmer is left with a hierarchical tree of modules. Each module will be easy to understand and straightforward to code, such that:

(a) It will only have ONE entrance and ONE exit.
(b) It will perform only ONE program function.

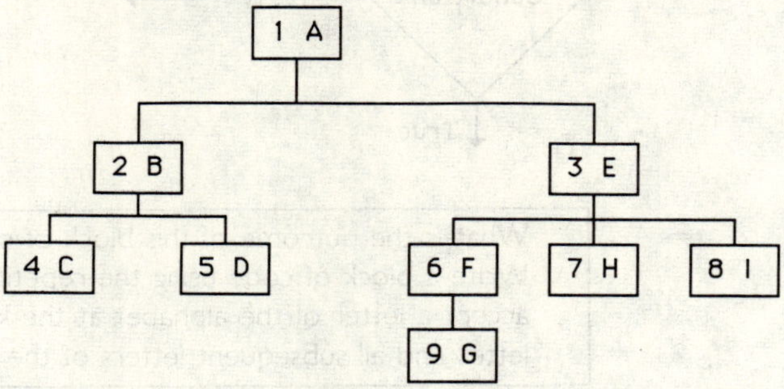

3.17 A hierarchical tree

Library project
Describe the structure of the problem posed in the library project as a hierarchical tree like the one shown.

Hierarchy plus Input Processing and Output (HIPO) charts

11 In addition to the structure diagram a diagram is also useful that relates to the structure diagram and at the same time distinguishes those parts of the structure that deal with input, those that deal with output and those that deal with processing. This can be done with a **functional diagram.**

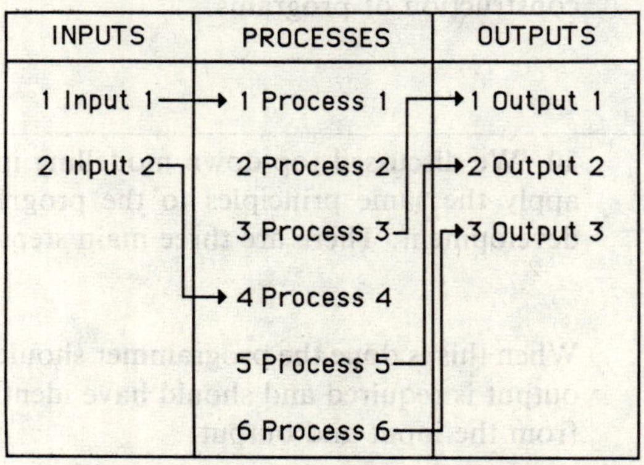

The structure tree coupled with the functional diagram form the HIPO—hierarchy plus input processing and output charts.

> **Library project**
> Construct the input-output chart for the library project.

Designing the algorithm

12 The third phase of the development process is to design algorithms for each of the modules. The algorithm will consist of a set of instructions designed to achieve the objective of the module. In designing the algorithm only the three control structures are to be used. At this stage the algorithms will be coded in pseudocode. The order in which the modules are coded will be either by level or by path.

By level The coding follows the numerical sequence shown in the hierarchical tree from 1 to 9.

By path The coding follows the alphabetical sequence shown in the tree, i.e. from A to I.

> **Library project**
> describe the two alternative coding sequences for the library project. Which of the two do you think is most suitable and why?

Coding the program

13 When the problem has been broken down into all its component modules and an algorithm has been designed and pseudocoded for each module, the entire system is ready for conversion to computer code.

Surprisingly, if the previous steps have been carried out with care, the effort of coding the final version is greatly eased. All that is required is a familiarity with the command codes for the particular language that you are using.

When coding each module two rules must always be obeyed.

- document each module
- indent the code within each control structure

Documenting each module

14 Every module must be documented with comments to describe what the module does and if it is not immediately obvious from the coding, how it does it. This is essential to inform anyone who may wish to read the coding at a later time.

> Document each of the control structure examples given earlier in this chapter.

Indenting the code within each control structure

15 You will notice that in each of the examples following the description of the control structures, the code was indented. Indentation has the effect of visually separating one control structure from another and making them easier to read. In this way anyone reading the coding will be able to see where any one control structure begins and ends, especially when two or more control structures are nested together.

Testing and debugging the program

16 When its coding is complete the whole program must be tested using test data that produces known results. This does not prove that the program is totally accurate because you may have accidentally chosen test data that does not pick out a particular fault. However, if all the test data works then you can assume that the program is correct although you must always be prepared for bugs to appear at any time during its operational lifetime. Three types of test data should be used:

Normal data

Normal data is the data that would be normally used during the day-to-day execution of the program. Samples of this type of data can be obtained from the existing system and used to test the program.

Exceptional data

Exceptional data is incorrect data. For example, if the program is expecting input in the form of numbers it should not be capable of accepting letters of the alphabet. A further example is the program expecting either a Y or an N in answer to a question with a yes or no answer. The program must be coded in such a way that if anything other than a Y or an N is entered then it is not accepted and the question is asked again to allow the answer to be re-entered. Remember that in situations such as these, both upper and lower case should be catered for.

Extreme data

Extreme data is data at the boundary of normal experience. For example, if the program is expecting a customer's name to be entered and has reserved only 20 characters then any customer with a name longer than this should be accepted but cut off after the 20th character. Extreme numbers should also be catered for, for example, if the application is generating invoices then the total value capable of being entered onto the invoice should exceed the normally expected maximum. In other words if experience dictates that all invoices are less than £1000 then they should be capable of accepting £10 000 at least.

When gathering test data it should always be remembered that the repetition of a successful test run with similar data does not prove anything. Good test data is defined as the smallest amount of data necessary to complete the testing satisfactorily.

> **Library project**
> What test data would you use for the library project? Would it be likely to detect all possible errors in the system? Why?

When testing a program it is likely that bugs will appear which may be of three forms:

Syntax errors

17 These are the most common types of error and arise from a misuse of the language commands. For example, a command may be misspelt such as PRNT instead of PRINT or it may be incorrectly completed such as a selection control structure IF with the ENDIF omitted. Syntax errors cause the execution of the program to stop when they are encountered, but once located they can be easily overcome by a simple amendment. One method of locating them is to use the operating system to put a trace on the execution of the program so that when the program is executed the actual commands executed are displayed on the screen as they are executed, so indicating where in the program the fault is located.

Logic errors

18 Correct preparation beforehand should have ironed out all the logic errors in your program. However, they do sometimes occur in the coding stage such as using a + sign instead of − sign. They do not cause the program to cease execution but will produce incorrect results, and as a consequence, can be very difficult to locate.

Run-time errors

19 A run-time error can occur if an incorrect data type is input into the system or if a printout is expected when the printer is switched off. Errors such as these cause execution to stop and often for an error message to appear to describe the fault. Run-time errors usually occur because program controls are absent.

Summary

A good program is one which is correct and bug-free, easy to understand and maintain, and is efficient, reliable and flexible. To achieve this a structured approach must be adopted when writing a program. There are three control structures that are used in combination to program a problem. The control structures are sequencing, selection and repetition. The program is first broken down into its smallest modules—top-down modular approach—and then described by HIPO charts. Each module is then simply coded following either a route by level or by path. Each module is documented and all code with a particular control structure is indented. Once written, the program is tested and debugged. Test data should include normal, exceptional and extreme data. Bugs appear as syntax errors, logic errors or run-time errors.

Key points

Programming concepts, program qualities, structure, sequence control structure, selection control structure, repetition control structure, top-down modular programming, defining the output, refining the processing unit, hierarchy plus input and output (HIPO) charts, designing the algorithm, coding the program, documenting each module, indenting the code, testing and debugging, normal data, exceptional data, extreme data, syntax errors, logic errors, run-time errors.

Student self assessment

1 Describe one consequence of bad programming practice. (1)
2 List the two topics that need to be considered when developing programming style (1)
3 What qualities should a good program possess? (2)
4 List the three control structures. (3)
5 Describe the sequence control structure. (4)
6 Describe the selection control structure. (5)
7 List two variants of the selection control structure. (5,6)
8 Describe the two variants of the selection control structure. (5,6)
9 What is repetition control structure? (7)
10 Describe and compare the two repetition control structures. (7,8)
11 What is wrong with GOTO? (9)
12 What is top-down modular programming? (10)
13 What features does the structure of each module possess? (10)
14 What is a hierarchical tree? (10)
15 What are HIPO charts? (10)
16 Describe the two sequences of programming modules. (12)
17 What two features must the code of a module possess? (13)
18 What is meant by documentation of a module of code? (14)
19 What is meant by indentation of code? (15)
20 What is meant by testing a program? (16)
21 What is normal test data?
22 What is exceptional data?
23 What is extreme data?
24 What is meant by debugging a program? (16)
25 What are syntax errors? (17)
26 What are logic errors? (18)
27 What are run-time errors? (19)

Exercises

1 Which of the following requires a binary decision?

are you male or female?
how old are you?
what is your lucky number?
what time is it?

2 State two reasons, other than speed, why writing a computer program in which the user selects commands from a menu might be better than typing in the commands themselves.

3 As details of candidates for examination are being prepared for entry into a computer, a name is input incorrectly. Is this detected by

a check digit
a range check
using a trace
verification

4 Computer programs are often split into modules, each of which is written separately. One reason for this is

so that one programmer can do the whole job
so that the program can be used on several makes of computer
to identify and correct errors more easily
to provide work for several programmers

5 A computer system is used in a company to calculate the worker's wages and print their wage-slips. Give a brief description of three different tasks of the computer staff.

6 A date is to be entered into a computer program in the form ddmmyy, where dd is the day of the month, mm is the month and yy is the year. For example 240589 would be the 24th May 1989.

(a) Describe clearly the three following validation techniques that could be used to test the data.

(b) Explain the terms verification and validation.

(c) Name two reasons why a date should be coded rather than stored in full.

7 A keyboard operator enters information into a computer system. The information is read from the data capture forms and typed in. Describe a method of verification which would help reduce errors.

8 A computer program is written to process marks out of 100. If a number is not in the range 0 to 100 a validation routine shows an error message, after writing the routine the programmer uses test data.

(a) What is meant by test data?

(b) Suggest three different numbers which would be suitable test data.

9 The clocking in and out times of a company's workers are recorded on time sheets. There is no night shift. The format for each sheet is: a five digit works number, followed by 5 or 6 pairs of times in 24 hour clock notation, (time of arrival followed by time of leaving), each field separated by a slash /. An example is shown below. It has three errors in it.

20023/0900/1703/1706/0859/0885/1659/0901/1702
/0859/17084/0900/1330

(a) Write down the three errors.

(b) For each error give a validation rule that might be used in the data entry program to detect it.

10 (a) When a program has been planned, it is often given a dry run. Explain what is meant by a dry run.

(b) When a program does not work, a trace is sometimes used. How will the use of a trace help?

An electricity board uses a computer-based system to charge customers for the electricity they use. A meter records the amount of electricity used for each customer (see diagram below). Every three months a meter reader visits the customer's house to read their meter. The new meter reading is written on a data collection form next to the customer's account number. Using the new meter reading and the previous meter reading the amount of electricity used can be calculated so that the customer's electricity bill can be produced.

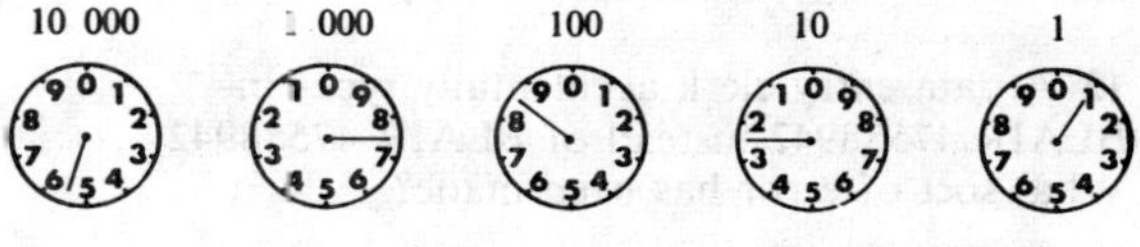

The readings on the above electricity meter would be recorded i.e.

5 7 8 2 1

(a) Design a suitable data collection form to allow the new meter reading to be recorded for each customer. Show clearly which information is printed by the computer and which is written by the meter reader.

(b) The electricity board keeps a record of each customer's details. Describe the different fields that you would expect to find in each customer's record to enable the system described above to function.

(c) A customer receives an incorrect bill for about £1,000,000.

(i) Explain how this could happen.
(ii) What steps could be taken to prevent this?

(d) Customers often telephone the electricity board to enquire about bills, etc. The telephone operator must be able to access each customer's details immediately in order to answer their enquiries. Describe a suitable computer-based system to achieve this. Make specific reference to the required Hardware, Operating System features and Method of Access to the data files.

11 The following algorithms are intended to print out integers from 1 to 10 inclusive

Algorithm 1
set count to 1
while the count is less than 10 **do**
  add 1 to the count
  output the value of the count
endwhile

Algorithm 2
set count to 1
repeat
  output the value of the count
  add 1 to the count
until the value of the count is 10

Algorithm 3
for count going from 1 to 10 **do**
  add 1 to count
  output the value of the count
endfor

In fact, none of these algorithms works correctly. Rewrite the algorithms so that they work.

12 A data entry clerk accidentally types in BLAIR 47538942 instead of BLAIR 47588942
What sort of error has been made?

a collection error
a logic error
a syntax error
a transcription error

12 An automatic car wash is controlled by a microprocessor and offers a number of alternative programs. The microprocessor is connected to a number of sensors and activators.

(a) What is the purpose of

(i) a sensor
(ii) an activator?

(b) The following algorithm describes briefly how a customer operates the car wash.

select a program for the car wash and pay
REPEAT
  drive forward into the car wash
UNTIL a red light comes on
REPEAT
  wait for the car to be washed
UNTIL a green light comes on
drive out of the car wash

(i) Name two types of sensor that the car wash might include, giving in each case, a reason why the sensor is needed.
(ii) What additional hardware would be needed to implement the system shown in the algorithm?

5 *Implementing and maintaining the system*

Objectives

1 To explain the need for adequate testing of solutions.
2 To describe the various implementation strategies.

Implementation strategies

1 The implementation of an information system requires careful planning and an orderly execution. It must always be borne in mind that the information system involves hardware, software, personnel and procedures or work practices.

A number of possible different strategies can be adopted when implementing the new information system:

- direct implementation
- parallel implementation
- pilot implementation
- phased implementation

Direct implementation

2 With direct implementation the new system replaces the old system immediately. The danger with this is that if the new system does have errors in it then there is no fall-back position to the old system and the new system has to continue while the errors are corrected.

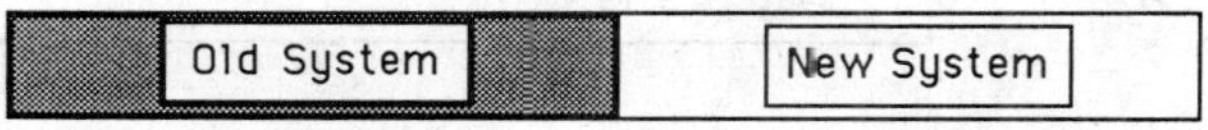

> Some systems have to be directly implemented because it would be impossible to run the old with the new, for example, any system that depends on personnel to the extent that there would be no time to run two independent systems. Can you think of an example.

Parallel implementation

3 The most common implementation strategy is to run the old and the new simultaneously for a limited period of time. Then if any

problems occur with the new system the old one can be used while it is amended and corrected.

Pilot implementation

4 During a pilot implementation, only a small part of the new system replaces the same part of the old system. When the changeover of that part of the system is satisfactorily completed the new system takes over completely from the old.

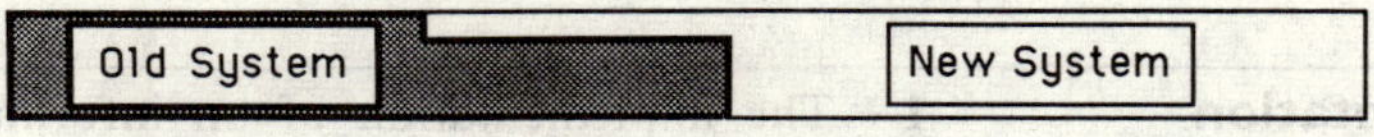

Phased implementation

5 A phased implementation means that sections of the new system are implemented at different times. The changeover process is gradual and minimises the risk involved in converting from one system to another. It does, however, take the longest time and is, consequently the most expensive.

> Do you think that parallel implementation would be a good way to implement a computer controlled payroll system? Why?
> Why do you think that pilot implementation would be suitable for a customer sales order processing system.
> What form of implementation would you choose for the library system and why?

Installation of hardware

6 The physical installation of the hardware requires careful planning. Adequate space must be found to locate not only the computer but also the peripheral equipment such as printers and VDU terminals. Paper documentation will also need to be accommodated in a place that is conveniently accessible to the computer, as will magnetic media both as a renewable resource and as a backup store.

The personnel who will be operating the system and their comfort must also be considered especially as many of them will be sitting at a keyboard for large periods of time.

Once the space has been located it must be wired for power to the appropriate places in the room, with all cables safely installed and switches easily accessible.

Assuming that all these provisions have been made and the hardware successfully purchased and installed, the system must be tested. This will ensure that all peripheral devices are functioning correctly and that the whole system works smoothly and without any interfacing problems.

> **Library project**
> What hardware will be required for the library project?
> Find out how much this is likely to cost.

Installation of software, file creation and testing

7 The next task is to install the software and test that it operates correctly. Before the software can be put into full operational use a number of files may have to be created. For example, a job costing system would require a detailed employee file, which could be transported from an existing computerised file by downloading or created from scratch. The systems analyst is responsible for organising this.

> **Library project**
> What files will be needed to run the library system?
> Do any already exist as computer files on another computer? If so, how can they be transferred to your computer? What plans need to be made for creating new files?

Training

8 If the personnel in the system are to be effective their needs must be considered. They must become familiar with the new system which will involve some measure of training. This can be of two forms:

- operational training
- system familiarisation

Operational training

9 The operational personnel must become familiar with both the input and the output processes of the system. They will need keyboard skills, and the ability to transpose written input into a machine readable form. This may involve the sole use of the keyboard or of other peripheral devices such as a mouse, bar reader or document reader. When handling output it is essential that operators are familiar with such devices as printers, and that they are able to load paper, change the ribbon and if necessary change the format of the print using the printer's internal control system.

System training

10 All operational personnel should be familiar with the basic processing stages of the information system enabling them to feel part of the system. This will improve their performance if they know what to expect at any stage in the operational cycle.

> **Library project**
> Is it likely that any library personnel will require training to operate the new system? If so, what form should that training take? How long will the training take? How much does a commercial trainer charge?

Documentation and maintenance

11 We have already stressed the importance of documentation. This must be made available from day one and in a readable form appropriate to the level of expertise of the reader.

As the information system is used on a day-to-day basis, experience will undoubtedly show up any shortcomings in the system. These may be due to a lack of foresight at the terms of reference stage or to fresh developments in the field that need to be incorporated. The business world is constantly changing so the system must be flexible enough to be modified to incorporate changes. For example, if the current VAT rate is 15% the system should be easily adaptable to any other VAT rate. The process of modifying the system is called maintenance and this continues throughout the operating life of the system.

It is possible that in time the system may have been modified to such an extent that it has become very inefficient. The system must be studied again with a view to replacement. In other words, the Information System Life Cycle has come to an end and the whole process must start again.

> **Library project**
> Can you anticipate any new features that might need to be introduced as the new library information system is used? Will the introduction of new features mean that the system will have to be completely re-written? Why?

Summary

There are four methods of implementing a new information system: direct, parallel, pilot and phased implementation. The choice of which implementation strategy to adopt depends upon the circumstances of the particular application. Hardware is installed and tested prior to the installation of the software and when it has been successfully located, the software is installed and tested. Any files that need to be created before the system can operate will be created now. All personnel who are going to be involved with the new system will need some form of training. This will take the form of operational and system training. The amount of training will depend upon the complexity of the system and the previous experience of the personnel. Once installed with its complete documentation, the system must be maintained during its operational life.

Key points

Implementation strategies, direct implementation, parallel implementation, pilot implementation, phased implementation, installation of hardware, installation of software, file creation and testing, training, operational training, system training, documentation and maintenance

Self assessment questions

1 List the three implementation strategies. (1)
2 What is direct implementation? (2)
3 What is parallel implementation? (3)
4 What is pilot implementation? (4)
5 What is phased implementation? (5)
6 What needs to be considered when installing hardware? (6)
7 When software is installed what two tasks are required before the system is operational? (7)
8 List the two types of training associated with an information system. (8)
9 What is operational training? (9)
10 What does system training involve? (10)
11 What does a system require during its operational lifetime? (11)

Exercise

A firm intends to install a computer. It has asked a computer company for help. The systems analyst has investigated the firm's method of manual stock control. Describe two further jobs that would be required of the systems analyst before the computer system was fully ready to replace the manual system.

6 Computer personnel

Objectives

1 To describe the tasks of various personnel in the workplace.
2 To describe the various employment opportunities within the computing industry.

Working for a large organisation

1 A large organisation will have its own computer department employing personnel responsible for both the day-to-day data processing of the organisation and the installation of new systems within the organisation.

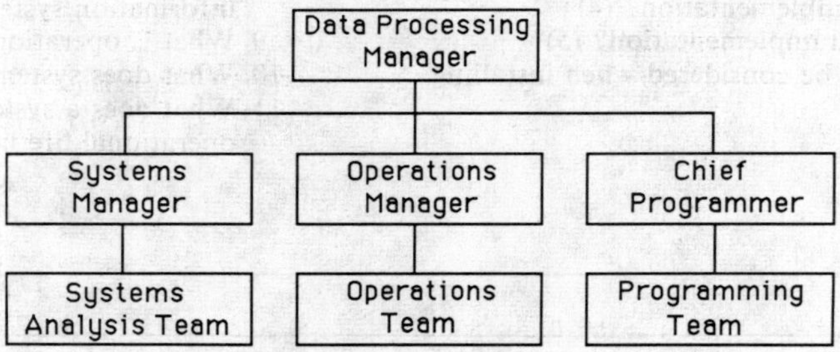

The data processing manager

2 The DP manager is responsible for overseeing all the computing operations of the department. Immediately responsible to him are the:

- systems manager
- chief programmer
- operations manager

Systems manager

3 The systems manager will be a senior systems analyst heading a team of systems analysts and designers. Systems analysts oversee the design, development and installation of any new computer system as well as maintaining the old systems. They must therefore interact with all personnel in the department to ensure that any system initiated fits in with the smooth running of the department as a whole.

Chief programmer

4 The chief programmer heads a team of programmers whose responsibility is to see that the specifications laid out by the systems designers are carried out satisfactorily.

Operations manager

5 The operations manager leads a substantial team of individuals and is responsible for ensuring that the physical process of the company's data processing are performed satisfactorily.

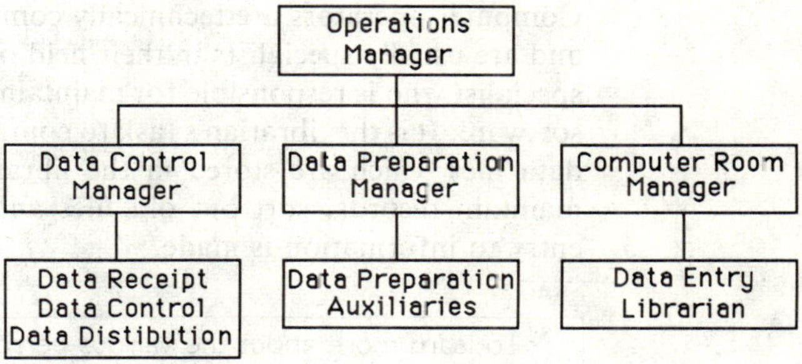

Data processing

6 There are three main areas of activity associated with data processing:

- data control
- data preparation
- computer operation

Data control

7 The data control manager is responsible for ensuring that all jobs are processed and that nothing is omitted or duplicated. All jobs are logged and it is the job of the data control section to ensure that not only are jobs sent to the computer but also returned so that the output can be sent to the appropriate parties.

Data preparation

8 The data preparation department receive their work from the data control section. When data is received it may not be in a form suitable for entry into the computer. There are a number of ways of making data suitable for this. At one time this was done by transferring the data onto punched cards using a key-punch machine. More efficient now is the key-to-disk method in which data is transferred into machine readable form using a workstation for putting the data onto a disk. Within this section a number of auxiliary staff will be employed to ensure the smooth running of operations and to be responsible for secretarial work and other non-input tasks.

Computer operation

9 As soon as the data has been translated into machine readable form it must be fed into the computer. This department is responsible for ensuring that all aspects of the physical computer system are operational and that jobs are initiated and completed according to schedule. Computer operators are technically competent to handle the hardware and are usually specialists in their field of work. The librarian is also a specialist who is responsible for maintaining the security of all data and software. It is the librarian's task to control and maintain programs and data files which are stored in the library on disks and tapes and to maintain records, sort out old files and ensure that only authorised entry to information is made.

> To learn more about the various personnel employed within a large computer installation, talk to your careers teacher. If you are interested in computing as a possible future career it would be worthwhile to arrange a visit to a large installation. The reality of working in such an environment can then be discovered first hand.

Working for a small organisation

10 In a small organisation a similar structure applies except that the number of staff is significantly less. The systems analyst, designer and programmer may be the same person although the duties will remain the same and the operation of the DP department will follow the same structure.

Typical examples of small computer organisations are:

- computer service bureaux
- software houses

Computer service bureaux

11 Computer service bureaux provide computing facilities to other organisations ranging from data processing to simple payroll accounting. They may also offer time-sharing on their own computer. If a company requires the use of a computer on the premises, but is unable or unwilling to invest in an expensive machine, it can link into a computer bureau computer which becomes dedicated to the company's use on a time sharing basis.

Software house

12 Software houses specialise in providing software and systems analysis. Much of this software may be commercially available with the software house acting as an agent for the makers. Other software may be bespoke in which case it will act as systems analyst to determine your needs and provide the solution. Software houses are becoming more widespread as more microcomputers are being adopted into the commercial and business world. This is largely because there are so many user-friendly applications packages written for the microcomputer, although minicomputer and mainframe users are now finding that more user-friendly applications software is also becoming available to them. Despite this growth in mini and mainframe software, the trend is for the centre of gravity of computing activity to move towards the microcomputer. With sophisticated networking facilities, multi-megabyte hard disk and optical disk storage and gigabyte primary storage becoming available on a desktop it is hardly surprising.

> Working in a Software House can be very interesting because computer equipment will be supplied to a wide variety of commercial and business concerns. Look up Software Houses in the Yellow Pages and arrange a visit to one of them.

Working for yourself

13 As the computer invades the work place at such a rapid pace the need for computer personnel increases proportionately. To meet the demand some computer professionals act as freelance contract personnel. These people, largely programmers and systems analysts, offer their services to companies who have a specific problem to solve. They will contract to work for a set period of time, after which the company no longer has any responsibility for them. This is of benefit to both the individual and the company using their services. The individual is exposed to a wide variety of situations and programming problems across the entire spectrum of industry and commerce. The company does not have the person contracted on the permanent payroll and thereby only pays for what is asked for. Freelance work does however require a number of years' experience in the computer industry first.

Computer qualifications

14 There are many varied ways of obtaining the necessary qualifications to work in the computer industry.

As with all careers there is a ladder from the bottom to the top and where you get on the ladder depends upon your starting qualifications. If you leave school immediately after GCSE or A-levels you will start at the bottom of the ladder and receive training both on the job and possibly through day release at technical college or night school. The drawback to this is that as you proceed through the industry you may find that you have insufficient general qualifications to proceed further up the ladder. It is therefore better to obtain general qualifications before specialising.

There are two main computer qualifications. One offered by the British Computer Society and one by the Institute of Data Processing.

The British Computer Society (BCS)

15 Four levels of qualification are offered by the BCS

(a) Student membership You must be at least 17 years of age and possess 5 GCSEs including English and Mathematics, and be taking an approved course.

(b) Associate membership You must be at least 18 years of age and be in approved employment. You will have passed Part 1 of the society's examinations or have gained exemption through possessing an HND or degree pass in Computer Science or other approved qualification.

(c) Licentiate membership You must be over 21 years old, have had at least three years experience of computing and have passed Part 1 and Part 2 of the society's examinations. Exemption from the BCS examinations is obtained by possession of a degree, together with approved practical experience.

(d) Member of the British Computer Society (MBCS) To be a full accredited member you must be over 25 with at least five years experience and suitable qualifications.

Institute of data processing

16 There are two levels of membership of the IDP.

(a) Student membership You will need 4 GCSEs in approved subjects OR be at least 19 years of age and able to submit evidence that you will be able to pass the institute's examinations.

(b) Associate membership of the Institute of Data Processing AIDP You will have passed Parts 1 to 4 of the institute's examinations or have an HND/BEC equivalent and have spent three years working in the area of Data Processing.

If you are interested in a career in computing then it will be useful to become a student member of either of these institutions. For further details their addresses are:

The British Computer Society 29 Portland Place LONDON W1N 4HU	The Institute of Data Processing Walter House 418–422 Strand LONDON WC2R 0PW
Tel: 01-637 0471	Tel: 01-240 3106

Keeping up-to-date

Formal education in computing and data processing opens the doors of the industry to you. Yet, because of the speed at which the industry is changing, it is essential that you keep up-to-date with new developments. There are a number of ways to do this:

(a) Professional associations Membership of BCS or IDP will put you in touch with the latest developments through the monthly magazines and newsletters.

(b) Magazines and books Computer magazines abound ranging from those that deal with very specific issues such as networking to those that deal with quite general issues such as PC's.

(c) Exhibitions Every year major exhibitions are held in various parts of the country dealing with all aspects of computers. The Human Resources exhibition held each year in the Barbican Exhibition Hall in London deals primarily with issues involving the use of computers in the workplace and their effects on the labour force.

(d) Workshops and seminars Professional associations, universities and polytechnics all run workshops and seminars during the year. These can range from advanced concepts to quite general issues.

Summary

The particular tasks performed by the various computer personnel depend upon the organisation for which they work. A large computer installation will employ a large staff of computer personnel led by the data processing manager. Directly responsible to the DP Manager are the systems analysts led by the systems manager, the programmers led by the chief programmer and the operational personnel led by the operations manager. The operational personnel consist of people involved in data control, data preparation, computer operation and a number of auxiliary personnel.

A small organisation such as a computer service bureau or a software house will employ fewer people but similar tasks will be done. The advantages of working for smaller organisations such as these is that they work for larger companies and in doing so expose their personnel to a wide variety of applications. When a computer professional is sufficiently experienced, self-employment is a valid option.

To be employed within the computer industry a person needs qualifications. These qualifications can be obtained in a variety of ways, including through the various grades of membership of the British Computer Society or the Institute of Data Processing.

Because the computing arena is changing so rapidly, keeping up-to-date with the latest technology is essential. This can be done in a variety of ways including reading magazines or attending seminars and conferences.

Key points

Working for a large organisation, the data processing manager, systems manager, chief programmer, operations manager, data processing, data control, data preparation, computer operation, data processing, working for a small organisation, computer service bureaux, software houses, working for yourself, computer qualifications, the British Computer Society, the Institute of Data Processing, keeping up-to-date, professional associations, magazines and books, exhibitions, workshops and seminars.

Self assessment questions

1 List three types of employment in the computer industry. (1)
2 Who heads the computing department of a large computer installation? (1, 2)
3 Name the three people who are directly responsible to the DP manager. (1, 2)
4 What is the role of the systems manager? (3)
5 What is the role of the chief programmer? (4)
6 What is the role of the operations manager? (5)
7 Who are the three people directly responsible to the operations manager? (5, 6)
8 What does data control involve? (7)
9 What does data preparation involve? (8)
10 What does computer operation involve? (9)
11 What is the librarian's responsibility? (9)
12 List two smaller computer organisations. (10)
13 What is the role of a computer service bureau? (11)
14 What is the role of a Software House? (12)
15 Why is the centre of computing activity moving towards the microcomputer? (12)
16 What sort of employment can a freelance self-employed computer professional expect to be offered? (13)
17 What do you need before you can expect to be employed within the computing industry? (14)
18 Name two sources of computer qualifications. (15, 16)
19 How can a computer professional keep up to date with all the latest technological developments? (17)

Exercises

1 Checking batch totals would be the job of a

chief programmer
data control clerk
file librarian
punch operator

2 Which of the following is a manual information retrieval system?

a database
an encyclopaedia
teletext
viewdata

3 Clean & Fresh plc are a company who make bathroom fittings. The company has recently installed a computer system to calculate the workers' wages, and print their wageslips. It will also calculate and print the bills as well as keep all the company records. Clean & Fresh have decided to set up a computer department and have appointed several computer staff rather than employ an external bureau.

(a) Describe briefly three tasks that the computer staff might be expected to carry out.

(b) Shiney Fittings plc, a rival company, also make bathroom fittings from their factory in another town. They have also decided to computerise and plan to use the services of a computer bureau to calculate and print the workers' wageslips.

(i) Suggest one advantage of their decision compared with that of Clean & Fresh.
(ii) Suggest one disadvantage of their decision.

(c) Next year Clean & Fresh plan to use the computer to help design new bathroom fittings. Describe one task of the designer that will be changed considerably by using the computer.

(d) How will Shiney Fittings' decision to use a bureau cause them further problems if they intend to develop computer aided design of their fittings?

Section four

1 Case study 1: *The word processor*

Objectives

1 To derive the information requirements for the solution to a problem in terms of the output needed.
2 To select and implement suitable methods of communication between people and computers.

Mail Order Supplies Limited

1 Mail Order Supplies Limited is a company that provides services to mail order companies.

Mail order companies sell their goods by sending circulars through the post to householders. Circulars may be accompanied by a catalogue or by a competition encouraging the householder to enter.

2 One problem facing mail order companies is in deciding who to send the circulars to. Sending letters through the mail is expensive so the company must try to select only those people who are likely to buy the goods and services. For example, a circular advertising Time-Share holidays is less likely to appeal to a person renting their home than one who owns their home because it involves buying a portion of a property on a time basis.

3 Rather than sifting through names and addresses of residents in the UK to find potential customers, mail order companies buy lists of potential customers from firms such as Mail Order Supplies Limited, which devote their energies to creating lists of names and addresses to match any given requirement. This company also provides folding and stuffing services and from their lists, prints off names and addresses on to sticky labels to be transferred to the envelopes that are to be stuffed.

Personalised circulars

4 The management of Mail Order Supplies Limited have decided that they wish to extend the services that they offer to their clients. They have decided that designing and creating the circulars for their clients will not only bring in extra work from current clients but will also encourage new companies to use their services. Not only could they produce circulars but, by taking advantage of their mailing lists, they could create personalised circulars.

5 A personalised circular contains references in the body of the circular to the person who receives it. This makes it less impersonal and because the reader sees their own name in the letter it makes them take it more seriously than its impersonal counterpart.

The following letter is a typical example of a personalised circular:

```
                    SUPERIOR SALES BY MAILS

Mr AB Cook
123 High Street
Lowtown
LT1 2AQ

Dear Mr Cook,

You  have  been  personally selected to receive 10 numbers to be entered
into  our  free  prize draw.  Do you know, Mr Cook, that the FIRST PRIZE
is a Two Week Holiday For TWO in the glorious SEYCHELLES.

I  would  urge  you Mr Cook to post your acceptance of our special offer
today.   When we receive your acceptance your 10 numbers will be placed
into our computer ready for the draw.

If  you  reply within one week Mr Cook an extra 10 numbers will be given
to you.

Do not hesitate Mr Cook, post your acceptance NOW.

Yours most sincerely


Prize Draw Manager.
```

6 Mail Order Supplies were unsure about how best to proceed, so a consultant analyst was approached and asked to find the best way of implementing this new service.

The consultant explained to the management how a system such as this was implemented and told them that the first requirement would be the terms of reference provided by the management.

Terms of reference

The terms of reference were set out as follows:

- Design a system to enable Mail Order Supplies Limited to offer its customers a service of designing and producing a personalised circular to accompany their mailing list services.
- The hardware that is currently available consists of a number of PCs, letter quality printers and dot-matrix printers. The software available is a word processing package of professional quality.
- Mail Order Supplies does not wish to invest too much capital in the venture but rather to use the facilities that are currently available.

7 From the terms of reference the consultant then prepared a feasibility report.

Feasibility report

By talking to management and the company personnel involved, the consultant came to the following conclusions:

- The software that they currently possessed was adequate for the job; their comprehensive word processor also contained a simple graphics facility to incorporate straight lines and shading into a document.
- Should the management wish to incorporate more sophisticated computer graphics into their documents, then a desk-top publishing package would be required. A desk-top publishing package is a sophisticated text and graphics editor which can be used to produce near type-set quality print.
- The computers that they already possessed were also adequate—they already ran the software. The only problem was the printers: the dot-matrix printers would not be of a high enough quality and the letter quality printers, although able to produce the quality of print that was required, would be too slow. To produce personalised circulars each letter was to be printed by the computer and because they would be required in batches of thousands, a fast, letter quality printer was essential.
- The consultant advised Mail Order Supplies to invest in a laser printer which would combine both excellent reproduction and speed.

The feasibility report also contained a detailed breakdown of costs including the consultant's fee. After some deliberation, management decided that the benefits they would accrue would more than offset the cost of the laser printer so they asked the consultant to proceed.

System design and development

8 The system design and development concerned the establishment of procedures from receiving a request for producing a circular to mailing it. No programming would be involved because the circular would be designed using the word processor with which the company personnel were already familiar. The only facet of the software that needed to be considered was training in the use of the mail-merge facility.

Mail-merge concerns the merging together of two documents at the printer. When the circular was ready to be printed, each copy was to have a person's name and address on it as well as the person's name at various places in the circular. To do this the circular document and the names and addresses document would be mail-merged together. We shall see how this is actually done in the consultant's system documentation.

When the personalised circulars were printed they were ready to be folded and stuffed into envelopes for mailing. The only other problem to be solved was the addressing of the envelopes.

Addressing envelopes is a straightforward process for non-personalised circulars: each name and address is printed on a sticky label which is then transferred to the envelopes, all of which will contain identical letters.

With personalised circulars there is the added problem of putting the correct label on to the correct envelope. There are two approaches to solving this problem.

Stuffing and labelling envelopes The envelope can be stuffed and labelled at the same time. There is always, however, a chance that an incorrect label could be put on an envelope which would totally negate the point of a personalised circular.

Using windowed envelopes To avoid any mislabelling, an envelope with a transparent window could be used. If the letter were printed and folded correctly, the name and address would show through the window, avoiding any need for labelling.

It was decided to adopt the latter course of action and the consultant now only had to produce a manual to describe how to operate the mail-merge system.

Mail-merge documentation

9 The mail-merge manual was in two parts:

- principles of mail-merge
- procedures to follow

Principles of mail-merge

10 Mail-merge is the merging of two documents. It is called mail-merge because the most typical application is the merging of a general letter with a personalised name.

To operate a mail-merge system two word processor documents are needed, for example a letter and a list of names and addresses. We shall refer to the letter as the circular document and the list of names and addresses as the data document.

When the circular document is created with the word processor the places where the name and the address are to go are left empty. These will be filled later by data i.e. the appropriate names and addresses from the data file.

The circular document has the locations specially marked where information from the data document is to be placed. The merge is achieved by the computer being prompted by the marks as the circular document is being printed. The computer then reads the appropriate

```
                        SUPERIOR SALES BY MAILS

<<name1>>
<<address1>>
<<address2>>
<<post code>>


Dear <<name2>>,

You have been personally selected to receive 10 numbers to be entered
into our free prize draw.  Do you know, <<name3>>, that the FIRST PRIZE
is a Two Week Holiday For TWO in the glorious SEYCHELLES.

I would urge you <<name4>> to post your acceptance of our special offer
today.    When we receive your acceptance your 10 numbers will be placed
into our computer ready for the draw.

If you reply within one week <<name5>> an extra 10 numbers will be
given to you.

Do not hesitate <<name6>>, post your acceptance NOW.

Yours most sincerely


Prize Draw Manager.
```

Data document

```
Mr AB Cook
123 High Street
Lowtown
LT1 2AQ

Mr Cook
Mr Cook
Mr Cook
Mr Cook
Mr Cook
```

data in the data document and writes it into the circular document in the space marked. The computer reads from the data document one item at a time progressively. Since the circular document has six references to the name of the addressee, then an extra five names have to be added in the data document after the name and address.

Procedures to follow

11 Finally the consultant produced the mail-merge system in the form of a document of procedures.

1 Receipt of request to produce a circular.
2 Meeting with mail order client.
   (a) Obtain terms of reference containing outline and preliminary layout of contents.
   (b) Ascertain if it is to be a personalised circular.
3 Produce feasibility report and costing: determine whether clients' wishes can be met and if not propose alternatives.

4 Design circular in liaison with client until client is satisfied.
5 Produce the finished product in single copy form: obtain client's approval to proceed with print run.
6 Amend the data document so that it will provide the desired data items.
7 Print all the circulars.
8 Fold circulars.
9 Stuff envelopes with folded circulars:
   (a) if a personalised circular, use windowed envelopes
   (b) if a general circular, print names and addresses on sticky labels and transfer to envelopes.
10 Mail circulars.

Implementation

12 When the overall procedure and mail-merge documentation was complete the consultant analyst delivered it to Mail Order Supplies Limited. The next stage of implementation involved training and ensuring that all personnel involved in the system knew what was expected of them.

Training was a straightforward process because the personnel involved already knew how to operate the word processor. Nonetheless the consultant had to make sure that they really did understand how the mail-merge operated so that they would be confident of the system from the start.

> To become familiar with your word processor copy the circular document of this chapter and mail-merge it to everyone in your class.

Summary

Mail Order Supplies Limited decided to offer their clients a service to produce circulars, including personalised circulars. To effect this they:

(a) Used a word processor facility to produce the circular document. The circular document was the circular to be mailed and the data document contained the names and addresses to be either printed on to labels or inserted into a personalised circular.

(b) Used the mail-merge facility of the word processor to produce the personalised circular.

(c) Used a laser printer for speed and near type-set quality print.

(d) Used windowed envelopes to avoid having to address the envelopes containing personalised circulars.

Key points

Mail order companies, personalised circulars, terms of reference, feasibility report, system design and development, mail-merge, stuffing and labelling envelopes, using windowed envelopes, mail-merge documentation, principles of mail-merge, procedures to follow, implementation.

Self assessment questions

1 How do mail order companies sell their goods? (1)
2 What problems do mail order companies have with their mailing lists? (2)
3 How do mail order companies resolve their mailing list problems? (3)
4 What is a personalised circular? (4)
5 Why are personalised circulars used by mail order companies? (5)
6 What is a desk-top publishing package? (7)
7 What is mail-merge? (8)
8 How can you avoid having a letter addressed to one person and an envelope to another when sending a personalised circular? (8)
9 How does mail-merge work? (10)
10 In what ways are the 'procedures to follow' similar to the general procedures to follow when solving someone else's problem? (11)

Exercises

1 How is the expression **merging** two files best defined?

combining them
comparing them
replacing them
updating them

2 A company is soon to computerise the office accounting system.

(a) Describe two ways in which the change from the manual system to the computerised system could take place.

(b) Describe one way in which this change is likely to affect the work done in the accounts department.

3 Mr Simpson owns a home computer system which consists of the computer, a keyboard, a disk drive, a monitor and a daisy wheel printer.

(a) Name two situations where interrupts would occur when using the system.

(b) Mr Simpson writes programs for his computer. His programs never work the first time they are run so he uses a trace and a breakpoint to debug the program. Explain these terms.

(c) Mr Simpson buys equipment so that he can receive satellite transmissions of weather data. He uses his computer to translate the data into diagrams and requires an accurate hard copy in colour.

An output device would produce better results than his daisy wheel printer. Name the output device that would be most suitable and give one reason for your choice.

4 A word processor is used by a school to produce a large number of standard letters. The letters are sent to parents informing them of the details of examination entries for their children. A data file containing details of each student's entries is merged with the document shown below to produce the letters.

DATA A, B, C, D, E, F, G

Middleton High School,
Middleton,
Middleshire

Dear *A*

I am pleased to inform you that *B* *C* will be entered for the following GCSE examinations in June 1989. I would be very grateful for your support in encouraging your son/daughter to attend school for these examinations on the correct days and at the appropriate times. A timetable of examinations is included with this letter.

D   *E*
F   *G*

Please complete the enclosed form of acknowledgment and return it to the school as soon as possible.

Yours sincerely.

A Prentice
Headmaster.

(a) While part of the document above will **not** be printed out when letters are sent to parents, some parts will be replaced with items from the data file during the merge.

Which part will neither be printed nor replaced when letters are sent to parents?

(b) The following data represents part of the data file. It includes one full record and part of two other records.

Computer Studies
Mr Hewitt
Paul
Hewitt
Mathematics
French
English
Art
Mr & Mrs Roberts
Sally

Explain how each field in the full record above would be included in the document to produce a letter that could be sent to a parent.

(c) Name four ways in which a word processor could be used to improve the appearance and accuracy of letters such as these.

2 Case study 2: *The spreadsheet*

Objectives

1 To describe the use of a spreadsheet in an application design and development.

2 To describe the use of top-down modelling and the use of pseudocoding.

Rapid Sales Limited

1 Rapid Sales Limited is a company that sells catering equipment and supplies to hotels, restaurants and retail kitchen shops. Their speciality is fast delivery using 132 sales representatives who are on the road every day selling directly to their customers.

To achieve their fast delivery commitment, each sales rep is equipped with a lap-top computer, a modem and a car phone. When the rep receives an order it is entered into the lap-top computer, which is then connected through the modem to the car phone and the order is immediately transmitted to the Rapid Sales computer located in the warehouse in Leeds.

As soon as the order is received in Leeds, all the necessary paperwork such as delivery note and invoice are automatically generated and the order is made up and despatched. Delivery is either by rail or road depending upon the availability of road transport and the existence of other orders in the same area.

Rapid Sales guarantee that they will deliver to any part of the country within 24 hours of receiving the order. If they are late then the customer gets the order free of charge no matter how large or small it is.

The offer of this facility has resulted in a rapid growth of the company and the sales force has achieved remarkable results. To maintain the operation, the company uses two minicomputers—one in its warehouse at Leeds and the other in its administrative centre in Bradford. These two computers run and organise the entire system and are operated by teams of qualified computer personnel.

The problem

2 During recent months the management of Rapid Sales have noticed that their sales have started to level off. They are unsure whether this is because the sales force has reached its maximum selling capacity or

because the sales force, being on the road and operating individually, have become complacent. Rather than employ more sales reps they have decided to run a competition to see if their existing sales force can be persuaded to increase productivity.

The terms of reference

3 After much discussion management have approached their systems analyst with a view to installing a computerised system to organise their competition. They have given the systems analyst the following terms of reference.

- Develop and install an information system that will organise and manage a competition among the sales force. The rules of the competition are as follows:
- Every day each sales representative's daily sales will be totalled. At the end of each month the top 20 sellers receive bonus points ranging from 20 points to the top seller, 19 to the next and so on.
- At the end of each month the top sales representative will be awarded a free gift.
- At the end of the year, the five representatives with the most accumulated bonus points will each win holidays for their families. Holidays can be anywhere in the world, with travel and accommodation paid, plus a generous cash award to cover expenses.
- The system must be run on existing equipment and must require little or no human intervention.

Feasibility report

4 The systems analyst has considered the problem posed by the terms of reference and included the following conclusions in the feasibility report.

- To operate the system, each sales representative's daily sales will be totalled every day. This is easily achieved as their sales records are contained on the company's computer and each sales record is updated every time an order is received.
- Using an existing microcomputer located in one of their offices and a COMMUNICATIONS PACKAGE they can link directly to the minicomputer and download this information from the mini to the micro into a text file at the end of each day's trading.
- This information can then be entered automatically into a SPREADSHEET which will automatically sort the sales figures into descending order.
- The top 20 representatives each month will then have points awarded and recorded on the worksheet. The names and points of the top scorer at the end of each month will be printed out for notification purposes.

- This process will be repeated every month until the year end when the top five representatives will be identified.
- Only existing hardware and software will be used and the only human intervention will be starting up the running of the program each day and closing it down.

Management have received this feasibility report favourably and decided to go ahead with the project.

System design and development

5 We have seen that many systems are constructed in levels and this system will be no exception. When the user runs the system the computer monitor screen will display a message to indicate that the user is at the top level of the system. This message will be in the form of a menu of options from which the user can choose.

There are three parts to the information system that can be accessed from the top level:

- capturing data from the minicomputer
- managing the competition
- QUITTING the system

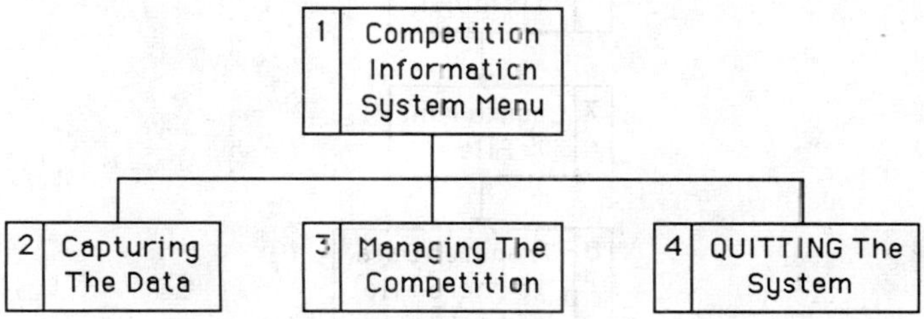

Capturing data from the minicomputer

6 As each sales rep transmits an order from a customer, the sales are recorded in a file. This is necessary because the reps are paid a commission, so a record of their weekly sales must be maintained. By using a simple communications link between a micro and the mini, the micro can be arranged to emulate a dumb terminal and download this data into a text file on the hard disk. The data will be stored in a text file called SALES and will be in the form of a column of cash values. These values will be arranged in the order of the reps' identification numbers which range from 1 to 132. A text file is a store of information, and unlike a database file is not made up of fields and records, but instead stores information in the form of text as though it were a single document.

Capturing the necessary data involves four processes using a **communications package**.

(a) **Connect the mini and the micro** The physical connection will be made when the system is implemented. Making the connection here refers to logging the micro on to the mini using the communications package.

(b) **Emulating a dumb terminal** The micro switches itself to dumb terminal mode to allow the host minicomputer to communicate to it.

(c) **Locate the mini file** The reps' sales figures are listed in the mini file called SALES. Using the facilities of the communications package, the mini is told that the information in SALES is to be downloaded onto the micro's hard disk into a micro text file called MICSALES.

(d) **Downloading the data** The data is downloaded into MICSALES, the micro logged off and control returns to the introductory competition information system menu screen.

The following structure diagram describes the processes involved in capturing data.

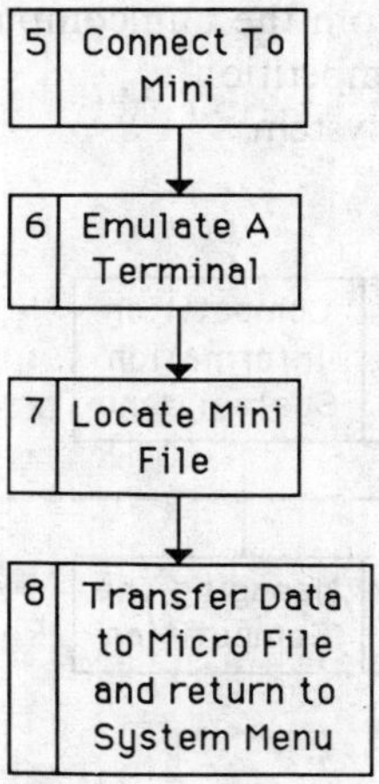

When this has been done this text file can be used as a source of data when running a program on the micro.

Managing the competition

7 The best way to manage competition is to use a spreadsheet package. The following worksheet has been devised to manage the competition:

	1	2	..	32	33 ..	35	..	46	47	48
1	Rapid Sales Ltd			Salesforce Competition				Date		
2	Number	Day 1	..	Day 31	Total	Month 1	..	Month 12	Name	Points
3										

The worksheet is subdivided into 48 columns and 134 rows (notice the row and column labels down the left hand side and along the top respectively).

The first row contains the identification of the worksheet. Note that the first cell of the first row is not large enough to contain the title of the worksheet so the cell has been expanded to allow it to fit in. The following cell contains the DATE. This is automatically generated whenever the computer is switched on and can be simply arranged by using the DATE function.

The second row contains the headings for each of the columns.

Column 1 contains the sales reps' identification numbers 1 to 132.

Columns 2 to 32 are reserved for daily data to be read in from the external text file resident on the micro's hard disk. The column chosen to have data read into it on any particular day is determined by the day number in the DATE. For example, if the date is 31st March the day number is 31 so the day will be read into the column headed Day 31—the 32nd column.

Column 33 contains the accumulated totals of all the sales figures in columns 2 to 32.

Columns 35 to 46 contain the bonus points awarded for each month's sales performance. The column chosen to contain bonus points is selected in any particular month from the month number in the DATE. For example, March will have a month number of 3 so the points will be placed in the column headed Month 3—the 37th column.

Column 47 contains the names of each sales rep and these will be entered from the keyboard when the worksheet is first constructed.

Column 48 contains the accumulated totals of all the monthly bonus points entered into columns 35 to 46.

Having decided on the use of a spreadsheet as the basis of the information system the management of the competition can be broken down into four separate tasks:

Entering daily sales

Data is automatically read from the text file on the hard disk into the cells of the appropriate column of the worksheet. The column number will be obtained from the day number in the date.

The accumulated sales total in column 33 is also updated automatically.

Entering monthly bonus points

The bonus points are automatically entered into the appropriate cells in the monthly column selected from the month number contained in the date and the accumulating totals in column 48 automatically updated. This is combined with

Identifying the month's winner

The names and accumulated points of the sales force are automatically printed out for that month to determine the month's top sales rep.

Identifying the annual winner

The last column is automatically sorted and the top five reps' names and points printed out in order.

Returning to system menu

8 All three previous options take the user deeper into the system. An option to move in the opposite direction must also be given and this is provided by the option to move back to the system menu.

The management modules

9 Since all the reading of data, calculating of bonus points and selection of winners is done automatically, no human intervention is required except for switching the system on and selecting the option required.

For this reason the management of the competition is designed to be run from a menu. The following diagram shows the menu module and the subsequent four modules that can be selected from the menu.

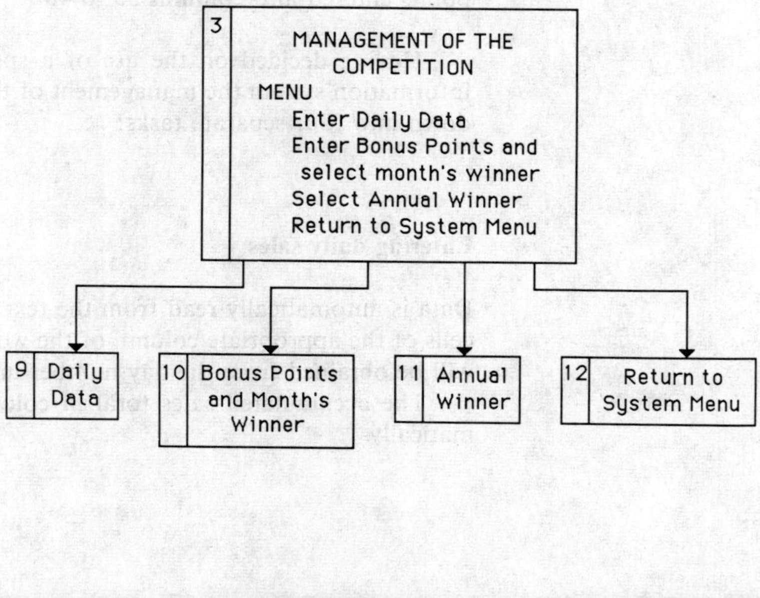

Whenever a menu is presented to the user, the options take the user further into the structure of the system to a lower level. However, the user may wish to move up a level and this can be catered for by adding a return option to the list of options displayed in the menu. When return is selected the user is then moved up a level through the system. There are four modules accessible from the management module:

Daily data

Order entire sheet on column 1 (Salesperson's Numbers).
Obtain value of DAY VARIABLE from date.
Goto Column number equal to day variable plus 2.
Read text file data into column.
Update total sales column.

Bonus points

Order entire sheet on totals column in descending order.
Obtain value of MONTH VARIABLE from date.
Goto column number equal to month variable plus 34.
From rows 1 to 20 fill with numbers from 20 to 1 descending.
Update total points column.
Goto names column.
Print out names and accumulated points in columns 47 and 48.
Top person in the list is that month's winner.
Clear sales figures from all day columns to prepare for next month's figures.

Annual winner

Go to Points column.
Order entire sheet on points column.
Print out first 10 rows from names and points columns.
Clear monthly bonus points from months columns to prepare for next year's competition.

Pseudocoding the eight management modules

10 The system has been designed with 12 modules. The next stage in the development process is to write out each module in pseudocode and this is done from the top level down.

System menu module

Note that in this module we have used all three control structures (*see* page 274). Each has a head and a tail to show where it starts and where it ends and the coding inside is indented to make it easier to read the program.

Communications system modules

The communications option from the system menu involves four separate processes. These processes are sequential and are governed by the command structure of the communications package used. Instead

```
*********************
*  MAIN SYSTEM MENU *
*********************

          BEGIN screen print

               Please make your selection from the possible options
               1.  Transfer data from mini computer to micro computer
               2.  Operate the competition system
               3.  QUIT the system

          END screen print
          * * * * * * * * * * * * * * * * * * * * * * * * *
          * SELECTION OF 1, 2 OR 3 INPUT AT THE KEYBOARD  *
          * * * * * * * * * * * * * * * * * * * * * * * * *
          BEGIN
               REPEAT
                input choice1
                UNTIL choice1 equals 1, 2 or 3
          END
          * * * * * * * * * * * * * * * * * * * * * *
          * VALUE OF choice1 DETERMINES OPTIONS *
          * * * * * * * * * * * * * * * * * * * * * *
          BEGIN
               IF choice1 = 1, choice1 = 2, choice1 = 3
                 DO Capture Module
                 DO Management Module
                 DO Quit Module
               ENDIF
          END
```

of writing them as four separate modules it will be sufficient to describe them collectively in one module.

This single module represents five communication operations.

```
************************
* COMMUNICATIONS MODULE *
************************

     BEGIN communications

          log  onto  mini  computer  using  communications  package
          commands
          emulate a dumb terminal
          download data from host file SALES to text file MICSALES

     END communications
```

It is assumed that the command sequence to execute this module will be available in the communications package manual. This command sequence must be described in detail when writing the manual for this system.

Management menu module

```
***************************************
* COMPETITION MANAGEMENT MENU MODULE *
***************************************

    BEGIN screen print

          Please select from the following options

          1. Enter daily sales figures
          2. Enter bonus points and identify this month's winner
          3. Identify the year's overall winner
          4. RETURN to the system menu

    END screen print

    * * * * * * * * * * * * * * * * * * * * * * * * * *
    * SELECTION OF 1, 2, 3 OR 4 INPUT AT THE KEYBOARD *
    * * * * * * * * * * * * * * * * * * * * * * * * * *

    BEGIN
          REPEAT
           input choice2
          UNTIL choice2 equals 1, 2, 3 or 4
    END

    * * * * * * * * * * * * * * * * * * * *
    * VALUE OF choice2 DETERMINES OPTIONS *
    * * * * * * * * * * * * * * * * * * * *

    BEGIN
          IF choice2 = 1, choice2 = 2, choice2 = 3, choice2 = 4
           DO Daily Enter Module
           DO Bonus Module
           DO Annual Module
           DO RETURN Module
          ENDIF
    END
```

Daily enter module

```
******************************
* DAILY ENTRY OF DATA MODULE *
******************************

     * * * * * * * * * * * * * * * * * * *
     * LOAD WORKSHEET COMP INTO MEMORY *
     * * * * * * * * * * * * * * * * * * *

     BEGIN
          load worksheet COMP
     END

     * * * * * * * * * * * * * *
     * DETERMINE DAY NUMBER  *
     * * * * * * * * * * * * * *

     BEGIN
          daynumber = DAY(DATE)
     END

     * * * * * * * * * * * * * * * * * * * * *
     * READ DATA FROM MICSALES INTO SHEET  *
     * * * * * * * * * * * * * * * * * * * * *

     BEGIN
          goto column number = daynumber + 1
          read data from text file MICSALES
     END

     * * * * * * * * * * * * * * * * * * *
     * UNLOAD WORKSHEET COMP ONTO DISK *
     * * * * * * * * * * * * * * * * * * *

     BEGIN
          save worksheet COMP
     END

     * * * * * * * * * * * * * * * * * * * *
     * RETURN CONTROL TO MANAGEMENT MENU *
     * * * * * * * * * * * * * * * * * * * *

     BEGIN
          do management menu module
     END
```

Bonus points and monthly winner module

```
************************************
* BONUS POINTS AND MONTHLY WINNER *
************************************

     * * * * * * * * * * * * * * * * * * *
     * LOAD WORKSHEET COMP INTO MEMORY *
     * * * * * * * * * * * * * * * * * * *

     BEGIN
          load worksheet COMP
     END

     * * * * * * * * * * * * * * *
     * DETERMINE MONTH NUMBER  *
     * * * * * * * * * * * * * * *

     BEGIN
          monthnumber = MONTH(DATE)
     END

     * * * * * * * * * * * * * * * * * *
     * ORDER SHEET ON TOTALS COLUMN   *
     * * * * * * * * * * * * * * * * * *

     BEGIN
          goto column 33
          order sheet in descending order
     END

     * * * * * * * * * * * * *
     * AWARD BONUS POINTS   *
     * * * * * * * * * * * * *

     BEGIN
          goto column monthnumber + 34
          set rownumber = 0
          FOR row = 3 to 22
               goto row
               enter 20 - rownumber
               rownumber = rownumber + 1
          NEXT row
     END

     * * * * * * * * * * * * * *
     * SELECT MONTHLY WINNER *
     * * * * * * * * * * * * * *

     BEGIN
          print contents of cells r3c47:48
     END

     * * * * * * * * * * * * * * * * * * *
     * UNLOAD WORKSHEET COMP ONTO DISK *
     * * * * * * * * * * * * * * * * * * *

     BEGIN
          save worksheet COMP
     END

     * * * * * * * * * * * * * * * * * * * *
     * RETURN CONTROL TO MANAGEMENT MENU *
     * * * * * * * * * * * * * * * * * * * *

     BEGIN
          do management module
     END
```

Selecting the annual winner module

```
*******************************
* SELECTION OF ANNUAL WINNER *
*******************************

     * * * * * * * * * * * * * * * * * * *
     * LOAD WORKSHEET COMP INTO MEMORY *
     * * * * * * * * * * * * * * * * * * *

     BEGIN
          load worksheet COMP
     END

     * * * * * * * * * * * * * * * * * *
     * ORDER SHEET ON POINTS COLUMN  *
     * * * * * * * * * * * * * * * * * *

     BEGIN
          goto column 48
          order sheet in descending order
     END

     * * * * * * * * * * * *
     * SELECT THE WINNERS  *
     * * * * * * * * * * * *

     BEGIN
          print contents of cells r3:135c47:48
     END

     * * * * * * * * * * *
     * CLEAR MONTH CELLS *
     * * * * * * * * * * *

     BEGIN
          goto column 48
          FOR row = 3 to 135
               enter 0
          NEXT row
     END

     * * * * * * * * * * * * * * * * * * *
     * UNLOAD WORKSHEET COMP ONTO DISK *
     * * * * * * * * * * * * * * * * * * *

     BEGIN
          save worksheet COMP
     END

     * * * * * * * * * * * * * * * * * * * *
     * RETURN CONTROL TO MANAGEMENT MENU *
     * * * * * * * * * * * * * * * * * * * *

     BEGIN
          do management module
     END
```

Return to system menu

```
***************************
* RETURN TO SYSTEM MENU *
***************************

     BEGIN
          do system menu module
     END
```

Finally, the last module to pseudocode is the third module at the second level—the module that permits the user to leave the system.

Quit the system module

```
****************************
* QUIT THE SYSTEM MODULE *
****************************

     BEGIN
          quit application
     END
```

The final coding

11 The coding of each module is done by the company's resident programmer using the 4GL that accompanied the spreadsheet. The actual coding is not reproduced here but is left as an exercise for you to complete.

Implementation and documentation

12 The final working program is installed and tested on the company's mirocomputer. For the test data the week's accumulated sales data is used repeatedly, making it easy to check that everything has worked satisfactorily.

The user manual has been written and includes a brief description of the system and how it works. The operating instructions are minimal because the system is menu-driven.

> Use your spreadsheet to duplicate this case study. If your spreadsheet does not have its own 4GL a number of the automatic procedures described here will have to be done manually. Describe how they would appear in a user's manual.

Summary

Rapid Sales Ltd decided to run a competition amongst their sales force. Each month the top sales rep received a free gift and the top rep of the year won a free holiday. Bonus points were awarded to the top 20 reps on a weekly basis and accumulated over every month and over the year. To organise the competition they used a spreadsheet and a communications package. The communications package downloaded the weekly sales figures into a text file on the microcomputer's hard disk. The spreadsheet then read this data into a worksheet, sorted in descending order and awarded bonus points to the highest 20 figures. The system was menu-driven and, apart from the communications package, used eight modules on a number of levels. The modules were described using an hierarchical tree and then pseudocoded before being coded in the spreadsheet's 4GL. Being menu-driven the documentation describing the operation of the system was necessarily brief.

Key points

Rapid Sales Ltd, the problem, the terms of reference, feasibility report, system design and development, capturing data from the minicomputer, connecting the mini and the micro, emulating a dumb terminal, locating the mini file, downloading the data, managing the competition, entering daily sales, entering monthly bonus points, identifying the month's winner, identifying the annual winner, returning to system menu, the management modules, daily data, bonus points, annual winner, pseudocoding the eight management modules, final coding, implementation and documentation

Self assessment questions

1 What is a menu? (5)
2 List the three modules accessible from the top level. (5)
3 What is a text file? (6)
4 List the four steps involved in downloading data from the mini to the micro. (6)
5 How was the computer managed? (7)
6 How was the weekly data entered into the spreadsheet? (7)
7 Why is there a 'return to systems menu' module? (8)
8 List the four management modules. (9)
9 What is an hierarchical tree? (9)
10 What is pseudocoding? (10)
11 What is meant by indentation and why is it used? (10)
12 What is meant by the program being menu-driven? (12)

Exercises

1 The following is part of an employee's weekly payslip.

employee number	employee name	gross pay	deductions
025143	J. Franklyn	£400.00	£140.00
			net pay
			£260.00

To produce this payslip the employee number, employee name, deductions and rate of pay per hour are required. Name one other piece of data that is required.

2 A form is to be designed to enter pupils for examinations in the simplest manner.
Each line of the form must contain space for the person's surname, initials, date of birth and their four digit candidate number.

The following diagram shows that 28 boxes are available for entering personal details. The remaining boxes will be used for the subject details.

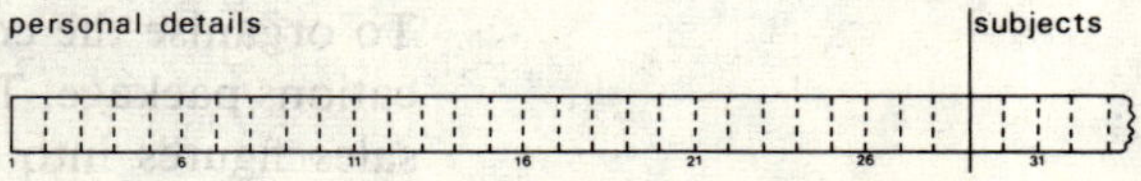

(a) Which columns on this diagram will be used to divide the different fields in the records? The dividing line and label for subjects is already shown.

(b) The candidate number uniquely identifies the candidate. Give one reason why it is also necessary to have the candidate name on the above form.

3 A library lending system keeps records of its customers and books on computer files.

(a) A book in the library is being borrowed by Miss Jones. Neither Miss Jones's name nor the book title will be entered at the time of borrowing the book.

(i) What data will be entered?
(ii) How would this data be entered?
(iii) Apart from details such as author, title and publisher, what other item of information should be stored about the book?
(iv) Name two alterations that must be made to the files after the book has been borrowed?

(b) The library lending system is an applications package. Write down an example of a utility program and explain how this differs from an applications package.

(c) The library system package comes with an instruction manual for the librarian. Which two of these following items would be found in the instruction manual?

flowchart, program listing, operating instructions, circuit diagrams, error messages, list of variables

(d) In another section of the library, terminals are on-line to the same database which is used by the lending system. These are available to all users of the library.

(i) A password system is used to prevent users of the library from gaining access to certain parts of the database. State one reason why the password system is necessary.
(ii) Name two examples of information which the user of the library could obtain by using these on-line terminals.

3 **Case study 3:** ***The file management***

Objectives

1 To introduce a file management system.
2 To demonstrate a sample of 4GL coding.

ActionLine Publications Limited

1 ActionLine Publications Ltd is a publishing company specialising in sports manuals. These manuals are comprehensive guides to any particular sport, each describing a particular sport and the history of its development. They also contain a full compendium of the rules of play as well as an instruction section which details coaching guidance for coaches and players. Every manual is written by an expert in the particular sport, in close consultation with a company editor. All the manuals have the same format and at the back of each manual is a detailed index.

When a book is written it is given to the publisher in typewritten form. The publisher typesets the book and produces a proof copy which is checked by the author for mistakes, after which the mistakes are corrected and the book is ready for printing.

At this proof stage, the index must be constructed which involves listing references in the text and key topics in alphabetical order.

ActionLine Publications Ltd, having experienced continual delays in publication because of index construction have decided to develop a computerised index creation system. On their staff is an editor who has an experience and understanding of file management systems and has been given the task of creating the system.

Terms of reference

2 The terms of reference are

- To design, develop and install an index creation system for use on either a company PC or a client's PC.
- To allow the application to be copied and for each copy to be sufficiently cheap to allow a copy to be given to the author free of charge.

Feasibility report

3 There are two aspects to this problem.

Designing and developing the system

4 There are a number of file management applications generators. Purchasing one of these and developing the index creation application would be quite simple.

Copying the application

5 Copyright laws prohibit any unauthorised copying of commercial software and the penalties are severe. If anyone copies software without authorisation, they are denying the author of the software the financial compensation due.

However, for many applications it has to be done, and there are two ways of approaching the problem. Authorisation can be obtained from the software authors although this is not usually possible, and instead the authors supply, at a reduced cost, a suite of programs that will allow a particular application to run but without providing the full facilities of the application generator. This is called a run-time version of the software. You can run the application on a run-time version but you cannot change it into another different type of application.

The application generator that the editor has in mind also provides a run-time version that will allow copies to be made. For each copy made a new run-time version will have to be purchased but the cost of each version is sufficiently low to warrant each copied application being given away to its authors.

The ActionLine management agrees with the editors' findings as described in the feasibility report and decides to proceed with the project.

Designing and developing the system

6 The task of creating an index to a book starts with the page-numbered proof copy. Using this, the author searches each page for items for inclusion in the index, each of which is recorded, together with its page number and category. For example, in a sports manual about golf, the word putter on page 10 will also be recorded under the category golf clubs. Having selected all the entries for the index the author then has to place them in alphabetical order both by item and by category. For example, Irons, Putters and Woods would each appear in their appropriate places in the alphabetical listing. In addition, they would appear under the category for Golf clubs;

Golf clubs	9
Irons	10
Putters	10
Woods	11

7 In addition to this, any item that appears more than once will

require multiple entries to be recorded. For example

Caddy 13, 65

Using a file management system to create the index, each record in the file will contain an item to be included in the index and the page number on which it appears. If an item is categorised, then the following record will contain both the category and the item. For example if record number 30 contains the item PUTTER on page 10 then record number 31 will contain the category GOLF CLUBS as well as a repeat of the item PUTTER and the page number 10.

8 To accommodate this each record must have three fields:

Number field

This field will record the page number. Because the records will never have to be sorted into page number order this field is not a key field.

Major item field

This will be an alphanumeric field and will contain the items for alphabetical listing. Because these items will be alphabetically sorted this will be a key field.

Minor item field

This too will be an alphanumeric field and will contain items that are to be listed within a group of items under a category, the category being in the major item field. This will be a minor key field to the previous major key field, which means that it will permit an alphabetical listing within another alphabetical listing.

For example, if a file has records with a major and a minor key field and seven of these records have the following entries:

Record 1	Major Field: C
	Minor Field: (blank)
Record 2	Major Field: B
	Minor Field: c
Record 3	Major Field: D
	Minor Field: x
Record 4	Major Field: B
	Minor Field: b
Record 5	Major Field: A
	Minor Field: (blank)
Record 6	Major Field: B
	Minor Field: a

Record 7	Major Field: D	
	Minor Field: w	

then if these records are sorted against the major key field with a sub-sort against the minor field they will appear in the following order:

Record 5	Major Field: A
	Minor Field: (blank)
Record 6	Major Field: B
	Minor Field: a
Record 4	Major Field: B
	Minor Field: b
Record 2	Major Field: B
	Minor Field: c
Record 1	Major Field: C
	Minor Field: (blank)
Record 7	Major Field: D
	Minor Field: w
Record 3	Major Field: D
	Minor Field: x

9 The system is to be menu-driven to make it simple to operate. The following modular structure is decided upon.

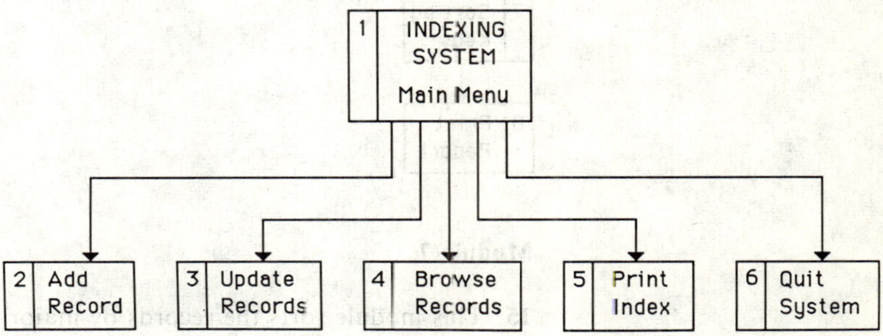

Module 1

10 This module is the entry module to the system. It will display a menu from which the user can choose any one of four modules to go to the next level and one module, number 6, that allows the user to quit the system.

Module 2

11 This module permits records to be entered.

Module 3

12 This module will permit any previously entered records to be amended should they require correction.

Module 4

13 This module permits the user to see all the records that have been entered into the system. It is necessary because the entire index may not be created at a single session. By browsing through the records the author can see the last record that has been entered.

Module 5

14 When all the records have been completed the index will need to be created. This is the module that looks after that process and is divided into two separate modules.

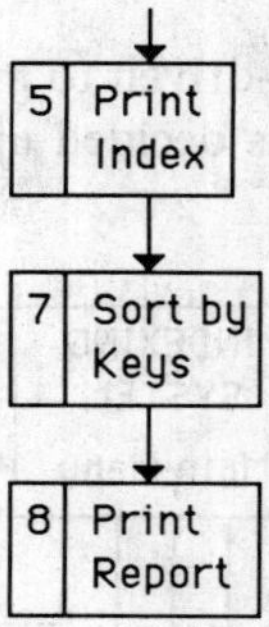

Module 7

15 This module sorts the records by major and minor keys.

Module 8

16 This module will print the index, which will be in the form of a report in which each record from the alphabetically ordered list will be printed in the following form:

Major key field .... Page Number
Minor key field .... Page Number

If a number of successive records has the same entry in the major key field then only the first record will provide the major key field entry: all the others will be suppressed. In this way the index will be printed out.

Data dictionary

17 The template for each record in the file has to be defined using a data dictionary.

	Field Name	Field Type	Size	Key	Key Type
1	Page Number	Numeric	3	N	
2	Major Field	Alphanumeric	20	Y	Major
3	Minor Field	Alphanumeric	20	Y	Minor

This data dictionary is constructed using the facilities of the file manager. Defining the data dictionary in this way automatically creates the file called INDEX—it is now ready for information to be entered into the records.

Screen design

18 If the file definition is left at that, the screen display for each record as it appears ready for data entry will look like this:

```
Page Number ---
Major Field  --------------------
Minor Field  --------------------
```

This does not give much assistance to an unfamiliar user, but by permitting a screen display to be created to accompany a record, the editor can produce the following:

```
ActionLine Publications Ltd------------------------------------INDEX

  Enter Page number here  ---

  Enter index entry here (Item or Category) --------------------

  Enter Item entry here  --------------------

            Press F10 when this record is complete
```

This screen is stored in a file called INDEXSCR.

Pseudocoding the modules

19 The modules are pseudocoded prior to coding in the 4GL.

Module 1 The introductory screen: name—MENU

```
***************************
* MENU FOR INDEX SYSTEM *
***************************

BEGIN screen display
     The following options are available;

           1. Enter Index Items
           2. Amend Index Items
           3. Browse Index Items
           4. Print The Index

           5. QUIT the system

     Please enter the number of your selection -

END screen display

* * * * * * * * * * * * * * *
* INPUT SELECTION FROM MENU *
* * * * * * * * * * * * * * *

BEGIN
     Input choice
END

* * * * * * * * * * * * * * * * * * * *
* EXECUTE OPTION ACCORDING TO choice  *
* * * * * * * * * * * * * * * * * * * *

BEGIN
     if choice = 1, choice = 2, choice = 3, choice = 4, choice = 5
          do ENTRY
          do AMEND
          do VIEW
          do PROUT
          do LEAVE
     endif
END
```

Module 2 Entering data into records: name—ENTRY

```
****************
* ENTRY MODULE *
****************

BEGIN
     enter data
END
```

Module 3 Amending data in records: name—AMEND

```
****************
* AMEND MODULE *
****************

BEGIN
     amend data
END
```

Module 4 Browsing records: name—VIEW

```
*****************
* BROWSE MODULE *
*****************

BEGIN
     browse records
END
```

Module 5 Printing data in records: name—PROUT

```
****************
* PRINT MODULE *
****************

BEGIN
     do SORT
     do REPORT
END
```

Module 6 Quitting the system: name—LEAVE

```
***************
* QUIT MODULE *
***************

BEGIN
     quit the system
END
```

Module 7 Sorting the records: name—SORT

```
***************
* SORT MODULE *
***************

BEGIN
     sort records against major and minor fields
END
```

Module 8 Printing the index: name—REPORT

```
*****************
* REPORT MODULE *
*****************

BEGIN
     print the pre-cefined report called REPINDEX
END
```

Coding the modules

20 The file manager has its own 4GL and the following modules are coded in this language. Explanations of certain commands are listed after the coding.

Module 1 The introductory screen: name—MENU

```
*************************
* MENU FOR INDEX SYSTEM *
*************************

menu print 10 10 1 0 The following options are available;
menu print 12 10 1 0 1. Enter Index Items
menu print 13 10 1 0 2. Amend Index Items
menu print 14 10 1 0 3. Browse Index Items
menu print 15 10 1 0 4. Print The Index
menu print 17 10 1 0 5. QUIT the system
menu print 19 10 1 0 Please enter the number of your selection -

* * * * * * * * * * * * * * *
* INPUT SELECTION FROM MENU *
* * * * * * * * * * * * * * *

menu input 19 55 1 0 1 choice

* * * * * * * * * * * * * * * * * * * * *
* EXECUTE OPTION ACCORDING TO choice   *
* * * * * * * * * * * * * * * * * * * * *

if choice = 1, choice = 2, choice = 3, choice = 4, choice = 5
     execute ENTRY
     execute AMEND
     execute VIEW
     execute PROUT
     execute LEAVE
     else transfer MENU
endif
```

Module 2 Entering data into records: name—ENTRY

```
****************
* ENTRY MODULE *
****************

load INDEX screen INDEXSCR
enter
key update
unload all
```

Module 3 Amending data in records: name—AMEND

```
****************
* AMEND MODULE *
****************

load INDEX screen INDEXSCR
update
unload all
```

Module 4 Browsing records: name—VIEW

```
*****************
* BROWSE MODULE *
*****************

load INDEX screen INDEXSCR
browse all
unload all
```

Module 5 Printing data in records: name—PROUT

```
****************
* PRINT MODULE *
****************

execute SORT
execute REPORT
```

Module 6 Quitting the system: name—LEAVE

```
***************
* QUIT MODULE *
***************

quit file manager
```

Module 7 Sorting the records: name—SORT

```
***************
* SORT MODULE *
***************

load INDEX screen INDEXSCR
order key [2;3]
```

Module 8 Printing the index: name—REPORT

```
*****************
* REPORT MODULE *
*****************

print report predefined REPINDEX
```

Coding commands

21 The 4GL that was used in the previous coding is similar to the 4GL that is provided with the SMART Integrated Software Suite. This is a package that contains a word processor, a spreadsheet, a database management system and a communications component, all of which are completely integrated and operable using the 4GL provided. The various commands that need clarification are as follows:

- **menu print a b c d** Here the 'a' refers to line number on the screen and 'b' to the column number at which the screen print will start. The letters 'c' and 'd' refer to the foreground and background colours to be used for the screen printing.
- **menu input a b c d e** Here the letter 'e' stands for the length of the input which in this case is just one number.
- **execute** This sends execution to the named module. In a procedural language this would be called a procedure. When the module is executed the control of the program is returned to the line following the execute command. Note that the value of the variable choice is maintained whenever execution moves to another module—we call such a variable a GLOBAL VARIABLE. If a variable has a value only in a particular module it is called a LOCAL VARIABLE.
- **transfer** This has the same effect as execute except that control does not return to the following line of control.

- **enter** This permits entries to be made into records one after another.
- **key update** This redefines the key files when new records are entered.
- **order key** [2; 3] This orders the major field (number 2) and the minor field (number 3).
- **print report predefined REPINDEX** The system has a report generator which is used to define the format of the printout. This predefined report can then be called into action in this way.

Implementation and documentation

22 The operation of this system is so straightforward that any author who uses a word processor will soon understand the system. The user manual provided is as follows;

User manual

The system

23 The index creation system has five parts:

- enter records to the file
- amend records already in the file
- browse records in the file
- print out the index

To use the system follow these instructions:

1 Switch the computer on with the orange switch and wait for the prompt A > to appear.
2 Place the floppy disk containing the INDEX SYSTEM into DRIVE A.
3 Type in at the keyboard the following:

INDEXAPP

and then press ENTER. After a few seconds the following screen will appear.

```
ActionLine Publications                                    INDEX

              The following options are available;

                   1. Enter Index Items
                   2. Amend Index Items
                   3. Browse Index Items
                   4. Print The Index

                   5. QUIT the system

              Please enter the number of your selection █
```

The screen presents you with all five options available within the index system.

Enter index items

24 If you select the number 1 from the main Index System Menu screen you will be presented with the following display:

```
ActionLine Publications Ltd                                    INDEX

  Enter Page number here  ---

  Enter index entry here (Item or Category) --------------------

  Enter Item entry here --------------------

            Press F10 when this record is complete

Insert ON  F3 - Prev fld  F5 - Not used  F7 - Fld delete  F9 - Repeat
F2 - Date  F4 - Next fld  F6 - Next Rec  F8 - Fld reform  F10 - Finish
```

You are now in a position to enter all the necessary details for an individual index item. These are;

- enter page number here This is the page number of the page that contains the item.
- enter index entry here (item or category) This is the item number or the category of the item on the previous record.
- enter index entry here This is the item repeated from the previous record entry: use only if the previous field is a category.

Amend customer records

25 If you select the number 2 from the main index system menu screen you will be presented with the following display:

```
ActionLine Publications Ltd                                    INDEX

  Enter Page number here  zz

  Enter index entry here (Item or Category) zzzzzzzzzz

  Enter Item entry here  zzzzzzzzzzzz

            Press F10 when this record is complete

Insert ON  F3 - Prev fld  F5 - Not used  F7 - Fld delete  F9 - Repeat
F2 - Date  F4 - Next fld  F6 - Next Rec  F8 - Fld reform  F10 - Finish
```

You can now amend all the necessary details for any index entry.

26 Note the key description underneath the index record—this enables you to amend records and refer to the function keys placed on the left hand side of the keyboard.

You can move to any field on an index record using the F3 and F4 keys on the left hand side of the keyboard.

You can move through the list of index records using the F5 and F6 keys.

When you wish to amend a field, place the cursor on that field and overtype anything that is already entered in that field.

When you have completed all your amendments, press F10 to return to the main index system screen.

Browse the index entries

27 Selecting number 3 in the Main Index System Menu will produce a display of all the records entered into the system. Use the function keys displayed at the bottom of the screen to allow you to move through the list.

Print the index

28 Select number 4 in the main index screen to automatically produce the index at the printer. Make sure the printer is switched on for this option.

> To fully appreciate your file manager, duplicate this system using your file manager or database management system.

Summary

ActionLine Publications Ltd decided to create a cheap give-away index creating system. They used a file manager whose supplier also provided a cheap run-time version for copying applications. The index system was developed in a modular structure and finally coded in the file manager's 4GL. The principle on which the system worked was that of ordering on major and minor key fields. Using this feature of the file manager, items for inclusion in the index could be inserted into their usual alphabetical listing as well as within an alphabetical listing under a category. The index itself was designed using the file manager's report generating facility. This enables the correct format for the index to be predefined and later called into execution during the running of the program.

Key points

> ActionLine Publications Ltd, terms of reference, feasibility report, designing and developing the system, copying the application, system design and development, data dictionary, screen design, pseudocoding the modules, coding the modules, coding commands, implementation and documentation, user manual.

Self assessment questions

1 Why is it a good idea to develop a computerised index creating system? (1)
2 What application package was used for the system? (1)
3 Is it difficult to locate a file manager? (3)
4 What is required to enable copies of commercial software to be made? (4)
5 What is a run-time version of an application package? (5)
6 What is a major key field? (8)
7 What is a minor key field? (8)
8 Describe the outcome of a sort against a major key field and a sub-sort against a minor key field. (8)
9 What does menu-driven mean? (9)
10 Describe the modular structure of the index system. (9–16)
11 What is a data dictionary? (17)
12 Why would you wish to be able to design screens to accompany data entry into a file? (18)
13 What is meant by pseudocoding? (19)
14 What type of language was used to code the final program? (20)
15 What is a 4GL? (20)
16 Can you remember the difference between a procedural language and a non-procedural language? Does the coding of the index system satisfy the definition of a non-procedural language? (20)
17 What is a global variable? (21)
18 What is a local variable? (21)
19 Why does the user manual describe the details of operation from switching on the computer? (22)
20 What other documentation should be provided with this system that is not shown here?

Exercises

1 A school uses a computer to store information on its pupils. The examination results of the pupils are held in coded form. Some of the fields used are as follows:

Subject	Level	Mark obtained	Date of examination

The codes used for each field are:

Subject	001 ≡ English	
	102 ≡ Maths	
	304 ≡ Physics	
Level	02 ≡ GCSE	
	03 ≡ A LEVEL	
	04 ≡ ORAL	

The 'mark' is a 3 digit number in the range 000 to 100; 'date of examination' is written in the following way:

1087 = OCTOBER 1987
0686 = JUNE 1986

(a) How would you interpret the following codes:
(i) 102020560585
(ii) 001040831187

(b) Encode the following; a mark of 65 in an 'A' level Physics examination taken in June 1984.

(c) It is possible to make errors when entering information. Give one example of an incorrect entry to
(i) the date field
(ii) the mark field.

(d) Give an example of one extra field that might be useful and give a reason for your choice.

2 If a store manager needs to alter items of data that are held on the stock file, what three different types of change might need to be made.

3 Many items now carry a bar code.

(a) The bar code could be read at the point-of-sale terminal by a bar code reader or a laser scanner.
(i) Which would be used in a food supermarket?
(ii) Why is this method preferred?

(b) A bar code on a tin of baked beans does not include the price.
(i) Explain briefly the reason for this.
(ii) How does the terminal find out the price to include in the bill?
(iii) Name an item where the price might be encoded in the bar code, and give a reason why it is then needed.

4 Name two methods of input not involving bar codes that are used for point-of-sale terminals, and give an example of the type of shop where each might be used.

5 Write down four advantages and two disadvantages of using electronic point-of-sale terminals as opposed to older types of tills.

6 (a) What is contained in the re-order level field in the stock file?

(b) Describe fully when and how this field is used in conjunction with the re-order file.

7 (a) Name one useful piece of information that the store management can find out from the till file.

(b) How is this information found out from the file?

8 A stock file is held on magnetic disk so that records can be read and updated in any order.

(a) What is this type of access called?

(b) How easily could the stock file be held on magnetic tape?

Explain your answer.

Section five

1 You and me

Objectives

1 To identify the implications of the use of computers for individuals, organisations and society.

2 To formulate a reasoned view of the potential effects of computer usage.

Introduction

1 In this chapter we trace the events of a typical day, pointing out some of the areas where the microprocessor chip is used. Many more are not mentioned here and you are encouraged to try to find as many as you can.

At home

2 It is 7 am on a bright, sunny, spring morning and you awake to the familiar tones of your favourite radio journalist. The digital clock on your bedside table has switched the radio on at this preset time—preset by you last night and remembered this morning by the chip inside the clock.

3 You rise and walk to your shower set at the temperature just right for you—set by you and remembered by the chip inside the heating system regulator on the kitchen wall.

4 Showered, dressed and ready for the day, you pick up the newspaper and notice how the photographs on the front page are crystal clear, with so much more detail than there used to be before the paper was typeset by computer. The print is not only clear, but there are no spelling mistakes: computerised spelling-checkers have picked out all the errors.

5 It is time for breakfast and a little breakfast television. You press the button on the remote control device and the chip inside selects the channel. Breakfast is fruit juice, cereal and coffee. The fruit juice comes from Florida, the cereal is made in Britain from wheat grown in Canada and the coffee comes from Kenya. The glass you drink the juice out of comes from France, the cereal bowl is made in England, the

cutlery comes from Japan and the coffee maker comes from Taiwan. Not one of them has ended up on your breakfast table without some form of computerised system coming into action.

6 Breakfast over, the day stretches out before you—a holiday with no pressing commitments apart from the date arranged for this evening through the computerised dating service. This is arranged by sending in details of your own personality, your likes and dislikes and your preferences in companions so that they can be matched with information relating to other people held on the computer's database. Once a match has been made then a meeting is arranged. You then remember, you must book the theatre and the restaurant for this evening.

7 To decide what to do this afternoon, you switch the TV to CEEFAX, the information channel with pages of information that have been input by using a computer's text and graphics facilities. Nothing inspires you on the entertainments page so you turn to the weather page. The weather should be good all day so you decide to spend the morning at home and the afternoon wandering around the town centre.

8 Meanwhile, the mail has arrived. There are four letters and this month's computer magazine. Two of the letters are from mail order firms trying to persuade you to buy. The introduction of computerised systems has made it much easier for them to keep track of their stock and their customers. As a result their catalogues are becoming more comprehensive and more widely circulated, tempting many people to

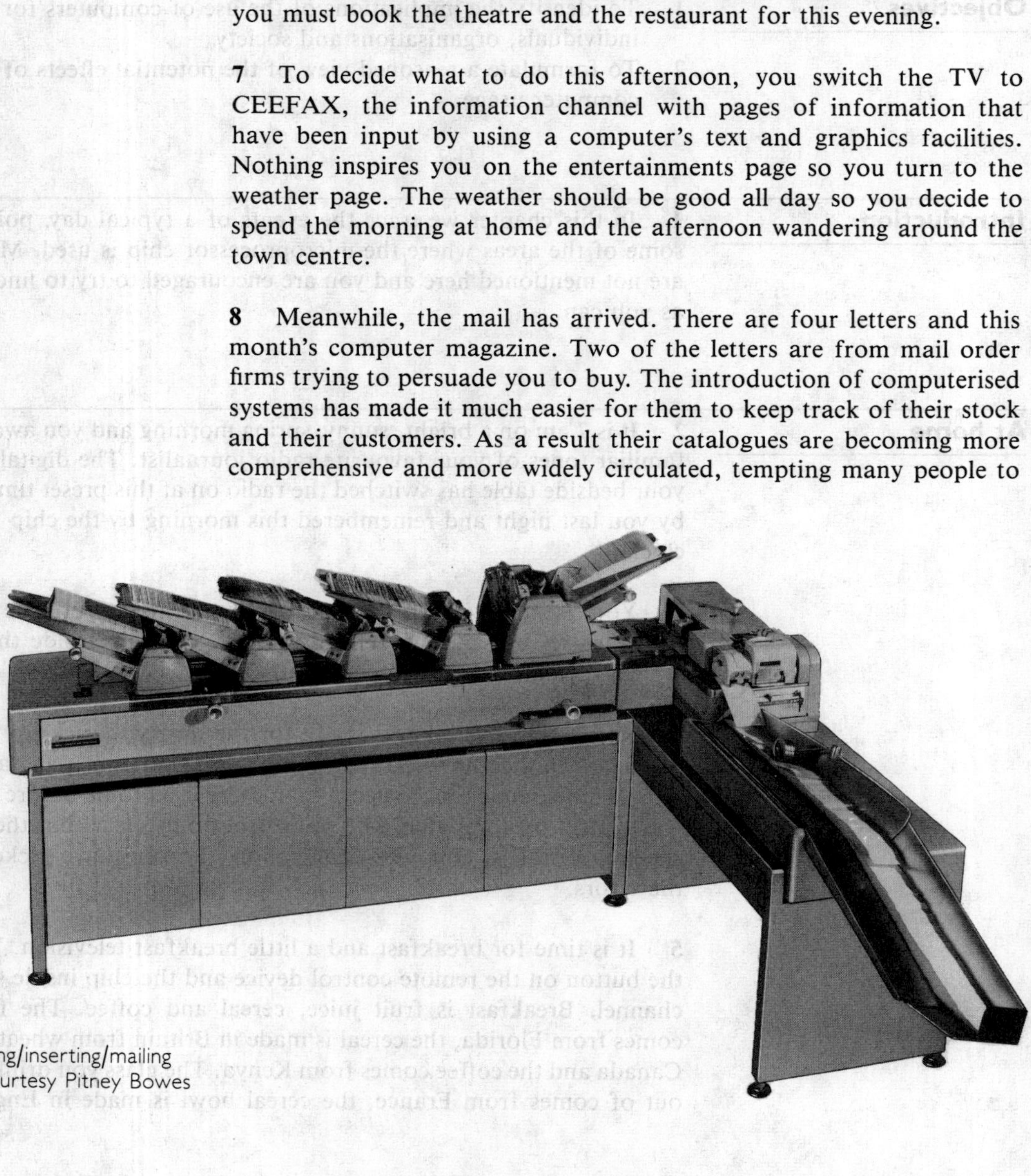

5.1 Collating/inserting/mailing machine; courtesy Pitney Bowes Ltd

buy from them. The third letter is from your college informing you that your Information Technology evening course will start at 6.15 pm tomorrow evening. The letter was only posted yesterday evening but because the post code has been used it has already arrived. By using the post code the automatic mail sorter in the Post Office knows exactly where the letter is being sent and sorts it into the correct place for collection by the postman.

9 The evening course in Information Technology, you are told, uses Computer Based Training (CBT) techniques, where the computer interacts with a video disk reader. Using this system you have the effect of a live TV presentation of the course material. The speed at which you are presented with new facts depends on your responses to the various questions asked so the pace is automatically set to suit you. You also have facilities to question the system yourself to review facts that you are not sure of while the teacher has time to talk to other students individually and clear up any problems they may be having.

10 In the fourth letter you find a cheque for £50—one of your premium bond numbers has been drawn by ERNIE. ERNIE stands for Electronic Random Number Indicating Equipment and is a computer that selects numbers at random to match the numbers on premium bonds. If a match occurs with one of the premium bonds in your possession, you win.

11 You turn to your computer magazine to find a special section dealing with aids for the handicapped. There is a picture of a man who is paralysed and the only parts of his body that he can move are his tongue, his eyes and some very slight movement of his head. By attaching sensors to his head he is able to communicate with other people using his computer screen and he can turn light switches on and off and summon help when he needs it. The extent to which the lives of handicapped people have been improved is a direct result of the use of the chip.

13 Before you leave the house for the afternoon you have some washing to do and lunch to prepare. You put your washing into the washing machine and set the washing cycle. The chip inside the machine takes in your instructions and organises the program to be done in your absence. Lunch comes out of the freezer and into the microwave oven, the chip inside the microwave organising the cooking.

14 You still have time to practice playing your electronic keyboard which can simulate an enormous range of instruments and can even be programmed to simulate a whole orchestra—all organised by the chip.

15 Before leaving you remember that there was a program on TV this afternoon that you wanted to record so you set the channel on the video recorder and the starting and finishing times. The chip inside the video recorder takes over from here. You then set the answering machine on the telephone for the chip inside to organise all incoming calls, and the burglar alarm, again activated by a chip.

> Make a diary of a day at home and a day at school. Keep a record of everything you do and note whether a chip has had any influence. If so, try to imagine what would happen if there were no chip. Would the event have been different in any way? Would the event still have happened? When you have done this compare your notes with the diaries of your friends. Check that you have not missed out times where the chip has been used in your day.

At play

16 The car you travel in has fuel injection—fuel is supplied to the engine, according to the car's speed and the load it is carrying, the whole process being organised by a chip. The digital display on the dashboard shows how much fuel you are using per mile, your current speed, the temperature of the engine and the level of the engine oil. Warning lights will come on when you are short of fuel, if your brakes are defective or when a light bulb is defective, all of which are organised by a chip.

17 On your way to town a computerised traffic light system is in operation. The traffic flow is controlled by a computer and there are no more traffic jams.

18 You arrive at the car park, take the ticket out of the machine and the barrier lifts up. You are counted as you go in and again when you leave. By subtracting the number of cars that have left from the number that have arrived, the chip inside the system can tell when the car park is full and light up a display outside that reads CAR PARK FULL. This saves you from driving around a full car park looking for a space that isn't there.

> Can you think of any other gates that are controlled by a computer?

19 Once in town, you remember that you need some cash. To save you from queuing, you take your bank card to the automatic teller, slot the card into the machine and type in your PIN number—Personal Identification Number. The automatic teller reads the brown magnetic strip on the back of the card to check that you have entered the correct PIN number. The details of your accounts are displayed and you decide to instruct the machine to transfer some money from your current account to your savings account before telling the machine that you wish to withdraw cash. You key in the amount, the machine counts out the cash and dispenses it to you with a small slip of paper which gives all the details of the transactions you have just made for your personal record. The chip inside the automatic teller has made it a much more convenient way to handle your financial affairs.

20 Next you set off for the photographic shop to pick up some prints that need to be developed. You pass the computer arcade and see the screens full of brightly coloured scenes of fighting space invaders, race track simulations, aircraft cockpit simulations and many more—chips again are hard at work.

21 Next to the arcade is the Quick Print shop where a number of duplicators are available for copying documents in either black and white only or colour. The shop also has a Fax facility which allows you to send a copy of a document anywhere in the country along the telephone lines, or anywhere in the world via satellite. All are controlled by chips.

> Who else in your town uses information and database query systems?

22 On the other side of the road is the travel agent where all the assistants use computer terminals to find out details about holidays they are selling all over the world. If you decide to book a holiday then that is also done at this terminal—trains, planes, hotels, tours or whatever you desire to make your holiday complete can all be booked and paid for at one of these computer terminals.

23 At the end of the block is the photographic shop which advertises in the window INSTANT DEVELOPING. Inside is a large machine into which your film is put and from which, minutes later, your prints are returned, all organised by a chip. The prints are not as good as you expected so the assistant suggests that the automatic light intensity setting is defective which means the chip may need replacing.

24 As you walk past a card shop you remember that your nephew has a birthday soon. Inside the shop you eventually choose a musical card suitable for a four-year-old which, by means of a chip inside plays 'Happy Birthday' when you open it.

25 You see from your digital watch that it is time for coffee and so make your way to a fast food hamburger restaurant. You ask for coffee and the counter assistant presses a button on the till. At the next till a customer wants three quarter pounders, two with fries one without, two milk-shakes, one coffee and three apple turnovers. This information all goes into the till, one button at a time. In the kitchen, the display shows exactly what has been ordered and then the tills automatically work out the cost of your purchases. The chips in these tills not only organise the immediate purchases but also retain the information and allow management to analyse their sales.

26 Coffee over, you decide to telephone the theatre in the next town to book your seats for tonight. When you have inserted your coins a chip controlled display tells you how much you have put in. You dial the number of the theatre box office and having made your booking you pay by giving your credit card number. The box office enters this number into their computer to check that you have the necessary credit available. It does this by talking over the telephone line to another computer owned by the credit company. You have enough credit so the transaction is completed and, when the call is over the chip inside the telephone returns to you the excess money you have paid.

What other shops can you go into in your town and see a computerised system being used?

27 After some more shopping you go home and decide to travel by public transport for your evening date. First you catch a bus at the end of your road. There is no conductor on this service; instead the driver collects the fares as you board by typing in your destination to the ticket machine, for the correct priced ticket to be issued. While the driver is able to concentrate on driving, the chip inside the ticket machine helps to keep the accounts straight.

28 Next you walk to the railway station where you are issued with a rail ticket with a magnetised brown strip on the back. There is no-one to check your ticket and instead you place it into a slot for the barrier to let you pass. On the platform the trains that are due to arrive and depart during the next hour or so are displayed on the TV screen suspended from the roof and connected to the station computer. The trains are also routed by computer.

29 At 7.30 pm, as you sit with your date in the theatre, the lights dim, the curtain rises and the stage is ablaze with colour. The effect of the lighting is dramatic. All the lighting changes have been preset during the dress rehearsal so that to effect a change of lights from one setting to another all that has to be done is to press a single button: the fading down and fading up of lights is done automatically.

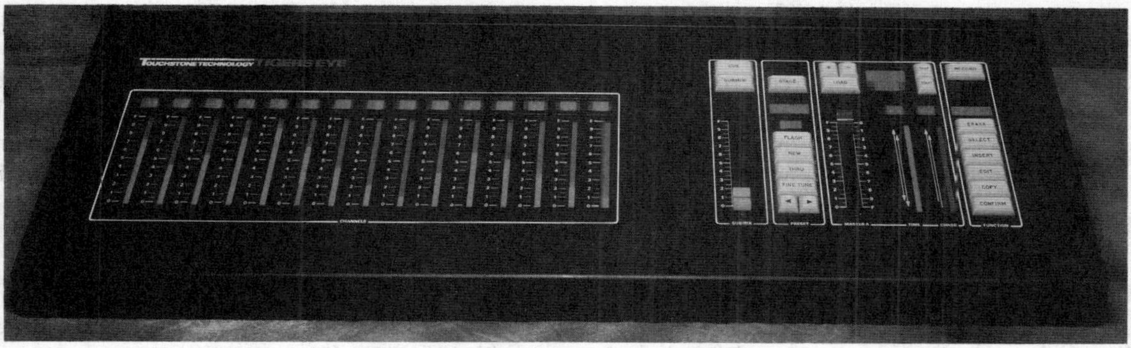

5.2 Theatre lighting console; courtesy Touchstone Technology

30 After the performance, you go to your favourite restaurant. On taking your order the waiter wipes a light pen over a bar code for each item and when the order is complete this light pen is slotted into a box on the head waiter's desk. The food order is then transmitted straight to the chef in the kitchen, the drinks order straight to the bar and the cost of each item is transmitted straight to the till. When the bill arrives after the meal it is clearly typed and because it has been calculated by computer is error free. To pay, you hand over your credit card and the cashier slides the card down a groove at the back of the till, making direct contact with the credit company computer to check that your credit is good.

31 You can now appreciate how much a microchip can feature in your daily life.

> Make a diary of a day out, away from home or school. Keep a record of everything you do and note whether a chip has had any influence. If it has, try to imagine what would happen if there were no chip. Would the event have been different in any way? Would the event still have happened? When you have done this, compare your notes with the diaries of your friends. Check that you have not missed out times where the chip has been used in your day.

Summary

The computer and the microprocessor chip are gradually affecting our daily lives more. At home clocks, heating systems, televisions, hi-fi units and many other devices are controlled by chips. Items that we use every day such as crockery and cutlery have all passed through some computerised system somewhere on their journey to our home. The newspapers are written and typeset by computer, the mail is sorted by computer and even cash prizes are selected by computer. Away from home the influence of the chip is still with us. The car may have a chip controlling its operation, traffic lights and parking barriers are both controlled by computer. Shops are also organised by computer as well as much of their equipment. From duplicators to film developers to money dispensers, the computer plays a vital role. Wherever you go and whatever you do a computer or microprocessor chip is likely to be involved.

Key points

Digital clocks, central heating regulators, newspaper typesetting, dating services, Ceefax, post codes, mail order, computer based training (CBT), ERNIE, handicapped aids, electronic keyboard, answering machine, video recorder, burglar alarm, fuel injection, traffic systems, automatic tellers, cameras, automatic photo developers, booking systems, fast food restaurants, public telephones, public transport, theatre lighting.

Self assessment questions

1 List three applications of the chip that you might encounter before breakfast. (2,4)
2 How does the chip affect your breakfast? (5)
3 What is Dateline? (6)
4 What is CEEFAX? (7)
5 Why do mail order companies use a computer? (8)
6 How does the post code help the Post Office? (8)
7 What is CBT? (9)
8 What do the letters in ERNIE stand for? (10)
9 What are premium bonds? (10)
10 List three computer controlled handicapped aids. (11)
11 Name two household appliances in common use that use a chip. (13)
12 Name one chip controlled musical instrument. (14)
13 Name one facility offered by a push button telephone. (15)
14 What does the chip do in a car's fuel injection system? (16)
15 What other facilities does a chip offer in a car? (16)
16 How can the computer assist traffic at an intersection? (17)
17 How can a computer assist in a car park? (18)
18 What is a PIN number? (19)
19 How do you operate an automatic teller? (19)
20 What facilities does an automatic teller offer? (19)
21 Name four places in the high street where you are likely to see computer controlled devices. (20–23)
22 What is a FAX machine? (21)
23 How do travel agents make use of the computer? (22)
24 Are you likely to find a chip in a card shop? (24)
25 What is a button till? (25)
26 Why are button tills used? (25)
27 How do button tills help to provide an efficient service in a fast food restaurant? (25)
28 What facility does the chip offer in a public telephone? (26)
29 How can you pay for a service over the phone? (26)
30 How does the chip assist the bus driver? (27)
31 How does your train ticket allow you on to the platform of an unmanned railway station? (28)
32 Where does the computer come into play in the live theatre? (29)
33 How can a light pen assist in the management of a restaurant? (30)
34 How can your credit rating be checked? (30)

Exercises

1 Many people now draw money from their bank or building society accounts by means of plastic cards.

(a) Name one advantage to the user of such a card.

(b) Name one advantage to the bank.

(c) Explain why it is important for the card holder to be careful with his/her plastic card.

(d) Describe four of the events that can occur when a card holder withdraws cash from a machine.

(e) Do you think it is likely that banks will attempt to withdraw their present counter facilities in favour of card dispensers?
Give one reason for your answer.

3 (a) Describe an on-line booking system that you have studied. Make specific reference to the hardware requirements as well as to the facilities provided by the system.

(b) Name the processes involved in the development of a computer-based system.

(c) With reference to part (b) above, which of these tasks would be carried out by

(i) a Systems Analyst,

(ii) a Computer Programmer?

(d) An existing manual booking system is to be replaced by a computer-based on-line booking system.

(i) Name one advantage and one disadvantage expected when the new on-line system is introduced.
(ii) What are two likely effects of the introduction of the on-line booking system on employees?
(iii) Give two examples of the improvements in customer service that may be expected as a result.

4 A microprocessor system is used to control the heating in a house. The heating can be set to come on and off at particular times, and the temperature in each room can be individually set. Within each room there is a temperature sensor, and an electrically controlled valve to turn the radiators on and off.

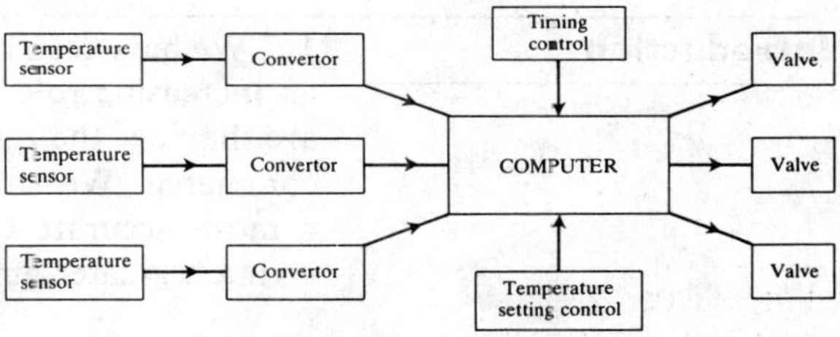

(a) Why are convertors needed?

(b) Discuss the advantages and disadvantages of using a computer controlled system over other control systems.

(c) Give a brief description of another way in which a computer might be used in the home to assist the householder.

2 *Business and other organisations*

Objectives

1 To recognise the advantages to organisations of using a computer.

2 To describe the ways in which computerisation is affecting the working lives of individuals.

Introduction

1 We have seen that computers and computerised systems are playing an increasing role in our daily lives but the place where these systems are having the greatest impact is in the world of business and commerce. We shall see in this chapter how the computer provides a more accurate control over management and production, thereby giving a greater amount of flexibility and financial saving.

Management and information

2 All organisations need to be managed. Management includes regulating and supervising the organisation's activities and controlling its money. For many years the computer has been available to process data relating to many aspects of management, often using large Mainframes. Since the introduction of the microprocessor, not only data, but also information can be processed by more people on smaller machines. Accurate information about the state of an organisation is essential for effective management. Information must be continually updated to maintain its accuracy.

> Ask your family and friends whether anyone you know has experienced the introduction of a computerised system. Ask their opinions and how it has affected their work.

3 In larger organisations information has to be shared and be accessible by many people. There are too many individuals, too much information and not enough time in the day for everyone to consult each other, hence the requirement of the computer. Information can be stored, regularly updated and as it changes it is accessible by anyone at a computer terminal. In this way the information relating to an

organisation becomes more accurate, more easily shared and more easily accessed and as a result, management is more effective.

> Your school is a large organisation. Who manages it? How are the school activities organised? Does a computer play a role in this organisation? Who organises all the timetables? Can you think of any area of school life that would benefit from the introduction of a computer? Why would it be of benefit?
> Try to find the answers to these questions by asking your teacher.

The computerised office

4 Perhaps the most obvious sign of modern technology being introduced into businesses and other organisations is the computerised office.

In many offices people no longer sit at a desk littered with paperwork but sit at what is called a workstation.

5 The workstation consists of a desk, complete with a small computer or computer terminal. Piles of paper are now replaced by word processor documents and database records that are accessible by using the computer. The computer communicates with other computers in the organisation, either through a modem connected to a telephone line or through a network and messages and memos are passed between individuals through the network or telephone link using their computer mail facility. The workplace is more efficient and less costly to operate. It also encourages the open-plan style of office layout, with a much more pleasant atmosphere in which to work.

6 The workstation arrangement is used by a wide variety of personnel in an organisation, the purpose to which the computer is put changing according to the job required to be done: a typist will use the computer as a word processor, an accountant will use a financial accounts system and, for a manager, the computer will operate a management information system.

> Next time you are in your town centre, see if you can find an open-plan office where computers are being used, for example, a building society. You could go in and try to find out what sort of work is done on the computers. Ask the people who work there if they enjoy their work and if they prefer the open plan office to the more conventional office. If there are older people working there, ask them how their job has changed as a result of computers being introduced.

Management and information systems

There are a variety of different types of management and information systems. Three examples are:

- the Sales Order Processing (SOP) system
- booking systems
- library systems

The Sales Order Processing (SOP) system

The sales order processing system is designed to accept and process incoming orders received over the telephone and entered on a computer. When the order is complete the computer enters these details into a despatch form which is then transmitted down the network to the despatch office, where the order is despatched to the customer.

8 At the same time an invoice will be created and sent down the network to the accounts office who will issue a printed copy to the customer. This method of using the computer to pass information from one department to another ensures that there is no duplication of effort and thereby no waste of time and money.

9 Such a sales order processing system not only automates the ordering, processing, despatching and invoicing of goods, but also creates a record of each transaction. These records represent a history of the company's sales and as such provide information that can be used for other purposes, in particular for updating the stock control system. As an item is sold and despatched it can be automatically recorded as having left the stock room and when the number of items in stock falls below a critical value a new batch of items can be ordered from the supplier. This can be arranged to be done automatically by the computer, thereby further increasing the efficiency of the firm.

> Can you think of other ways in which the information obtained from a sales order processing system can be used?

10 Details of items sold can also be used for marketing purposes. For example, when a particular item is not selling as well as it used to, the system can be arranged to detect this, enabling the sales team to find out why sales have dropped and try to rectify the situation.

11 Such a system would not operate in isolation from the rest of the company. The same customer list would be used by the order department as the accounts department, and the same stock list used by the order department as the despatch department.

12 Such interaction between departments using the same files makes it possible to obtain far more information about the state of the company than when all information was kept by different departments on different pieces of paper. This allows a company to plan both its current job scheduling and its future strategy more effectively.

> It may not be possible for you to see a sales order processing system in operation in your town. Instead, look in the shops to find one that uses a computer for checking on sales and stock. You should be able to tell quite easily: the till may be computerised or the items being sold may have card KIMBALL tags. When you have located such a store ask the manager to explain to you how their system works.

13 The same type of physical arrangement of a computerised reception operates at most hospitals.

As a patient is admitted to the hospital their details are entered into the hospital's database. These details include not only the patient's name and address but also information relevant to the proper management of the patient's needs and the hospital's management requirements. The result of placing all this information inside a computer file places all the information relevant to a patient in one place where it is easily accessible by doctors, nurses and management.

> Visit your local hospital to see how the computer plays a vital role in the hospital's organisation. Try to find out where the computer plays a significant role in the treatment of patients.

14 Two further examples of management and information systems are:

- booking systems
- library systems

Booking systems

15 The advantages of a booking system are particularly applicable to holiday companies. Every holiday they are offering can be made available to potential holidaymakers, and there is no need to rely on a travel agent to stock their leaflet. Consequently, there is a greater chance that all their holidays will be sold and because they have an accurate idea of the exact number of holidays they will sell, they can reduce their costs and hence the selling price of the holiday. The travel agent then knows that all the information about the holiday is accurate and that they can sell in confidence, knowing that all the paperwork will be taken care of by the computer. The customer also benefits from the speed and accuracy in obtaining the necessary details.

> Find a travel agent in your town that uses a computerised booking system and ask the manager to explain it to you.

Library systems

16 When you borrow a book from the library your reference number is read from your library ticket using a light pen. The reference number of the book you are borrowing is read by the same light pen and as a result, a record is made of who has the book, where it is and the date that it is due back. If you are late returning the book then the system detects this and issues you with a reminder to return it. This information can be used to find out which books are most popular and, as a result, when a particular book will have to be replaced or recovered due to wear. The advantages of a computerised system over a manual system are that fewer personnel are required to maintain the library records and more accurate records can be kept.

> Go to your public library and ask the chief librarian to explain to you the library computer system. Find out whether the system is used for anything other than lending, and what an ISBN number is. Find out about the National Lending Library at Boston Spa and the role that computers play there.

Business and commerce

17 The business and commercial world is a competitive place, requiring maximum efficiency in order to keep abreast of the competition. If you can manufacture goods or provide services at lower costs you can charge your customers less, thereby increasing their numbers. To reduce your costs you can employ computers which increase your efficiency. Computers are accurate: they can perform repetitive tasks without getting tired and do not need to be supervised like human beings—they are automatic. They are also cheap, requiring no wages, and can process vast amounts of information very quickly.

18 We shall look at two systems where the introduction of the computer has improved enormously both costs and efficiency, i.e. producing the same amount for less money *or* producing more for the same money. These are:

- financial systems
- manufacturing control systems

Financial systems

19 Every company is required to keep a set of accounts that contains the financial details of its trading. This information is contained in ledgers including the purchase ledger, the sales ledger, the cash book and the nominal ledger. The law demands that these ledgers be kept up to date. The purchase and sales ledgers keep a record of all the company's purchases and sales, the cash book records all receipts of money and the nominal ledger ties everything together, recording sales, purchases and cash receipts in detail, according to what initiated the transaction. Obviously this is an important task for a large organisation so the introduction of a computer system will make it more efficient and more reliable. In addition, the use of a computer makes it possible to access the financial information contained in the computerised ledgers enabling the company to make financial forecasts of future income and expenditure. It allows the company to budget and to keep a track of where financial problems are likely to occur.

20 A company must ensure that it has the ability to pay its debts. If a company owes more than it currently holds in cash then it may be unable to pay a particular bill. The finance department must ensure that the amount of cash it has available is more than the amount of money that it owes. In a large company this may be virtually impossible without the assistance of a computer.

> What other uses do you think can be made of information from a financial system?

21 Many customers buy on credit. Mostly they pay their bills on time but often they delay payment or they may not even pay at all. To ensure that the company does not lose money, the information stored on the financial and management information systems can be used to develop a credit control system. Records of past transactions with a particular customer can be kept to provide the company with information about that customer's credit worthiness, making a note of all delayed payments and all payments due.

22 From a history of the past financial records of particular jobs it is possible to develop a job costing system. This ensures that work is not costed too low, thereby losing profit, or too high, thereby losing deals. The larger the company, the larger the task of job costing, and the greater the need for a computer.

> Your Local Authority is likely to operate a computerised financial accounting system. Contact the finance department and ask if there is anyone willing to come to give your class a talk about the system they use. Ask about the ledgers, the payroll, the financial planning and how they calculate the rates.

Manufacturing and control systems

23 We shall look at two aspects of manufacturing systems:

- computer aided design and manufacture
- computer aided manufacturing

Computer aided design and manufacture

24 Before a company can manufacture a product it must be designed. A Computer Aided Design system (CAD) will speed up the time-consuming process of drawing the scale plans and models necessary.

Using these highly sophisticated drawing systems a designer can not only produce a design plan, but also a realistic three dimensional image of the design.

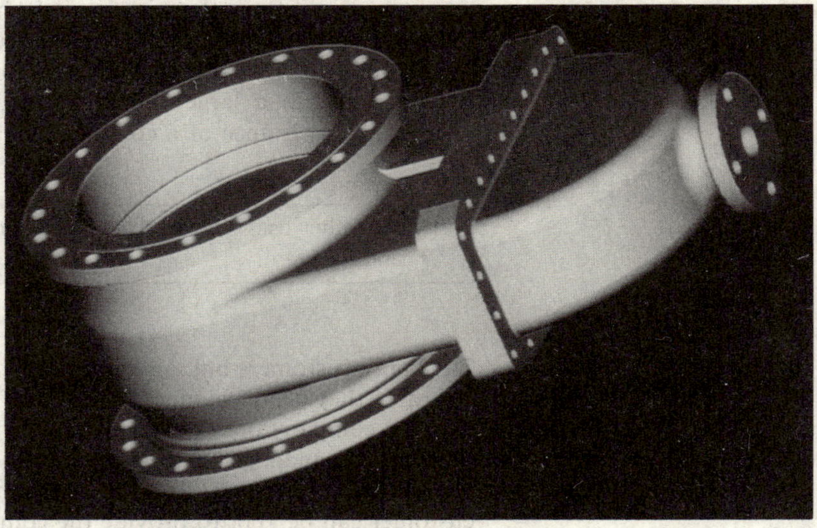

5.3 3D design on a computer

25 Furthermore, the design can be easily varied to find the best possible one. For example, car manufacturers use CAD systems by varying the styling of a particular bodywork component to find the design that produces the least air resistance or that produces the most stability. All these variations are done at the computer together with the necessary calculations to decide which is the best design: no longer do models need to be built and tested in wind tunnels. The saving in costs and the flexibility that these systems provide far outweigh the initial cost of their purchase.

It is worth while trying to view a computer aided design system in operation. You will probably find one in a Polytechnic or University near to your school. Perhaps your teacher could organise an outing to go to see it.

Computer aided manufacture

26 Computer Aided Manufacture (CAM) uses the computer to automatically control the manufacturing process. The basic essence of a

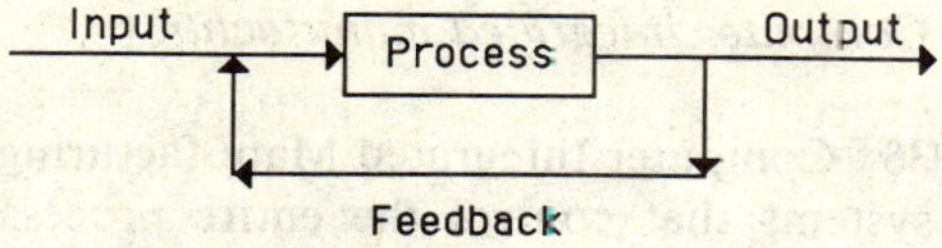

control system is the feedback. This may be in the form of information telling the user how to regulate the system or an automatic feedback in the form of signals from sensors.

Typical uses of feedback systems where the feedback is in the form of information acquired from sensors and automatically fed in, are:

- robotics
- computer integrated manufacture
- agriculture

Robotics

27 Many companies use computer systems to control their manufacturing processes. The assembly line in a car factory, the automatic welding of metal parts performed by robots, and automatic material handling are all examples of computerised control systems.

An assembly line consists of a continuous circuit along which the various stages of putting a product together are performed. Cars, televisions, and washing machines are common examples of products assembled in this way. A worker on an assembly line has one particular task to perform repeatedly during a working day which could vary from fitting an engine on to its mounting inside a car body, to fitting the knobs on to a television set. Obviously, such continual repetition became frustrating with the consequence that many of the assembled products were defective.

28 Today many assembly lines have been automated with robots taking the place of the human operatives. The result of this is few mistakes and continuous production over 24 hours a day.

29 Materials handling is more efficiently done automatically under computer control than by using manual labour. An example of this is the automatic warehousing system where goods are stored as and where the computer finds a place for them. There is no necessity for anyone to know exactly where a particular item is stored because the computer knows and whenever an item is needed the computer organises its retrieval.

> Try to see industrial robots in action if you can, for example, in a car manufacturing company. Most large manufacturers encourage visitors and organise special tours of their organisation.

Computer integrated manufacture

30 Computer Integrated Manufacturing systems (CIMS) are complete systems that control the entire process of manufacture. By linking together the manufacturing systems, the sales order processing systems, the stock control systems and the financial systems, everything proceeds under computer control with a minimum of manual assistance.

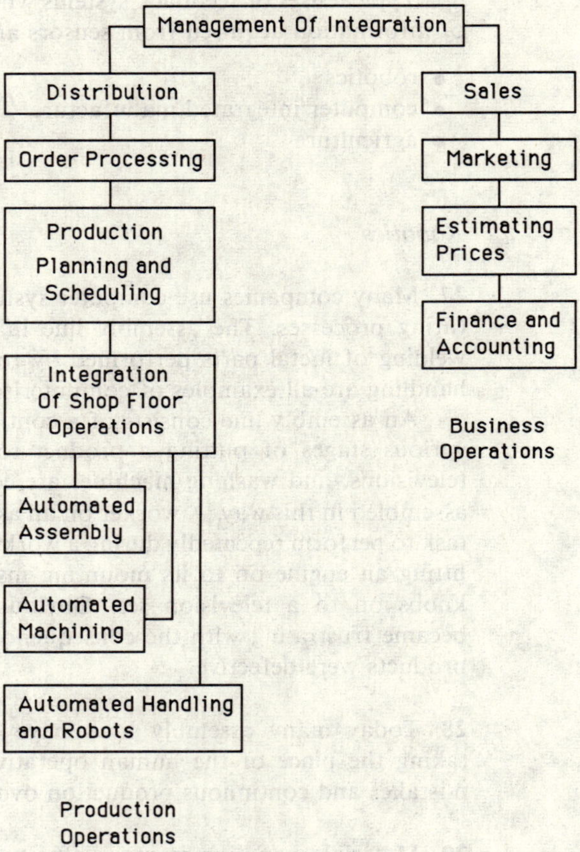

The diagram shows a typical integrated structure of a manufacturing system. At all parts of the structure the computer is used to regulate the system.

Agriculture

31 As well as using the computer to run a farm as a business, the computer helps the farmer to optimise crop production. Computer control systems look after the greenhouses, ensuring that plants are automatically fed and watered at regular, preset intervals. Sensors in the greenhouse measure the temperature and the humidity: if the temperature gets too low then heaters are automatically switched on, or if it gets too high, windows are automatically opened to provide cooling ventilation. Lettuces can be grown in this way, and when they are ready for market they are automatically picked and packed.

In this way the farmer can deliver his produce clean, packed and on time.

32 Animal rearing is also subject to computer control. Battery chickens can be regularly fed and watered automatically, living in a carefully maintained environment. In this way the farmer can save money on labour and provide an efficient service to customers.

Try to visit a farm that uses some form of computerised control.

Other organisations

33 There are numerous other organisations that use computers to make their operations effective.

Public order and emergency systems

34 The three organisations we shall look at are:

- the fire service
- the police
- the lifeboat service

The fire service

35 If you dial 999 to report a fire then you will be put in contact with the Fire Service's Command Control Centre. On the telephone you will be asked for relevant information such as the location of the fire, the state of the fire and your name.

From this information a message is sent through the computer network and via the telephone lines to the nearest fire station, notifying them of the location of the fire and indicating which fire tenders should be sent. The system is so efficient that the West Midlands Fire Service, for example, can usually get two tenders to a fire in the centre of Birmingham within 5 minutes of the caller first reporting the fire.

As the firemen proceed to fight the fire they keep a record of all their activities and their findings. Some of these messages can be transmitted to the Command Control Centre from a button box in the cab of the tender, others are transmitted via the in-cab radio transmitter.

These messages are then recorded in a log as and when they arrive, giving the Command/Control Centre an accurate assessment of the

5.6 Control room, West Midlands Control Centre; courtesy West Midlands Fire Service

5.7 In-cab button box; courtesy West Midlands Fire Service

current state of the fire. From this information the Control Centre can decide whether or not extra tenders are required, and if so, despatch them. This use of the computer in their communications system makes the most efficient use of fire engines, thereby making their fire fighting more effective and saving lives.

The police

36 The police have a similar command control centre from which operations can be monitored. This centre also contains records of crimes, criminals and cases currently under investigation. The West Yorkshire Command Control Centre is located in Bradford and is accessible by all police stations in West Yorkshire. The central computer facility consists of 10 Mcdonnel Douglas SEQUOIA Mainframes with terminals in each police station. As with the fire service, all 999 calls are immediately keyed into the system as they are received, with a continually updated log to record the action taken. Action on a 999 call is initiated by transmitting to the particular police station appropriate for the call. From this accumulated information the police are able to detect crime patterns in a locality, thereby making the solution of crimes more effective. To back up the regional police forces the Home Office maintains the Police National Computer in Hendon—a large system with numerous files for use by all the forces in the country. This system maintains records of wanted and missing persons, convictions, disqualified drivers, fingerprints, criminal names index and details of all licensed vehicles from the DVLC in Swansea. In the event of a major crime, an enquiry system is available called HOMES—the Home Office Major Enquiry System which is used when a major crime requires a large amount of information to be analysed in a short time.

> As a project, write a report on either computer usage by the police *or* computer usage by the fire service.

The lifeboat service

37 Lifeboats require very sophisticated assistance to guide them to ships that are in trouble. Often a lifeboat will be called out in terrible weather and probably at night. To ensure that they arrive at their destination in the shortest possible time they must know exactly where the distressed ship is located and what, if any, hazards there are between them. They need radar, depth sounding and navigation aids of a complexity and accuracy that only the chip can provide.

> Try to visit your local lifeboat. The Royal National Lifeboat Institution encourages the public to view their boats to find out first hand how they work.

Commercially available systems

38 Many systems are available and they come in three basic forms:

- off-the-shelf packages
- bespoke systems
- in-house developed systems

Off-the-shelf packages

39 There is a huge variety of off-the-shelf applications packages ranging in price from a few hundred pounds for a word processing package, for example, to tens of thousands of pounds for a CAD/CAM package. However, off-the-shelf packages might not be directly applicable to a particular company, and may require modifications to adapt them to a given situation. This is not usually possible because the people who write the programs do not make allowances for the purchaser to gain access to the code.

This drawback can be overcome by having a system designed and written especially for you—a Bespoke System.

Bespoke system

40 A bespoke system is a system that is specially written for a particular situation within an organisation or a company. Because the labour costs for developing and writing these packages are very high this is an expensive option, but the advantages are that it is tailored to your exact needs and is also amendable if you should desire it at a later date. Bespoke systems can be written either by a Consultant or, less expensively, in-house.

In-house development

41 Between the off-the-shelf packages and the consultants' bespoke packages lie the in-house developed packages. There are now various aids to help non-experts to generate their own systems. These are called Tools and Application Generators. For example, the SMART system consists of a database, a spreadsheet and a word processor all integrated together. It also has its own language, called a 4GL—a 4th Generation Language, which permits the relatively experienced user to create their own packages once they have analysed the system they wish to automate.

> Whenever you see a computerised system being used, try to find out whether it is an off-the-shelf system, a bespoke system or whether it was developed in-house. Try to find out how satisfied with it the user is and for what reasons. Is it easily amended and easy to use? Are there better systems available?

42 The following are some of the other tools used to help with in-house development.

43 Authorising systems allow teachers to enter course material that can be later accessed by students enabling them to learn independently of the teacher. These systems are so arranged that a person does not need to be a programmer to create a teaching program.

44 Case systems help with the analysis of systems prior to their being programmed. These systems will sort out the various stages that have to be gone through when constructing a system. In effect, they develop the structure of the problem which can then be used to model the solution.

45 Expert systems allow the expertise of a specialist to be stored in a database called a knowledge base. The knowledge base consists of a set of rules that an expert would make to solve a problem. This knowledge can then be accessed by anyone else, permitting decisions to be made that would ordinarily require an in-house expert to make. Again the various Expert System Tools permit useful systems to be developed by inexperienced users.

Summary

The computer plays a vital role in all organisations. With the advent of the fast microprocessor, the traditional role of the computer as a data processing system is being expanded into that of an information processing system. All parts of an organisation operate by manipulating information and as a result, all parts of the organisation are liable to computerisation. From the office workstation to the entire manufacturing process, the computer is taking control where once manual control was exercised. Financial management, stock management, sales order processing and production operations are all becoming more efficient as a result of the use of the computer. Our public order and emergency systems are also benefiting from the introduction of automated information processing techniques. For fire fighting, crime fighting and rescuing lives at sea, the microprocessor is playing an increasing role. Many of these systems are commercially available off-the-shelf, while many have to be written specifically for the application. With the expansion of the market for these special systems has come a collection of tools to assist the programmers. Just as data processing is being overtaken by information processing as a computer application, so traditional methods of programming code line by line are being overtaken by program construction using tools.

Key points

Management needs accurate information, computerised office, workstation, shared accessible information, Sales Order Processing (SOP), ordering, processing, despatching and invoicing of goods, stock control, hospital receptions, booking systems, library systems, financial systems, manufacturing control systems, CAD/CAM, robotics, CIM, agricultural systems, public order and emergency systems, fire, police and lifeboats, commercially available systems, off-the-shelf, bespoke and in-house development, software tools, authoring systems, case systems, expert systems.

Self assessment questions

1 What does the management of an organisation involve? (2)
2 What is essential for effective management? (2)
3 How is information stored? (2, 3)
4 Why do organisations store information on a computer? (3)
5 What is a workstation? (4, 5)
6 What are the advantages of a computerised office? (4, 5)
7 How are messages passed from one computer to another? (5)
8 How does the computerised office make for a more pleasant atmosphere in the workplace? (5)
9 Who would use a workstation? (6)
10 What is a Sales Order Processing system? (7–9)
11 How is a customer's order recorded in a computerised SOP? (7)
12 How is this information sent to the despatch department? (7)
13 How does the finance department know to send the customer a bill? (7)
14 Why are SOPs used? (8–10)
15 How would a SOP affect a stock control system? (9)
16 How could a SOP be used by the marketing department? (10)
17 What advantages are there in different departments using the same computer files? (11, 12)
18 How does a hospital's computerised reception operate? (13)
19 List two examples of management and information systems. (14)
20 What are the advantages of a computerised booking system over a paper booking system in a travel agents? (15)
21 How does the library computer system operate? (16)
22 What are the advantages of a computerised library system over a paper system? (16)
23 Why are computers becoming more widely used in business and commerce? (17)
24 List two systems adopted by business. (18)
25 Why are they adopted? (18)
26 How does a company keep track of its financial dealings? (19)
27 What is a ledger? (19)
28 List four ledgers used by companies. (19)
29 What is each ledger used for? (19)
30 How does a large company keep its ledgers up to date? (19)
31 What are the advantages of a computerised ledger system? (19)
32 Name three features of company business that are greatly assisted by using a computerised financial system. (20–22)
33 List two aspects of manufacturing systems that can be computerised. (23)
34 What is CAD? (24)
35 List the advantages of a CAD system. (24, 25)
36 What is CAM? (26)
37 List three areas where CAM is employed. (26)
38 Where are industrial robots used? (27)
39 Why are industrial robots used? (27, 28)
40 What is CIM? (30)
41 What is the main feature of a CIM system? (30)
42 List two farming activities where computer control is of great assistance. (31, 32)
43 Why would a farmer use either of these two systems? (32)
44 List three examples where public order and emergency systems are used. (34)
45 What happens when you dial 999 to report a fire? (35)
46 Give two methods by which a fire tender can communicate to command control. (35)

47 Why are the messages between the fire service command control and a fire tender recorded in a log? (35)
48 What happens when you dial 999 and ask for the police? (36)
49 What uses do the police make of computers? (36)
50 What do the letters HOMES stand for? (36)
51 When is HOMES used? (36)
52 What uses does the lifeboat service make of computers? (37)
53 List three types of commercially available systems. (38)
54 What are the advantages and disadvantages of off-the-shelf systems? (39)
55 What is a bespoke system? (39, 40)
56 What are the advantages and disadvantages of a bespoke system? (40)
57 What is an in-house system? (41)
58 Why is an in-house system a good compromise between an off-the-shelf package and a bespoke system? (41)
59 What are tools and application generators? (41)
60 What is a 4GL? (41)
61 What is the advantage of a 4GL? (41)
62 List three different types of software tools. (42)
63 What is an authoring system? (43)
64 What is a case system? (44)
65 What is an expert system? (45)
66 What is a knowledge base? (45)

Exercises

1 Which of the following computer based devices has changed the job of a typist?

electronic typewriter
photocopier
videotape recorder
word processor

2 Some airline pilots are partly trained by computer to fly new aircraft. The computer controls a machine that acts like the real aircraft and displays what the pilot might really see. The process the computer is carrying out is called

control
interfacing
interpreting
simulation

3 *Everybody*

Objectives

1 To describe the social changes which have occurred as a result of developments in microprocessor based devices.

2 To describe the social changes which may occur as a result of developments in microprocessor based devices.

Introduction

1 In this chapter we shall look at the ways in which the computer invasion has affected society in general, the changes in the quality of life and the coming together of the world of nations.

The quality of life

2 The Declaration of Independence of the United States of America, signed by the founding fathers in 1776 states that every citizen shall have a right to: **...life, liberty and the pursuit of happiness**.

By any standards these three rights describe the necessary components of human existence. Computers have changed and are continuing to change our lives. To measure the value of this change we must see to what extent they improve our

- life
- liberty
- pursuit of happiness

Life

3 There seems little doubt that the computer has contributed to the improvement of individual life. The role of the computer in medicine is becoming increasingly important, from the diagnosis, through intensive care to cure. Apart from the new systems that aid a doctor to diagnose an illness, computers are used to generate statistical information on a variety of complaints. A survey in the 1970s demonstrated a direct statistical link between smoking and both heart disease and lung cancer. This survey, which has been largely instrumental in changing the nation's smoking habits, would have been impossible without the aid of a computer to analyse the mass of data collected.

4 Patients who are critically ill or those recovering from major surgery need to be continuously checked to enable the nurses and doctors to monitor their progress and administer the appropriate medication and care when needed. Checking the functions such as heart rate, blood pressure, blood flow, temperature and brain patterns continuously, without the aid of computerised life support systems, would be impossible.

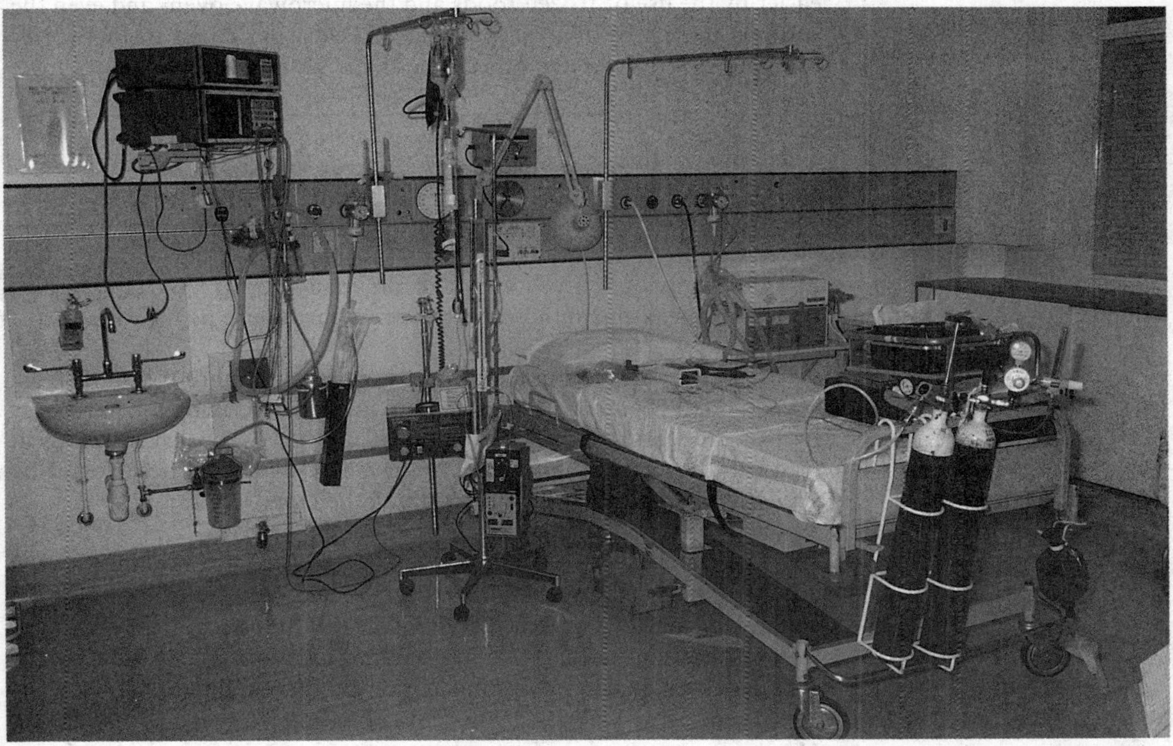

5.8 Intensive care unit; courtesy St Bartholomew's Hospital

5 The computer not only monitors the patient's health and well-being, but if their condition deteriorates the system will sound an alarm to summon a doctor or nurse. Such automatic monitoring also frees the nurses and doctors, to enable better care for the less critically ill patients.

6 The computer also comes into force in many residential homes for the elderly where individuals can be checked to see if they are well without them feeling that they are being pestered. Each room of an individual's apartment is equipped with a pull cord which, when pulled, will summon help from a resident nurse. Some local authorities install

these devices in homes that they rent to the elderly. The communication system that drives this alarm is controlled by a chip.

7 Even the healthy individual has benefited from the introduction of computer systems. At work they have taken the drudgery out of routine tasks while at home they have made for more efficient heating systems, more effective burglar alarms and a more comfortable life-style. Washing clothes is no longer a real problem, cooking has been made easier by the use of frozen foods and the microwave oven, and even the washing up can be done automatically. Television shows us the world, bringing events from the other side of the globe to our living rooms.

> Can you think of any other ways in which the computer has improved the quality of life? Can you think of ways in which the computer has caused our quality of life to worsen?

Liberty

8 Our individual freedoms take on many forms. We are free to travel, to speak our minds and to spend our leisure as we wish.

9 The computer has made travel far easier and more pleasant: from booking and departing to travelling to arriving. Booking a hotel in any part of the world is simply a matter of visiting your local travel agent who can then contact any hotel in the world by telephone, telex or by Fax. All this is due to the invention of the chip.

10 Travelling by air, sea or land is greatly assisted by the chip. Modern aircraft are extremely complex machines and only by using on-board computers can they be flown and navigated. Ships require a computer to give an accurate map reading of their location. Navigation by the stars has been replaced with navigation by the satellite.

11 Buying goods whilst in another country is now simple: Visa, Master Charge and American Express are accepted all over the world. The large computer data banks store all the details of your credit rating and can be accessed from anywhere in the world, either by telephone or by using a special terminal.

12 We are free to speak our own minds in Britain but it is best that we exercise caution. Apart from the danger of slander, it is best to be sure of the facts. By means of computerised communication systems the world of facts is at our fingertips. Prestel and Ceefax provide numerous pages of information, satellites provide twenty-four hour television news services and databases store facts and information on every subject.

> Can you think of any other ways in which the computer has improved our freedom? Has it reduced our freedom in any ways?

The pursuit of happiness

13 Whilst it is not possible to say that the computer is responsible for more happiness, it is possible to say that it has given more opportunities to pursue happiness to many more people. As well as travel, other activities such as sport, education and theatre are all improved by the use of computer systems.

Sport

14 Digital timing makes it possible to measure sporting records to the nearest one hundredth of a second. The quality of modern sporting equipment will have been tested using a computer. The organisation of major sporting events on the scale of the Olympics would be impossible without the use of a computer.

Education

15 Many of the high quality textbooks that you use in your studies have been written and typeset using a computer and thereby made affordable to schools. Computer Aided Learning (CAL) provides countless packages on any subject, enabling students to study individually and leaving the teacher free to help individuals overcome specific problems. An expertise in sitting examinations can also be acquired using several computer packages that test and mark without taking up the teacher's precious time.

Theatre

16 The movies that you see in the cinema have been made with the help of computers. Image and sound mixing, dubbing and editing all make use of computers. Live theatre uses computerised lighting equipment and the communication system between the stage manager, the box office, the front of house and the dressing rooms all use the chip.

> Can you think of any other ways in which the computer has improved our ability to pursue happiness? Can you think of ways in which it has hampered your pursuit of happiness?

The global village

17 The Canadian philosopher Marshall McLuan once referred to the world as The Global Village. He was making reference to the way television and modern communications technology was bringing the nations of the world closer together by the sharing of instantly communicated information.

The UK

18 Advances in communication put the country into more immediate contact with the rest of the world. The stock exchange operates almost twenty-four hours a day, trading all over the world. Computers in the UK access computers and their data banks in other countries, satellite TV brings other countries into our living rooms and classrooms instantaneously and international events affecting our own country can be witnessed first hand. The American Revolution was set off by what we now know as the Boston Tea Party. This relatively small squabble between American Colonists and some British soldiers was due to a lack of accurate information, exaggerated by King George and turned into a full scale Colonial revolt, with the result that eventually Britain lost the American colonies. Lacking such instantaneous communications today could have very serious international consequences.

> Name three situations where communications or lack of proper communications have been vital to this country's welfare. Did the chip play a role? Consider the possible outcomes both with and without the chip.

The European Community

19 The development of the United States of Europe as a single economic and political entity is becoming more of a reality. The DELTA Project has been started by the European Parliament and provides money to develop computerised educational systems. Its aim is to achieve a united approach to education in all countries of the European Community. By sharing information across the community, the DELTA Project is aimed to unify the educational systems of the entire EC. All the member states recognise that their individual welfare is best catered for within a larger community of states and as the EC grows, so the computer helps to keep it together and bring its peoples into closer communication and closer political union.

The world

20 What is happening in our own country is happening in all other countries to a greater or lesser extent. People are coming to realise that the world is a single community. Some of the more significant sights of recent history were the television pictures of the earth as seen from a satellite. As a result of the chip, for the first time the world saw itself as an island in a vast sea of space. In fact, the reason the chip was invented in the first place was to provide powerful information processing in a small space suitable for satellite and rocket technology.

> The chip is a direct consequence of President Kennedy's decision to commit the USA to land a man on the moon by 1970. Do you think that this would have been possible if the chip had not been invented? Why?

Summary

As time progresses changes in society affect everybody's quality of life. The value of an agent of change is measured by its effect on the quality of life and the computer is no exception to this rule. The way we live our lives has been improved by the introduction of computer systems. This ranges from the medical care we receive when we are ill to our daily, healthy existence. Our freedom becomes more assured as more people share accurate information. Many oppressive political systems depend upon the ignorance of the populace to maintain their power. With an educated and informed population, such oppression is much harder to maintain. Computerised systems have opened up more leisure opportunities to many more people. From sport to education to theatre, the chip has had a distinct influence. In the same way that the computer is an agent of change in the lives of individuals, so it is an agent of change to whole nations. As communications between countries improve and information flows freely from one side of the world to the other, the nations of the world come closer together. We are all a part of a single whole—the world—and the computer is helping us all realise that fact.

Key points

The quality of life, clinical care, hospital life support systems, emergency communication systems for the elderly, improved lifestyles, freedom to travel, worldwide personal credit, better and more information, improved sporting, education and leisure facilities, the global village, the UK, the European Community and the world.

Self assessment questions

1 List three components of human existence against which the quality of life can be measured. (2)
2 How has the computer benefited medicine? (3)
3 How has the computer assisted in changing the smoking habits of Britain? (3)
4 How does the critically ill patient benefit from computer technology? (4, 5)
5 How does the computer come into play in residential homes for the elderly? (6)
6 List eight ways in which the computer has benefited normal, healthy life. (7)
7 How has the computer benefited our liberty? (8–12)
8 How has the computer benefited travel? (9, 10)
9 How has the computer assisted you in your foreign purchases? (11)
10 List three credit cards that are accepted all over the world. (11)
11 What is PRESTEL? (12)
12 What does PRESTEL offer? (12)
13 How has the computer assisted us in our pursuit of happiness? (13–16)
14 List four areas where sport has benefited from the computer. (14)
15 How has education benefited from the computer? (15)
16 What is CAL? (15)
17 How has the theatre benefited from the computer? (16)
18 What is the global village? (17)
19 How have technological advances put this country into closer, more immediate contact with the rest of the world? (18)

20 How does the stock exchange benefit from the computer? (18)
21 What is a major benefit to nations of modern communications? (18)
22 What is the DELTA project? (19)
23 How will the DELTA project help to bring the countries of the EC closer together? (19)
24 Name some global effects of the computer development. (20)

4 Personal information

Objectives

1 To describe the computer applications which make use of personal data
2 To recall the potential dangers which are inherent in the use of computers to manage files of personal data
3 To identify safeguards which should be taken to prevent the possible misuse of personal data

Introduction

1 In this chapter we shall consider the consequences of the increasing amount of personal data that is being stored in computer files. We shall see that the problem revolves around the ability of unknown individuals to access this information and its ability to be easily changed.

Personal information

2 When you were born your parents had to go to the Registrar of Births, Deaths and Marriages to register your birth.

Your birth certificate contains the names of yourself and your parents, your date and location of birth and the occupations of your parents. This is the first record of personal information that concerns you and is stored on somebody else's files, and as you progress through life, more occasions will require you to reveal personal information that is to be stored by somebody else.

> Try to remember how often you have had to give information regarding your personal life, for example to the doctor, the dentist, a scout or guide troop. Make a list of different situations where you might be asked for personal details. Could anyone else gain access to this information? Would you object to anyone else seeing this information? Why?

3 All employees will have filled in a form giving details of their life history to date such as education, previous employment and medical details. This allows prospective employers to assess their suitability for a job.

This life history might contain information that an individual does not wish to be known by anyone else other than their employer.

> Can you think of any other situations where personal information is gathered that could be put to other uses, for example, going on holiday and telling the milkman not to deliver milk for two weeks? Try to think of two other situations.

The storage of personal information

4 Before the days of computerised personnel records, such life histories were written on sheets of paper and stored under lock and key in a filing cabinet in a secure office. Obviously access to those records was difficult without proper authorisation.

5 Today it is likely that they will be contained in computer files, saving space, and thereby money. But, as a result, the lock and key security is lost. As soon as a computer contains information there arises the problem of who has access to it—who can view it, who can amend it and who can manipulate it.

> A copy of everyone's birth, marriage and death certificates are kept in Somerset House in London. This vast store of personal information is open to the public. It can be used, for example, to discover your family tree. Can you think of any other uses that it could be put to? A politician called John Stonehouse put it to a special use in the 1970s. Find out what he did.
> Can you think of other stores of personal information that are open to the public?

The accessibility of personal information

6 Access to personal information no longer means asking the person with the keys to open up the filing cabinet. It is possible for unauthorised people at remote terminals to pry into these files unless some safeguards are taken.

7 The remoteness of the terminal is the disturbing factor. A number of people try to access as many private databases as they can for fun. These people are known as hackers and their success in accessing confidential files is a cause for concern. Because telephone lines connect the world and its computers together, the hacker can be in one country and the information in another.

8 Not only can information be viewed, it can also be changed. If we cannot regulate who views we cannot regulate who amends the

information, which means we cannot guarantee the integrity—the completeness and the accuracy—of the information.

> Can you think of any situations where personal information could be changed and adversely affect the individual? Try to think of at least three areas of activity where a change in the information would affect you, either for the better or the worse.

9 People are naturally very sensitive about the distribution of personal information relating to them so it is essential that proper safeguards are taken to ensure its security and integrity.

The security and integrity of personal information

10 The protection of computerised information has always been a problem but this problem has escalated as the amount of information to be stored has grown and more sophisticated computer communication and information processing techniques have been developed.

11 It is not only individuals who need to worry about the security of information. Companies are concerned that information relating to their trade secrets should not be seen outside the company. Governments store vast amounts of secret information on computers and they, again, are concerned that only those with authorisation should be able to access it. As a result of the problems surrounding the security and integrity, i.e. the accuracy of information, a number of protective measures have been devised.

- passwords
- access logs
- encryption
- physical isolation

Passwords

12 The first level of security is the password. This allows only those people who know the password to access protected information. With some systems there can be different levels of password. For example, your password may permit the viewing of information only whereas a superior may also be able to edit the information, or it may permit the viewing of a restricted amount of information whereas others may be able to view it all.

13 The issuing of passwords will be done by the Computer Manager although the actual password used will normally be devised by the user. Often users take their names or names spelled backwards or use their date of birth or their telephone numbers. While this makes it easier for the user to remember their password it also means that it can easily be guessed at by someone attempting to view or even amend data they are not supposed to have access to. This is the way the hackers operate by continuing to try different combinations until they eventually hit the right one. Prince Philip's private Prestel pages were once accessed by an unauthorised hacker—his password was just a sequence of 2s.

> If you were told to choose your own personal password up to 8 characters long what would you choose? For how long do you think you could remember it? Write it down and try to remember it next week. How easy do you think it is to devise your own password that is simple enough to remember but that no-one else will be able to guess?

14 One way of solving this problem is by asking the computer to generate a random sequence of characters as your password. Then you have only to remember it. However, it is easy to steal a password even though when you type the password into the computer nothing appears on the screen. Always make sure that no-one is looking over your shoulder when you are keying in your password.

Access logs

15 The second level of security is to log individuals who use their password to access the data. This is a useful device for locking out hackers. If anyone enters a password incorrectly more than twice then the system will lock them out, an effective method unless, of course, they get it right first time. The log also records the activities of genuine users, noting all the processing activities performed.

16 The log can then be used to locate the sources of any errors or misuse of the system. Another way of checking fraudulent misuse, particularly of Financial Systems, is the audit trail. This can trace step-by-step any transactions that have occurred within the computer system thereby exposing any erroneous or fraudulent transaction.

Encryption

17 Apart from the unauthorised viewing and editing of information, wholesale theft of information must also be guarded against. For example, one of the most valuable assets of a company is its customer file. This will not only contain the names and addresses of its customers but it could also contain details of their trading such as discounts given, prices charged and the value of their purchases. Such information would be invaluable to an unscrupulous competitor who might even attempt to steal it. Theft can be accomplished either physically by stealing the disks on which the file is kept or electronically by remotely accessing the file and downloading it into their own system. To prevent this information being of any use to a thief it could be coded into gibberish using a secret scrambling code. When the thief tries to read the data it then means nothing at all and without the key to the code the thief cannot de-code the information.

18 This is called encryption and is the means whereby governments communicate to their embassies abroad. Coded information is transmitted from the home computer to the embassy's computer through a telephone or satellite link. Anyone can intercept the information but only the embassy has the encryption key to de-code the gibberish into meaningful information. This level of security physically isolates the data by making it useless unless it is coupled with the encryption key in the embassy's computer.

> A very simple code is to relate letters of the alphabet written forwards with those written backwards
>
> a b c d e . . . . w x y z
> z y x w v . . . . d c b a
>
> Using this code the word BAD would become YZW. Write a code yourself. How easy do you think it would be to encrypt it?

Physical isolation

19 Data can also be physically isolated by storing it on removable disks and putting the disks under lock and key.

This by itself is inconvenient and does not avoid the hacker when it is installed and being accessed in the normal course of events. However, combined with the other methods of security it does provide a real protection.

20 A further variation of this is to allow only specific individuals to have physical access to the hardware by isolating it in a room. Access to this room would then be by password, usually imprinted on a magnetic card which causes the door to be unlocked to permit access. More sophisticated variations of this include the voice activated lock and the palm print identifier.

The 1984 Data Protection Act

21 Parliament has recognised that with the increasing use of computers to store personal information there is a growing problem of maintaining its security and integrity. Also as more information is shared, it may be possible for information collected for one reason to be used for another. For example, information that is collected through credit card purchases to enable the credit company to send you a bill could be sifted to build a picture of your movements and types of purchase and used by organisations who market specific products.

As a result of the Government's concern the Data Protection Act was passed by Parliament in 1985.

22 This Act demands that any organisation or individual storing personal information must register as doing so. When they register they must state:

- what data is being stored
- why the data is being stored
- where the data is being stored
- where the data was obtained

The data must be gathered, processed and retained only under these stated conditions. The information must be adequate and relevant for the stated purposes and it must be accurate and up-to-date. If there is any change in the use of the data from its original use then this must be notified to the registrar. Finally the data must be secure.

Individuals whose personal information is stored have, under the Act, the right to:

- know if personal data about them is being held
- view the data and to amend it if it is incorrect

If the data is inaccurate or it is unlawfully disclosed to anyone else then the individual has the right to gain compensation.

23 Anyone infringing these regulations is breaking the law and faces the possibility of legal sanction.

> Can you think of anything that the Data Protection Act has left out that should be included?

Backup and recovery

24 Apart from unauthorised access to computer information there is also the problem of accidental loss of information, which also includes vital personal information. What happens, for example, if a fire occurs in the office where the customer file is kept or if you spill coffee over your disks? What happens if, in the middle of a complicated piece of processing, the power fails and you lose information that was being stored temporarily in the computer's transient memory?

> What is the worst possible outcome from each of the following events?
>
> (a) A company loses its customer file in a fire
>
> (b) A warehouse manager wipes a magnet over the surface of a disk containing a complete record of the stock levels

(c) Your head teacher's dog chews up all the floppy disks that contain your 'mock' GCSE marks

(d) During the run of a payroll, the power fails. Some paypackets are complete with payslips and cheques but others are not.

25 Any one of these situations could spell disaster if the correct precautions had not been taken. These precautions concern the adoption of:

- back-up procedures
- recovery procedures

Back-up procedures

26 Back-up procedures are concerned with keeping a spare copy of any files that are used. This is known as backing up. Some files never change so they can be backed up and the copy stored in a secure place away from the computer. They must be stored away from the originals in case of, for example, a fire.

27 Other files may change continually so backing up becomes more involved. For example, a payroll system will consist of a master file and a transaction file. The master file contains information that rarely changes such as an employee's name and pay rate and information that

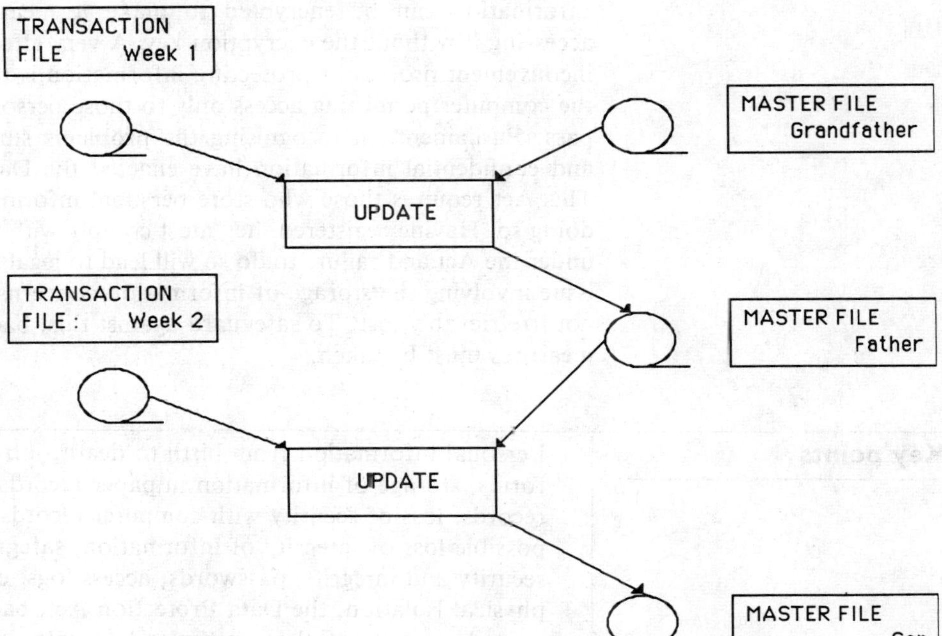

changes regularly such as the total amount paid to date. The transaction file will contain the data necessary for the computer to compute a week's pay for all the employees provided that it has access to the master file. Several generations of the master file will be retained as a precaution against accidental error or disaster. These generations of files are called grandfather—father—son files. When this week's payroll has been run, the updated master file is called the son. Last week's master file is called the father and the week's before that is called the grandfather.

Recovery procedures

28 Recovery procedures concern everything from the simple restoring of a file from a back-up to using another computer because yours has been destroyed. When designing systems it is important to be aware that unforeseen events can occur so that all reasonable precautions are taken and all reasonable alternatives planned in advance. Even if the computer installation is completely destroyed by fire a fall-back position should be available to allow the business of a company to continue.

Summary

Throughout our lives we give personal information to other people to be kept on record. When this information is kept on a computer problems arise from unauthorised access. Anyone who can access personal information can not only view it but also amend it or use it for other purposes. To prevent unauthorised access, various safeguards can be employed. Passwords and access logs can be used both to restrict unauthorised access and to maintain a check on authorised access. Information can be encrypted to make it meaningless to anyone accessing it without the encryption key. A very effective, though often inconvenient process of protecting information is to physically isolate the computer permitting access only to those personnel who possess a pass. Parliament, in recognising the problems surrounding personal and confidential information have enacted the Data Protection Act. This Act requires those who store personal information to register as doing so. Having registered they must comply with the rules laid down under the Act and failure to do so will lead to legal sanctions. Another issue involving the storage of information concerns ensuring that it is not irretrievably lost. To safeguard against this, back-up and retrieval measures must be taken.

Key points

Personal information from birth to death, job application forms, storage of information in paper records and computer records, loss of security with computer records, hackers, possible loss of integrity of information, safeguards to ensure security and integrity, passwords, access logs, encryption and physical isolation, the Data Protection Act, back-up procedures, grandfather, father and son files, recovery procedures.

Self assessment questions

1 Name two pieces of personal information that we all have recorded about us. (2)
2 Give an example of where you are likely to be asked for personal information. (3)
3 What are the problems that arise when personal information is stored in computer files? (4–7)
4 What is a hacker? (7)
5 Why can hackers be a problem? (7)
6 What is meant be the integrity of information? (8)
7 What information, other than personal information, do people wish to keep secure? (11)
8 List four measures that can be taken to make computer files secure. (11)
9 How does password security operate? (12)
10 Who issues the passwords? (13)
11 How are passwords devised? (13)
12 What problems are associated with passwords? (13,14)
13 Describe a situation where passwords are used frequently by people not familiar with computers. (14)
14 What is an access log? (15)
15 What is an access log used for? (15,16)
16 What is an audit trail? (16)
17 What is an audit trail used for? (16)
18 What is meant by encryption? (17,18)
19 How can encryption make information stored on a computer secure? (17,18)
20 Name an organisation which uses encrypted information. (18)
21 How can physical isolation make computer files secure? (19)
22 List three methods of restricting entry to a locked room. (19,20)
23 How can access to a physically isolated computer be controlled? (22)
24 How has Parliament acted to prevent the unauthorised use and misuse of personal information? (21)
25 List two reasons why Parliament enacted the Data Protection Act. (21)
26 What does the law require of an individual who stores personal information? (24)
27 List four requirements to be recorded about stored personal data when registering under the Data Protection Act. (22)
28 List four requirements concerning the gathering and storing of personal data under the Act. (22)
29 What rights do individuals have under the Data Protection Act if personal data is stored about them? (22)
30 What happens if anyone infringes these regulations? (23)
31 How can computer files be made secure from accidental loss? (24–8)
32 What does backing up mean? (26)
33 Distinguish between a master file and a transaction file. (27)
34 Explain the grandfather-father-son generations of backed up files. (27)
35 What are recovery procedures? (28)
36 Why are recovery procedures important? (28)
37 When should recovery procedures be planned? (28)

Exercises

1 Any computer system that holds personal, commercial, or military information must be protected from unauthorized access or use.

(a) For a central mainframe computer system there are varying possible ways of restricting access. Describe briefly three of the methods that might be used.

(b) For a personal computer state two precautions not already given in your answer above.

2 Guarding against illegal access to data can be done by which of the following

keeping an ancestral (grandfather-father-son) filing system
making multiple copies
using a write protect tab
using passwords

3 Which two of these applications are personal data?

payroll flight simulation stock control
credit card billing computer aided design

4 Many goods and services can now be purchased with plastic cards. The card companies use computers to work out the bills each month. This means that the card company's computers store much personal information about its customers and their purchases. If another organisation got hold of such information it could be used against the card holder.

(a) Name two organisations that might want to have access to this personal information.

(b) In what ways might the card holder suffer if these organisations did have access.

5 'Hacking' is the term for someone who tries to gain illegal access to a computer system. This is usually done using a remote terminal or microcomputer.

(a) Name one example of harm that a 'hacker' might cause as a result of breaking into a computer system.

(b) To protect computer systems from 'hackers' a system of passwords or codes can be used. These should be secret and known only to legal users. Some people use names of people close to them because they are easy to remember. Why should this be avoided?

(c) Suggest a suitable password for a remote access computer system and explain why you think it is suitable.

(d) Name one further simple method of protecting a computer system from 'hackers' trying to access remote terminals.

6 A mail order company has replaced its manual typewriters with word processors to produce letters from the management to customers.

(a) How will this affect the work done by

(i) the managers?
(ii) the typists?

(b) Some of the data held on the mail order company's central computer is personal data about its customers. In what way does the Data Protection Act attempt to protect the interests of the customer?

(c) Letters produced by the word processors could either be printed and posted to customers or sent via electronic mail. Why does the company need to use the postal system when electronic mail is much faster?

(d) When electronic mail is sent over normal telephone lines, why must compatible modems be used by both the company and its customers?

7 A university has a fire in the computer room and many magnetic tapes are totally destroyed. Some magnetic tapes were, however, held in a different building which was not affected by the fire.

(a) What would these other magnetic tapes be likely to contain?

(b) How could the computer staff retrieve most of the data that was held on the destroyed files?

8 In the following diagram, what sort of file is x?

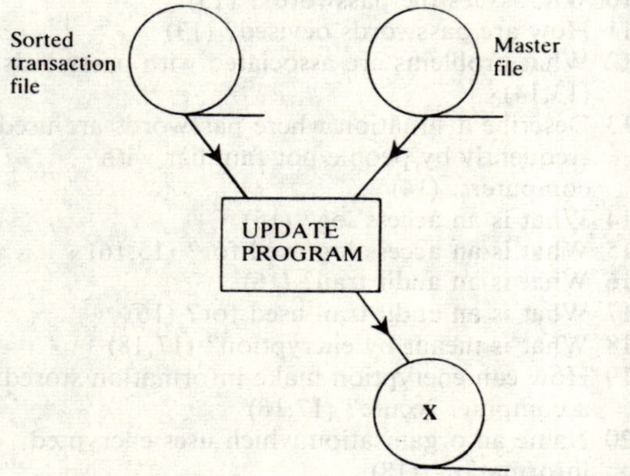

a grandfather file
a new master file
a new transaction file
an unsorted transaction file

9 A master file and a sorted transaction file are stored on magnetic tapes. The transaction file has been checked and is known to contain only new records to be inserted into the master file. Describe the way in which a new master file can be generated using the existing master file and the transaction file.

5 The invasion into jobs

Objectives

1 To outline the changes in employment being brought about by computer usage.

2 To give a reasoned description of the potential effects of computer usage for a range of applications.

Introduction

1 In the last chapter of Section 4 we looked at the employment opportunities that exist and are developing within the area of computing. We shall now look at the serious problem of unemployment that has become associated with the introduction of computer systems into the workplace. Unemployment is discussed within an historical perspective against the background of the Industrial Revolution and parallels are drawn with the current Computer Revolution. The effects of unemployment are considered and tentative solutions are suggested to lessen its effects.

Unemployment

2 The fact that computers can displace people is recognised as such by everyone involved with employment. While employers recognise the savings that can be made and the increased productivity that can be achieved in this way, trade unions recognise that the introduction of new technologies causes their members to be put out of work. The Government sees both sides of the picture: for the nation to remain competitive in the world its companies and corporations must introduce the new technologies, but at the same time it recognises the inevitable unemployment that this will cause. On the one hand the new technologies make some people redundant and on the other hand the same technology creates new business opportunities and hence more jobs. Whichever government is in power, it is a delicate task to maintain a balance.

3 What is not always recognised is the nature of the unemployment caused. To appreciate this we shall first take a brief look at another cause of unemployment—the introduction of mechanisation during the Industrial Revolution.

The Industrial Revolution

4 During the eighteenth century, Britain saw the end of the Agricultural Revolution, which had started during the Tudor period, and the beginning of the Industrial Revolution. Due to improvements in agriculture and medicine, Britain's population rose from 5 million in 1600 to 10.5 million in 1800. This growing population created an increased demand for food that the new agricultural methods could not meet. Food had to be imported and to meet the cost of these imports, British goods had to be exported—manufactured goods. As the population grew so the Industrial Revolution blossomed. By the early 1700s the increasing efficiency demanded of industry created the need to replace human and animal power with machines. This was the age of invention.

- In 1712 Thomas Newcomen invented the Steam Pump
- In 1732 Michael Menzies invented the Threshing Machine
- In 1768 James Hargreaves invented the Spinning Jenny
- In 1787 Edmund Cartwright invented the Power Loom

5 Unemployment followed in the wake of these and many other inventions. Men, women and children were cast aside as the nation's industries mechanised. There was no Welfare State to cushion the poverty and in 1834 Parliament enacted the Poor Law that established workhouses in which the poor and destitute could live.

> Trace a particular activity from its origins to its modern working. For example, books were originally written by hand but can now be written, typeset and printed using a computer. Find out how the numbers of people employed in your chosen activity have changed and how the activity has speeded up over the ages.

The computer revolution

6 Now, as we approach the end of the twentieth century, the population of Britain remains at around 55 million—a five-fold increase over the last hundred years. We need to continue to import food, raw materials and manufactured goods and to pay for these imports by exporting our own goods and services. The world is a competitive place and to compete successfully we must be efficient in production and able to offer cheap prices. This means embracing the new technologies, which in turn brings with it unemployment. The difference today is that whereas in the nineteenth century unemployment largely affected only the un-educated poor and the manual workers, now it is affecting everybody. To understand why this is so we must look at what it is that is causing unemployment.

7 The introduction of computers into the workplace is only the visible cause of unemployment. The root cause of unemployment is

what those computers represent, i.e. their ability to process information.

The information age

8 It has been emphasised throughout this book that everybody processes information to some extent. A production line worker filling boxes with biscuits processes less information checking that the biscuits are satisfactory than an airline pilot landing an aeroplane at a busy airport. But they both process information and it is here that the computer comes in.

Computers are efficient. They can process vast amounts of information very quickly and with complete accuracy. They can work 24 hours a day, every day of the year, do not need to be paid, and their running costs are very small in comparison to salaries. It therefore makes economic sense to use computers instead of people.

9 To illustrate this, in the wages office of a valve manufacturing company the wages used to be calculated from job cards and time cards by the wages manager and five assistants. Now, with two PCs in the office the same wages are calculated by the wages manager and one assistant.

10 Computers are machines that can be instructed to work. While manual workers can also be instructed to work, computers are more cost-effective. They can also be taught how to control other computers, so displacing supervisors as well as manual workers.

11 The people being displaced are those whose jobs demand a level of information processing that can be matched or bettered by the computer. As technology advances the invasion of the computer into jobs creeps higher up the scale and those people whose jobs demand high levels of information processing are also being displaced.

Think of three activities that you would not expect to be computerised. Discuss these with your classmates and see if they agree with you.

The effects of unemployment

12 Unemployment brings with it division. Those without a job and relying on Social Security neither progress nor prosper, while those still working share in the nation's wealth and prosper. As time moves on these differences become more noticeable, especially from the viewpoint of those without a job. Society becomes divided and as a result can become unstable. The French and Russian Revolutions were fuelled by just such social division. This changing pattern of society presents a problem that must be resolved.

Resolving the problem

13 The most important aspect of trying to solve a problem is in admitting that the problem exists. Recognising the problem for what it is gives us the positive opportunity to create the better society that the Information Age promises, rather than wait for technological and social evolution by natural selection. The opportunities for positive social change as a consequence of the computer revolution are almost boundless. If only a small measure of the creative imagination that has been invested in the development of modern technology were available to social development, the effect would not only be of immediate social benefit, it could alleviate many of the impending problems of the Information Age. There are signs that the problem is already being addressed. For example, in recognising the existence of the problem the Government has mounted an ambitious retraining scheme under the **Training Agency**—previously called the Manpower Services Commission (MSC).

Retraining

14 Computers not only displace people but also create jobs. The computer industry provides excellent career prospects for people with talent, imagination and a flexibility of outlook and even for people who are not computer professionals opportunities are still available. Computers require people to install, program and operate them and there is a growing shortage of people who possess these necessary skills. Retraining of the unemployed in basic computer skills is one way of providing these personnel.

15 This is, however, only a short-term attempt at a solution to the overall problem. It is possible for a person to be retrained for a job that could later be performed by a computer. This is perhaps a pessimistic view but its possibility highlights the true nature of the problem. Perhaps a more realistic approach to the problem is to encourage a change in the traditional attitudes to work within the social framework.

> How do you view work? Do you think it should be an important part of your life? Do you enjoy it? Can you imagine a life without a job? What would you do?
> Discuss these questions with the other members of your class and with your family and friends outside school.

Changing attitudes

16 It used to be the norm for people to leave school, get a job and remain in the same job until retirement. The job would occupy 8 or 9 hours a day for five or more days a week and would form an individual's basic activity. Life would be organised around the job. Holidays, leisure and relaxation would be indulged in when not working and at the convenience of the employer. This is the traditional attitude to employment. There are a number of ways this attitude could be changed both to accommodate the computer invasion and to help resolve the developing divisions within society. Three examples are:

- the reduction of the working week
- home working
- continued education

The reduction in the working week

17 The current average working week is approximately 35 hours. If this were reduced then more people could be employed to do the same amount of work. Everybody would have more free time which would lead to a lessening of the importance of 'being at work' and an increase in the importance of 'being at leisure'. There are, of course, arguments against this. Employing more people costs the employer more money and rewards each employee with less money. However, with the greater efficiency that will come by introducing the new technologies, greater profits will be made. These could be reinvested in a reduced working week, or an alternative would be the current practice of **job sharing**—a single job shared by two people. Again, each person has a reduced working week but at the same time they each have a reduced pay packet unless they take on a second job.

How would you like to share a job? List the advantages and disadvantages to the employee and to the employer.

Home working

18 A change in the attitude of employers over starting and finishing times has seen the introduction of **flexitime**. With this method an employee can choose when to be in work during certain hours of the day. With the introduction of the new technologies this flexibility can be extended to allow certain employees to work from home. A typist, for example, does not need to sit in a typing pool for eight hours a day. With a word processor at home they could be connected to a dictating machine via the telephone line and do all the typing at home on a terminal. The savings made in the costs of maintaining a typing pool could then be eliminated—this saving being passed on into a reduced working week. Telecommuting is being considered more often as a realistic approach to certain kinds of employment, especially when the costs of maintaining a large building in the city centre are considered.

> Would you like to have a job where you worked from home? Can you think of any drawbacks? Could you motivate yourself to work? What would be necessary to make you as efficient at home as you would be at a place of work.

Continuing education

19 At present it is accepted that having spent eleven years in the school system, an individual is equipped for life with the knowledge necessary to earn a living. Part of that knowledge will be an ability to communicate to obtain more knowledge, because no-one can learn all they need to know for life in just eleven years. However, the idea that formal education is no longer required beyond the age of seventeen is rapidly losing ground. More careers demand A levels or even a degree. To accommodate this demand by employers for higher qualifications, more higher and further education is needed and the approach to education is changing. People are coming to regard education as something to enjoy rather than something to endure and as most people take early retirement they are finding an increasing satisfaction in studying. Society functions best when the populace is educated and well informed. With the increased wealth created by the new technology, educational services could be widened in scope and extended in depth: more subjects could be introduced and carried through to a higher level and education could develop more into a system of learning for its own sake rather than training for future work. Flexibility could be introduced with opportunities to re-enter at any age—a feature that is becoming more necessary as job-changing becomes more widespread.

20 By changing attitudes to education, people could be encouraged to think of education as a life-long facility enabling them to develop within a career, to change career or to develop their own minds. A more educated society means a more forward-looking society with a desire and an ability to solve society's problems.

A caring society

21 The measure of any civilised society is assessed by the extent to which it cares for its members. If the work-ethic were to be supplemented by an invigorated society-ethic then life could greatly improve for every member of society.

History teaches us that life continually poses challenges and in that respect life today is no different from life in the past—except in the time scale.

Do you enjoy your education? Why? How could school life be changed to be more enjoyable? How would you feel if some of your classmates were the same age as your parents or even your grandparents? Would you enjoy being taught by a machine? Why? Would you prefer to learn without having to worry about passing or failing exams?
Discuss these questions with your friends.

Summary

As the computer invades areas of employment it brings with it unemployment. The type of unemployment it brings is different from that experienced during the Industrial Revolution. The Computer Revolution involves the displacement of human information handlers. As the computer becomes more sophisticated, so the level of information that it can handle and process becomes more sophisticated. This brings with it unemployment higher up the scale of information handling. The conclusion is that everyone could be liable to be displaced. Unemployment is insidious and creates social division. To anticipate the problems that come with social division it is suggested that a change in the traditional attitude to work may have to take place. It is not easy to say how this can come about because whatever is suggested today could become obsolete tomorrow by virtue of the newest technology. In recognising the problem, the Government is making an attempt to address the problem in its retraining schemes under the supervision of the Training Agency.

Key points

Unemployment by computers displacing people, unemployment is different from that of the Industrial Revolution, Computer Revolution unemployment caused by displacement of information handlers, everybody becomes potentially liable, the effects of unemployment, solving the problem, retraining, changing attitudes, the reduction of the working week, home working, continued education.

Self assessment questions

1 What is a common result of introducing computers into the workplace? (2)
2 Why are computers introduced into the workplace? (2)
3 Where does the Government stand in relation to the employers and Trade Unions with regard to the introduction of computers in the workplace? (2)
4 What was happening in Britain during the eighteenth century? (4)
5 By how much did Britain's population change between 1600 and 1800? (4)

6 Why did Britain's population increase so much between 1600 and 1800? (4)
7 What was the effect of the increase in population in Britain between 1600 and 1800?
8 How did industry meet the demands put upon it in the early 1700s? (4)
9 List four inventions of the eighteenth century that helped British industry mechanise. (4)
10 What were the consequences of the mechanisation of industry during the Industrial Revolution? (5)
11 Why was mass poverty such a problem during the Industrial Revolution? (5)
12 Describe one enactment of Parliament that was intended to relieve poverty in the nineteenth century. (5)
13 What is the current population of the UK? (6)
14 How can we feed and clothe ourselves? (6)
15 How can we ensure that Britain can continue to export its goods and services? (6)
16 Name one effect that will result from British industry embracing the new technologies? (6)
17 What is the root cause of the unemployment resulting from the introduction of computers in the workplace? (7–11)
18 Why is the unemployment created by the introduction of computers in the workplace different from the unemployment created by mechanisation during the Industrial Revolution? (8–11)
19 Give three examples of the introduction of computer systems displacing people. (9, 10)
20 What is the social effect of unemployment? (12)
21 Name one measure enacted by the Government to attempt to address the problem of unemployment. (13)
22 What can people be retrained for? (14)
23 What is the traditional attitude to work? (16)
24 Name three possible ways to change the traditional attitudes to work. (17)
25 What would be the effects of reducing the working week? (17)
26 What is meant by job sharing? (17)
27 What is flexitime? (18)
28 What is meant by home working? (18)
29 Why should continued education be encouraged? (19)

Exercises

1 (a) Explain why the introduction of a computer system may cause unemployment.

(b) How might incorrect use of a computer system result in a loss of privacy?

(c) What two methods are used to ensure that data held on a computer is secure?

2 A journalist writes stories about the news for a newspaper on a small computer which uses word processing software. They are sent to the editor via a modem and telephone. The editor checks the story and makes any changes that are needed, before sending it to a printing machine by another telephone link.

(a) Name one advantage to the journalist.

(b) Name one advantage to the newspaper owner.

(c) What is the disadvantage to the journalist of working from home in this way.

3 When computers are used to automate work, some human jobs disappear, some change, and some are created. If a car production line is automated, suggest, with a reason for each:

(a) a type of human job that will be lost

(b) a type of human job which will be altered

(c) a type of human job which will be created.

6 ... *And what of tomorrow?*

Objectives

1 To identify possible future developments within the computing industry.

2 To formulate a reasoned view of the potential effects of computer usage.

Introduction

1 This final chapter looks to the future. It is always difficult to predict the future especially when it relies on technologies that are not yet discovered. Consequently, this chapter looks to the immediate future and considers natural, anticipated extensions to systems that are currently in use. In time this chapter will become out-of-date but the final message will not.

Processing power

2 We have seen how in the 1960s minicomputers started to take the place of mainframe computers because a similar processing ability could be achieved at lower costs and how in the 1970s the microcomputer came in at the lower end of the processing scale in turn to invade the minicomputer realm. The invention of the silicon chip processor has made it possible to build physically smaller computers that can handle similar amounts of data and work at similar speeds to existing large computers. At the same time the development of highly sophisticated information processing systems as opposed to data processing systems has made the processing power of computers the major agent of change within society. The processing power of a computer can be measured by the number of instructions it can execute in a second. Because computers can execute instructions very quickly, this number is measured in millions of instructions per second—(mips). For example, a typical PC microcomputer can operate at around 1 mips whereas the Cray supercomputer operates at around 150 mips.

Large numbers are difficult to comprehend. How long does it take you to add two numbers together? Try using a calculator to see how long it will take you to add 1000 numbers together. Try it

> with 10 and multiply the time by 100. Now program your computer to add the numbers 1 to 1000 together and see how long it takes.

3 The reasons for attempting to produce computers that operate at ever faster speeds depends upon the applications to which they are put. A microcomputer usually spends much of its time accessing data that is resident on its media which takes a long time in comparison with its internal processor speed. For microcomputer applications that make use of peripheral devices, doubling the processor speed could make little significant difference to the overall performance in a particular application. However, in the area of multi-tasking where a single processor is time-sliced to execute a number of different programs sequentially, speed is clearly important.

4 Another application that depends critically on processor speed is one where vast amounts of data have to be continually accessed and updated. The DVLC in Swansea is a good example of this. To handle the system, the DVLC uses a computer that is large enough to hold vast amounts of data in memory. Clearly, the faster the processor, the greater the overall performance and in a situation such as this, processor speed is all important.

5 Two ways in which the processing power of a computer can be increased are by using the principles of:

- parallel processing
- superconductivity

Parallel processing

6 A processor can only execute one instruction at a time but 100 processors can execute 100 instructions simultaneously. If a calculation requires 100 arithmetic operations to be performed then performing them simultaneously will only take as much time as performing one operation. The process is speeded up 100 times. The following diagram shows how this can be arranged by using many processors connected in parallel.

7 This is the principle of parallel processing. A number of processors are arranged in parallel to accept input simultaneously, process simultaneously and produce a single output. Using this principle, Data General have developed a computer that can operate at 2000 mips. The Meteorological Office's computer, used to predict weather patterns, handles large amounts of data very quickly and operates at 3000 mips.

> Can you think of a type of arithmetic sum which has 100 or more operations in it and could be arranged to be done simultaneously.

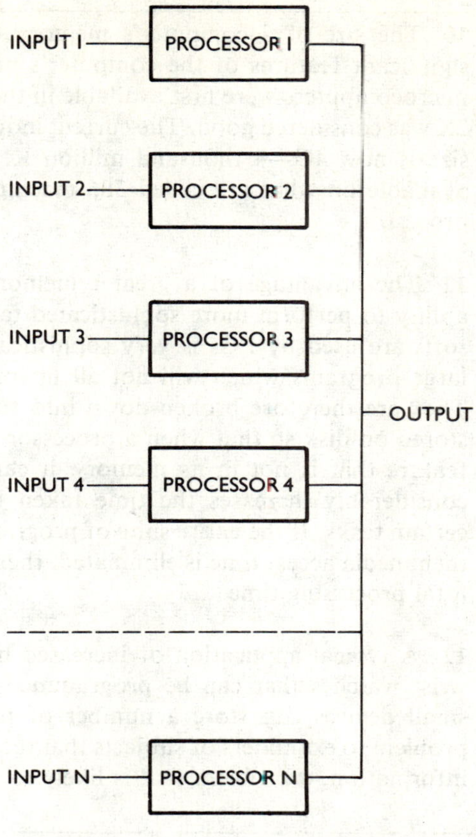

Superconductivity

8 When a current passes through a conductor it meets resistance which converts some of the electrical energy into heat energy. The electric fire is an example of this. A computer uses the same type of conductors—metallic wires—to connect its components together. Despite the fact that these conductors have a very low resistance, the result is that power is lost, heat is generated and inter-component communication is slowed down. There are certain substances that can conduct electricity but offer no resistance to the electric current at all. These are called superconductors. Until recently, all known superconductors operated at near absolute zero, − 273 degrees Celsius. Recent research has discovered materials that will superconduct at normal temperatures. If these substances were used there would be less power loss, less heat generated and inter-component communications would be greatly speeded up, thereby increasing the efficiency and performance of the computer.

9 As computers operate at faster speeds, so their applications will not only speed up but small computers will be able to perform more of the tasks currently done by larger computers. Their use will become even more widespread and more and more applications will be found for them.

Memory

10 The size of a computer's memory has become one of the most significant features of the computer's processing power. When small microcomputers were first available in the late 1970s, a memory size of 2K was considered good. The current industry standard for PC memory size is now 4G—4 thousand million K. This size of memory is now available on what are called 386 machines which use the Intel 80386 processor.

11 The advantage of a greater memory size lies in the computer's ability to perform more sophisticated tasks in less time. Much of the software used by PCs is very sophisticated, but this in turn requires large programs which will not all fit into memory at the same time. They are therefore broken down into suites of smaller programs and stored on disk so that when a processor requires a particular software feature that is not in its memory, it can bring it in from disk. This considerably increases the time taken by the computer to perform certain tasks. If the entire suite of programs can be resident in memory, then media access time is eliminated, thereby reducing considerably the total processing time.

12 A typical application of increased memory is exhibited in digital wrist watches that can be programmed to store text. Some of these small devices can store a number of pages of text and pose a real problem to examiners of subjects that require recall of large amounts of information, a problem that is likely to increase in time.

> Can you think of a particular type of examination where a text processing watch would give a cheater a great advantage? How would you design the examination so that the watch was of no use?

13 A computer's memory can be increased quite easily by simply adding more memory chips to the board but the result is very bulky. What is desired is to get more memory into the same space and this can only be done by shrinking the components of the chip to smaller dimensions. There is a lower limit to this: memory size is dictated by the smallest size that a metallic component on a chip can be made and to reach smaller dimensions requires moving to the molecular domain.

14 Molecules of crystals have what is called polarisation, in other words they either spin up or spin down—think of it as clockwise rotation or anticlockwise rotation.

15 This option between two states means that they can be used to store binary information: spin up = 1 and spin down = 0.

Much work is being done on molecular memories and if it should prove fruitful then even greater memories will become available in an even smaller physical volume.

How many molecules are there in a crystal of granulated sugar?

Media

16 The greater the amount of data that is available to a computer, the more work it can do. If the data cannot be stored in the computer's internal memory then it must be stored externally on media. Originally data was stored on punched cards but now it is stored on the magnetised surfaces of disks and tapes—magnetic media. Reading these magnetised surfaces takes a significant amount of time in comparison to processing speeds, but developments in compact disks have permitted stored data to be retrieved in much faster times.

17 A compact disk is read by a laser. In time it is anticipated that the Compact Disk (CD Roms) will also be available for writing to—the Compact Disk Interactive (CDI)—making available large amounts of storage space to be both read from and written to very quickly. In addition, it will have the ability to store digitised pictures in the form of images captured with a TV camera. These images will be in sufficient number and so quickly accessible that the computer's monitor screen will be used to display moving TV sequences. This has been available with CD Roms for some time—what is soon to be generally available is the ability to edit these images with graphics or text. Soon, the effects that we have all seen on television, where images can be mixed and merged with graphics and overlays, will be available to the PC user. What used to cost thousands of pounds to television companies will now cost just hundreds. This typifies the progress being made in computer technology.

Artificial intelligence

18 Computers were originally devised to 'crunch' numbers. Nowadays this represent a decreasing proportion of their roles. Computers can now manipulate text and with this facility vast amounts of non-numeric information. As the computer becomes more able to perform more of the tasks performed by human beings, it is natural to ask if the computer has intelligence.

19 If we define intelligence to be the power to reason and infer conclusions from facts, then the computer can be made to display apparent intelligence by giving a means to simulate reasoning. The most widely used aspect of this artificial intelligence concerns **expert systems**. In the manufacturing industry machines are becoming so complex that when they become faulty an expert is required to find the fault. Expert

systems are being used to diagnose faults and thereby reduce down-time and financial losses.

> The rules in an expert systems knowledge base are in the form of IF .. THEN .. . Can you think of a set of rules that you use that could form the knowledge base of an expert system?

20 Expert systems are becoming more widely used, especially where the rules are well documented. Many people use documented rules to make their decisions, for example, bus timetables decide for you when you can catch a bus. This information is very easily put into an expert system's knowledge base. If the rules are not well documented then the expertise of the expert has to be elicited in other ways.

> Can you think of any situations where an 'expert' uses rules that are 'rule-of thumb'? These rules are not well documented so how would you suggest they be found out so they could be used in an expert system?

21 More companies are turning to the use of expert systems to provide straightforward decision-making systems, thereby freeing the 'expert' for more important tasks. A particular area of their future use is to combine an expert system with another piece of software, thereby creating an **intelligent application**. For example, work is currently underway to develop **Intelligent Authoring Systems**.

22 This will permit a teacher to enter a course of study into a computer. At a later time a student would then access this information and, using the intelligent aspects of the system, be taught by the computer. The intelligent aspects of the computer would enable it to respond to the student's responses in an intelligent manner, picking out the student's strengths and weaknesses, and coaching him or her in the most appropriate manner.

> Do you think the quality of your education would improve if you learnt by CBT under the guidance of your teachers?

Learning machines

23 Much work is being done in developing computers that can learn. Chess programs are typical of this. As the computer plays chess against an opponent, so its skill improves, making it harder to beat the computer. Another example of a learning machine is a robot working in a continually changing environment that can adapt to the changes.

Neuron modelling

24 The application of facts to rules may not be the way human intelligence operates. Many people think laterally—they reason by making analogies with similar but different problems. Another model of human intelligence concerns the physical structure of the human brain which consists of a large number of nerve centres called neurons, each of which is connected to a number of other neurons.

Research is being carried out to develop such models on computers using the principles of parallel processing. What the eventual outcome of investigations into machine intelligence will be is not known although more human functions are being effectively simulated. Whether the time will come when we invent a computer that has an intelligence greater than our own is impossible to predict. It is, however, an imaginable idea.

Communications

26 Another important aspect of life that has created a terrific demand for computerisation is in **communications**. We can pick up a telephone and talk to another person anywhere in the world within a few seconds.

5.13 A dealing room Courtesy The Stock Exchange

This facility has spawned so many uses that it is no longer a novelty, it is essential. The vast money markets of the world depend upon twenty-four hour communications between countries: the global weather patterns are used to co-ordinate farming and international news is transmitted around the world on a minute-by-minute basis. As communication methods become more reliable and more cheaply available, so more communication will take place, making the world appear to be a smaller place.

26 Fibre optics permit computers to talk to each other without loss of power in the signal. This makes them more reliable. As they become more reliable they become more depended upon, and hence more used. As a result they become cheaper and so even more used.

> How do you feel about being able to receive hundreds of TV programmes via satellite TV? Do you think it will improve the quality of your TV viewing?

Sophisticated tools

27 Programmers less frequently sit down writing lines and lines of code but instead make use of tools—software that makes the creation of systems much quicker and easier, and in which many instructions are given to computers over and over again.

28 For example, these instructions may store data in a file on a disk, sort names into alphabetical order or find the largest number out of a large collection of numbers. To make the computer perform these tasks requires many lines of code. It makes sense to reduce a complex set of instructions into one or two simple words: for example, sort numbers is a much simpler instruction to code than the actual code necessary to sort numbers. This simplification is achieved by making use of a 4GL—a fourth generation language.

Many versions of them exist and the programming of highly sophisticated systems has been brought down to the level of the relatively inexperienced programmer. As the tools become more sophisticated, so do the eventual products of the progammers, from graphics to even more complicated systems. It is even likely that voice activated systems will become available, with the input taking the form of the user talking to the computer.

Applications

29 There are many applications of these future possibilities that we could discuss. We shall consider four:

- data bank access
- vehicle guidance

- book readers
- remote education

Data bank access

30 The ability to access the data banks of the world by more people will bring the world closer together by making it ever more interdependent.

Vehicle guidance

32 Vehicle guidance will become an important aspect of travel. As more traffic uses the roads and motorways, they become less and less useful as a means of rapid transit. If vehicles could be automatically guided, then many of the traffic hold-ups could be eliminated. A step is being taken in this direction by Autoguide, a computerised system for directing traffic from departure to destination.

32 A vehicle equipped for Autoguide has an on-board computer that receives messages from beacons situated at important road junctions. By entering the starting point and destination the driver is guided at each junction by an arrow appearing on the screen, indicating which way to proceed.

> The technology is available for pilotless flight. How do you think you would feel boarding a plane to Australia knowing there was no pilot on board?

Book readers

33 Work is being done in the area of converting visual impressions to sound. This would enable a book to be read by a computer and its words vocalised into human speech synthesised by the computer. The world of literature would open up to the blind and avoid the necessity of translating books into hefty Braille tomes.

Remote education

34 The Open University has already established the principle of remote education via the television and radio. With more sophisticated communications linking schools, universities and polytechnics around the world, education direct from the leading centres of excellence all over the world could become as commonplace as the public library.

> Who do you think would benefit most from remote education?

Postscript

35 The most important outcome of the introduction of the chip into our lives is that we are all going to experience change which will be on a scale and at a pace that the world has never seen before.

36 Even at the end of the last century, the main mode of travel was the horse. The car had been invented but the mass of the population either walked or travelled by horse, not necessarily on horseback but in a horse-drawn tram, for example.

Using horse power as a means of moving around had been the mode of travel for thousands of years. There were no planes, few cars, little electricity, no radio or television, and it took a week to get to America and a month or more to get to Australia. Look at the world now, and the change that has occurred within the last hundred years.

37 In 1980 I sat in front of a microcomputer for the first time. It had a 4K memory! I am writing this on a PC with a 640K memory. If I could afford it I could buy a 386 PC with 4 000 000 K memory. The difference is only eight years.

38 The world is changing and we must all accept that; even in the 'good old days' there were people talking of the 'good old days'. As I said in the first section of this book, some change is for the better and some is for the worse.

39 Whenever one problem is solved it throws up other problems. That is life and the human spirit is there to overcome all the new problems. The world is getting smaller and the barriers between countries are coming down. People can see people on the other side of the world, talk to them, and visit them.

The society we create is every bit as much a part of us as our minds are. We cannot isolate ourselves from society, we are a part of it and it is a part of us. One of our primitive instincts is to run with the herd. Life is more secure that way. But the herd is getting bigger, the community is changing and only we ourselves remain physically the same.

As you move into the future keep your eyes open, your minds open and most of all keep your hearts open. To paraphrase Rudyard Kipling

There are more things in heaven and on earth, Best Beloved,
than are dreamt of in your philosophy.

Summary

The significant feature of computer development concerns the processing power which can be measured by the number of instructions that can be executed in a second. The unit of measurement is the

MIPS—millions of instructions per second. At present processing power ranges from 1 MIPS on the PC to 150 MIPS on the Supercomputers—large serial processing machines, and 2000 and 3000 MIPS on large parallel processing machines. It is only natural to assume that in the future, as memory size and processing power increases, so computer applications will become more sophisticated and more widely applied. Memory size may be increased by employing molecular memories and processing power can be increased by using superconducting circuits and parallel processing. Advances in media, such as the Compact Disk Interactive, will give the users of small computers access to larger and more varied disk based data storage. The use of television images displayed on the computer's monitor and overlaid with graphics and text will no doubt feature in the future generations of software. Other areas of future applications concern a greater tendency to imitate the human being.

Robots already imitate human physical attributes and developments in artificial intelligence are aimed at imitating human intellectual attributes. Expert systems are used to imitate human decision-making processes and these will become more sophisticated as more success is achieved in areas such as learning machines and neuron modelling. Developments in communications using fibre optics will permit more and more accurate and reliable interaction over larger distances. The effect of this can only be to make more people better informed and thereby bring the peoples of the world closer together. As more powerful computers with larger memories and more diverse storage and communication facilities become available to more people, so the ability to generate more sophisticated systems will become more generally available. This will be facilitated by sophisticated software tools enabling inexperienced users to have available techniques currently only available to professional programmers.

The hallmark of the future will be rapid change. Humanity will be able to adapt to this change provided people and society can be sufficiently flexible in outlook. The future offers a tremendous challenge and we should all be prepared to meet it head on.

Key points

Increased processing power, superconductors, larger memories, molecular memory, more sophisticated media, CDI, artificial intelligence, expert systems, learning machines, neuron modelling, fibre optic communications, sophisticated programming tools, data bank access, vehicle guidance, book readers, remote education, the pace of change and the challenge of the future.

Self assessment questions

1 How can we measure the processing power of a computer? (2)
2 What does MIPS stand for? (2)
3 What is the processing power of a typical PC microprocessor? (2)
4 Why is the processing power of a microcomputer less significant than that of a larger computer? (3,4)
5 In what sort of application is the processing power of a computer significant? (4)
6 Name two ways in which higher processing powers can be achieved. (5)
7 What is meant by parallel processing? (6,7)
8 What sort of processing power can be achieved by a parallel processing system? (7)
9 What is meant by superconductivity? (8)
10 How may developments in superconductivity increase the processing power of computers in the future? (8,9)
11 What are the advantages of a larger memory? (10,11)
12 How large a memory has the Intel 80386 chip? (10)
13 Give a typical example of the use of large memories available in a small physical space. (12)
14 How can a computer's memory be increased? (13)
15 What are the physical properties of crystals that would permit them to act as computer memories? (14,15)
16 What developments are likely to improve data storage facilities? (16,17)
17 What is meant by CDI? (17)
18 What features of data storage does a CDI disk have that ordinary floppy disks do not currently have? (17)
19 What is meant by intelligence? (18, 19)
20 Why are we concerned to make connections between computers and intelligence? (18)
21 What is an expert system? (19)
22 What is a knowledge base? (19)
23 What are expert systems used for? (20,21)
24 What possible future use could be made of expert systems? (21)
25 What is an authoring system? (22)
26 Give an example of a learning machine. (23)
27 What is meant by lateral thinking? (24)
28 What is a neuron? (24)
29 How will improvements in communications affect the future? (25)
30 What will be the role of fibre optic cables in developments in communication? (26)
31 What is a 4GL? (27,28)
32 What are 4GLs used for? (28)
33 How will more sophisticated software tools affect the future? (28,29)
34 List four possible areas of computer applications that could significantly affect the future. (29)
35 What are some benefits of universal data bank access? (30)
36 What is Autoguide? (31)
37 How might vehicle guidance affect travel in the future? (31,32)
38 How could the world of literature be opened up to the visually handicapped in the future? (33)
39 What is meant by remote education? (34)
40 How will possible developments of remote education affect education in the future? (34)
41 What will developments in computer technology cause us to experience? (35)
42 What is the challenge of the future? (36,39)

Index